Global Airlines

*To my wife Janet
and my daughter Helen*

Global Airlines

Competition in a transnational industry

Third Edition

Pat Hanlon
University of Birmingham

AMSTERDAM • BOSTON • HEIDELBERG • LONDON • NEW YORK • OXFORD
PARIS • SAN DIEGO • SAN FRANCISCO • SINGAPORE • SYDNEY • TOKYO
Butterworth-Heinemann is an imprint of Elsevier

Butterworth-Heinemann is an imprint of Elsevier
Linacre House, Jordan Hill, Oxford OX2 8DP, UK
30 Corporate Drive, Suite 400, Burlington, MA 01803, USA

First edition 1996
Second edition 1999
Third edition 2007
Reprinted 2008

Notice
No responsibility is assumed by the publisher for any injury and/or damage to persons
or property as a matter of products liability, negligence or otherwise, or from any use
or operation of any methods, products, instructions or ideas contained in the material
herein. Because of rapid advances in the medical sciences, in particular, independent
verification of diagnoses and drug dosages should be made

British Library Cataloguing in Publication Data
A catalogue record for this book is available from the British Library

Library of Congress Cataloging-in-Publication Data
A catalog record for this book is available from the Library of Congress

ISBN: 978-0-7506-6439-4

For information on all Butterworth-Heinemann publications
visit our website at books.elsevier.com

Printed and bound in *Hungary*

08 09 10 10 9 8 7 6 5 4 3 2

Contents

Figures

Tables

Preface to the Third Edition

Since publication of the second edition in 1999 the airline industry has experienced a great deal of turbulence. The date of 11 September 2001, or 9/11, is now firmly imprinted in the memories of almost everybody on the planet, as a result of four commercial airliners being put to uses entirely different from those intended for them. The tragic events in the US have certainly heightened tensions over security, as have the subsequent military action in Afghanistan, the war in Iraq, the continuing Arab-Israeli conflict, the terrorist attacks in Bali, Madrid and London and, of course, the uncovering of a suspected plot to bomb aircraft flying across the North Atlantic. These events led in the short term to some sharp falls in passenger traffic; but they also pose some challenging questions that could well have longer-term repercussions way beyond the more immediate concerns over safety.

In addition to terrorism, the industry has had to contend with the effects of a number of oil price hikes, a cyclical downturn in economic activity, and the related stockmarket declines that began in the early months of the year 2000; and a number of other events exerted negative influences upon airline traffic, like the SARS (severe acute respiratory syndrome) outbreak in the Far East, foot-and-mouth disease in the UK, and the Asian' flu epidemic. At the time of writing, an avian flu pandemic has not been visited upon the world, but the dangers from the deadly virus are so serious that all businesses, but especially airlines, need to consider what precautions they can take just in case.

All this has come at a time when the industry is undergoing the radical restructuring highlighted in previous editions. Privatization and deregulation are both having major effects in liberalizing the industry from constraints on competition; and in recent years competition has intensified, with the spectacular growth of 'low-cost' or 'no-frills' carriers presenting big challenges to the position of the traditional 'legacy' or 'full-service' airlines. Hereinafter, competition between the two is referred to simply as low-cost carriers versus full-service airlines, although it is recognized that some full-service airlines might consider themselves to be operating at relatively low cost, whilst some low-cost carriers might claim to be offering at least some frills. This competition is examined as a topic in its own right in a new Section 2.5, but it is also discussed at various points throughout the text.

Another recent development warranting greater space is the increasing use of e-commerce in air transport. Use of the Internet and electronic ticketing are changing the face of airline sales and distribution, with relatively less reliance being placed on selling through travel agents. Some low-cost carriers do not use them at all. Further advances in this direction will reduce airline costs, as will the growing tendency to outsource various functions to places where the cost of labour is lower. These trends are discussed in a new Section 3.4.

Many forecasts predict that air traffic will grow at a long-term average rate of 5 per cent per annum. But many airports across the world are approaching their capacity limits. Given that there is also pressure from environmentalists to reduce aircraft noise and air pollution, there are some huge issues here. These are discussed with particular respect to the implications for airline competition, and for the possible emergence of a transnational industry. The question of how airport slots are allocated and the importance of airport capacity constraints for the future of hubbing are examined in a revised Chapter 5.

Low-cost carriers generally avoid busy hub airports by flying to/from secondary and regional airports, enabling some passengers to bypass the hubs. An important question is how far capacity constraints at hub airports can be alleviated, either through the use of larger aircraft or through greater use of direct point-to-point flights. In this regard airlines serving long-haul markets will in future face an interesting choice between two different kinds of aircraft, the Airbus A380 to serve markets via hubs and the Boeing 787 (Dreamliner) to operate direct on point-to-point routes. This is discussed briefly in Section 5.8.

Another major development is the increasing awareness of the contribution which aviation makes to the problem of climate change. This is a huge topic, one justifying a book on its own. But in the present volume some attention is paid to some of more important issues in the latter half of Section 2.4 on airline operating costs.

With so many developments taking place it is time to take the story forward. As well as the updating tables and figures the text has also been revised to reflect progress towards globalization. A further move in the direction of full-blown transborder mergers has been taken by the recent amalgamation between Air France and KLM (discussed in Chapter 7); and greater liberalization in the matter of route access may soon develop, with the possible establishment of an Open Aviation Area between the EU and the US (discussed in Chapter 8).

In making the revisions I have been greatly assisted by Sally North and Francesca Ford at Elsevier Butterworth-Heinemann, both of whom have been very patient and have given me much useful advice. Then there is my wife Janet who has, as usual, performed wonders in re-typing large portions of the text. Finally, my daughter Helen somehow found time in her crowded schedule to help in the assembly of the figures and tables, as well as from time-to-time acting as my 'computer tutor'. My most grateful thanks to all.

Pat Hanlon, 2006

Preface to the Second Edition

In the years that have passed since the first edition of this book appeared much has happened in the airline industry. Perhaps the single most important development has been the clear emergence of Oneworld, Star, Wings, and Atlantic Excellence as four major alliance groupings with firm intentions to set up and operate global networks. More and more airlines are aligning themselves with one or other of these groupings and there is currently an intensive focus on the pro- and anti-competitive effects to which these global alliances may lead. The development has been attended by a great deal of publicity in the trade and national presses, with issues like the British Airways/American alliance, the shortage of airport slots, the advent of specialist low-cost airlines, the marketing of customer loyalty schemes, etc. all receiving extensive coverage. All these things are reflected in the revision, updating and expansion of this book, which nonetheless retains its original theme of charting the progress of the industry as it moves from one dominated by national firms in public ownership to one in which the major players are global entities all in private ownership.

Once again it behoves me to thank various people who have helped in the preparation of this book. My wife Janet (with some assistance from Christy Ringrose) has somehow found the time to re-type whole chapters and many other portions of the text. David Allen skilfully updated most of the drawings while adding a number of completely new ones. And at Butterworth-Heinemann, Catherine Clarke and Kathryn Grant have, as always, been extremely efficient in dealing with all my correspondence whilst at the same time giving me a lot of encouragement. Finally, I would also like to record my appreciation of the many comments made by Prof. Kidani (of the University of Hiroshima) who supervised the translation of the first edition into Japanese. I am most grateful to all these people. Their help is much appreciated.

Pat Hanlon, 1999

Preface to the First Edition

Stephen Wheatcroft, a well known authority in the field of air transport, explained at the beginning of his book *Air Transport Policy* (Wheatcroft, 1964) the problem he encountered in keeping up with a constant flow of new material. If that was a problem then, it is certainly no less of one now. Hardly a day goes by without the announcement of some new development in the airline industry. At the time Wheatcroft was writing the main concerns were with the reasons why governments needed to control entry to routes, the capacities supplied by each airline and the fares and rates airlines charged; with the national interests governments were pursuing in regulating an industry very largely in public ownership; and with the economic impact of larger and faster aircraft. Today the focus of attention has shifted to deregulation and privatization; to the emergence of global carriers in a transnational industry; and to the problems posed by an increase in industrial concentration and by capacity constraints at major airports. But many of the issues Wheatcroft addressed still find their parallels in current debates. So, following Wheatcroft's good example, the present volume lays rather less emphasis on reporting the details of the very latest developments and rather more on the underlying trends and policy issues.

This book is addressed to policymakers and managers, not just in airlines, but also in government departments, regulatory authorities, international organizations, and other bodies concerned with civil aviation. There are many important questions to be resolved, as the industry moves from one dominated by flag carriers owned or supported by national governments to one in which privatized airlines pursue more purely commercial objectives. For policymakers, the issues involve trade-offs between pro- and anti-competitive effects, weighing positive, efficiency enhancing effects, against any adverse effects flowing from increases in market power. For managers, fundamental changes in the industry are throwing up some crucial strategic decisions on network configurations, sales distribution systems, relationships with other carriers, and so on. This book is also written for students. Those who may find it useful are likely to be following courses in business, economics, management or tourism, or preparing for professional examinations of bodies like the Chartered Institute of Transport. The transition taking place in the airline industry has attracted some attention in the microeconomics and strategic management literature, recent texts in these fields often containing a number of vignettes on the experience of airlines in the process of profound and continuous change. In many ways the airline industry provides a kind of 'test bed' for theories on deregulation, contestable markets, alliance formation, etc. This book goes into these matters in far greater depth than is possible in more general texts, and as such it is hoped it will be useful for essays, projects, dissertations, and theses as well as supplying a reference to support lecture courses and classes.

In one way or another a great many people have helped me prepare this book, none of whom can in any way be held responsible for any errors that may appear in it. At the University of Birmingham I have received much encouragement from my Head of School, Colin Rickwood, and from my Head of Department, Noel Kavanagh; and I have benefited from some useful discussions with other colleagues, especially John Burton, John Driver, Stephen Littlechild, and Roger Sugden. Two people who, at one time or another, used to be at Birmingham University have also been helpful: Rigas Doganis, Head of the Department of Air Transport at Cranfield University and recently appointed Chairman of Olympic Airways, the Greek national flag carrier; and Nigel Dennis, of the University of Westminster, who was one of my PhD research students. I also wish to acknowledge the stimulation provided by BCom undergraduates, in particular those who chose to write their final year dissertations in this field. Their intelligent and searching questions forced me to clarify quite a few points.

From the airline industry itself a lot of people helped to shape my thoughts, by supplying comments, data, and ideas. The individuals involved are too numerous to mention, but I am especially indebted to managers in British Airways who have always been very helpful to me. Managers in other airlines have been helpful too, including in particular those in Aerolineas Argentinas, Air India, American, Delta, KLM, Lufthansa, Swissair, and United. Some enormous benefits have been derived from discussions and correspondence with officials in various regulatory bodies, especially the UK Civil Aviation Authority and the US Department of Transportation. In search of source material, librarians at the CAA, Royal Aeronautical Society, and Chartered Institute of Transport were helpfulness itself when, on frequent occasions, they assisted me in tracking down references.

In the production of the manuscript I received a great deal of assistance from my wife Janet, who, despite the fact that she never trained as a secretary, was able to word process the book from start to finish. Her skill in doing so was remarkable, especially since she was looking after me generally at the same time! I was fortunate to secure the services of Rachel Southall, of the Public Affairs Department at the University of Birmingham, for the drawing of the majority of the diagrams, which she accomplished with consummate skill and my 12-year-old daughter, Helen, was also able to contribute something to the drawings, using her graphics package. Finally, the staff at Butterworth-Heinemann gave much helpful advice. I am extremely grateful to all these people.

Pat Hanlon, 1996

1

Introduction

Air transport is now big business. Its origins can be traced back so far as 1919, just after the First World War; but it was not until peace was restored after the Second World War that the era of major expansion really began. More than half a century on an air transport is now a key element in the 'world's largest industry', travel and tourism, which takes almost 11 per cent of consumer spending, and employs roughly one in every nine people in the global labour force. But air transport is also a significant industry on its own, contributing much to economic development.

It has been estimated that air transport supports a grand total of 29 million jobs (Air Transport Action Group, 2005). This total includes direct, indirect, induced, and catalytic effects. The *direct* effects, adding up to approximately 5 million jobs, are made up of the following: an estimated 2.1 million people working for airlines, for example as flight crew, check-in staff, maintenance personnel, etc.; a further 1.9 million working on sites at airports in retail outlets, restaurants, hotels, etc.; around 730 000 people working in civil aerospace sector on the manufacture of aircraft systems, frames, engines, etc.; and about 330 000 people working directly for airport operators in airport management, maintenance, security, and so on. The *indirect* effects are essentially jobs, around 5.8 million of them, which are supported through purchases of goods and services by firms in the air transport industry, examples including: jobs in the energy sector generated through the purchase of aircraft fuel; employment in the IT sector providing computer systems for the air transport industry; and the workers needed to manufacture goods required by airlines and airports. As for the *induced* effects, these are the jobs, estimated in the region of 2.7 million, which are supported by employees in the air transport industry – whether direct or indirect – using their incomes to purchase goods and services for their own consumption. Finally, the *catalytic* effects, which are essentially spin-off benefits to other industries, are by far the most difficult to quantify, but include about 15.5 million direct and indirect jobs in tourism, jobs that are supported by the spending of international visitors arriving by air.

Estimates of these effects should always be treated with some degree of caution. To begin with a certain netting off might be called for, insofar as similar effects might have been generated in other areas of economic activity with an equivalent amount of resources. There is sometimes a risk of overemphasizing the 'multiplier' effects in creating new jobs. For the net benefit of these jobs to the economy as a whole can be quite small, especially if they merely reflect transfers from existing jobs in other industries or from one region to another. Even so, there is now a fair amount of evidence to suggest that the wider benefits of air transport can often outweigh its effects on employment. In a study conducted by Oxford Economic Forecasts (2005) an analysis of data from 25 European Union (EU) countries showed that these wider benefits contributed an additional 4 per cent to European GDP. The same scale of impact at the global level would imply a contribution to world GDP of around US $1550 billion in 2004. And these supply-side catalytic effects are additional to those arising from trade and tourism.

In transporting some 2 billion passengers annually (and carrying around 40 per cent of inter-continental exports by value), air transport's overall global impact has been estimated at US $2.96 trillion, roughly equivalent to 8 per cent of world GDP. But there is another side to this, as the President of the International Civil Aviation Organization has explained:

> While aviation is a catalyst for social and economic development around the world, it is also a source of pollution. While aviation's total emissions are modest compared with other sectors they are not expected to decrease in the coming years.
>
> (Assad Kotaite, 2006)

Air transport makes a material contribution to greenhouse gas emissions and other things affecting climate change. Broadly speaking, 1 kg of jet fuel causes 3 kg of CO_2 to be released into the atmosphere. But in quantitative terms airline emissions are still comparatively small when set against those in other industries. Across the 15 member countries of the EU airline emissions account for just 4 per cent of total CO_2 emissions, compared to 34 per cent for power generation and 20 per cent for road transport (Frontier Economics, 2006). The problem though is how this will increase in the years ahead, given that air transport is a high-growth industry.

Air transport has always been a high-growth industry. Very few industries, if any, have enjoyed such growth for such a long period of time. Over the past 60 years its growth rate has been consistently well above that of world GDP. Between 1945 and 2000 world passenger traffic grew at an average annual rate of 12 per cent per annum, although that figure is influenced by particularly high growth from a small base in the early part of the postwar period when the industry was still relatively immature. From 1960 to 2000 the growth in passenger traffic was at an average rate of 9 per cent per annum. Freight and mail have also grown rapidly, at average rates since 1960 of 11 and 7 per cent per annum, respectively. And only twice in all this time has world air traffic actually fallen, in 1991 and in 2001. These of course were years marked by some exceptional events: the Gulf War, the economic recession in the early 1990s, the 9/11 attacks on the US, and threats of international terrorism generally. The falls may have been relatively small in relation to the overall level of traffic (see Table 1.1) but they were sufficient to set off considerable alarm throughout the industry. Traffic growth did resume

Table 1.1 Development of world scheduled passenger traffic, 1990–2004. *Source*: International Civil Aviation Organization

	Passengers carried		*Passenger-kilometers*	
	Millions	*Annual change (%)*	*Billions*	*Annual change (%)*
1990	1165	5.0	1894	6.5
1991	1135	−2.6	1845	−2.6
1992	1146	1.0	1929	4.5
1993	1142	−0.3	1949	1.1
1994	1233	8.0	2100	7.7
1995	1304	5.8	2248	7.1
1996	1391	6.7	2432	8.2
1997	1457	4.7	2573	5.8
1998	1471	1.0	2628	2.1
1999	1562	6.2	2798	6.5
2000	1672	7.0	3038	8.6
2001	1640	−2.0	2950	−2.9
2002	1639	0	2965	0.5
2003	1691	3.0	3019	2.0
2004[a]	1887	12.0	3442	14.0

[a] Provisional estimates.

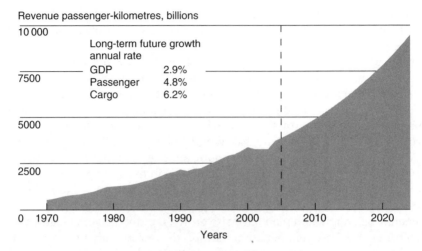

Revenue passenger-kilometres, billions

Figure 1.1   One view of future growth in world passenger traffic (*Source*: Boeing)

fairly quickly after the 1991 fall; and there are now clear signs that high growth is returning following the disturbances in 2001–03.

Forecasts vary of how air traffic will grow in the future, but most predictions centre on an average growth in passenger traffic of around 5 per cent per annum. At this rate of growth passenger traffic will nearly triple by 2025. One forecast of passenger traffic growth is illustrated in Figure 1.1.

Figures on total traffic conceal variations from one part of the world to another. There has been burgeoning growth in the Asia/Pacific region, with more modest growth in Europe and Africa. The rapid growth of Asian airlines, such as Cathay Pacific, Malaysian Airlines, and Singapore International Airlines (SIA) has effected some considerable changes in the structure of the international industry. Thirty to forty years ago airlines of the Asia/Pacific region were responsible for not much more than 10 per cent of the world's air passenger traffic but now account for something over a quarter, as shown in Table 1.2 and Figure 1.2. Future growth is expected to continue being rather uneven, just as in the recent past when the effects of the SARS (*Severe Acute Respiratory Syndrome*) epidemic and financial contagion in the so-called 'tiger' economies of the Pacific Rim put a sharp brake on growth in the Asia/Pacific region. But this region is expected to regain momentum and re-establish its position as one of the fastest growing markets. In the short term, up to 2007, the fastest growth is forecast to take place in the Middle East, with the lowest percentage growth rate being recorded in the most mature market of all, North America (Table 1.3). But in absolute terms and over a longer period, airlines in North America are expected to enjoy the greatest increase in revenue passenger-kilometres

Table 1.2 Passenger traffic by region, 1985–2004. *Source*: International Civil
Aviation Organization

Region of airline registration[a]	Passenger-kilometres performed by scheduled airlines					
	1985		2000		2004	
	Billions	*Total (%)*	*Billions*	*Total (%)*	*Billions*	*Total (%)*
Africa	36.7	2.7	66.4	2.2	75.2	2.2
Asia/Pacific	222.3	16.3	735.5	24.4	903.7	26.3
Europe	428.2	31.3	801.4	26.6	919.9	26.8
Middle East	42.7	3.1	93.8	3.1	148.3	4.3
North America	569.2	41.6	1175.7	39.0	1247.3	36.2
Latin America/ Caribbean	68.3	5.0	141.8	4.7	147.3	4.3

[a] For the geographical boundaries of each region, see Figure 2.2.

(Figure 1.3). The explosive growth in China, at a little less than 9 per cent
per annum, is from a smaller base than traffic in North America, but it is
clear that, with its huge population and latent demand, the Chinese market
(like that in India) is going to become one of the biggest in the years to
come. Lower rates of growth are expected in the European market, and also
in Africa and in the Latin America/Caribbean region.

One possible explanation for the variation in growth rates by region is that
regions are at different stages in the life cycle of the industry (Figure 1.4).
A possible hypothesis is that growth follows an S-shaped pattern over
time: slow to begin with, then very rapid, and finally slow again when the
industry reaches maturity. On this interpretation, Africa would appear to
be in transition from the beginning to the rapid growth stage; Asia and the
Middle East would seem to be well in the rapid growth stage; and North
America and Europe now show signs of reaching the end of the rapid growth
stage before entering the mature stage.

The airline industry may often have achieved high rates of traffic growth,
but this has not generally been accompanied by high rates of profitability,
quite the opposite. Airline profit margins have been well below average
compared with firms in other industries, and in some years there have been
some heavy losses indeed, especially in recent years. It has been estimated
that airline members of the International Air Transport Association lost a
total of US $36 billion between 2001 and 2004, with a further loss of US $6
billion expected for 2005 (Bisignani, 2005). There were a number of reasons
for these heavy losses, principal among them being declining revenue yields,
rising fuel costs, and excess capacity in the industry.

It is against this background that the industry is undergoing some radical
restructuring. For most of the post-war period the industry was dominated

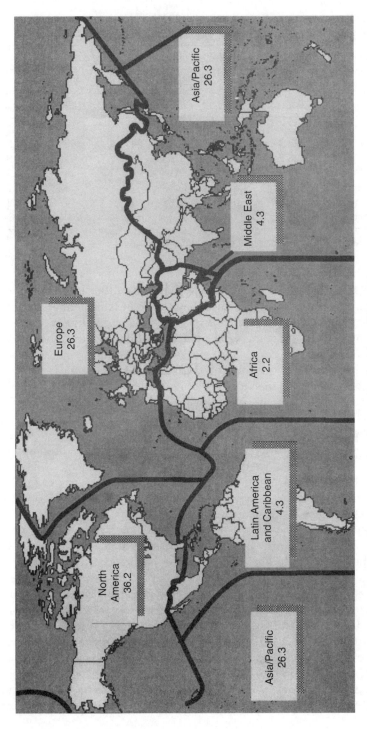

Figure 1.2   Distribution of world passenger traffic (*Source:* Derived from Table 1.2)

Table 1.3 Scheduled passenger traffic growth forecasts by region. *Source*:
International Civil Aviation Organization

	Av. Annual growth 1994–2004 (%)	Forecast 2005 (%)	Forecast 2006 (%)	Forecast 2007 (%)
Africa	4.8	6.5	6.6	5.5
Asia/Pacific	6.2	9.2	8.4	8.3
Europe	5.8	7.6	6.6	6.5
Middle East	9.1	11.8	12.0	8.8
North America	3.7	6.3	4.5	4.2
Latin America/ Caribbean	3.4	6.2	5.5	5.6
World	5.1	7.6	6.5	6.2

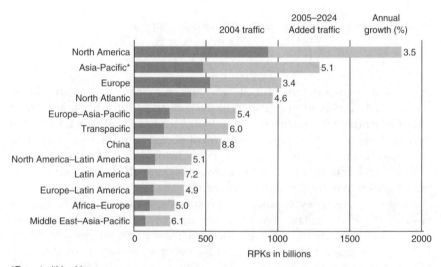

*Except within china.

Figure 1.3   Variations in growth rates by major market areas, 2005–24 (*Source*:
Boeing)

by state-owned airlines, called 'flag carriers', and the governments which
owned them often subsidized and used them as instruments to further
their mercantilist interests or to promote their countries' status, power, and
prestige. Where airlines were in private ownership (e.g. in the US) governments still exercised close control over where they could fly and the prices
they could charge. In the international sphere the system of government
regulation was established by the Chicago Convention signed in 1944. This
led to a complex web of bilateral agreements between pairs of countries,

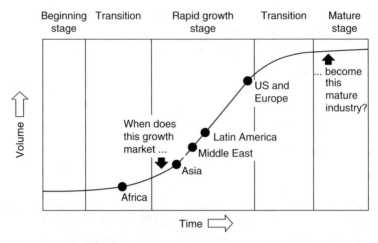

Figure 1.4   Life cycles of airline markets (*Source*: Boeing)

under which government officials and airline representatives are almost continuously involved in negotiating the exchange of traffic rights. These inter-governmental agreements have had a profound influence upon the development of air transport. Government protection of flag carriers often produced 'artificial' markets, in which the profitability of individual airlines was determined more by the number of competitors allowed on particular routes than by the quality and pricing of their services.

A series of recent developments is threatening to overwhelm the current system, in which regulatory mechanisms are increasingly coming into conflict with the objectives and aspirations of the airlines themselves. Many airlines are seeking to break free from the constraints that bilateral negotiations impose on their route networks. They are investing in foreign airlines and forming all kinds of alliances in order to gain access to traffic for which they would otherwise not be able to compete. In particular, major US airlines are making determined efforts to expand their markets by developing their international networks, because of intense competition and reduced prospects of profitability in their deregulated domestic market. At the same time the mounting cost of supporting state owned flag carriers is forcing all governments to examine the option of privatization. In some cases the prospects for privatization could be considerably enhanced if existing restrictions on foreign ownership were to be relaxed, and more and more governments are beginning to show their willingness to do this. Governments are also increasingly willing to relax controls over route entry and pricing. What they are less willing to agree to is anything that implies the surrender, or even the partial surrender, of their sovereignty in the matter of traffic rights. Therein lies the biggest conflict of all.

Air transport has always been a *global industry*, but one served by national firms. Some airlines now want to become *global firms*, but to do so they may in the end have to lose their nationalities, if they are going to be able to conduct their business in much the same way as global firms in other transnational industries do. This is being inhibited by governmental restrictions on foreign ownership. Governments still largely adhere to the principle that airlines should be 'substantially owned and effectively controlled' by nationals of the state in which the airline is registered. Ownership clauses in bilateral air service treaties in effect limit the grant of traffic rights to airlines registered in one or other of the two states involved. So, if an airline of one state were to take over an airline of another state, serious doubts would arise over traffic rights on international routes. The merger might invalidate the rights previously held by the airline being taken over (which largely explains why the merger between Air France and KLM took the form it did). Other states might no longer recognize it as a national airline of its original home state. At present the risk of losing traffic rights constitutes a deterrent to full cross-border mergers; and this explains the current preference for alliances over mergers. In order to enhance 'global reach', the kinds of alliance airlines are most interested in these days are not (as in the past) those with partners based in neighbouring countries but those with airlines operating complementary networks in other parts of the world.

The book proceeds as follows. Following a survey of some key factors affecting the airline industry in Chapter 2, a number of important issues are addressed in Chapter 3 concerning the consequences of liberalizing competition. When airlines are given greater freedom, both to fly where and when they want to and to determine the levels and structure of their fares, competition has in many places become more intense, especially where traditional full-service airlines are being challenged by recently established low-cost carriers. At the same time there is a marked tendency for the industry to become more highly concentrated in the hands of just a few large airlines or consortia of airlines bound together by alliances. It is explained that the trend towards increased concentration can have positive and negative effects. On the positive side efficiency may be enhanced when large airlines are able to reap certain economies not available to the same extent to smaller carriers; but on the negative side there is the fear of large carriers becoming so dominant that they can exert considerable market power. So one central issue discussed in this book is how to weigh the efficiency-enhancing effects against the market power effects.

The present constraints on how airlines can configure their route networks are discussed and illustrated in Chapter 4. If there is one single most important lesson to be learnt from deregulation, it is that there are some enormous economies of scope to be derived from operating a large extensive network. The discussion in Chapter 4 explains how airlines are seeking to extend their networks, within the limitations set in bilateral agreements, by such means as franchising, codesharing, and block spacing.

Full-service airlines derive many operational advantages from scheduling services through hubs and these are discussed in Chapter 5. Here the question is examined whether the pro-competitive effects of hubs are likely to outweigh any anti-competitive ones. A crucial aspect of freer competition concerns how airlines price their services. When is it desirable for airlines to engage in discriminatory pricing and when is it not? How can it be established if airlines are engaging in a predatory manner? And where it is thought that they are, what might be done to inhibit this behaviour? All these issues are discussed in Chapter 6.

In Chapter 7, concerned with mergers and alliances, consideration is given both to the strategies being pursued by airlines and to the policies adopted by governments. When heavily regulated, airlines had a long tradition of colluding with one another; and so the question naturally arises as to whether mergers and alliances are merely going to be another way of achieving the same end result (i.e. suppressing competition). This of course is a major concern for competition authorities in adjudicating upon proposals from the three major transatlantic alliances: Star, oneworld and SkyTeam. It is argued that the net effects of alliances upon competition may depend largely upon the particular kind of merger or alliance being entered into. In replacing agreements between airlines with complementary networks, and in substituting intra-alliance co-operation for multilateral co-operation under the auspices of the International Air Transport Association, links between airlines based in different parts of the world can generate some important pro-competitive effects. On the other hand these same links can leave alliance partners with substantial market power in certain city pair markets, especially on routes between the hub cities of the airlines involved. Hence there are trade-offs between pro- and anti-competitive effects that the competition authorities have to evaluate, as in the case of the alliance being developed between American Airlines and British Airways.

Finally, some thoughts on possible future developments in the emergence of transnational airlines are presented in Chapter 8. Here it is suggested that government-imposed constraints on foreign ownership will be progressively relaxed, so that alliances may prove to be precursors to full-blown cross-border mergers. Eventually the concept of an airline's nationality will lose most if not all of its significance, something which raises major questions over the bilateral system of negotiating traffic rights and whether (and how or by whom) competition between airlines can be regulated in a truly transnational context.

2

The airline industry

2.1 Airlines around the world

The 2006 edition of the annual *Flight International World Airline Survey* lists a total of over 1400 airlines of one description or another: full-service airlines, low-cost carriers, charter operators, regional airlines, air taxis, freight-only carriers, etc. Airlines exist in many different shapes and sizes. Even just amongst full-service airlines offering scheduled passenger services over international routes there is a wide range. Two of the very largest are American Airlines and Delta Airlines. These two airlines each carry around 100 million passengers annually and operate fleets of 500 (Delta) to 725 (American) aircraft. At the other extreme one of the smallest airlines is Druk Air, the national airline of Bhutan, which carries less than 10 000 passengers per annum on just two British Aerospace 146 aircraft.

In terms of fleet size and passenger-kilometres flown, 6 of the 10 largest airlines are registered in the US (Figure 2.1). And whether it is in terms of sales revenue, passengers carried or number of employees, the list of the top 100 airlines is dominated by airlines based in North America, Western Europe, and the Asia/Pacific region

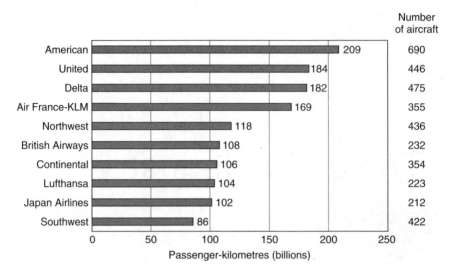

Figure 2.1   Ten largest airlines in 2004 (*Sources: Airline Business* and *Flight International*)

(Table 2.1). Beyond the top 100 there is a whole host of smaller airlines. Virtually every country in the world has its own national flag carrier and there are numerous charter airlines as well as hundreds of small regional carriers serving short-haul routes.

Most national airlines depend for their livelihood on international traffic. Geographic and demographic factors justify significant domestic networks in only a few countries. The existence of so many different nationalities amongst the carriers of international traffic owes much to the bilateral bargaining process under which countries exchange route traffic rights with each other, in the form of air service agreements signed more or less as international treaties. In this process political considerations have often played a more important part than economic factors.

Airlines of nations contracting a bilateral air service agreement receive the right to enter the industry, at least on routes to and from the home countries, even though some of them would not belong in the industry on economic grounds.

Many airlines are still owned by state governments. Non-scheduled charter airlines have always been privately owned but, until the trend to privatization that began in the 1980s, there was only a handful of international scheduled airlines that were not completely or largely owned by governments. Airlines in the US have never been in government ownership; but these apart, the only other non-government firms amongst major international airlines were Cathay Pacific, Korean Air, Canadian Pacific (now part of Air Canada) the French company UTA (now in partial state ownership

Table 2.1 The top 100 airlines in 2004 ranked by passenger-kilometres. *Sources:* Compiled from *Airline Business* (August 2005) and *Flight International* (*29 March– 4 April, 5–11 April, and 12–18 April 2005*)

		Passenger-kilometres (millions)	Passengers (millions)	Employees (number)
1	American	2 09 217	91.6	93 500
2	United	1 84 286	70.8	63 000
3	Delta	1 82 317	110.0	70 600
4	Air France-KLM[a]	1 68 998	64.1	1 06 183
5	Northwest	1 17 958	55.4	39 100
6	British Airways[a]	1 07 892	35.7	51 939
7	Continental	1 05 766	42.7	37 680
8	Lufthansa	1 04 064	50.9	34 559
9	Japan Airlines[a]	1 02 354	59.5	20 231
10	Southwest	85 950	70.9	31 011
11	Qantas	84 762	31.5	33 862
12	Singapore Airlines[a]	77 594	15.9	14 010
13	Air Canada	69 874	27.6	29 198
14	US Airways	64 302	41.5	26 659
15	All Nippon[a]	57 645	48.6	12 277
16	Cathay Pacific	57 283	13.7	15 040
17	Emirates[a]	51 398	12.5	16 119
18	Thai Airways	50 633	19.5	25 884
19	Air China	46 645	24.5	23 000
20	Iberia	45 924	26.7	26 314
21	Korean	45 879	21.3	15 352
22	Malaysian[a]	44 226	17.5	17 839
23	America West	37 544	21.1	12 756
24	China Southern	37 196	28.2	17 569
25	Alitalia	33 860	22.3	20 653
26	Virgin Atlantic	30 222	4.3	8264
27	China Airlines	29 567	8.9	9124
28	Varig	28 297	12.3	10 572
29	China Eastern	27 581	17.7	16 435
30	SAS[b]	26 443	23.8	9147
31	Alaskan	26 116	16.3	10 040
32	Saudi Arabian	25 825	15.8	25 000
33	JetBlue	25 310	11.8	7596
34	Air New Zealand	24 352	11.2	10 394
35	ATA Airlines	23 314	10.6	7918
36	South African	23 080	6.7	11 201
37	EVA Air	21 755	5.4	4469
38	easyJet	21 566	25.7	3226
39	Condor Flugdienst	21 520	7.1	2400
40	Austrian	21 277	9.4	5163
41	Britannia Airways[c]	21 245	8.7	3175

Table 2.1 *Continued*

		Passenger- kilometres *(millions)*	Passengers *(millions)*	Employees *(number)*
42	Aeroflot	20 648	6.6	14 714
43	Swiss	20 596	9.2	9570
44	Ryanair	20 055	27.6	2288
45	Asiana	19 724	12.3	6411
46	MyTravel Airways	19 323	6.7	1900
47	Air-India[a]	18 990	4.3	15 189
48	THY Turkish	18 575	12.0	10 956
49	LTV International	18 400	5.9	2610
50	Gulf Air	17 863	7.5	5183
51	Air Berlin	17 274	12.0	2300
52	Hapag-Lloyd[d]	16 631	7.1	2450
53	Finnair	15 604	8.2	8711
54	First Choice Airways	15 420	6.1	2000
55	LAN	15 125	6.6	11 173
56	Virgin Blue[a]	15 000	12.8	3446
57	Hainan Airlines	14 839	11.0	8000
58	Aeromexico	14 512	9.1	6730
59	EL Al	14 364	3.2	5417
60	Thomas Cook Airlines (UK)	14 338	5.0	1804
61	Garuda Indonesia	14 137	9.8	6251
62	AirTran Airways	13 643	13.2	6000
63	Pakistan Int'l Airlines	13 641	5.1	19 128
64	TAP Air Portugal	13 640	6.5	5750
65	TAM Linhas Aereas	13 447	12.0	6309
66	Philippine Airlines	13 380	5.5	7270
67	Mexicana	13 174	8.4	6500
68	Monarch	12 807	5.0	1704
69	Corsair	12 349	2.1	–
70	Qatar Airways	12 171	4.5	3257
71	ExpressJet	11 935	13.7	6100
72	Air Europa	11 630	7.7	2379
73	Aerolineas Argentinas	11 353	4.4	7016
74	Aer Lingus	11 291	7.0	3906
75	Hawaiian Airlines	10 138	5.7	3276
76	Frontier Airlines	10 118	6.4	3380
77	WestJet Airlines	10 100	7.8	3900
78	Comair (US)	10 090	12.6	5500
79	Air Transat[e]	9933	2.4	1800
80	Sibir Airlines	9871	3.7	4950
81	Egyptair	9654	5.2	–
82	Indian Airlines	9386	6.9	19 520
83	American Eagle	9361	14.9	7886
84	SkyWest	8924	13.4	5880

85	Vietnam Airlines	8530	5.1	8500
86	Iran Air	8325	7.6	8887
87	SriLankan Airlines	8143	2.4	5004
88	Mesa Air[f]	8102	10.2	–
89	Martinair	7950	1.8	3490
90	Spirit Airlines	7833	4.8	2700
91	Atlantic Southeast	7673	10.4	5809
92	Shanghai Airlines	7498	5.7	3401
93	Royal Air Maroc	7317	3.7	5719
94	Kuwait Airways	7285	2.5	4291
95	TACA	7000	–	–
96	Jet Airways[a]	6992	8.1	6685
97	Xiamen Airlines	6826	6.2	4556
98	Olympic Airlines	6824	5.8	1799
99	LOT Polish	6822	3.9	4042
100	Excel Airways	6460	2.4	600

–Not available.
[a] To the year ended 31 March 2005.
[b] Includes Braathens.
[c] Includes Thomsonfly.
[d] Now sometimes also known as Hapagfly.
[e] To the year ended 31 October 2004.
[f] To the year ended 30 September 2004.

following the takeover by Air France) and the Brazilian carrier Varig. All the rest were in majority state ownership, with many owned 100 per cent by their national governments. A lot of national airlines were started in the early postwar period, at a time when nationalization was fashionable and at a time when defence considerations placed a high value on the national airline as a military reserve. Without state investment many national airlines would not have been able to afford up-to-date aircraft and would have found it difficult to survive in the limited markets of the time. Governments subsidized them in order to protect local employment, to promote trade and tourism, and to help the country's balance of payments. Another reason for government involvement is quite simply, prestige. A flag carrier is often seen as a status symbol, an indicator of national 'virility', especially in developing countries.

Many countries still support their airlines with state aids, but an increasing number has decided to privatize them. From 1985 to 2002, no less than 130 states announced privatization plans, or expressed their intentions to privatize, approximately 190 state owned airlines. During this period, about 90 of the targeted airlines have been fully or partially privatized. The number of national flag carriers remaining totally in state ownership is dwindling year by year. In search of greater operating efficiency, and to reduce the burden on the public purse of financing capital investment in new equipment, more and more countries are offering shares in flag carriers both to the private sector and to other airlines. This is taking place faster in some parts of the world than in others (Table 2.2). Following recent privatizations, for example Air Canada, the two Mexican airlines (AeroMexico and Mexicana), the Colombian carrier Avianca, and also Lan-Chile, state ownership has become very much the exception amongst major airlines in North, South and Central America, especially now that Air Jamaica is fully privatized. This contrasts with the situation in Europe where British Airways (BA), Iberia, and Lufthansa are still the only major flag carriers entirely without a government shareholding. Some European carriers, while not completely privatized, have substantial private shareholdings (like Air France, SAS, and Austrian) and elsewhere governments have signalled their intentions to sell their flag carriers at some time. For almost 70 years national airlines in state ownership dominated air transport in Europe; but now there are only 8 airlines in 100 per cent – or close to it – state ownership (in Table 2.2 Air Malta, Bulgarian, Croatia Airlines, CSA Czech, Olympic Airlines, Malev, TAP Air Portugal, and Tarom).

The French government decided upon a partial privatization of Air France, progressively diluting its equity holdings, so that the sale of a further tranche of shares just after the merger with KLM in 2004 reduced the government's equity to just under 20 per cent. But it may be some time before the likes of Olympic Airlines and TAP Air Portugal can be privatized given the large deficits these airlines have been incurring. It is, of course, difficult to privatize firms that would be effectively bankrupt without the aid they receive from their government owners. This is also the case for a number of airlines in the Middle East and Africa, where governments are keen to privatize but where operating losses are likely to deter most purchasers. Privatization is proceeding apace in the Far East however, with Air New Zealand, Singapore International Airlines (SIA) and Japan Airlines already transferred into the private sector and with Malaysian, in which private shareholders already hold substantial stakes, due to join them. And the process of airline privatization has also started in the People's Republic of China. In that country the two largest regional airlines, China Eastern, and China Southern, have between 30 per cent and 40 per cent of their share capital listed on stock exchanges. It is possible that further partial privatizations will soon follow, perhaps in the long term that of the flag carrier Air China.

Although there have been one or two cases in which state holdings have actually been increased in recent years – e.g. the Italian Government in 2002 raising its stake in Alitalia from 53 per cent to 62.4 per cent – the trend towards privatization is almost universal. Of the top 100 airlines listed in Table 2.1, 60 are in 100 per cent private ownership, 15 are partially privatized and the remaining 25 are in full state ownership or very close to it. The predominance of privately owned carriers is greater still when one looks at the ranking by sales: only four state owned airlines appear in the top 25; and privately

Table 2.2 Ownership of flag carriers, 2004–2005 (percentages of share capital held by state governments). *Source*: Compiled from *Flight International* (29 March–4 April, 5–11 April, and 12–18 April 2005)

Africa	%	Asia/Pacific	%
Air Algerie	100	Air China	69
Air Malawi	100	Air New Zealand	77
Air Mauritius	9.25	Air Niugini	100
Air Namibia	100	Air Pacific	51
Air Tanzania	51	Air Seychelles	100
Air Zimbabwe	100	Air Tahiti Nui	61.4
Cameroon	96.43	Air Vanuatu	100
Airlines		Air-India	100
Egyptair	100	All Nippon	0
Ethiopian	100	Bangladesh Biman	100
Kenya Airways	22	Cathay Pacific	0
L.A. de Mozambique	80	China Airlines	0
Royal Air Maroc	95.95	China Eastern	61.64
South African Airways	100	China Southern	50.3
Sudan Airways	100	EVA Air	0
TAAG Angolan	100	Garuda	100
Tunisair	74.42	Indian Airlines	100
		Japan Airlines	0
Americas	%	Korean	0
		Malaysian	69.3
Aerolineas Argentinas	5	Philippine Airlines	4.26
Aeroperu	20	PIA	87
Aeromexico	0	Qantas	0
Air Canada	0	Royal Brunei	100
Air Jamaica	100	Royal Nepal	100
American	0	Singapore Airlines	0
ATA Airlines	0	Solomon Airlines	100
BWIA	75	SriLankan Airlines	51
Continental	0	Thai Int'l	53.98
Copa Airlines	0	Vietnam Airlines	100
Cubana	100	*Europe*	%
Delta	0		
Lacsa	0	Aer Lingus	85
Lan Airlines	0	Aeroflot	51
Lloyd Aero Boliviano	48.3	Air France-KLM	20
Mexicana	0	Air Malta	98
Northwest	0	Alitalia	62.3
Pluna	49	Austrian	39.7
TAM Linhas Aereas	0	British Airways	0
United	0	British Midland	0
Varig	0.43	Bulgarian	100
Vasp	40	Croatia Airlines	94.55

Table 2.2 *Continued*

CSA Czech	97.92	*Middle East*	%
Cyprus Airways	69.62	El Al	70
Estonian Air	34	Emirates	100
Finnair	58.43	Etihad Airways	100
Iberia	0	Gulf Air	100
Lot Polish	67.96	Iran Air	100
Lufthansa	0	Kuwait Airways	100
Luxair	23.1	Middle East	99.37
Malev	97	Airlines	
Olympic Airlines	100	Oman Air	33.8
SAS	50	Qatar Airways	50
Swiss International	32.5	Royal Jordanian	100
Airlines		Saudi Arabian	100
TAP Air Portugal	100	Syrianair	100
Tarom	99.72	THY Turkish Airlines	75.2
Ukraine Int'l	61.5	Yemenia	100
Virgin Atlantic	0		

owned airlines take 9 out of the top 10 positions. Airlines in full state ownership account for only a tenth of total sales made by the top 50. This of course is influenced by the inclusion of ten large airlines from the US, but even without the US carriers privately owned airlines still predominate over state owned carriers, especially when one considers the non-scheduled (charter) sector, the rapidly growing sector of low-cost carriers and the many hundreds of small regional airlines almost all of which are in 100 per cent private ownership.

Accompanying the trend towards privatization is a trend towards foreign ownership. Foreign ownership is not something entirely new. In the 1940s and 1950s, some well-established US and European airlines often took stakes in foreign airlines just starting up. For example, Pan American took minority stakes in many Latin American airlines; Air France bought shares in a number of African airlines, especially those in former colonies; and the two British airlines, British European Airways (BEA) and British Overseas Airways Corporation (BOAC), often did the same, not just in Commonwealth countries but in other countries as well: at one time BEA held 40 per cent of Alitalia and BOAC 50 per cent of Egyptian Airways and also 47 per cent of Middle East Airlines. The airline ownership map was then redrawn on more nationalistic lines, so that in the 1960s and 1970s few airlines held a stake, even a minority stake, in the airline of another country. This is now changing again, with many privatized airlines seeking to take equity stakes in airlines based in other countries that have complementary networks, as when in December 1999 Singapore Airlines purchased 49 per cent of the share capital in Virgin Atlantic.

What is new in foreign ownership is the holding of shares in privatized airlines by people living outside the country in which the airline is registered. For instance, when BA was floated in February 1997, some 17 per cent of its shares was purchased by foreign nationals. By March 1992 the figure had grown to the maximum permissible level of 41 per cent, although it has slipped back somewhat since. Over the same period share ownership of the airline has become more concentrated, the total number of shareholders falling from 1.1 million at flotation to around 233 000 in 2006. A large proportion of BA shares held by foreign nationals are held in the US, although the nationality spread amongst shareholders as a whole covers more than 100 countries throughout the world (British Airways, 2006).

A further trend in the ownership of airlines is an increase in employee participation. This is most noticeable in the US where a number of major carriers have swapped shares in the company in return for concessions on wages, pensions, and working rules. The first to do so was Northwest, which exchanged $886 million worth of concessions for one-third of the shares in the company and three seats on the board of directors. The buyout of United Airlines left employees with 55 per cent of shares and three directors. The deal struck by TWA gave employees 45 per cent of shares and four directors in return for $660 million of concessions. And USAir agreed to turn over 20 per cent of its shares to its pilots in return for a 21.6 per cent pay cut.

Employee ownership is not limited to the US and there are signs that it is spreading to Europe and elsewhere. Employees were given preferential terms in the purchase of BA when the airline was fully privatized in 1987. The airline also runs a 'sharesave' scheme for staff members. Almost half of BA employees now hold shares in the company; and employees' total stake in BA share capital now comes to around 10 per cent. The proportion is higher, at around 15 per cent, in the soon-to-be-privatized Irish carrier Aer Lingus, whilst Alitalia employees hold 12 per cent, Air France employees 11 per cent, and those in Iberia 9 per cent. When Aeroflot became a joint stock company in March 1997, the Russian government retained a majority 51 per cent of the shares, with all the remaining 49 per cent passing to the airline's employees.

2.2 Demand for air travel

Three fundamental factors affecting passenger demand are incomes, fares, and service levels. One view of the relative importance of these factors is given in Figure 2.2. The concept of elasticity refers to the responsiveness of quantity demanded, for example the number of passengers, to a change in any one of the factors affecting demand. Some broad estimates of aggregate elasticities imply that demand is highly elastic with respect to income,

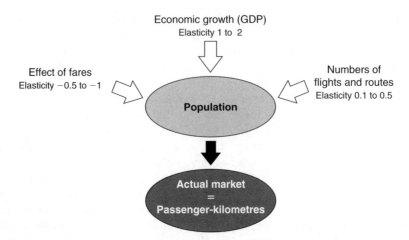

Figure 2.2 Components of air travel demand (*Source*: Airbus Industrie)

rather less elastic with respect to price (i.e. fares) and relatively inelastic with respect to service levels.

The concept of demand elasticity is one of the most basic concepts in economics and yet at the same time a very slippery one. It is also rather crucial to the pricing and competition issues that are discussed later on in this book. Hence it is worthwhile to give some brief consideration here to how it is defined, how in theory it should be measured and how in practice it might be estimated. All this can be explained just in terms of price (or fares) elasticity, since the principles involved can easily be extended *mutatis mutandis* to other elasticities of demand, those with respect to income, to service levels, and also to advertising (or marketing in general) since that too is often a significant factor affecting demand.

Price elasticity

In economics price elasticity is defined as the ratio of the proportionate change in quantity demanded to the proportionate change in price, when the price change is small. The coefficient of price elasticity (E_p) is thus

$$E_p = \frac{\text{proportionate change in quantity demanded}}{\text{proportionate change in price}}$$

and as such can be viewed as the relationship between a percentage change in quantity demanded and a given percentage change in price. For example, if a 10 per cent increase in quantity demanded results from a 5 per cent reduction in price, $E_p = -2$.

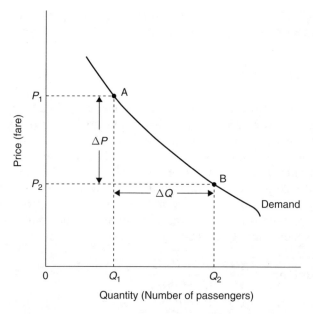

Figure 2.3 A demand curve

Elasticity can be measured in two main ways, both of which can be illustrated by reference to a demand curve, like that portrayed in Figure 2.3. It can be measured *either* between two points *or* at a single point on the demand curve. The former kind of measurement is known as *arc elasticity* and the latter as *point elasticity*. But the value of an elasticity ratio varies a lot with the points at or between which it is measured. In algebraic terms the elasticity ratio can be expressed as:

$$E_p = \frac{\Delta Q/Q}{\Delta P/P} = \frac{\Delta Q}{\Delta P} \cdot \frac{P}{Q}$$

where Q = quantity demanded, where P is price and where the Δ symbol denotes a 'change in'. As an example of arc elasticity consider the demand for a particular air service. If the initial fare P_1 is £60 at which level the number of passengers Q_1 is 100 (point A) and if the fare is then reduced to P_2 at £48 and this induces an increase in passengers to Q_2 at 140 (point B) the measurement of arc elasticity from point A to point B is:

$$E_p\{A \rightarrow B\} = \frac{140 - 100}{48 - 60} \cdot \frac{60}{100} = -2$$

This implies that a 10 per cent reduction in fare leads to a 20 per cent increase in passengers. But if the elasticity ratio is measured the other way around, from point B to point A, a somewhat different value would result. For taking the arc measure from point B to point A,

$$E_p\{B \rightarrow A\} = \frac{-40}{12} \cdot \frac{48}{140} = -1.14$$

implying that a 10 per cent increase in fares leads to an 11.4 per cent reduction in passenger demand. Thus we arrive at significantly different magnitudes of the elasticity ratio despite the fact that both measures are taken from one and the same demand schedule. The problem is essentially a numerical one: should a change in fare (ΔP) from £60 (P_1) to £48 (P_2) be considered a 20 per cent change (in the downward direction) or a 25 per cent change (in the upward direction). To overcome this problem it is conventional to take measures of arc elasticity at the midpoints between the observations on P and Q, that is:

$$E_p\{midpoint\} = \frac{\Delta Q}{\Delta P} \cdot \frac{(P_1 + P_2)/2}{(Q_1 + P_2)/2}$$

$$= \frac{\Delta Q}{\Delta P} \cdot \frac{P_1 + P_2}{Q_1 + Q_2}$$

In the example the midpoint measure of arc elasticity is thus:

$$E_p\{AB \text{ midpoint}\} = \frac{-40}{12} \cdot \frac{60 + 48}{100 + 140} = -1.5$$

implying that a 10 per cent change in fares is associated with a 15 per cent change in the number of passengers.

A similar numerical problem exists in the measurement of point elasticities. The concept of point elasticity is more precise than that of arc elasticity. If two points on a demand curve are moved closer and closer together, they finally merge into a single point, and point elasticity is simply arc elasticity when the distance between the two points approaches zero. The numerical value of point elasticity varies all along the demand curve – in theory from minus infinity where the curve meets the vertical axis to zero where it meets the horizontal axis. So, once again, in order to abstract from this, it is conventional to take some kind of middle value, in this case to measure the elasticity ratio at the mean values of price and quantity, $\bar{P}$ and $\bar{Q}$. Thus the point measure of price elasticity is:

$$E_p = \frac{dQ}{dP} \cdot \frac{\bar{P}}{\bar{Q}}$$

where d denotes the first derivative of quantity with respect to price.

More strictly, given that there are a number of different factors affecting demand, not just price, measure of price elasticity should recognize the implicit *ceteris paribus* (other things being equal) assumption and be given as:

$$E_p = \frac{\partial Q}{\partial P} \cdot \frac{\bar{P}}{\bar{Q}}$$

where ∂ is the first partial derivative.

Whether the measures are taken at mean values or midpoints, it is customary to distinguish between five degrees of price elasticity. These are illustrated in Figure 2.4. The polar extremes are: (i) *zero elasticity* and (ii) *infinite elasticity*. In the former, any change in fare produces no change in passengers; and in the latter an infinitesimally small change in fare causes an infinitely large change in passengers. Midway between the extremes is (iii) *unit elasticity*, where a given proportionate change in fare induces exactly the same proportionate change (albeit in the opposite direction) in passengers. Most interest focuses on where the real demand curve lies in relation to the unit elasticity curve, which is a rectangular hyperbola. If the real demand curve has a gentler slope than the rectangular hyperbola, as is the

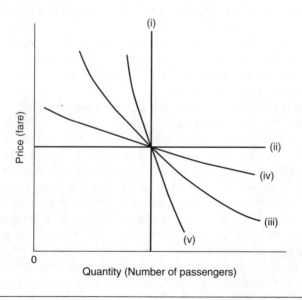

(i) zero elasticity	$E_p = 0$	(iv) elastic demand	$E_p < -1$
(ii) infinite elasticity	$E_p = -\infty$	(v) inelastic demand	$0 > E_p > -1$
(iii) unit elasticity	$E_p = -1$		

Figure 2.4 Degrees of price elasticity of demand

case with curve (iv), then we have a situation of *elastic demand*, which obtains when a given proportionate change in fare leads to a greater than proportionate change in the number of passengers. Finally, if the real demand curve has a steeper slope than that of unit elasticity, as curve (v) has, then we have *inelastic demand*, when a given proportionate change in fare leads to a smaller proportionate change in passengers.

The discussion above is couched in terms of what is known as 'own-price' elasticity of demand; and this can be distinguished from 'cross-price' elasticity, which refers to the change in the quantity demanded of one service, service a, in response to a change in the price of some other service, service b. The mean value point measure of cross-price elasticity is:

$$\frac{\partial Q_a}{\partial P_b} \cdot \frac{\bar{P}_b}{\bar{Q}_a}$$

Note that, in contrast to the coefficient of own-price elasticity, the coefficient of cross-price elasticity is expected to assume a positive sign, when it relates to services which substitutes for one another (but again negative when relating to services which are complementary to one another). Cross-price elasticity is often important in analysing competition issues, for example in examining the effects of customer loyalty schemes discussed in Chapter 3.

In order to measure own-price or cross-price elasticities of demand one must first derive estimates of the relevant demand curve. This may be not at all easy. For at any one moment in time all that can be observed directly is a single co-ordinate, at the existing price and quantity. So there is the problem of how to generate variation in P and Q, a problem to which there are, broadly speaking, three alternative approaches. It is possible to conduct a market survey in which passengers are asked to respond to a question such as: how many flights would you take if the fare were to be reduced by x per cent? But such a question is so hypothetical that considerable doubt must be attached to the reliability of any responses given. Alternatively there may be opportunities to conduct controlled experiments, in which the fare is varied and changes in passenger demand monitored. But such experiments are likely to be very costly and disruptive to the normal working of the air travel market, and so in most cases this is not a practicable possibility. Because of the unreliability of market surveys and the expense of market experiments, the estimation of demand curves is usually attempted by means of statistical analysis. And a large number of empirical studies have been undertaken aimed at statistical estimates of demand elasticities.

A useful review of studies which produced estimates of demand elasticities has been presented by Gillen, Morrison and Stewart (2004) This report identifies six distinct markets for air travel across the world and gathers together estimates of own-price elasticity for each of these markets

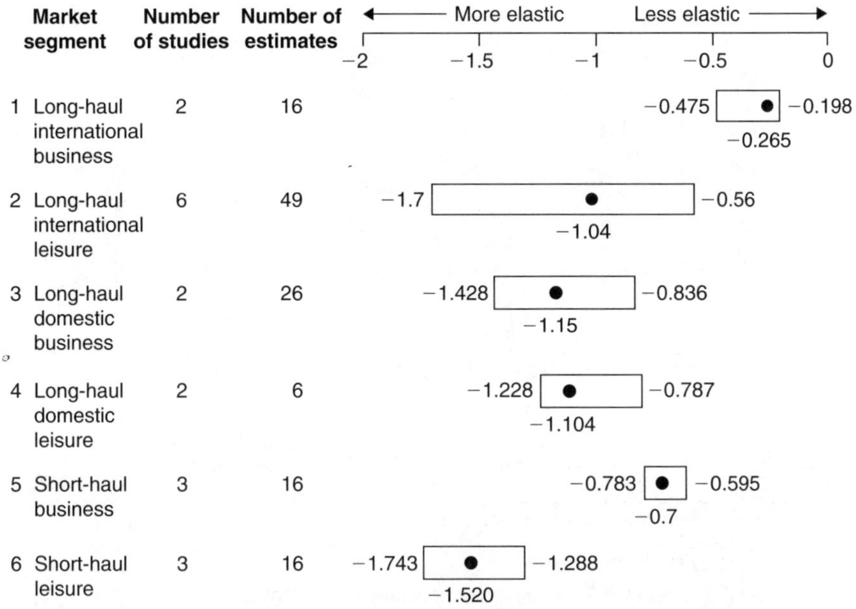

Market segment	Number of studies	Number of estimates				
			◄——— More elastic		Less elastic ———►	

Figure 2.5 Estimates of own-price demand elasticities for air travel showing a scale from −2 to 0, labelled "More elastic" on the left and "Less elastic" on the right, with gridlines at −2, −1.5, −1, −0.5 and 0.

Market segment	Number of studies	Number of estimates	Range (middle half)	Median
1 Long-haul international business	2	16	−0.475 to −0.198	−0.265
2 Long-haul international leisure	6	49	−1.7 to −0.56	−1.04
3 Long-haul domestic business	2	26	−1.428 to −0.836	−1.15
4 Long-haul domestic leisure	2	6	−1.228 to −0.787	−1.104
5 Short-haul business	3	16	−0.783 to −0.595	−0.7
6 Short-haul leisure	3	16	−1.743 to −1.288	−1.520

Note: The range of elasticity ratios shown captures the middle half of the estimates and encompasses the median values, which are represented here by black dots.

Figure 2.5 Estimates of own-price demand elasticities for air travel (*Source*: Gillen, Morrison and Stewart, 2004)

separately. These are summarized in Figure 2.5. In general terms, business demand is less price elastic than leisure demand, long-haul demand is less elastic than short-haul demand and international travel less elastic than domestic. Much depends on the availability of substitutes: the closer the substitutes, the more elastic is passenger demand. Since the availability of alternative modes of transport diminishes with distance traveled, it is expected that the demand for air travel will be less price elastic for longer flights than for shorter flights. Given that international travel tends to be spread over more time, with longer stays at the destination, the air fare tends to be a smaller part of overall trip costs and this makes international demand on long-haul routes relatively less sensitive to changes in fare than demand on domestic short-haul routes.

Income elasticity

Air travel demand generally appears much more elastic with respect to income. The latter is often proxied by gross domestic product (GDP). Although air travel tends to grow faster than GDP – about twice as fast – it still follows the same cyclical pattern as GDP. A time-series relationship

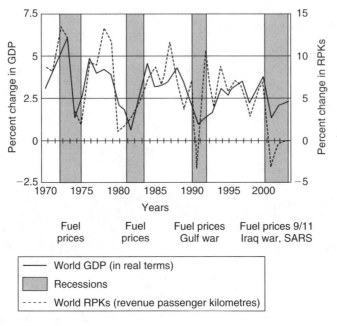

Figure 2.6   Relationship between GDP and air travel (*Source*: ICAO)

between air travel (revenue passenger kilometres) and GDP is portrayed in Figure 2.6, in which there appears to be a remarkably high correlation between annual percentage changes in air travel and annual percentage changes in GDP. This of course is a short-term year-to-year relationship. For a longer-term perspective cross-section comparisons can be drawn across countries, relating in a given year air travel per capita to GDP per capita. Comparisons of this kind are given in Figure 2.7, which reveal that every US citizen made on average 2.2 trips a year when the corresponding figure for India was just 0.02 trips a year and that for China 0.06. But the two Asian giants are in the midst of an economic transformation which, it might be anticipated, will turn them into the world's largest consumer markets over the next 25 years (with their combined purchasing power becoming five times greater than that of the US today). There is therefore huge potential for air travel growth amongst people in these and other emerging and developing countries.

It is however important that the magnitudes of income elasticities are not exaggerated. Air travel growing at twice the growth rate in GDP does not in itself mean that the income elasticity ratio is +2, because some account should be taken of other factors stimulating air travel growth over the same period of time. For instance, over the past 35 years or so, average passenger

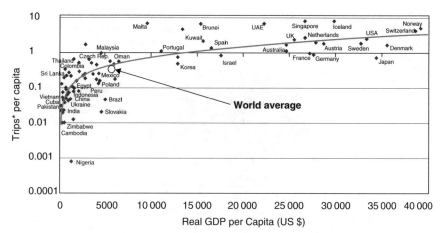

* Passengers carried by airlines domiciled in the country.

Figure 2.7 International comparisons of air travel related to GDP, 2004 (*Source*: Airbus Industrie)

fare levels, as represented by average airline revenue yields, for example in terms of US cents per passenger kilometre, have fallen by around 50 per cent (Doganis, 2002). Hence much of the growth in air travel should properly be ascribed to price elasticities, before arriving at estimates of partial elasticities with respect to income. Historical growth rates may indicate that air travel does indeed grow at some multiple of GDP growth, but the historical rate is the sum of two very different kinds of demand growth: *underlying growth*, which occurs naturally over time and is driven by factors external to the industry; and *induced growth*, which occurs in response to changes in things that airlines control, like fares (Boston Consulting Group, 2006). Forecasts of future demand that rely on the extrapolation of induced demand can be very misleading and may result in some overly optimistic estimates.

That being said there is no denying that income levels constitute a powerful driver of air travel demand. It is primarily the rich people who fly. There is a pyramidal structure to the penetration of air travel in different income bands, as illustrated in Figure 2.8. The fact that air travel demand comes first and foremost from high-income passengers is also evident in data relating to UK airports (Figure 2.9). The average annual income of passengers using a dozen of the top airports in 2003 ranges from £72 000 at London City down to £36 000 at Nottingham East Midlands; and although incomes at provincial airports tend to be half, or not much more than half, incomes at London City or London Heathrow, they are still a long way above average incomes for the population at large. The incomes factor is also reflected in comparisons of propensities to fly (Figure 2.10) where, apart from the special case of

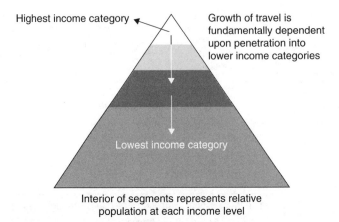

Highest income category ◄ ─── Growth of travel is fundamentally dependent upon penetration into lower income categories

Lowest income category

Interior of segments represents relative population at each income level

Example of air travels penetration (%) in the US

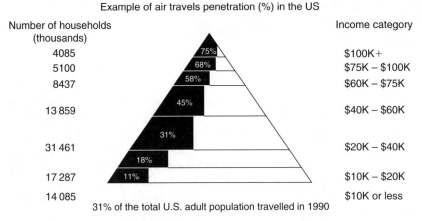

Number of households (thousands)		Income category
4085	75%	$100K+
5100	68%	$75K – $100K
8437	58%	$60K – $75K
13 859	45%	$40K – $60K
31 461	31%	$20K – $40K
17 287	18%	$10K – $20K
14 085	11%	$10K or less

31% of the total U.S. adult population travelled in 1990

Figure 2.8   Air travel and income categories (*Source*: Boeing)

Scotland, there is a clear north–south divide just as there is in many other respects, the frequency at which air journeys are taken being very much greater in London and the Southeast than in other parts of the country. (Scotland is a special case because of its relative remoteness from other regions, and consequently its high level of demand for domestic flights, plus the fact that inbound tourist traffic is also relatively high in per capita terms.)

Estimates of partial income elasticities were reviewed in the Gillen, Morrison and Stewart (2004) study whose findings are summarized in histogram form in Figure 2.11. There is a wide variation from one air travel market to another, some studies producing unexpectedly negative income elasticities at one end, whilst at the other some income elasticities were found in the range +7 to +11.5. But the estimates centre around +0.5 to +2.5.

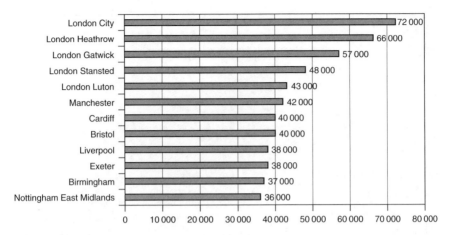

Figure 2.9 Average passenger incomes at major UK airports, 2003 (*Source*: Derived from Civil Aviation Authority Survey)

Many forecasts of future demand are based upon extrapolations of past trends (preferably in underlying demand) and on the assumption that a mature market is one that grows at more or less the same rate as GDP. It is recognized that the lower rates of growth in the more mature markets apply to far higher levels of traffic, but who is to say exactly when a market has reached maturity, even in the most developed countries? One possible approach is to look for indications of latent demand. One such indication is the percentage of people who have never flown. In the US this percentage fell sharply during the 1970s from 50 per cent down to 33 per cent, but it has remained fairly constant within the range 30–35 per cent since 1984 (James, 1993). The percentage of non-flyers is higher in Europe and elsewhere, but is there some particular minimum below which a mature or saturated market cannot go. One suggestion is that it is around 20 per cent, or that the maximum potential market, even in the most high-income countries, is 80 per cent (Graham, 1995). A certain number of people might never fly because of some infirmity or disability, and some people may decide never to fly because they entertain strong fears of flying. Fear of flying, or *pteromerhano* to give it its medical name, is a well-known phenomenon that probably had the effect of slightly slowing down the development of air travel in the past, when it especially affected older people at a time when air transport was not as commonplace as it is today. Younger people tend not to be so susceptible. Yet a not insignificant number of people, across all age groups and from all walks of life, find air travel so frightening that some airlines, like for example Virgin Atlantic, have launched 'Flying without Fear' courses in attempts to allay these peoples' fears and to help them overcome anxieties about their next air trip. (In two notable cases, the fears of soccer stars Dennis Bergkamp of Arsenal and Holland and the late Jimmy Johnstone of

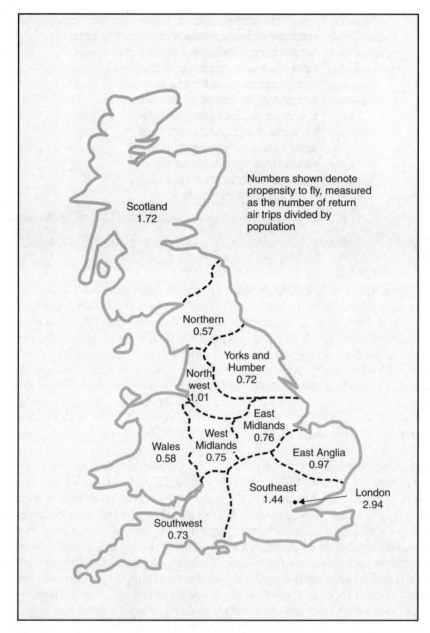

Figure 2.10   Propensity to fly by UK Planning Region, 2003 (*Source*: UK Department for Transport)

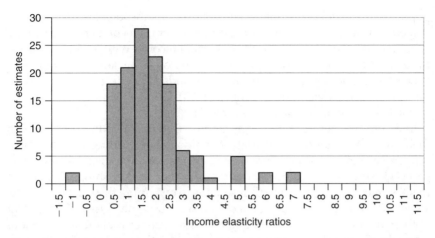

Figure 2.11 Estimates of income elasticities of demand for air travel (*Source*: Gillen, Morrison and Stewart, 2004)

Celtic and Scotland were such as to pose some ticklish problems for their clubs when playing the away legs of European cup ties!)

'Maturity' in this sense can be taken as a decline to unity in income elasticity and 'saturation' as when income elasticity drops to zero. In an interesting paper Graham (2000) suggests that air travel markets can go through five different stages as follows:

Income elasticity	Market maturity or saturation
Constant and substantially >1	Stage 1 (full immaturity)
Decreasing but still >1	Stage 2
Approaching 1	Stage 3
1 or below	Stage 4 (full maturity)
Zero	Stage 5 (full saturation)

As pointed out by the Civil Aviation Authority (2005b) this is much like the normal product life cycle, under which products start their lives as highly income elastic, becoming less so as they become more commonplace, eventually approaching saturation with zero income elasticity. Generally speaking, the speed at which this cycle proceeds is slower for broader categories of product (e.g. air travel) which are less subject to changes in fashion and somewhat faster for narrowly defined products (e.g. package tours).

Leisure and business travel

What constitutes a saturation level may itself rise over time in response to economic, social and demographic developments. For instance, the increasing proportion of relatively healthy and prosperous retired people in the population should contribute some increase in the demand for leisure-related air travel. In many empirical studies of air travel demand, the income factor has been represented simply as current income, with no recognition of the effect that wealth or assets (financial and non-financial) has on demand. When wealth, or 'permanent' income, is included the effect can be quite significant, as Alperovich and Machnes (1994) found in estimating demand elasticities for international routes to/from Israel.

In a country like the UK, where about 70 per cent of households own their own home, house price inflation could well be exerting a considerable influence upon air travel demand, in the same way that the associated 'feel good' factor could be affecting demand for many other things. Moreover, there is an increasing trend for households to own more than just one home, some 150000 English households own a second home abroad (36 per cent of them in Spain, 25 per cent in France). This number is about 1 per cent of all English households. But a recent survey of passengers passing through Stansted Airport found 15 per cent of them owning a property abroad. This suggests a very high propensity to fly amongst households owning abroad, just as one would expect (Civil Aviation Authority, 2005b).

Elsewhere the impact of increasing wealth is more direct and in some cases more dramatic. In China for instance, year-on-year increases in air traffic of 20 per cent are not uncommon, this explosive growth being quite graphically illustrated in Figure 2.12, which compares how domestic air routes have changed over the past 20 years. International travel from China has also grown very fast, the histogram in Figure 2.13 showing that the whole of the increases has been in leisure travel, with business travel remaining more or less constant. Sharp increases in leisure travel in recent years, whether on domestic or international routes, reflects the booming Chinese economy and the emergence of a sizeable 'middle class' of affluent consumers, a class that is expected to more than double its present size by 2020 (Figure 2.14).

Ageing populations in some mature markets could contribute significantly to continued air traffic growth insofar as older people tend to have both greater personal wealth and more time available for travel. But there is another side to this: with people living longer, greater expenditure tends to be made on medical care, leaving that much less of discretionary income, or wealth, to be spent on things like travel. Wheatcroft and Lipman (1990) have attributed to increased spending on medical care the fact that for the previous 15 or 20 years the percentage of spending by US consumers on travel recreation had remained remarkably constant. This means that expenditure on travel has increased only at the same rate as the increase in consumer incomes, implying an income elasticity of no more than unity, the indicator of a mature market. Wheatcroft and Lipman noted that the proportion of US consumer expenditure spent on medical care rose from only 4.7 per cent in 1950 to over 13 per cent by 1990, but considered that expenditure on medical care will likely reach a peak allowing other expenditures, including travel,

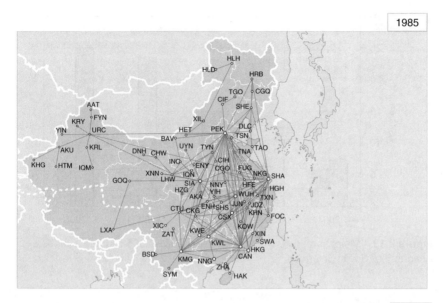

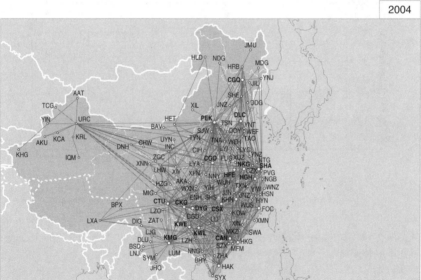

Figure 2.12 Network of domestic routes within China, 1985 and 2004 (*Source*: Airbus Industrie)

to increase somewhat more rapidly in the future. This is possible, at least in a country like the US where provision for medical care has been largely a matter for private finance for a long time. In European countries, where there has been more of a tradition of state support for health and pensions,

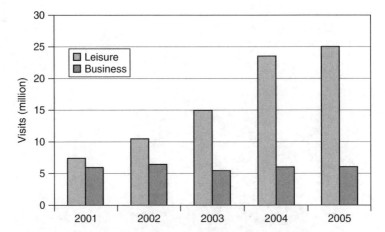

Figure 2.13 Visits abroad by Chinese citizens, 2001–2005 (*Source*: Chinese Academy of Social Sciences)

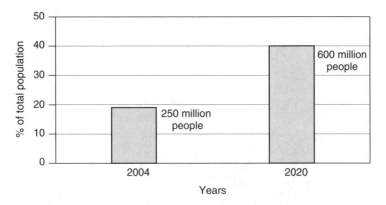

'Affluent middle class' is defined here as households with the
equivalent of US $18 000 and US $36 000 of assets

Figure 2.14 Affluent middle class consumers in China, 2004 and 2020 (*Source*: Airbus Industrie)

a rise in consumer expenditure on such things might be expected, as the number of governments seeking to shift part of the finance burden from public to private funds increases.

Whilst recognizing these points, there are other socio-economic factors which might cause saturation levels to rise. A decline in average family size should encourage a shift in the air/surface modal split, since intercity trips by smaller travelling parties are more likely to be made by air. A continued increase in paid holidays and in the number of two-income families should bring more people into the category of those able to afford at least one, and perhaps two, overseas holidays a year. The influence of increased higher education should also have a positive impact on air travel demand, especially if the globetrotting activities of university students (another group with more time for travel than most!) are anything to go by. The growing economic integration in North America and Europe might exert some positive effect on the demand for air travel within those regions, as might increasing liberalization of airline competition, provided that congestion problems, both in the air and on the ground, can be overcome without some very sharp increase in costs.

Leisure travel has been growing more rapidly than travel on business and this is something that affects the aggregate price elasticity of demand. The demand for leisure travel is price elastic, but that for business travel is price inelastic. Across the world as a whole the leisure/business breakdown is now approximately 80/20, virtually reversing the position as it was in the early postwar period, when it was business travel which predominated. The business travel share varies widely, often being much higher on domestic routes. It also varies a lot by airline. But the declining proportion of business travellers means that total demand has in aggregate been getting more price elastic over time. It might also be getting relatively less income elastic, at least in highly developed economies. In a further paper by Graham (2006) it is suggested that, whilst income elasticity still plays a significant role in stimulating air travel to grow faster than GDP in less developed economies, in the more developed economies it is price elasticity which is increasingly likely to exert the greater influence. Lower fares, with more flexible booking arrangements, are encouraging a trend to substitute frequency of travel for length of stay, that is travellers flying more often but not staying at the destination very long on each trip.

Business travellers are very important to the airlines. For it is mainly these passengers who pay the high fares (first, business or full economy) that yield a lot of revenue. The proportion of total revenue earned from the high-fare passengers can be quite large. In the old days, that is before deregulation and liberalized competition, there used to be the so-called '80:20 rule', meaning that 80 per cent of airline revenue came form just 20 per cent of its passengers. And not so long ago it was possible to cite an even more striking example: in the case of BA, passengers travelling in business class on long-haul routes (marketed by the airline as its 'Club World' product) used to account for just 5 per cent of BA's total passengers but generated as much as 25 per cent of the airline's total revenue. But this is changing, as business travellers become much more price elastic in their demand. More and more business travellers are giving preference to price over service, sacrificing flexibility and frills in return for lower fares (Alamdari, 2004). In Figure 2.15, the percentage of business travellers flying with BA who travelled in business

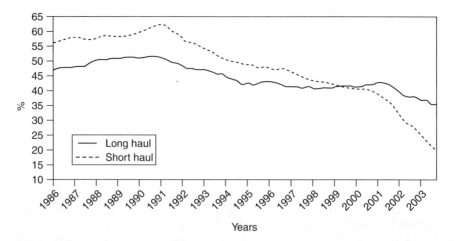

Figure 2.15   Percentage of business travellers flying on BA in first and business class, 1986–2003 (*Source*: British Airways)

Table 2.3 Capacities, revenues, and operating ratios by class of service, IATA airlines, 2002. *Source*: IATA

Class of Service	Capacities (seat Kilometres) (%)	Revenues (US $) (%)	Operating ratios (revenues as % of costs)
First	2.4	3.8	73
Business	14.8	28.1	129
Economy	82.8	68.1	105

class was almost 65 per cent in 1991 but had declined to 25 per cent by 2003 and is expected to have fallen to 15 per cent before the end of 2006. However, business travellers are still vitally important for airline profitability. First of all the decline in long-haul business class is not so marked; and also, as indicated in Table 2.3, the overall operating ratio for International Air Transport Association (IATA) airlines' business-class service is much higher than that for economy class and higher still than that for the generally unprofitable first-class service (which explains why many airlines have withdrawn first-class service from short-haul routes). Even although a lot of travellers have been 'trading down', business class still generated 28 per cent of total passenger revenues from a capacity share of a little less than 15 per cent.

There has been some discussion about the possible effect on business travel of dramatic improvements in global electronic communications, through such innovations as e-mail, the Internet, video teleconferencing, etc. Such innovations have already reduced the need for some business travel and might be expected to continue to do so as electronic communications systems are refined and introduced more widely. But electronic communications are unlikely to prove to be anything more than a partial substitute for business air travel. Far from air travel, the kind of 'journeys' most influenced by these developments have so far been visits within company establishments from one office to another, with external marketing trips, visits to suppliers and journeys to customers to provide technical sales service much less affected. Indeed it is not beyond the realms of possibility that new forms of electronic communications may act more as a *complement* to air travel and rather less as a substitute for it. Some years ago it was suggested that greater use of telephones, and then fax machines, would largely replace postal and courier services. But of course nothing of the kind has taken place, these two forms of communications having grown in parallel with each other. Similarly, e-mail, the Internet, and teleconferencing may actually stimulate some kinds of business travel, especially international travel. This was one of the points to emerge from an earlier study undertaken by the author into the demand for supersonic air services (Hanlon, 1973). A survey of large companies heavily involved in international business travel revealed that the purpose of overseas visits was such that they could not be replaced simply by fax message or videoconference. Day-to-day routine matters can be dealt with through such media, but important decisions and technical problems usually require face-to-face contact on the ground, as does the search for new business. Air travel and telecommunications tend to reinforce one another in this respect. Both have played a part in making it easier for large multinational companies, with a presence in many different countries across the world, to centralize many functions that would otherwise require staff on the spot. Business travel may now be a much smaller proportion of total travel, but this is because leisure travel has been growing so much faster. Business travel is still growing in absolute terms, despite periodic downturns in times of economic recession. It is possible that a lot of the recent growth in the use of electronic means of communication has been due to firms responding to recessions – and also to greater competition in final product markets – by cutting travel costs rather than to any great increase in business efficiency from these means of communications. In the longer term the increased globalization of business in general is likely to foster the continued growth of both travel and telecommunications.

2.3 Factors affecting airline operating costs

One of the most crucial factors affecting airline operating costs is the average stage length over which it flies its aircraft. Other things being equal, the longer the stage length the lower the cost per unit. Unit cost declines rapidly as stage length increases because many of the costs in operating a flight are incurred in take-off, landing, climb, and descent. Also higher block

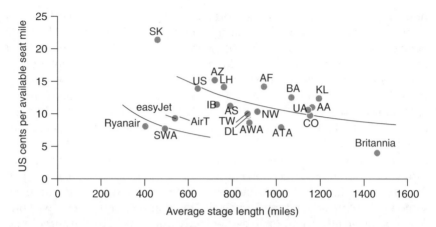

Figure 2.16 Unit operating costs as a function of stage length (*Source*: Booz Allen Hamilton)

speeds and better fuel economy are achieved on the longer sectors. The L-shaped relationship between unit cost and stage length is a fundamental characteristic of airline economics, and the airlines with the lowest costs per seat mile, or cost per tonne kilometre are those operating large aircraft over long stages, like Virgin Atlantic, Qantas, SIA, etc. (Figure 2.16).

Allowing for stage length it has been clear for some time that full-service airlines in Europe have relatively high costs. This was one of the problems identified by the Comité des Sages (1994). The Comité found European air-lines' operating costs to be between 40 per cent and 50 per cent higher than those of comparable airlines in the North America and the Far East. It was widely believed that costs associated with employment were largely responsible for this.

There is considerable variation in salary levels from airline to airline (Table 2.4). Too much should not be read into the precise figures here, since the comparisons of averages are affected by, amongst other things, currency fluctuations, cost-of-living differences, the mix of staff, and so on. The variation is especially wide for pilots, and this is only partly explained by differences in the aircraft they fly or in their average ages and seniority levels. In North America, where airlines buy their labour in a single market, salaries tend to be fairly similar across airlines, at least across airlines of a similar kind, although there are some wide differences between full-service airlines, low-cost airlines, and regional carriers. At the extremes Continental Airlines' pilots are paid more than four times what pilots flying for Continental Express receive. On the other side of the Atlantic some rather striking differences appear between airlines in Western Europe (e.g. Iberia) and airlines in Central Europe (e.g. Estonian). And in the Far East there are some wide differences between neighbouring countries, with pilots flying for Malaysian being paid less than half the salaries

Table 2.4 Average annual remuneration for different categories of airline staff (year ended 31 December 2000 to the nearest $100 at current exchange rates). *Source*: ICAO

	Pilots and co-pilots	Cabin attendants	Maintenance personnel	Ticketing, sales and promotions staff
North America				
Continental	166752	41981	90004	34330
Delta	150549	19519	62432	68985
United	148094	35604	49525	38816
American	138295	34288	49078	38515
Northwest	134177	32098	52881	61810
USAir	121404	35604	49525	41912
Canadian	117997	34499	–	–
Southwest	110601	30745	64839	35188
TWA	106170	34364	39680	39516
America West	94425	28998	49023	22624
Spirit Airlines	71176	–	43020	–
Sun Country	66031	–	42752	41692
JetBlue	55493	27734	20100	–
Vanguard	53058	14736	69607	–
National	51956	18954	36659	21049
Atlantic Southeast	43493	8585	28053	36128
Trans States	42072	30159	26583	–
American Eagle airlines	41302	28305	37587	–
Horizon Air	36715	32295	34711	27999
Continental Express	36310	19858	46329	30894
Latin America/Caribbean				
Aeromexico	136476	33751	–	–
Mexicana	133196	25700	26134	11177
Aerolineas Argentinas	95703	23215	21947	28482
Austral	93849	19693	32320	20648
TACA	77822	–	–	7141
Transbrazil	70733	27295	19397	14269
Varig	51262	18016	11079	12615
Nordeste	49245	21452	23431	16008
Aces	41156	10306	17300	–
Vasp	35599	23227	14135	7354
LAB	32218	7808	10518	6728
Aerosur	25950	6064	9794	9333
Sansa	17116	–	–	7141
Ecuatoriana	12433	2957	4136	4783
Cubana	9059	3885	4066	1501
Europe				
Iberia	160222	52887	34651	35048
KLM[a]	159542	40157	37458	37501

Table 2.4 *Continued*

	Pilots and co-pilots	Cabin attendants	Maintenance personnel	Ticketing, sales and promotions staff
Air France[a]	1 55 076	47 152	38 808	37 526
Lufthansa	1 53 334	45 939	–	–
SAS	1 48 510	61 480	55 069	50 440
TAP Air Portugal	1 31 253	41 207	26 563	30 105
British Airways	1 12 431	29 454	45 327	31 894
Spanair[b]	99 126	30 678	22 328	–
EasyJet	94 831	22 434	–	17 424
British Midland	91 764	27 247	49 766	29 177
Virgin Atlantic	91 179	19 787	45 890	31 306
Monarch Airlines	87 628	19 883	–	28 554
Finnair	80 459	24 268	30 578	29 178
Air Nostram	67 395	10 316	32 491	–
CityFlyer Express	64 161	21 834	44 252	27 821
Olympic	62 328	25 104	31 004	15 045
British Regional	58 759	20 453	46 610	29 816
Jersey European	48 936	14 170	–	20 530
Loganair	48 086	22 906	32 310	13 285
Maersk Air	39 554	15 183	19 830	18 815
Estonian Air	28 704	9851	16 202	11 544
Czech Airlines	18 280	7126	6698	5209
Lithuanian Airlines	14 106	6715	5614	5324
Asia				
Japan Asia Airways[a]	2 31 592	44 123	1 56 794	91 259
Cathay Pacific	2 06 399	41 960	55 092	32 329
Japan Airlines[a]	2 01 698	79 448	–	–
All Nippon[a]	1 94 085	42 352	68 844	68 535
SIA	1 44 171	35 646	46 851	82 203
Thai Int'l[c]	1 00 195	18 450	20 163	34 661
Air-India[a]	62 899	12 046	14 776	11 345
Korean	61 384	32 141	35 055	34 527
Asiana	61 316	23 725	42 649	51 985
Malaysian[a]	60 189	21 506	16 191	23 582
Air Mauritius[a]	53 218	7953	11 593	6999
PIA	27 238	6101	6280	9417

[a] To the year ended 31 March 2001.
[b] To the year ended 31 October 2000.
[c] To the year ended 30 September 2000.
–Not.

earned by SIA pilots. As they stand the figures point up some extraordinary comparisons: pilots employed by Olympic, Air-India, Varig, and JetBlue all earn less than cabin attendants working for Japan Airlines! Wide international differences like this are only possible because of restrictions on the employment of non-nationals. And a huge question is to what extent (or how soon) increasing liberalization and globalization (whether through outright mergers or through alliances) will lead to some easing of these restrictions and a certain levelling out of salaries across airlines.

The matter is naturally of some concern to the unions. The Airline Pilots Association (ALPA) has been particularly concerned. ALPA fears a number of repercussions from further liberalization/globalization. First it is concerned that US airlines could substitute lower-wage workers from abroad for personnel based in the US, either directly or through some form of wet lease arrangement, under which the US airline hires not only an aircraft but also its crew (as opposed to a dry lease which only involves the aircraft). A second, related, concern is that foreign airlines will increasingly be able to exploit wage differences to win business, which might result in US employees either losing their jobs or seeing detoration in their pay, terms and conditions. Then there is the possible adoption of 'flags of convenience', if US airlines become free to base themselves in low-wage countries without endangering traffic rights on international routes. This too could mean a certain equalization of salary levels across countries, although the attractions of flags of convenience might not be as great as they are in international shipping because there are smaller potential cost savings through less regulation.

These issues have been examined by, amongst others, the UK Civil Aviation Authority (2004). The Civil Aviation Authority (CAA) concludes that fears of the US being overrun by a sudden influx of pilots from Central and Eastern Europe are very largely unfounded. In the CAA's view, there are certain 'natural' restrictions on labour substitutability in air transport that do not apply so much in other industries. In manufacturing for instance it is relatively easy to envisage 'lift and shift' policies under which firms can move production from one part of the world to another. But in air transport the airline really must be near its market with geographic 'centres of gravity' at either end of the routes it serves. Hence it is necessary for the airline to employ people in those locations in order to maintain operational efficiency. Also, there are simply not at present large numbers of qualified pilots elsewhere who could take jobs away from EU and US pilots. Of course that situation might change in the future if the effects of liberalization and globalization include some significant relaxation in international markets for labour.

The inter-airline differences noticeable in Table 2.4 might, in freer labour markets, provide some quite strong incentives for pilots – and other airline staff – to move from low-salary countries to high-salary ones. But there are other factors involved, such as different tax regimes, different costs of living, different social benefits, different pension entitlements, and so on. From the airline's point of view the average annual renumeration statistics presented in Table 2.4 do not tell the whole story. For the airline also incurs some non-wage costs in employing people. These can represent anything between 15 per cent and 33 per cent of total labour costs, the proportion varying widely across the EU, from Sweden at the top end to Ireland and the UK at the bottom. The US lies towards the lower end of the European spectrum (but is still above Canada in this respect). When differences in social costs are put alongside differences in salary levels, the gaps between airlines in different parts of the world became even wider.

Some airlines have been seeking to narrow these gaps by moving some of their activities to countries where labour costs are much lower. Two early examples of airlines which went down this path were Lufthansa and (the former) Swissair, both of which transferred some of their aircraft overhaul requirements to Shannon Aerospace in Ireland. In the future it is quite possible that many more airlines will subcontract work to partners based in low-wage economies – 'outsourcing' as it is known – and that more airline jobs will be exported out of high-wage economies. But so far the scale on which this has been entered into has been rather small. Mostly the outsourcing undertaken so far has been of 'common service' functions like complaints handling, call centre operations, IT support, etc. The business has usually gone to Asia. The BA for example, has outsourced some of its IT support functions to India, although this is very much an exception to general practice within the company. Since 1992 by far the greater change to BA's employment situation has been the shift of some non-core activities away from London to other locations in the UK (call centre operations to the Northeast of England and some engineering to South Wales).

After labour, the next major component of operating costs is fuel. Across the world's airlines as a whole fuel can represent something between 15 per cent and 25 per cent of total operating costs depending on the international price of oil. Fuel costs also exhibit marked variation between airlines, not only because of factors like stage length but also on account of the costs of transporting fuel to the airline's main airports and the local rates at which tax is levied on it. Indeed for some particular airlines fuel can be the largest single item of cost, an extreme example being Indian Airlines, a carrier which has to pay both federal and state government taxes on its purchase of fuel and for which fuel can represent over 40% of operating costs (Hanlon, 1986). Europe tends to suffer from relatively high fuel costs too, having to pay somewhat more per gallon than airlines in the US. But *all* airlines are having to pay substantially more than they did in the past, as a result of some very sharp increases in international prices for fuel (Figure 2.17). These have clearly had the effect of inflating airlines' total bill, both in absolute terms and as a proportion of operating costs (Figure 2.18). The need to economize

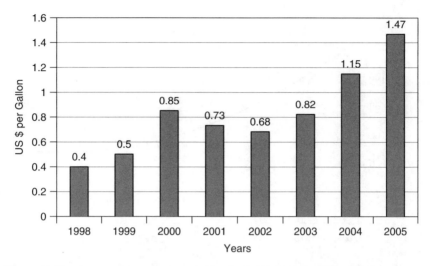

Figure 2.17 Average annual prices for jet fuel, 1998–2005 (*Source*: US Government Accounting Office)

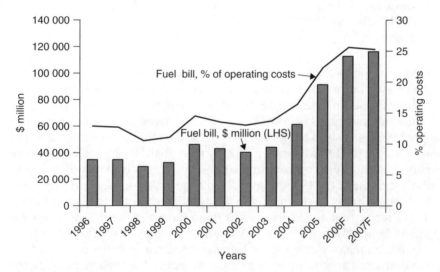

Figure 2.18 Total fuel bill incurred by IATA airlines, 1996–2007 (*Source*: IATA)

on fuel has never been greater. The question is to what extent fuel economies can be won from further advances in aircraft design.

In the past the unit operating cost of air transport has declined quite a lot as a result of aeronautical innovation. From the Douglas DC-3 to the introduction of jets there was a gradual fall, in real terms, in the unit cost of aircraft operation of some 30 per cent. A fall of roughly the same magnitude came with the appearance of the first generation of jet aircraft; and there were

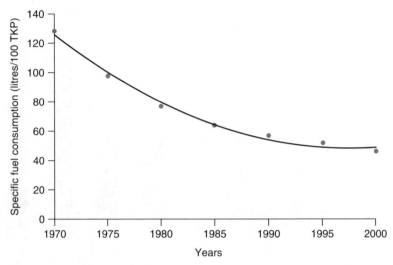

TKP: Tonne kilometres performed.

Figure 2.19   Average fuel efficiency across IATA airlines' aircraft fleets, 1970–2000 (*Source*: Frontier Economics, 2006)

further reductions when turbo-fan and wide-bodied jets were introduced. These falls in unit cost came partly from increases in speed, but mainly from increases in aircraft size. But there are now indications that innovation in aircraft types is, in these respects, running into diminishing marginal returns. Instead the focus has switched to reducing fuel consumption, which since the 1970s has fallen a lot, by more than 50 per cent, although the curve relating fuel consumption to line has certainly flattened out since the beginning of the 1990s (Figure 2.19). One main contribution to reduced fuel consumption has been a cut in the number of aircraft engines (e.g. from 4 to 2 for transatlantic service) but there have also been some improvements in aerodynamic design. Aircraft technology is constantly improving, but no major technological leap has occurred recently and none is on the horizon. Various advances leading to reduced operating costs are still possible; and various improvements embodied in new long-haul aircraft, like the Airbus A380 and Boeing B787, should offer some savings in fuel costs. In aerodynamics, developments are currently focused on airflow control to effect significant reductions in drag, by drilling tiny holes in wing skins to suck away the secondary layer. So far as airframe structures are concerned, there is potential for greater use of composite materials, stiffer and lighter than the present metallic structures, which could reduce the empty weight of an airliner by as much as 30 per cent, which in turn could reduce fuel consumption. The use of improved materials could also result in better engine performance. But none of these kinds of development seem to offer the prospect of a large discrete fall in unit cost in the way that earlier innovations did. For further reductions in unit cost airlines may have to look more at improvements in managerial efficiency rather than relying on technological innovation. But whatever savings can be made through advanced technology, they are going to assume ever more importance. For there are increasing pressures for airlines to be made more accountable for the external costs they impose on the environment.

Environmental costs

Fuel and labour are costs which are internal to the airline. The airline meets these costs directly. The costs of any adverse effects on the environment do not necessarily show up in airline company accounts and because of that they are regarded as external costs. An underlying tenant of government policies is that these external costs should, so far as practicable, be internalized in some way so that full account of them is taken in airline decision-making. The main kinds of external environmental costs are noise, air pollution, and contributions to climate change. The issues involved are so huge as to justify a book on their own; and there have been a number of extensive studies dealing with all these issues (e.g. CE Delft (2003)). Here the focus is on climate change and in particular on how the airline industry should be made responsible for its contribution to CO_2 emissions, a matter under serious consideration by the EU.

At some time a final decision needs to be reached as to whether or not the EU Emissions Trading Scheme (ETS) should be extended to include air transport. The ETS has been in operation since January 2005 and covers 11 500 installations, mainly in heavy industries, which together are responsible for nearly half of total EU CO_2 emissions. The contribution of aviation to CO_2 emissions is still relatively small – around 3 per cent to 4 per cent within the EU-15 countries – but this expected to grow quickly alongside the fast growing demand for air travel. Further, the ETS only covers CO_2 emissions and not the other global warming effects of aviation, namely nitrous oxides (NO_x) and condensation trails in the upper atmosphere. Emissions of NO_x result in the production of ozone (which can be a warming effect) and the destruction of methane (which can be a cooling effect) and condensation trails, or contrails, induce cirrus clouds which can also cause a warming effect. There is much scientific uncertainty over the size of NO_x and contrails effects. The jury of scientists is still out on these, although it is known that they are driven, to a greater or lesser extent, by where an aircraft flies rather than what it emits. This and their rather short lives result in ephemeral regional effects rather than the global effects of CO_2 which are cumulative and can last a hundred years.

It may fairly readily be accepted that aviation's contribution to global warming through CO_2 emissions is, or will become, sufficiently serious to warrant some attention. But why a tradable permits system rather than a fuel tax or emissions charge? In theory the reason is that a tradable permits system can provide the same environmental benefit at a lower cost to society. In a tradable permits system a cap is set on total emissions, but the market is left to decide where, how, and when emission reductions can be made most economically. It is true that much the same kind of effect can be achieved with a fuel tax or emissions charge, but by focussing directly on the quantity of emissions rather than their price, a tradable permits system gives airlines stronger incentives to reduce emission levels, for example through adopting cleaner technologies like newer/more fuel-efficient aircraft. Where a tax or a charge is levied, a large part of this might be passed onto passengers in the form of higher air fares (just like fuel surcharges) especially where it is possible to discriminate and concentrate the increases in some of the more price-inelastic segments of the air travel market.

There can be a further problem with taxes or charges. If they are not levied across an airline's network, in the same form and at the same rates, they might induce all manner of instrumental behaviour designed to reduce the burden of them. One practice which might be encouraged is that of 'fuel tankering', that is picking up more fuel than absolutely necessary at points where it is cheap in order to reduce the impact of higher prices elsewhere. To the extent that variations from airport to airport reflect real cost differences in supplying fuel at different locations, the practice might seem harmless enough but even then it can have adverse consequences in environmental terms. On a flight over a given sector, unit operating costs are greater where a greater weight of fuel is uplifted; and it is even possible, especially where high temperatures prevail, for the carriage of additional fuel to entail the sacrifice of some payload capacity. Carting additional fuel across the sky does in itself increase fuel burn which in turn increases CO_2 emissions. Hence it would be highly desirable for any fuel taxes or charges to be made uniform over as wide a geographic area as possible. In the case referred to earlier of Indian Airlines, in 1984/5 the carrier was met with an extraordinarily wide range of post-tax prices for aviation fuel, from R_s 410 at Porbandar to R_s 4320 at Chandigarh, a ten-fold difference! This was the combined effect of variations in pre-tax supply price plus the levy, on top of the central government's excise duties, of sales taxes and *octroi* set by individual states at varying *ad valorem* rates ranging from 8 per cent in Uttar Pradesh to just over 25 per cent in Gujarat (Hanlon, 1986). This example is admittedly a most extreme one but , unless fuel taxes or emission charges are levied uniformly, from country to country, the scope for airlines to engage in tankering could be quite wide. If the EU does decide to impose a tax on aviation fuel and/or levy a CO_2 emissions charge upon airlines, then it should do so in such a way that the tax and/or charge is effectively the same across all EU member countries. Even that would not eliminate instrumental behaviour altogether, but at least the scope for tankering would be rather limited if it could in effect only take place on routes in and out of the EU.

Since the problem of CO_2 emissions is one of *global* warming it would be ideal if the relevant ETS were to be global too. Unfortunately, achieving agreement right across the world on a matter like this is just too formidable, this despite the fact that emissions trading has been endorsed by the International Civil Aviation Organization (ICAO). The prospects for emissions trading are to be re-visited at a major ICAO conference in 2007. But the chances of this resulting in any degree of unanimity on the subject seem remote.

Nor is there unanimity within the EU. Airlines like BA, SAS, and Air France-KLM are very much in favour, but the idea is being opposed by Lufthansa. The German airline believes the ETS would burden carriers with what it considers to be an 'unacceptable cost risk'. Its Chief Executive has argued that since climate change is a global issue it would be better to wait for a worldwide scheme rather than seeking a solution just within Europe. But the problem with that is that the wait might be an unacceptably long one.

Another objection comes from the European Low Fares Airline Association (ELFAA), an organization representing easyJet, Ryanair, and 9 other carriers. The ELFAA claims that its members could be disproportionately affected, given that they generally operate only intra-EU flights on short-haul routes, so that fuel costs make up a much higher proportion of total operating costs for ELFAA members than they do for full-service airlines which also operate some long-haul services. In principle the ETS should include all flights departing from EU airports, to cover the entire contribution of EU aviation to CO_2 emissions, some 40 per cent of which arise from intra-EU flights and some 60 per cent from flights to/from third countries outside the EU. There is however a great practical difficulty in this: considerable dubiety attaches to the question of whether the EU can unilaterally impose a scheme upon non-EU airlines. There is some uncertainty regarding the legality of this under the 1944 Chicago Convention which still applies to many aspects of international air transport. Clearly this uncertainty should be resolved before the matter goes any further. For it is possible that the EU will be forced into introducing a scheme applying to intra-EU flights only and that non-EU airlines will be able to challenge being included even in just that. And legal obstacles might also impede EU attempts to impose fuel taxes or emissions charges on non-EU airlines.

Before an ETS goes ahead simply on the basis of intra-EU flights flown by EU airlines, a little thought might be given to some possible implications of this for other changes taking place in the airline industry. Liberalization has already gone quite a long way, but the next step might entail relaxing, or even abolishing altogether, controls over foreign investment and ownership, something that is discussed later in this book. That would open the way for full cross-border airline mergers to be consummated, accelerating a process of consolidation in the industry, which so far has been restrained by being limited to mergers between airlines registered in the same country (with the two notable exceptions of Air France-KLM and Lufthansa-Swiss). A combined airline formed by the merger of two (or more) airlines in different countries (or even on different continents) might be able to exercise some choice in the matter of where it is registered. If an ETS applies in the EU, but nowhere else, the merged airline might prefer to become a non-EU airline, adopting something akin to a 'flag of convenience,' just like in shipping.

It is understandable if many airline managers greet the prospect of emissions trading or fuel taxes/charges with something less than unbounded enthusiasm. For they already seem to have their hands full dealing with some severe (and in some cases enduring) financial problems, with rising oil prices, depressed revenue yields, pension deficits, and so on. Nonetheless widely expressed concerns about the relationship between air transport and climate change are encouraging political support in favour of airlines bearing more of their environmental costs. (And some rather strong views on the subject have recently been reported in the press, including those by the so-called 'greens' and also a statement by the Rt. Revd. Richard Chartres, Anglican Bishop of London, the third highest ranking prelate in the Church of England, who said that 'flying on holiday or buying a large car are a symptom of sin'.)

2.4 Financial performance of the industry

If a capitalist had been present at Kitty Hawk back in the 1900s, he should have shot Orville Wright. He would have saved his progeny money. But seriously, the airline business has been extraordinary. It has eaten up capital over the past century like no other business because people seem to keep coming back and putting fresh money in . . .

. . . I have an 800 [free call] number now that I call if I get the urge to buy an airline stock. I call it at two in the morning and say 'I'm an aeroholic'. And then they talk me down

Warren Buffett, aka 'The Sage of Omaha'

The airline industry has just experienced one of the most turbulent periods in its entire history. In the accounts of a great many airlines the red ink has flowed copiously over the past 5 years. The recent fortunes of the industry can be viewed in two sets of time series presented in Table 2.5 and Figure 2.20. The former is derived from data collected by the ICAO and covers the results of all scheduled airlines registered in any one of the

Table 2.5 Operating and net margins of world scheduled airlines, 1984–2004. *Source*: ICAO

	% of operating revenues	
	Operating margin	*Net margin*
1984	4.8	1.9
1985	3.7	1.9
1986	3.7	1.2
1987	4.9	1.7
1988	6.1	3.0
1989	4.3	2.0
1990	−0.8	−2.3
1991	−0.2	−1.7
1992	−0.8	−3.6
1993	1.0	−1.9
1994	3.1	−0.1
1995	5.1	1.7
1996	4.4	1.9
1997	5.6	2.9
1998	5.4	2.8
1999	4.0	2.8
2000	3.3	1.1
2001	−3.8	−4.2
2002	−1.6	−3.7
2003	−0.5	−2.3
2004[a]	0.9	−1.1

[a] Preliminary estimates.

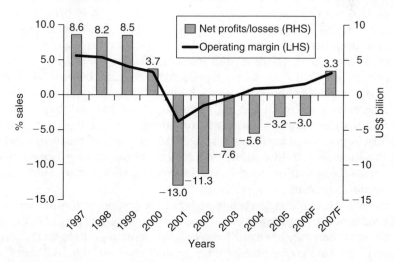

Figure 2.20 Operating margins and net profits/losses, IATA airlines, 1997–2007 (*Source*: IATA)

ICAO Contracting States; the latter relates only to those airlines – generally speaking the larger ones – which are members of the industry trade association the IATA. The present period of difficulties is by no means the first the industry has had to contend with. In the one before, in 1990–94, there was an economic recession in the major world economies which began in 1990 and this was accentuated by the Gulf War which broke out in 1991. The industry as a whole managed to keep in the black during the middle and late 1990s, before the cycle turned again in 2000, with the 'dot com' collapse in share prices triggering a downturn in economic activity, in particular in Japan, Germany, and the US. Then there were the horrific events of 9/11, but the industry was already in financial difficulties before the terrorist attacks, and these just served to make matters very much worse. The year 2001 is one that can lay claim to being the worst ever for the airline industry. IATA airlines sustained a 2001 net loss amounting to 13 per cent of sales revenue; and they have posted losses in each year since. Between 2001 and 2005 IATA airlines lost a grand total of US $43 billion, described by the organization's Director General as a 'financial disaster' (Bisignani, 2006). There are some signs that the industry is pulling out of its financial doldrums and, in a cautiously optimistic forecast for 2007, IATA airlines are predicted to record their first overall surplus for 6 years, albeit a rather small one. There are however still some concerns about rising fuel prices, higher interest rates and a slowdown in the world economy which, together with continued instability in the Middle East, could mean the industry suffering further net losses in aggregate terms.

In terms of its profitability, the airline industry is both cyclical and very marginal (Doganis, 2006). It is relatively easy to understand why it is cyclical, given high-income elasticities of demand for air travel and a very close correlation with changes in economic activity. But why is profitability so marginal in this industry? Even in years of surplus the financial performance has been disappointing. So that their investors receive a rate of return commensurate with relative risks involve, airlines should be achieving net profits of around 7 per cent or 8 per cent per annum. But this is not often achieved, despite air transport being a high-growth industry. It is not always the case that high growth and high profits go hand in hand. Experience in other industries indicates that firms sometimes struggle to maintain profitability in periods of rapid expansion. But in the case of the airline industry, the high-growth-low-profits syndrome seems to have been around forever, as the quotation from the world's second richest man which began this section suggests.

One possible explanation is that many of the best opportunities for making profits out of fast growth are accruing more to other players in the aviation sector than they are to airlines. This was a main point to emerge from a study of value chain profitability conducted jointly by IATA and the McKinsey consulting firm (International Air Transport Association, 2006).

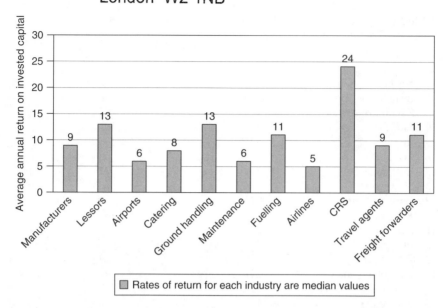

Figure 2.21   Returns on invested capital in aviation-related industries, 2004 (*Source*: IATA)

As illustrated in Figure 2.21, the highest average annual rate of return on invested capital, one of no less than 24 per cent, was earned by computer reservations systems (CRSs). The next highest were aircraft lessors and ground handling firms, both of which achieved 13 per cent, followed by fuel suppliers and freight forwarders on 11 per cent, aircraft manufacturers and travel agents 9 per cent, caterers 8 per cent, airports and aircraft maintenance firms 6 per cent each. Down at the bottom of the list came airlines with only 5 per cent. Comparisons like this may suggest that firms in other industries connected to aviation have greater market power to earn profits than airlines do.

Some airlines have shown themselves able to weather financial crises better than others. The 20 most profitable airlines are listed in Table 2.6 and the 20 heaviest loss-makers in Table 2.7. The comparisons should be treated with caution, since accounting practices vary around the world and also because the net results are taken after all costs, extraordinary items and contributions from subsidiaries have been taken into account. But accepting this qualification there are still some points one can draw from these comparisons. The successful carriers are those which are efficiently managed, have their costs under control, have good yield management procedures and generally have responded well to the more competitive environment. It is noticeable that all bar two of the ten most profitable airlines have strong long-haul networks over which they carry significant volumes of

Table 2.6 Twenty most profitable airlines, 2005. *Source: Airline Business*

		Net profit (US $ million)	*Net margin (% of sales revenue)*
1	Air France-KLM	1108	4.3
2	British Airways	829	5.5
3	Singapore Airlines	747	9.3
4	Emirates	674	10.7
5	Iberia	635	10.5
6	Qantas	575	6.0
7	Lufthansa	561	2.5
8	Southwest	484	6.4
9	Cathay Pacific	424	6.5
10	Ryanair	380	18.1
11	Air China	294	6.3
12	FL Group	274	274.2
13	ANA Group	235	2.0
14	ACE/Air Canada	221	2.6
15	Gol Transportes Aeros	213	212.6
16	Korean Air	196	2.6
17	Aeroflot Russian	190	7.5
18	Thai International	169	4.2
19	LAN	147	5.9
20	Saudi Arabian Airlines	137	3.5

high-revenue business travellers. The two exceptions are the two most successful of the low-cost airlines, Southwest and Ryanair (leaving aside the truly exceptional cases of the FL Group and Gol Transportes Aeros). In the other direction the four heaviest loss-makers were all US airlines, all of which operate extensive networks of domestic routes within the US routes on which they face extremely fierce competition. In fact three of them applied for bankruptcy protection and their 2005 losses were greatly affected by charges made to their accounts to cover costs of re-organization. But even subtracting these extraordinary items, their losses were still the heaviest.

Almost all of the US $43 billion losses in the past 5 years were in fact sustained by US airlines. These airlines also received a US $5 billion aid package from the US Government to help them get over the aftermath of 9/11. In 2005 US airlines were still losing money, to the tune of US $10 billion, whilst airlines in the rest of the world made net profits of US $4 billion (although that still came nowhere near the 'cost of capital' rate of return required to ensure value for shareholders). A graph of net margins over time (Figure 2.22) shows US airlines incurring some very heavy losses in 2001 and 2002 but recovering by 2006 to move closer to margins

Table 2.7 Twenty heaviest loss-making airlines, 2005. *Source: Airline Business*

		Net loss (US $ million)	Net margin (% of sales revenue)
1	United	−21176[a]	−121.9[a]
2	Delta	−3818[b]	−23.6[b]
3	Northwest	−2533[c]	−20.6[c]
4	American	−861	−4.2
5	Varig	−612	−29.8
6	ATA	−445	−42.3
7	Malaysian	−421	−13.4
8	JAL	−416	−2.2
9	US Airways	−237	−2.2
10	China Southern	−226	−4.8
11	Alitalia	−208	−3.5
12	Austrian	−160	−5.2
13	Air Berlin	−144	−9.5
14	Swiss	−142	−5.0
15	Kuwait Airways	−82	−9.6
16	PIA	−74	−6.9
17	Garuda	−71	−6.0
18	Continental	−68	−0.6
19	Midwest	−65	−
20	China Eastern	−57	−1.7

[a] Affected by re-organization charges of US $20.6 billion.
[b] Affected by re-organization charges of US $889 million.
[c] Affected by re-organization charges of US $1.1 billion.
− Not available.

achieved by airlines elsewhere. Against the background of an expanding US industry there have been a number of major airline liquidations, most happening in or just after a period of economic recession (Figure 2.23).

There might have been more liquidations but for the protection afforded to airlines under the US Bankruptcy Code. In this two major provisions are relevant to airlines in financial difficulties: Chapter 7 which is in effect a straight bankruptcy, when a trustee is appointed to sell off available assets to repay creditors; and Chapter 11 which governs business re-organizations. Amongst other things, Chapter 11 allows companies, with court approval, to reject agreements made under collective bargaining and to renegotiate contracts with creditors. The intention behind Chapter 11 is to give a firm under pressures of financial liquidity some 'breathing space' in which to shelter from its creditors and to gain some time to re-organize its affairs in an attempt to stay in business. From deregulation in 1978 up to 2005 there have been 162 airline filings under the Bankruptcy Code, 22 of them in the past 5 years. These are listed in Table 2.8 which details the chapter under

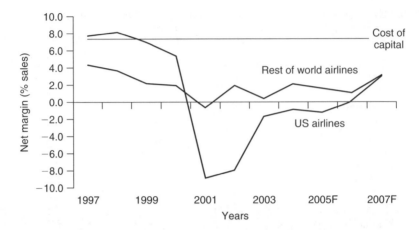

Figure 2.22   Airline Profitability: US airlines compared to airlines from the rest of the world, 1997–2007 (*Source*: Air Transport Association)

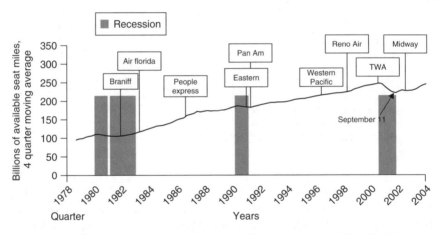

Figure 2.23   Growth in US airline industry capacity and major airline liquidations, 1978–2004 (*Source*: Air Transport Association)

which each filing was made (three under Chapter 7, the rest under Chapter 11) and the eventual outcome.

There has been a lot of controversy about the effect of the Chapter 11 provision. Some have argued that it serves to artificially prolong the lives of 'failed' carriers. This is a subject on which there is further discussion in the following chapter on competition issues. There have of course been bankruptcies outside the US. A list of failed airlines in Europe since 2000 is given in Table 2.9. Apart from Sabena and Swissair, the other airlines that have gone out of business have been relatively small, new entrant airlines rather than large, long established ones.

Table 2.8 US airline bankruptcy filings 2000–2005. *Source:* US General Accountability Office

Filing	Airline	Chapter filed	Outcome
29 Feb 2000	Tower Air	11	Ceased operations
1 May 2000	Kitty Hawk	11	Emerged from bankruptcy
19 Sep 2000	Pro Air	11	Ceased operations
27 Sep 2000	Fine Air Services	11	Emerged from bankruptcy
3 Dec 2000	Legend Airlines	11	Ceased operations
6 Dec 2000	National Airlines	11	Ceased operations
3 Aug 2001	Midway Airlines	11	Ceased operations
10 Nov 2001	Trans World Airlines	11	Acquired by American Airlines
2 Jan 2002	Sun Country Airlines	7	Liquidated[a]
30 July 2002	Vanguard	11	Ceased operations
11 Aug 2002	US Airways	11	Emerged but later re-filed[b]
9 Dec 2002	United Airlines	11	Still in bankruptcy
21 Mar 2003	Hawaiian Airlines	11	Emerged from bankruptcy
30 Oct 2003	Midway Airlines	7	Ceased operations[c]
23 Jan 2004	Great Plains Airlines	11	Ceased operations
30 Jan 2004	Atlas Air/Polar Air cargo	11	Emerged from bankruptcy
12 Sep 2004	US Airways	11	Merged with America West
26 Oct 2004	Southeast Airlines	7	Ceased operations
30 Dec 2004	Aloha Airlines	11	Still in bankruptcy[d]
14 Sep 2005	Delta Airlines	11	Still in bankruptcy[d]
14 Sep 2005	Northwest Airlines	11	Still in bankruptcy[d]

[a] New owners acquire assets and resume operations.
[b] In 2004.
[c] Originally ceased operations in 2002 before filing for Chapter 7 in 2003.
[d] At the time of writing.

Another factor that is relevant when comparisons are being made of the profitability of international airlines is the influence of foreign exchange rates. An international airline typically earns a large proportion of its revenue, and incurs a large proportion of its costs, in its own national currency, the currency of the country in which it is based. But whilst large,

Table 2.9 Airline failures in Europe 2000–2006.[a] *Source*: Compiled by the author from various sources

2000	Debonair	UK
	AB Airlines	UK
2001	Gill Airways	UK
	Sabena	Belgium
	Swissair	Switzerland
2002	British World Airways	UK
	HC Airlines	UK
2003	Euroceltic	UK
	Aero Lloyd	Germany
	Air Lib	France
2004	Duo Airways	UK
	SkyNet	Ireland
	JetGreen	Ireland
	JetMagic	Ireland
	Sobelair	Belgium
	V-Bird	Netherlands
	Volare	Italy
	Air Polonia	Poland
	Air Littoral	France
	Flying Finn	Finland
2005	EUJet	Ireland
	Hellas Jet	Greece
2006	Air Wales	UK

[a] This list is not exhaustive.

these proportions are not necessarily dominant (Hanlon, 1981). Some airlines can earn more than half their revenues in foreign currencies while incurring the vast majority of their costs in their national currency. So when exchange rates fluctuate this can have a significant impact upon an airline's profit and loss situation. Airlines based in countries with 'hard', appreciating, currencies are disadvantaged by a rise in the exchange value of their national currencies, while the opposite is the case for airlines based in countries with 'soft', depreciating, currencies. In the future, the effects of market liberalization and globalization could mean that such currency gains and losses largely disappear, or at least become much less significant, as airlines get greater freedom to switch their costs out of hard currencies and also greater freedom to enter what have hitherto been traditionally regarded as national carrier's 'home' markets. The introduction at the beginning of 1999 of the new EU currency, the Euro, reinforcing this trend, while at the same time ensuring greater transparency in the relative levels of air fares charged in different countries.

2.5 Full-service versus low cost

The financial situation faced by large airlines in the US has to be considered an extremely serious one. Large US airlines occupy 6 out of the top 10 positions in terms of airline size (Table 2.1) but only one of them is earning profits (Tables 2.6 and 2.7) whilst three of them are under Chapter 11 bankruptcy protection (Table 2.8). The seeds of this situation were sown long ago; and a brief historical outline of how some famous airlines have been forced out of the industry – but usually only after a long struggle – might help to place it all into perspective.

Just 2 years after the passing of the US Airline Deregulation Act in 1978 the once-mighty Pan American Airways, a household name but one which was in desperate need of some liquidity, decided to raise cash by selling off its most valuable and prized assets at fire-sale prices. (The assets included its landmark building in New York, the Intercontinental chain of hotels, and its Pacific, North Atlantic, and Latin American route traffic rights.) The money raised enabled Pan Am to limp through another decade before finally succumbing to a further series of losses. In a similar way, Eastern airlines filed for Chapter 11 in 1989, having had net losses ever since 1980. Eastern had above-average labour costs and also had to contend with a devastating strike by its mechanics and pilots. A continuation in labour unrest forced it to shut down for good in January 1991. Another famous airline to suffer through years of losses after deregulation was Trans World Airways. To begin with it seemed as though TWA was going to be able to ride out the crisis, aided by some labour concessions and also by a buoyant economy. But when (at the time of the Gulf War) it needed further help, the unions refused; and the expedient of selling off assets (route, property, and equipment) proved not to be enough and so TWA made the first of what turned out to be three petitions for bankruptcy in 1991. The airline managed to struggle on for another 10 years until, on the verge of liquidation in 2001, it was taken over by American Airlines.

Continental is the only pre-deregulation airline to emerge successfully from bankruptcy protection; and it survives to this day. In the early years of deregulation it suffered heavy losses essentially because of its inability to compete against new entrants' lower labour costs. In its first period in Chapter 11 (1983–86) it reduced salary and benefit packages and terminated its existing pension plans. But a few years later it had to return to Chapter 11 (for 1990–93) and this time the cuts it made were more widespread amongst the staff. It also negotiated deferrals for future pay increases so that when it emerged from bankruptcy it had the lowest-cost structure of any major pre-deregulated airline.

The above airlines, along with American, United, Delta, Northwest, and the recently merged US Airways/America West, can all be termed 'full-service' airlines, alternatively known as 'network' carriers, or, especially in the US, 'legacy' airlines ('legacy' because they existed on the major trunk and/or international routes before deregulation). The financial performance of these so-called full-service airlines in the deregulated era has become so precarious as to lead some to suggest that the fundamental business model is broken (Tretheway, 2004). It is broken because of fierce competition from rapidly expanding 'low-cost' airlines, which are sometimes alternatively described as 'budget' or 'no frills' airlines. (The terminology used in this book is to regard the alternative labels, whether for 'full service' or 'low cost', as synonyms.) In the US the three largest and most successful low-cost airlines are Southwest, JetBlue, and AirTran.

Across the world as a whole full-service airlines still predominate. Around two-thirds of the top 100 airlines in Table 2.1 can be classed as full-service airlines. The top 25 low-cost airlines are listed in Table 2.10, a list which expressly excludes the charter airlines which exist mainly in Europe and which can be regarded as a special form of low-cost air transport. Charter airlines have recently been consolidating into three large groups, details of which are given in Table 2.11. The more successful of them have been adopting hybrid business models, by which is meant that they market low-fare seat-only services alongside their traditional business of packaged tours. (Two examples of this are the independent operator Monarch and Thomsonfly, part of the TUI Group.)

Much has been written about the low-cost business model pioneered in the US by Southwest Airlines, replicated and extended by Ryanair in Europe and copied in one way or another by a large number of start-up airlines all across the world. A very good discussion is given by Doganis (2006) whose book contains an entire chapter devoted to the subject. So all that is attempted here is a brief summary.

The key concept in a low-cost model is *simplicity*. Low-cost airlines offer a simple product produced through simple operations. The product is sold at low fares, or sometimes very low fares, that are for the most part unrestricted but which permit no refunds and no interlining. Seats are sold ticketless, online and mostly direct from the airline itself (with very little business, if any, going via travel agents). In-flight service is either non-existent or has to be paid for separately by the passenger. Many low-cost airlines have dispensed with seat assignment, passenger choosing their own seats when on the aircraft. Point-to-point services are flown at high frequency, often on routes bypassing full-service airlines' busy hubs. Partly as a result of this, punctuality is usually very good.

The simplicity of their operations is seen first and foremost in low-cost airlines' standardized fleets. In many cases only one aircraft type is employed, maybe in a number of different variants. The most popular equipment is

Table 2.10 Top 25 low-cost airlines ranked by passenger numbers, 2004.[a]
Source: *Airline Business* (May 2005)

		Country	Low-cost launch	Passengers (thousands)	Aircraft current on order	
1	Southwest	USA	1971	70 909	420	80
2	Ryanair	Ireland	1991	27 594	86	78
3	easyJet	UK	1995	24 300	95	87
4	AirTran	USA	1993	13 170	91	48
5	Air Berlin	Germany	2002	12 037	44	60
6	JetBlue	USA	2000	11 783	73	210
7	Virgin Blue	Australia	2000	9537	45	2
8	Gol	Brazil	2001	9204	30	21
9	Song	USA	2003	8000[b]	36	12
10	WestJet	Canada	1996	7836	57	13
11	Independence	USA	2004	7059	88	57
12	Frontier	USA	1994	6420	48	15
13	Lion	Indonesia	2000	6100	19	
14	Ted	USA	2004	5000	49	6
15	Spirit	USA	1990	4777	32	35
16	flybe	UK	2002	3962	31	25
17	germanwings	Germany	2002	3474	17	
18	bmibaby	UK	2002	3200	16	
19	DBA	Germany	2003	3000	16	
20	AirAsia	Malaysia	2001	2839	19	60
21	Hapag-Lloyd Express	Germany	2002	2700	14	
22	Cebu Pacific	Philippines	1996	2450	15	14
23	Norwegian	Norway	2002	2074	12	
24	Virgin Express	Belgium	1997	2051	11	
25	Monarch	UK	1986	1860	–	

[a] The definition of a low-cost carrier adopted in this table is one of an airline flying point-to-point intra-regional scheduled services with no interlining. The airline will have a stand-alone management team and market itself with a single-class service, selling most of tickets through direct sales via the Internet. There will be few frills on board; and carriers will have simplified fleet structures and fast turnarounds at airports. Five other notable carriers in this sector are: Sterling (Denmark), Kulula.com (South Africa), Thai AirAsia (Thailand), MyTravelite (UK), and Germania Express (Germany).
[b] Estimated.
– Not available.

the Boeing B737 airliner. Aircraft are flown at high utilization rates which means that they are often in the air for over 11 hours a day. Flights are more often than not operated in and out of non-congested secondary, down-town, regional or local airports at which some very rapid turnarounds (15–20 minutes) can be achieved.

Table 2.11 The three large European charter groups in 2004. *Source: Airline Business* (September 2005)

	Charter Traffic	
	Passengers (thousands)	Passenger-kilometres (millions)
TUI Group	19 500	55 600
Thomsonfly[a]	8100	20 400
Hapagfly	7100	16 800
Corsair	2100	12 200
Britannia Nordic	1150	4059
TUI Belgium[b]	1000	2300
Thomas Cook Group	14 500	40 868
Condor Flugdienst	7110	21 520
Thomas Cook Airlines (UK)	5010	14 338
SunExpress	1160	2629
Thomas Cook Airlines (Belgium)	970	2381
MyTravel Airways	9280	25 671
MyTravel Airways (UK)	6380	17 941
MyTravel Airways (Denmark)	2900	7730

[a] including Britannia Airways.
[b] commenced operations in April 2004.

What traditionally has been offered by full-service airlines is by contrast very much more complex. It is aptly described by Tretheway (2004) in the following terms:

> In the period from 1945 to the end of the 20th century, the world's airline industry built a remarkable product. A passenger almost anywhere in the world could purchase a ticket to seamlessly fly to almost any other part of the world. This remarkable feat did not require an industry structure consisting of a single global airline. Rather, it used a complex, but effective set of relationships among hundreds of individual air carriers. Individual airlines invested in internal systems, infrastructure and procedures to connect passengers within their own network, and to the network of other airlines, including competitors… …. Travellers enjoyed low transaction costs – a single call to one airline or travel agent would procure for them a ticket to anywhere, potentially using the services of many carriers, and allowing refundability, flexibility, and in a large number of cases, transferability.

All this came at a cost.

The comparative economics of full-service and low-cost airlines can be examined most clearly by using data supplied in the same form by both kinds of airline. Such data is supplied to the US Department of Transportation and this has been analysed by the US General Accountability Office (2005) whose

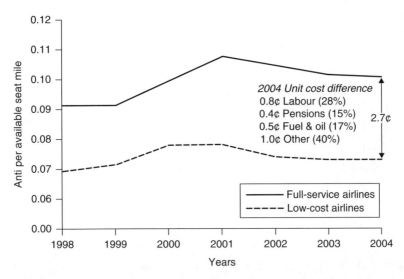

Figure 2.24 Unit cost differentials, US full-service versus low-cost airlines, 1998–2004 (*Source*: Adapted from US General Accountability Office, 2005)

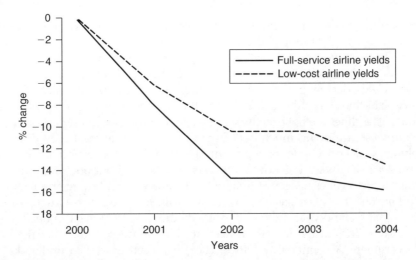

Figure 2.25 Percentage changes in passenger revenue yields, US full service versus low-cost airlines 2000–2004 (*Source*: Adapted from US General Accountability Office, 2005)

results on costs, revenues, and profitability are given in Figures 2.24–2.26. The finding on costs is that full-service airlines are at a disadvantage of about 2.7 cents per available seat mile. Both kinds of airline are experiencing declines in yields, the amount of revenue airlines collect for every mile a

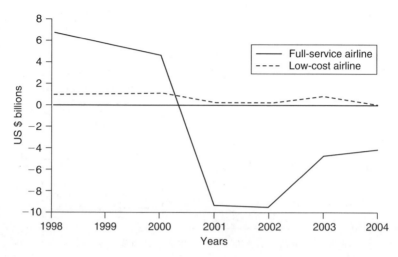

Figure 2.26   Operating profits and losses, US full service versus low-cost airlines, 1998–2004 (*Source*: Adapted from US General Accountability Office, 2005)

passenger travels. The declines reflect the increased intensity of competition and the consequent loss of airlines' pricing power in the UK domestic market. This has affected full-service airlines more severely and the percentage decline in their yields is therefore that much steeper. With higher costs and with yields declining faster, it is no surprise that the profitability of full-service airlines has fallen below that of the low-cost airlines. As a group the low-cost airlines are not exactly making a lot of profits – although some, like Southwest, are doing much better than others – but at least they did not plunge so deeply into losses as the full-service airlines did, especially in 2001 and 2002. The point has now been reached where all but one of the major full-service airlines has spent time under Chapter 11 bankruptcy protection; and the one that so far has not, American Airlines, posted such a huge loss in 2005 that some people are wondering whether it is to be next in line. Full-service airlines in the US are in deep trouble, so deep in fact that the US Government Accountability Office (2006) has been moved to undertake a special study into the question of whether re-regulating the airline industry would at this stage be desirable. The conclusion reached by the GAO is that it would not be, because it would likely reverse much of the benefits travellers have gained in the more competitive environment since deregulation.

3

Competition issues

3.1 The regulation versus competition debate

For many years air transport was a closely regulated industry, both domestically and internationally. Governments had a whole host of reasons why they were not prepared to leave the industry entirely to the forces of free and unfettered competition. This regulation versus competition debate spawned a large literature in the 1960s and 1970s (see Richmond, 1962; Caves, 1962; Wheatcroft, 1964; Levine, 1965; Kahn, 1970; Keeler, 1972; Douglas and Miller, 1974; White, 1979). All that is presented in this section is some brief discussion of the fundamental issued involved.

Governments traditionally regarded air transport as, in some sense, a public utility. Strictly speaking, it is not. Economists prefer to reserve the term 'public utility' to enterprises that have characteristics of natural monopoly. Natural monopolies exist where the advantages of size are so great that a service can only be provided at least cost if it is supplied by one, and only one firm. A single firm becomes a monopolist because the average cost of providing the service reaches a minimum only when an output rate large enough to satisfy the entire market has been reached. In a situation of this sort competition will not be sustainable. If there is more than one firm, each of them must be producing at a higher-than-minimum level of average cost; and so each will have a motive to cut price to raise output and thereby reduce average cost. The result is likely to be economic warfare, the outcome of which will be the survival of just one firm, the natural monopolist. The monopolist may then in the interest of maximizing its own profits, raise price and restrict output, producing at a rate at which costs are not minimized. Hence the rationale for government regulation: to prevent the firm from using its monopoly market power to move away from satisfying total market demand at least cost by charging a higher-than-competitive price for the service.

There is general agreement on the need for regulation in natural monopoly industries. These are industries in which the ratio of fixed (inescapable) to variable (escapable) cost is often very high. The fixed costs are often associated with heavy infrastructure investment, which often generates some enormous economies of scale, with average costs falling as output expands. Telecommunications, gas and electricity distribution, and water supply are often cited as examples of natural monopolies. If there were several firms supplying a given local area, this would result in multiplication of cables, transformers, pipelines, and so on. Consequently it is much more efficient if local monopoly rights are granted to just one firm. But to prevent this firm exploiting its monopoly position, regulation is required to restrain prices. This is why the UK government, having decided to privatize telecommunications, power, and water utilities, also decided to impose upon them price caps related to the rate of general price inflation. It is also the reason why similar public utilities in the US are subject to rate-of-return constraints in their pricing.

The UK government applied the same principle when privatizing the British Airports Authority (BAA), and imposed caps on the charges the BAA can make for aeronautical activities at Heathrow, Gatwick, and Stansted. Similar caps have been applied at Manchester Airport. It is recognized that there are elements of natural monopoly in the supply of airport facilities. But are there any in airline operations? Where airport authorities supply runways and terminals, where navigation and air traffic control facilities are supplied by governments, and where the 'track', or airspace, is god-given, airlines are very much in the position of having their infrastructure provided for them. They have no heavy investment to make in fixed assets with inescapable or sunk costs. The major investment an airline has to make is in the acquisition of a fleet of aircraft. An aircraft is a sophisticated, hi-tech piece of equipment and as such can be a rather expensive asset to acquire, costing many millions of dollars to purchase. But an airline does not necessarily have to purchase aircraft; it can lease them. And even if it does purchase aircraft, the costs involved are by no means inescapably sunk, in the same way as infrastructure investment often is. For by its very nature, an aircraft is a very mobile asset, and can be considered as 'capital on wings'. There is a well-developed market for second-hand aircraft and, to be disposed of, an aircraft can be flown to the other side of the world if need be. Hence an aircraft is in no sense a fixed asset and can be redeployed relatively easily.

It is generally accepted that the airline industry is characterized by a relatively low fixed-to-variable cost ratio. Most of the costs incurred are escapable. This is not to say that there are no sunk costs at all. As discussed later expenditures on advertising are, to all practical intents and purposes, sunk costs. Nor is it true to say that there are absolutely no elements of natural monopoly in the airline industry. Investment in sophisticated computer reservations systems (CRSs) involves a great deal of capital expenditure and the average cost of running a system falls sharply as the number of bookings increases. This too is discussed later in the book. But generally speaking, the a priori expectation is that sunk costs in the airline industry are very low by the standards of many other industries. Also there is no particular a priori reason to expect the long-run average costs of airline operation to fall with increases in output. Nor does the empirical evidence suggest this. A whole army of scholars in the US has over a long period been engaged in testing this hypothesis (Koontz, 1951, 1952; Proctor and Duncan, 1954; Cherington, 1958; Caves, 1962; Gordon, 1965; Straszheim, 1969; White, 1979; Crane, 1954). The general findings of these studies was that the average cost per seat-mile bore no statistically significant relationship to the total number of seat-miles flown, or that long-run average cost was more or less constant with respect to output levels. Caves (1962) concluded that, once some minimum efficient size has been attained, scale of operations plays an insignificant role in determining average costs, and that very large size may even be slightly disadvantageous. Both theory and evidence strongly suggest that the industry is characterized by constant returns to scale, at least so far as the costs of airline operation are concerned. On this view, large airlines would have no cost advantages over small airlines and therefore the latter would face no insuperable entry barriers.

Airlines may not qualify as public utilities under an economist's natural monopoly definition, but governments have often treated them as though they do, regarding them as 'quasi' public utilities (Wheatcroft, 1964). There are a number of reasons for this. The most general argument is that civil aviation, like other transport industries, generates important external benefits. The returns from air transport are not limited to those accruing to the industry itself, but encompass wider effects on the economy at large. Governments often see airlines as instruments to promote special national interests. The national airline can be looked upon purely and simply as a prestige symbol; or as a means of encouraging trade and foreign investment; or as a way of stimulating the development of tourism; or as an important source of foreign exchange; or as a vehicle for providing support to home industries in the aerospace sector; or as a way of guaranteeing the availability of a standby fleet, with fully trained crews, in the event of an emergency. Governments have many different objectives to pursue, and there can often be conflicts between these and the commercial objectives of airlines themselves. So countries have often tried to avoid these conflicts by conferring monopolies on their national airlines, protecting them from free and unregulated competition on international routes. The importance governments attach to these nationalistic and mercantilist objectives may have been declining somewhat over time, but they are still highly significant.

In discussions of airlines as quasi public utilities, the question of safety is often the question raised. Air transport is a fail-dangerous activity, a fail-extremely-dangerous one. It has always been regarded as having unique safety problems because of the nature of its vehicle. There is a widely held view that market forces alone cannot be expected to elicit from all airlines a sufficiently high and consistent degree of attention to safety standards. It is true that airlines have strong commercial self-interests in safe operations. Nobody will want to fly on an airline with a poor safety record. But most people would prefer to prevent accidents by regulation, rather than wait for an airline to lose passengers' confidence. While the airline may be acquiring a reputation for unsafe operations, many people could actually be killed. The need for technical regulation of safety is one of the few things on which governments have reached unanimous agreement. Under the aegis of the International Civil Aviation Organization, governments have agreed standards of airworthiness, maintenance, aircrew qualifications, flying hours limitations, and other operational requirements. It is fair to say that technical regulations of this kind have met with a fair measure of success. The number of passengers killed has fallen over time, despite substantial growth in traffic; and accident rates, however these are measured – per passenger-kilometre, or per landing – all show considerable declines (Figure 3.1). Across the world in 2001 there were 11 fatal accidents on scheduled services, involving 439 passenger fatalities (Table 3.1). This is equivalent to 1 death for every 3 billion passengers-kilometre flown, a rate eight or nine times better than that which prevailed in the early 1970s. On the whole scheduled airlines' safety record is impressive both in its own right and in relation to other modes. But there are some wide variations by country (Taylor, 1988). One of the best records is the US, where deregulation since 1978 does not, on the face of it, appear to have had any significant effects on total or fatal accident rates, which have continued to fall. In the US the safety record on all four main modes of transport has improved quite significantly over the past 15 years or so (Figure 3.2). In statistical terms bus, rail and air all appear much safer than the private car; and the fatality rate (Table 3.2) in air transport is considerably below that in either

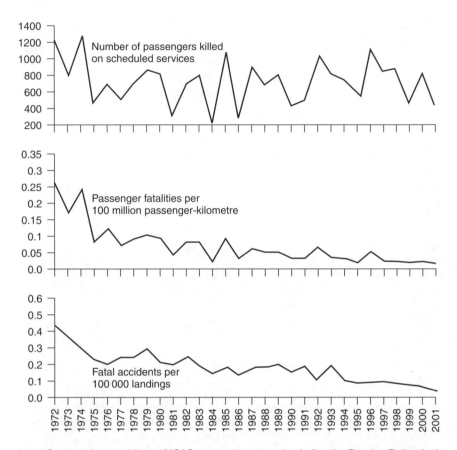

Note: Graphs relate to airlines of ICAO contracting states (excluding the Russian Federation)

Figure 3.1 Fatal accident rates on scheduled services, 1972–2002 (*Source*: International Civil Aviation Organization)

bus or rail transport. But of course there is another aspect to this, the problem of terrorist attacks on civil aviation. Some data collected by the International Civil Aviation Organization (Table 3.3) has shown that while the number of acts of unlawful interference have if anything declined, the numbers of people injured or killed (while include people on the ground) have varied quite a lot. The horror of 9/11 is reflected in the figures for 2001. In just 1 year more people were killed this way than in the previous two decades.

Another argument advanced in favour of regulation is that the airline industry, if not a natural monopoly, is naturally oligopolistic, at least at the level of the individual route market. Oligopolistic industries are ones in which most of the output is produced by just a few large firms. When there

Table 3.1 Aircraft accidents involving passenger fatalities on scheduled air services, 1982–2001[a]. *Source*: International Civil Aviation Organization

	Aircraft accidents	*Passengers killed*	*Passenger fatalities per 100 million passenger-kilometres*	*Fatal accidents per 100 000 aircraft landings*
1982	25	762	0.08	0.25
1983	21	817	0.08	0.20
1984	16	218	0.02	0.14
1985	25	1037	0.09	0.21
1986	19	427	0.03	0.15
1987	23	889	0.06	0.18
1988	26	712	0.05	0.19
1989	29	879	0.06	0.21
1990	23	473	0.03	0.16
1991	24	518	0.03	0.17
1992	24	972	0.05	0.17
1993	31	806	0.04	0.21
1994	23	961	0.05	0.14
1995	20	541	0.02	0.12
1996	21	1125	0.05	0.12
1997	24	859	0.03	0.13
1998	20	904	0.03	0.11
1999	20	498	0.02	0.10
2000	18	755	0.03	0.09
2001	11	439	0.02	0.05

[a] Statistics relate to airlines of ICAO contracting states, excluding the USSR up to 1992 and the Commonwealth of Independent Stated thereafter.

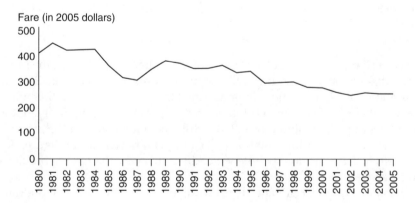

Figure 3.2   Median round-trip fares in real terms, US domestic routes, 1980–2005 (*Source*: US General Accountability Office)

Table 3.2 Fatality rates[a] in the US by mode of transport. *Source*: US National Safety Council

	Car[b]	*Bus*[c]	*Rail*	*Air*[d]
1989	1.12	0.04	0.06	0.09
1994	0.91	0.03	0.04	0.06
1999	0.83	0.07	0.10	0.003
2003	0.75	0.05	0.02	0.005

[a] Per 100 million passenger miles.
[b] Including taxis; drivers considered as passengers.
[c] Excluding school buses.
[d] Excluding cargo airlines.

Table 3.3 Aviation security, 1982–2001. *Source*: International Civil Aviation Organization

	No. of acts of unlawful interference	*No. of persons injured or killed during acts of unlawful interference*	
		Injured	*Killed*
1982	36	119	14
1983	45	70	15
1984	41	249	68
1985	40	243	473
1986	14	235	112
1987	13	121	166
1988	12	21	300
1989	14	38	278
1990	36	145	137
1991	15	2	0
1992	10	123	10
1993	30	2	28
1994	37	53	36
1995	14	3	0
1996	15	54	130
1997	6	0	1
1998	9	1	0
1999	6	2	2
2000	11	20	0
2001	21	3205[a]	3520[a]

[a] The number of deaths and injuries on the ground on 9/11 estimated from various sources.

are only a few firms in the industry, each firm, when deciding on price and other marketing strategies, must take the likely reactions of its competitors fully into account. A price cut, for example, may be advantageous to one firm considered in isolation, but if this results in other firms also cutting their prices to protect their sales, then all firms might suffer reduced profits. Consequently, oligopolists are expected to avoid price competition, colluding to co-ordinate their prices either with one-firm acting as price leader or with all firms joining a cartel. In those situations the oligopolists can seek maximum joint profits, setting prices at levels similar to those that would prevail under monopoly. In avoiding price competition, the oligopolists then channel most of their competitive efforts into various forms of non-price competition, advertising, and other kinds of product differentiation. Price cutting may be seen as a fairly dangerous thing to do, since it can start a price war that may have grave consequences for the stability of the industry, while advertising and product differentiation may be viewed as much less risky ways of winning customers away from competitors. But expenditure on such non-price forms of competition may only have the ultimate effect of raising the costs of the entire industry, because of mutually offsetting effects, one firm's efforts in this direction being cancelled out by those of another; and the higher costs may be passed on to the customer in higher prices. Hence, to prevent firms colluding, or to prevent the instability caused by price wars, it was argued that oligopolistic industries like the airline industry should be regulated, with prices set by a government regulatory authority.

A similar argument questions whether a deregulated air transport market can be viable in the long term, or whether the inherent characteristics of the industry are such that competition would ultimately prove destructive. This is an issue that has been around for a long time and it is one that tends to attract more attention during economic recessions. Air transport markets often exhibit a lot of instability over time, due to high-income elasticities of demand, as discussed in Chapter 2. But in addition to this there is the question of the existence or not of a so-called 'empty core' (Button, 1996, 2002; Telser, 1978). Simply put, a core implies that competition leads to the optimal level of supply in the market, but where there are indivisibilities competition could destabilize the market and lead to a sub-optimal level of supply or no supply at all. The core is then said to be empty. For example, in the present context, a route might ideally, given the level of demand, be served by one and half flights a day, but naturally only one or two flights can in fact be flown. One airline might operate a single flight but its high profits might attract a second carrier. Two airlines on the route might not be able to generate sufficient revenue to make a profit, so that one or both might abandon the route. The result might be no flights at all or just one operated as a local monopoly. If such an empty core exists there can be benefits for both the airlines and their passengers if the airlines get together and co-operate with each other. But if airlines are permitted, or more than that encouraged, to co-operate, it might be difficult to distinguish between situations in which such co-operation is desirable for the establishment of stable market equilibria and when it merely serves a cloak for anticompetitive collusion to enable the carriers to earn monopoly profits. If any kind of collusive behaviour is to be sanctioned by government authority, it is important to consider how best to regulate such collusion once it is allowed.

Arguments about external benefits, safety, market stability, etc., led to the establishment in 1938 of the US Civil Aeronautics Board, which for the next 40 years regulated the prices charged by scheduled airlines operating interstate domestic routes in the US and also controlled entry to these routes. There was much criticism of regulation by the CAB (Caves, 1962). Much of this criticism centred on the CAB's entry policies: between 1938 and 1977, the CAB permitted no entry at all into city-pair markets that already had two or more carriers, and even in markets with no non-stop service or where there was only one carrier, there was little new entry. The critics argued that new entry was important for promoting competition and stimulating efficiency. There was also criticism that airline fares were considerably higher than they would have been under competition. This was largely attributed to airlines competing mostly in terms of frequency of service and in-flight frills like gourmet meals and not in terms of fares. Some economists (Douglas and Miller, 1974) suggested passengers would gladly trade frequency and frills for substantially lower fares. At the same time more and more people began to question the merits of regulation when they could see what appeared to happen when regulation was absent. CAB regulation only applied, at the federal level, to interstate routes. Routes within individual states were unregulated and fares there were very much lower than on interstate routes, some comparisons throwing interstate fares into a bad light. In particular, reference was made to the so-called 'Californian experience' (Levine, 1965). Some very cheap fares were available on routes like San Francisco–Los Angeles and these fares (and also some on routes within Texas) compared very favourably with equivalent fares on interstate routes of approximately the same distance on the East Coast. For example, standard coach class fares for intrastate routes in California were often about half (and sometimes less than half) those for interstate routes from cities like Chicago, Boston, and Detroit (Table 3.4). Many people blamed regulation for the high fares on interstate routes, so the Federal Government decided to deregulate interstate routes, passing the Airline Deregulation Act in 1978.

The above arguments were clearly very influential in persuading the US government to deregulate when it did. But there were also perhaps some other, more underlying, factors involved. The effect that the suppression of price competition had in channelling airline competition into aspects of service quality had implications for airlines' choice of equipment and thus for aircraft manufacturers. At a time of rapid technological advance in aircraft design, airlines stood to lose market share unless they matched

Table 3.4 Comparisons of fares on interstate and intrastate routes within the US, 1975. *Source*: Civil Aeronautics Board

City-pair	Distance (miles)	Coach class one-way fare ($)
Los Angeles–San Francisco (intra)	338	18.75
Chicago–Minneapolis (inter)	339	38.89
Los Angeles–Sacramento (intra)	373	20.47
Boston–Washington (inter)	399	41.67
San Francisco–San Diego (intra)	456	26.21
Detroit–Philadelphia (inter)	454	45.67

their competitors in using the latest type of aircraft available, because the most up-to-date aircraft had greater passenger appeal.

The advent of pressurized cabins, the replacement of piston-engined aircraft by turbo-props, and then the substitution of turbo-props by jets, all tended to mean that aircraft were retired from front line service before they were fully amortized in the operator's accounts, having been rendered prematurely obsolescent by more advance types. For this reason airline executives sometimes complained that the rate of aeronautical innovation was too fast for the financial health of their companies. Had airlines been free to compete in terms of fares, it is possible that the rate of innovation might have been appreciably slower. But each technological leap in aircraft design brought with it a substantial gain in productivity, reducing seat-mile costs; and the pressure on airlines to adopt new aircraft had important advantages for the manufacturing sector. If there appeared to be no significant economies of scale in airline operations, there certainly were some enormous ones in aircraft manufacture. The cost per aircraft declines very steeply as the rate of output of a particular type increases, as development and set-up costs are spread over more and more units and as the manufacture moves down the 'learning' curve. From this point of view the main beneficiaries of regulation may well have been not the airlines themselves but rather their suppliers. But that was then. The circumstances now are somewhat different. Since the introduction of the first wide-bodied airliner powered by turbo-fan engines there have been regular improvements in aircraft design, but no major advance has occurred recently and there is no new technological leap on the horizon. For the first time in the history of the industry, aircrafts are being retired more because they have reached the end of their physical lives than because of obsolescence. Diminishing marginal returns have set in the field of aeronautical innovation and there are fewer external benefits from regulation to flow from this direction: hence the shift in focus to efficiency in airline operations, sought by deregulation and by allowing greater price competition.

If, as some have argued, the airline industry is naturally oligopolistic, would the outcome with deregulation simply be that firms would recognize their mutual interdependence and continue to avoid price competition through collusion? This is where another set of arguments, made in reference to the theory of contestable markets, came in.

3.2 Contestable markets

The theory of contestable markets was developed in the early 1980s. The key point in this theory concerns the *threat* of competition, as distinct from *actual* competition. According to the theory, firms in oligopolistic industries will still price at the same levels as they would in more competitive industries, provided a threat of competition exists. For the threat of competition to be credible and for a market be classed as contestable a number of preconditions must be met (Baumol, 1982; Baumol, Panzar, and Willig, 1982). First, there should be no barriers to the entry of new firms to the market. What this means in economic terms is that there should be no extra costs borne by new entrants that are not borne by incumbent firms already in the industry. If for instance incumbent firms enjoyed economies of scale, as in a natural monopoly situation, new entrants would be at a cost disadvantage, and then the threat of their entry would not be all that credible. The second condition is that there should be no heavy 'sunk' costs. A sunk cost is a cost that, once incurred, is inescapable. For its entry to be a real threat, a new firm must be able, if it wants to, to engage in 'hit-and-run' entry. It must be able to go into the market, make profits for a brief period of time and, if things look as if they are not going to work out on a long-term basis, get out of the market again without having irrevocably committed a lot of resources and without losing a lot of money. If hit-and-run competition is profitable, any attempt by incumbent firms to raise price above competition levels will provoke entry. But entry to some industries does involve substantial costs. In manufacturing, for instance, investment in fixed plant and equipment, such as a factory, is a heavy sunk cost; and for this reason many manufacturing industries are not contestable markets. What is also necessary for successful hit-and-run entry is a third condition, which is that the time it takes incumbents to respond to new entry by varying their prices is longer than the time the new firm needs to make its entry profitable. In other words there must be some delay in the reaction of incumbent firms; otherwise the incentive for entry, that is the existence of prices above competitive levels, could be withdrawn as soon as entry takes place, making entry an unattractive proposition.

How far are these conditions met in markets for air travel? As discussed earlier, there appear to be no elements of natural monopoly in the airline industry, nor much evidence of significant scale economies. Hence new entrants would not on these accounts be at any cost disadvantage compared with existing firms and the condition that there are no entry barriers might appear to be met. Then what about the condition that there should be no sunk costs? If a new airline wants to enter the industry, it is going to need some aircraft. An aircraft is a sophisticated, hi-tech piece of equipment and as such can be a rather expensive asset to acquire, costing many millions of dollars to purchase. But expenditure on aircraft is not a sunk cost in the same way that plant and equipment in manufacturing is. For an aircraft may be considered as 'capital on wings' and by no means a fixed asset but, by its very nature, a highly variable one. It is something that can be disposed of fairly easily, flying it to the other side of the world if need be. The main fixed assets used by airlines are in fact provided for them by governments and airports. So can new entrants succeed in hit-and-run competition? It was thought that the entry/exit process could be a rather quick one and certainly quick enough in relation to incumbents' ability to change fares, alter schedules, etc., since in the past such changes had always been subject to some delay.

So, with all three conditions apparently met, the proponents of contestability considered the airline industry as almost a textbook example of a contestable market (Bailey, Graham, and Baumol, 1984) If that is so, it does not matter so much if there is little actual competition on a particular route, so long as there is plenty of potential competition, with a lot of new entrants ready to come in if incumbent airlines exert market power and charge high fares. But a decade and a half of experience with deregulation in the US and elsewhere has cast a lot of doubt on this proposition.

Experience of deregulation

There have been many studies of US deregulation (Civil Aeronautics Board, 1982; Bailey et al., 1985; Brenner, Leet, and Scholt, 1985; Levine, 1987; Kahn, 1988; US Department of Transportation, 1990; Keeler, 1991; Dempsey and Goetz, 1992; Williams, 2002). These all provide detailed accounts of the effects on airline costs, fares and profits, on industry concentration, on the intensity of competition, etc. and so only a very brief commentary focusing on the fundamental issues is presented here. There are also studies covering the effects of deregulation in Canada and Australia (Button, 1991), but since the effects in Canada and Australia have been very similar to those in the US, the discussion here focuses on US experience.

At first it seemed that the advocates of deregulation were to be vindicated by events. Deregulation brought in a lot of low-cost new entrant airlines and released airlines hitherto confined to intrastate routes. Airlines like People Express, AirCal, Air Florida, and so on began challenging the established trunk airlines on interstate routes. This had a dramatic impact on industry structure. The number of carriers offering scheduled services on trunk routes rose from 36 in 1978 to over 120 by 1985; and by 1985 the top five carriers accounted for 57 per cent of the US industry's output, compared with 69 per cent in 1978. So industry concentration fell; fares and costs also fell; and profits rose, as airlines became more efficient. All in all, things looked good. Two economists at the Brookings Institution in Washington DC (Morrison and Winston, 1986) set out to estimate the benefits of deregulation, comparing the situation in 1983 with that in 1977, 1 year before the airline Deregulation Act was passed. They made the comparison by constructing a 'counterfactual' 1977 scenario, developing a model to give a picture of how the industry would have looked had there been no regulation in 1977. The results of this study indicated annual gains to passengers of at least $6 billion and to airlines of at least $2.5 billion (both figures at 1977 price levels). Given all this, deregulation was hailed as an unqualified success in the mid-1980s. But what happened then?

From 1985 onwards the industry entered a period of consolidation. Fierce competition pushed a number of airlines into bankruptcy or merger. Many of the established airlines, shaken in the early years of deregulation, by now had recovered, having cut costs and having learnt to exploit some of their advantages to force competitors out. Aggressive pricing and scheduling behaviour proved to be more effective competitive weapons than some advocates of deregulation had foreseen. Concentration in the industry began to rise again. Hardly any of the original new entrants survived as independent operators; and the industry has become more oligopolistic than it was before deregulation, the top five carriers now accounting for 70 per cent of the industry's output.

The theory revisited

Does this show that contestability no longer applies? Or was it not really applicable in the first place? US experience of deregulation suggests that, contrary to earlier a priori reasoning, none of the pre-conditions for contestable markets is wholly met in the airline industry. Some of the leading figures who initially suggested that air transport may be 'naturally' contestable subsequently changed their minds:

> We now believe that transportation by trucks, barges and even buses may be more highly contestable then passenger air transport.
>
> (Baumol and Willig, 1986)

To see why a different view is taken now, let us reconsider the conditions for contestability, taking them in reverse order.

What is now abundantly clear is that new entrants cannot really engage in hit-and-run entry, but only 'hit-and-get-hit-back' entry. It is not realistic for new entrants to expect some delay before incumbent airlines respond to their entry. Where there is any delay, it is getting shorter and shorter all the time. Under regulation there were relatively few fares and these changed relatively infrequently. But, as everyone now knows, in liberalized markets fares can be changed many times, almost at a moment's notice, the changes being notified to travel agents more or less instantly via extensive networks of computer reservation systems. The number of fare changes airlines make is rising rapidly. In the past, the Airline Tariff Publishing Company, a co-operative venture between airlines to process changes in ticket prices, considered 25 000 changes a day to be a large number. But by 1988, somewhere between 40 000 and 60 000 was not unusual (and in one peak week nearly 600 000 were processed, United Airlines along filing around 30 000 a day (Hamilton, 1988)). It is clear that incumbent airlines can now react very swiftly when they see any of their traffic threatened by a new entrant. Or they can even forestall entry by announcing fare changes in advance of the entrant commencing operations on the route or routes in question, something discussed further in Chapter 6.

It is also questionable whether the no-heavy-sunk-costs condition is met. The costs of acquiring aircraft may not be sunk costs, but there are other items of airline expenditure that are, such as advertising expenditure. Money spent on advertising cannot be recouped if the airline decides to withdraw from the industry. It is inescapably sunk. And this can now be quite a heavy sunk cost. One result of deregulation has been to increase the relative importance of advertising and sales promotion in general. For reasons discussed below, to be a major carrier in deregulated markets, an airline needs a fairly extensive network of routes. It is possible for some airlines to operate as 'niche' carriers, specializing on certain types of routes for certain types of traffic; but to enter into competition with the large network airlines, a new entrant would need to commit a lot of non-recoverable resources to advertising the launch of a network and thus would have to incur a lot of sunk costs.

Sunk costs in advertising and difficulties with the idea of hit-and-run entry are serious enough objections to the notion of contestability in air transport. But the most compelling reason for rejecting its application to airline competition is the discovery that there are some 'new' forms of entry barrier. The airline industry may not be like public utilities in having strong elements of natural monopoly, nor like capital intensive manufacturing industries in having significant economies of scale in production; but there are nonetheless some very important advantages in large firm size in this industry. There is no particular advantages in large size per se, as some airlines have discovered (e.g. Aeroflot, Pan American, TWA and Air France, perhaps) and the benefits of large size derive not from conventional economies of *scale* as such but from greater opportunities to reap economies of *scope*.

The distinction between economies of scale and economies of scope can be explained as follows. With economies of scale, the average cost per unit of output declines as the level of output increases. Where economies of scope exist the cost of producing two (or more) products jointly is less than the cost of producing each one alone. Formally, if C denotes cost and Q output, economies of scale mean that C/Q falls as Q expands. Economies of scope can be gauged from the relation:

$$S = \frac{C(Q_1) + C(Q_2) - C(Q_1 + Q_2)}{C(Q_1 + Q_2)}$$

where $C(Q_1)$ is the cost of producing Q_1 units of the first product alone, $C(Q_2)$ is the cost of producing Q_2 units of the second product alone, and $C(Q_1 + Q_2)$ is the cost of producing Q_1 units of the first product in combination with Q_2 units of the second product. Where there are economies of scope $S > 0$ because the cost of producing both products together is less than the cost of producing each alone, that is $C(Q_1 + Q_2) < C(Q_1) + C(Q_2)$. The larger the value of S the greater the economies of scope.

The scope economies large airlines are able to reap lie mainly on the marketing side, most of them related to network size. Airlines serving large and widespread networks can more easily afford large-scale marketing campaigns which are much more efficient than promotions of individual routes, but which are beyond the means of many small airlines. Quantity discounts in media purchasing mean that advertising costs rise much less than in proportion to the number of city-pair markets served. Also, advertising an entire network gives large airlines a strong sense of identity in the public mind. The marketing advantages of large networks are reinforced by the use of sophisticated CRSs and loyalty marketing schemes. CRSs generate economies of scope, insofar as they permit the booking system to be centralized and they also have useful some spin-offs like, for example, facilitating the airline's yield management procedures. These are discussed in Section 3.4. Loyalty marketing schemes, in the form of frequent flyer programmes (FFPs), travel agency commission overrides (TACOs) and corporate discounts, require extensive networks to be most effective, and these are discussed in Section 3.3. But the most important source of economies of scope – and arguably the most profound change induced by deregulation – are the economies of route traffic density airlines can reap by configuring their networks in the hub and spokes pattern. By combining passengers and groups of passengers an airline can carry the total more cheaply than if it carried the passengers separately. This is what might be achieved by routing through hubs, which has the effect of increasing traffic on each sector flown. The impact of hub and spokes networks is discussed more fully in Chapter 5.

If economies of scope have become so important in deregulated air transport, why were they not evident before? They were not uncovered in the many studies referred to above that investigated relationships between size and efficiency in air transport. There are two possible explanations. First, the researchers were examining the influence of output level Q, on average cost, C/Q, and not directly seeking a measure of scope economies, S. Second, it could have been that regulation itself prevented large airlines from exploiting their size advantages, given that route entry was controlled and airlines had limited freedom to pursue scope economies by reconfiguring networks.

If economies of scope give large airlines significant advantages over smaller ones and in this way it reduces contestability, how has this affected the benefits of deregulation? There is no doubt that average fares paid by passengers have fallen in real terms, after allowing for inflation. What is a little less clear is how far this is due to deregulation and how far it is the result of other factors. A study by the US Government Accountability Office (2006) found that fares on US domestic routes in 2005 were in real terms almost 40 per cent lower than they were in 1980 (Figure 3.2). The extent to which this fall can be attributed to deregulation, as opposed to other factors such as advances in technology, has been matter of debate and some controversy. Dempsey and Goetz (1992) have taken the view that falls in the early post-deregulation period had less to do with deregulation per se and rather more to do with fuel prices, which actually fell in real terms at that time. That certainly has not been the case recently. As shown in Figure 3.3,

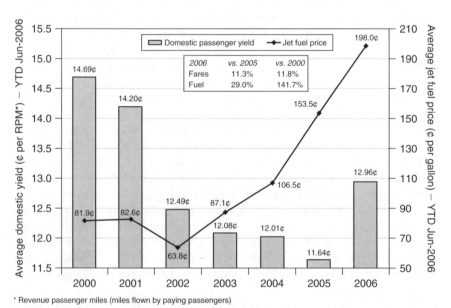

Figure 3.3   Jet fuel prices and airline yields, US domestic routes, 2000–06 (*Source*: Air Transport Association)

in which fares are represented by yield per revenue passenger mile, fuel prices have risen steeply, whilst fares have continued on their downward trend. But Dempsey and Goetz also contend that the fall in air fares has merely been the continuation of a long-term trend established in the pre-deregulation period. A more widely supported view is that expressed by Pickrell (1991), an economist at the US Department of Transport, whose review of various estimates of deregulation's effect on fares led to the conclusion that on average fares paid are some 15 per cent lower than they would have been if the regulatory regime had continued in force.

With fares in real terms having fallen by 40 per cent, should this not be reflected in the growth of passenger demand? Passenger traffic has indeed grown strongly, but traffic growth on US domestic routes has not been particularly exceptional when compared to growth on domestic or international routes elsewhere in the world. This is a point that has in the past been raised by the UK Civil Aviation Authority, raising the question of how large estimated gains from deregulation to US consumers can be reconciled with traffic demand only increasing at rates commensurate with the growth in air travel across the world as a whole, when in some parts of the world, outside the US, government regulation has not disappeared completely.

There are of course many factors determining passenger demand and those affected by deregulation (primarily fares and service frequencies) could have been outweighed by other more exogenous factors. For example, the US market for air travel is one of the most mature and in mature markets one might expect growth rates in passenger demand to be lower then elsewhere, as explained in Chapter 2. So, the fact that US traffic has grown at approximately the same rate as world traffic could still be, at least in part, a positive result of deregulation.

Re-regulation?

What some airlines might consider to be a negative outcome of deregulation is the financial insecurity that seems to go with it. The losses incurred by full service airlines have been so heavy that, on some calculations, the sum total of deficits could be seen as exceeding all profits accumulated since the invention of powered flight, as it has been put in some press articles. No surprise then if, seeing this, airlines elsewhere have occasionally viewed the prospect of deregulation with something less than unbounded enthusiasm. And within the US, with so many airlines having to file for bankruptcy protection, the question has from time to time been raised as to whether, in the interests of industry stability, there should be a return to government regulation and control. But the majority of studies in which this issue has been given serious consideration have been fairly unequivocable in concluding that the industry should not be re-regulated.

Airlines' financial position in the first half of the 1990s brought into question whether the two goals set for President Clinton's National Commission to Ensure a Strong and Competitive Airline Industry (Clinton Commission, 1993) are compatible: is it really possible to achieve both a strong and competitive industry at one and the same time? In the depths of a recession there tended to break out a number of spectacular 'price wars', which lent some credence to the view that the industry is susceptible to destructive competition. The Clinton Commission received a lot of complaints about the way in which the bankruptcy laws are administered, in particular the Chapter 11 provision. It was submitted that Chapter 11 bore a heavy responsibility for the industry's poor performance overall, insofar as it served to artificially prolong the lives of failed carriers, giving them temporary relief from the need to service their debts and encouraging them to offer deep discounts on fares just in order to generate sufficient cash flow to keep going. This, it was argued, obliged other carriers to follow suit, the ensuing price wars plunging the whole industry into losses. The Clinton Commission did not altogether accept this, although it did conclude that some reform to bankruptcy law was desirable, to reduce the time bankrupt airlines are given to file re-organization plans.

In an updated application of their 'counterfactual' methodology for estimating the welfare effects of deregulation, Morrison and Winston (1995) found that travellers' benefits were still accruing at very healthy annual rate of US $18.4 billion (at 1993 price levels). Accordingly these authors rejected calls for the industry to be re-regulated, notwithstanding the lack of profitability and the instability that goes with it. Morrison and Winston subjected the question of how far the industry's financial losses could be attributed to the pricing behaviour of carriers operating under Chapter 11 to econometric analysis. Their conclusion from that is that the effect was quite small. (Interestingly, it was found that the net revenues of some airlines were actually enhanced through the tarnished image of its bankrupt competitors, for example Delta in competition with Eastern – although those of some of the others were actually damaged by the lower marginal costs and fares of competitors in Chapter 11, for example American and United competing against TWA.)

In a more recent study conducted by the US Government Accountability Office (2006) the overall conclusion drawn is that re-regulating the industry 'would likely reverse consumer benefits . . . especially lower fares'. The GAO noted that numerous industries had been deregulated in the US over the past 30 years, but that very few had been re-regulated. The few instances in which an industry was re-regulated stemmed from inadequate competition (such as occurred in the cable television industry after it was deregulated). Aside from concerns about lack of competition at some heavily congested hub airports, the same cannot really be said about air transport, especially now that the low-cost carriers are presenting such a challenge to the full-service airlines.

Contestability in a broader sense?

William Baumol, one of the original exponents of the theory of contestable markets recently presented a paper (Baumol, 2005) in which he made the following observation:

> ... *margins in air passenger transport tend to be higher when a fewer number of carriers serve a given route. This phenomenon has been widely interpreted to imply that* ... *the firms possess market power and, more broadly, that the observation refutes the conjecture that the air markets are highly contestable. I had previously accepted those conclusions but am now forced to recant. Although passenger air transport may or may not approximate a high degree of contestability* ... *the number of airlines serving a route does not settle the issue.*

Thus it appears that Baumol, who once considered air transport highly contestable – indeed almost a textbook example of it – and who later saw reason to change his mind on that, has now changed it back again, at least in part.

Perhaps the kernel of the matter is what is meant by 'a given route'. In the most fundamental terms a route is the physical path an aircraft takes between take-off at one airport and landing at another. So a route is essentially that which links together an airport-pair. But this is not necessarily the same thing as a 'market'. In one, fairly narrow, sense a market is made up of all passengers who want to travel from a specific origin to a specific destinations, and of all airlines which provide service from that origin to that destination. In this respect there is often an important distinction to be made between the *city-pair* market and the *airport-pair* route. The former relates to the passenger's true origin and destination; and in hub and spokes systems many passengers travel on two or more different routes but participate in just one market. It is the city-pair market to which contestability should refer. There are of course cases where the airport-pair route can be the city-pair market as well; but there are also cases in which one city-pair can be served, even directly, by two or more airport-pairs. Contestability is unlikely to be high in hub-to-hub city-pair, except possibly where there are alternative (secondary or downtown) airports in one or other of the cities involved. Consider for example a city-pair like Houston–Chicago. The route between Houston International (IAH) and Chicago O'Hare (ORD) is a hub-to-hub airport-pair. (Continental operates its largest hub at IAH, while American and United both operate hubs at ORD.) But the overall city-pair market should include routes to/from other airports in each metropolitan area, principally in this case Chicago Midway (MDW) and Houston Hobby (HOU).

The concept of contestable markets naturally tended to appear less convincing when, in the deregulated US industry, the entry of a lot of new airlines was followed in quick succession by their exit, either to bankruptcy or through a takeover. Since deregulation in 1978 well over 200 new entrant airlines have come and gone through bankruptcy or takeover. In retrospect it could be that many of these new entrants were seeking to contest the wrong market, or at least contest it in the wrong way. This possibility can be examined by comparing and contrasting the experience of two low-cost airlines making their way into the industry in the early years of deregulation: People Express and Southwest Airlines.

People Express entered the industry in 1981 as a low-cost (and certainly no frills) airline. By 1985 it had become the fifth largest airline in the US, with flights to most major US cities as well as some transatlantic long-haul services. As an entry strategy, it attempted to establish a low-cost hub and spokes system, all centred around its hub at Newark, New York. Its expansion was at a particularly explosive rate. It also pursued an aggressive acquisitions policy, taking over Frontier Airlines, Britt Airways, and Provincetown-Boston Airlines, all within a short space of time. In 5 short years the number of miles flown annually by People Express had reached 92 million. But this rapid expansion came with a number of problems. One of these was the strong competitive reaction from full service airlines operating the same routes. Two carriers in particular, American and Northwest, engaged in price wars with People Express (see Chapter 6). Facing competition as fierce as this, loaded down with debt and struggling to integrate the operations of the airlines it had acquired, People Express was forced to sell itself to Texas Air Corporation; and it ceased to exist as a separate carrier on 1st February 1987, when its routes and assets were merged into the operations of another Texas Air subsidiary Continental Airlines. Thus People Express first enjoyed rapid growth but then met with sudden failure.

The entry strategy and initial growth aspirations of Southwest Airlines were altogether more cautious. As it turned out, Southwest has achieved some very high growth rates, often much higher than other airlines in the industry. But it did not set out to achieve growth at all costs. Nor did it seek to become a hub and spokes airline, at least not in the conventional sense. It does of course have a number of large bases across the country, but these are not hubs in quite the same way as Atlanta is for Delta Airlines, Minneapolis is for Northwest, Dallas-Fort Worth for American, and so on. Southwest pioneered the concept of a low cost, no frills airline which mostly involved flying short haul point-to-point services at high frequency, utilizing secondary airports. It is not true to say that Southwest avoids major airports completely, since it does fly into LAX, Phoenix Sky Harbor, Cleveland Hopkins, Pittsburgh and, invading a major hub for US Airways, Philadelphia. But the really heavily congested and slot-constrained hubs are still off-line to Southwest: ORD, Boston Logan, Washington Reagan and the three large airports in New York, Kennedy, La Guardia, and Newark. Southwest serves the New York metropolitan area at MacArthur Airport in the small town of Islip (population 20 000) on Long Island. This is a long way out of Manhattan – the rail service takes 1 hour 25 minutes. But any additional access/egress time on ground transportation is at least partly offset by a saving of some 15 to 20 minutes in average flight (block) times as a result of less taxing on the ground and less 'stacking' in the air. Southwest has been consistently profitable ever since 1973. Its original mission was to make flying less expensive than driving. The airline often entered markets not so much as to compete against other airlines as to attract traffic from the roads. It offered fares 50 to 60 per cent below those of other airlines at the time. At these fares the airline could only be profitable with lean operations and high rates of utilization of both aircraft and crews. The success of its business model led to the low-cost-high-profits phenomenon being named after the company: the 'Southwest Effect', in which the key concept is that when a low-cost airline enters a market, the market itself changes, so that a 50 per cent drop in fares is met by not just a doubling but maybe even a quadrupling of passenger demand. Southwest has been an inspiration to other low-cost airlines. Its original business model has been repeated many times around the world. Its two best-known disciples in Europe are easyJet and Ryanair. Indeed it has been said that Ryanair is now the best illustration of what a low-cost model entails, in that it goes to greater extremes in reducing costs and eliminating service frills (Tretheway, 2004). But if Ryanair is considered as one of the best examples, People Express might count as having been one of the worst. People Express sought to win business by charging low fares, but its costs were not particularly low because it chose to enter the industry as a hub and spokes airline. Its basic business model was therefore not a recipe for profitability. It is possible to identify other reasons why People Express ended up the way it did. Some suggest it was because it expanded too rapidly – it took Southwest 17 years to reach the annual mileage figure which People Express had attained in 5 years (Rhoades and Tiernan, 2005). It also had labour relations problems and some difficulties in integrating the operations of Frontier. But more fundamentally than that it was probably seeking to contest markets already well served and to contest them by doing much the same thing as airlines already there were doing.

Baumol's point about the number of airlines on a route not settling the issue can be readily accepted if, by 'route', he has in mind an airport-pair. For there is a great multitude of airport-pairs which are served by just one airline. It would not necessarily be sensible to regard all these as monopolies causing concerns about competition. To cite an extreme example: at the time of writing Ryanair's operations at London Stansted cover 86 airport-pairs, in many of which Ryanair is the only airline involved, such as Stansted to places like Haugesund, Bydgoszcz, Esbjerg, Carcassonne, and so on. But the particular airport-pair, or even in some instances the particular city-pair, is not broad enough to define the market. Destinations can compete for passengers just as airlines do. The fact that Southwest is the dominant carrier in 90 of its top 100 airport city-pairs is no real cause for concern either, especially when fares are low.

These points may be insufficient to rehabilitate fully the application of contestable markets theory to air transport. The problems over its underlying premises of no insuperable entry barriers, no heavy sunk costs, and profitable hit-and-run entry still very largely remain. Also remaining are a number of questions about airlines' business practices. One of these concerns airlines' use of loyalty marketing schemes.

3.3 Loyalty schemes in airline marketing

Loyalty schemes form part of an airline's overall marketing strategy, and expenditure on loyalty schemes is much like expenditure on other forms of marketing such as advertising. Marketing expenditure has two fundamental purposes. One is to increase the airline's share of passenger demand; the other is to make that demand less-price elastic. These objectives are illustrated in Figure 3.4.

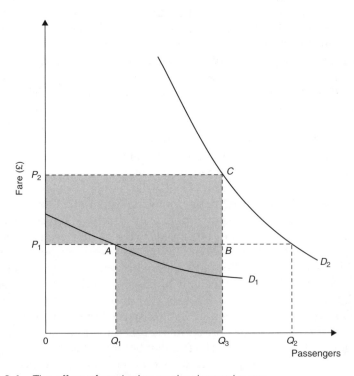

Figure 3.4   The effect of marketing on the demand curve

The original demand curve, before anything is spent on marketing, is represented by D_1. On this schedule, if the fare charged by the airline is P_1, the number of passengers carried by the airline is Q_1. Following a marketing campaign the demand curve shifts to the right and acquires a steeper slope. The rightward shift allows an increased number of passengers (Q_2) to be attracted to the service at the original price, and the steeper slope enables the airline to raise the fare and still have a substantial increase in passengers. Thus, in Figure 3.6, the fare can be raised to P_2, at which passenger demand is Q_3, still well above the original level of Q_1.

The airline benefits both from an increase in passengers and from a higher fare per passenger; its total gain in revenue is the shaded area, area Q_1ABQ_3 from the increase in passengers plus area P_1BCP_2 from the increase in fare. So long as this additional revenue is greater than the costs associated with the marketing campaign, the airline increases its profit.

Reducing price elasticities is an underlying objective that loyalty schemes have in common with advertising and other forms of marketing. Advertising is an attempt to reduce elasticities by persuading passengers that one airline's service is much superior to those of others, whereas loyalty schemes seek to achieve the same effect by raising passengers' 'switching' costs, making it relatively expensive, in terms of lost rewards, to transfer their patronage from one airline to another. If price elasticities or more particularly cross-price elasticities are reduced, this lowers the incentive for competitive price cutting and increases the scope for enhancing revenues by raising fares.

Loyalty schemes can often be more profitable than other forms of marketing. It often costs more in marketing terms to generate new customers than to retain existing ones. A major advantage in loyalty schemes is that they provide a valuable source of data about customers on whom the greatest amount of profit is earned, enabling firms to target these customers that much more effectively (Reichheld, 1996).

Airlines tend to focus loyalty schemes on passengers whose demand is already less price elastic; that is, on passengers prepared to pay premium fares for first, business, and fully flexible economy class travel. To these passengers, price is usually a far less important factor than factors related to the quality of service, factors like frequency, seat access, convenience in making/changing bookings, in-flight comfort, and so on. And the fares such passengers pay are often some multiple of the fares paid by passengers from price elastic segments of the market, passengers who travel on promotional fares like the advance purchase excursion (apex), passengers for whom price is the most important factor. Because the amounts they pay are so much higher, passengers travelling on first, business and unrestricted economy class fares typically contribute a disproportionately large share of the airline's total revenue. And the share they contribute to airline profits can be even more disproportionate. The profit per passenger is often much greater in the higher fare categories, and passengers seated towards the front of the aircraft are usually those on whom the lion's share of airline profit is earned.

Hence it is towards the high-fare traffic that airlines mainly direct the marketing of their loyalty schemes, of which there are essentially three kinds: FFPs, corporate discounts, and travel agency commission overrides (TACOs).

FFPs

FFP is a purchase incentive plan which rewards the passenger for repeat patronage of the services of a particular airline. For each eligible ticket bought, the passenger accumulates mileage points according to distance travelled and according to the type of ticket bought, first and business class passengers receiving points at multiples of the basic rate. Once earned the passengers can exchange the mileage points for rewards in the form of free or discounted tickets, upgrades from one class of travel to another, special concessions on car hire and hotel accommodation and other benefits in the form of free gifts, dedicated lounges at airports, and so on.

The first FFP was launched by American Airlines in 1981 and this was so successful that other US airlines decided to follow suit. The growth in FFP awards has been truly spectacular, from 4.1 billion miles awarded in 1981 to 1646 billion in 2002 (Table 3.5). American's 'AAdvantage' programme now has 48 million members, while United Airlines' FFP 'Mileage Plus' has around 43 million and Northwest's 'WorldPerks' about 25 million (Table 3.6). All told about one in every five or six people in the US is a member of a FFP. The popularity of the programmes run by US airlines meant that European airlines had to introduce schemes of their own, albeit somewhat reluctantly at first. The first European carrier to have one was British Airways (BA), with its original 'Air Miles' scheme which is now known as 'Executive Club', followed by Lufthansa with its 'Miles and More' programme. Now virtually all major airlines have FFPs, under their own distinctive brand-names, such as 'Flying Blue' of Air France/KLM (combining the former 'Frequence Plus' (AF) and 'Flying Dutchman' (KL)) SAS's Eurobonus, British Midland's 'Diamond Club', Virgin Atlantic's 'Flying Club', and so on. Membership numbers vary a lot from airline to airline according to size and depending upon whether or not it is a significant player in markets for international business travel.

A recent survey by *Official Airline Guides* found that 90 per cent of the world's business travellers participated in a FFP. Participation is highest in the US where travellers participating in FFPs belong to an average of 4.6 schemes each. In Europe the highest participating rates are to be found in France, the Netherlands and the UK, and the lowest in Belgium and Germany. Across the world as a whole, 120 million people are members of an FFP, 24 million in Europe and 21 million in Asia. Just over a quarter of these people are active FFP members.

Table 3.5 Mileage awards, redemptions and FFP liabilities, US Airlines 1981–2002. *Source: www.webflyer.com*[a]

| | No. of miles (billions) | | Accumulated liability for unredeemed[b] |
	Awarded	Redeemed	
1981	4.1	1.9	2.2
1982	16.8	12.9	6.1
1983	38.3	28.6	15.8
1984	65.1	41.9	39.0
1985	94.3	57.3	76.0
1986	123.8	72.8	127.0
1987	163.0	81.3	208.7
1988	282.1	90.8	400.0
1989	337.1	120.4	617.2
1990	394.1	133.4	877.9
1991	443.3	155.3	1165.9
1992	498.8	178.6	1486.1
1993	583.0	202.1	1867.1
1994	644.0	278.6	2232.4
1995	661.0	284.8	2608.6
1996	830.0	255.3	3183.3
1997	980.0	271.8	3891.5
1998	1120.0	403.0	4608.5
1999	1290.0	358.8	5539.7
2000	1440.0	349.5	6630.2
2001	1600.0	341.6	7888.6
2002	1646.0	402.9	9131.7

[a] Data derived from the 10-K reports that airlines file with the US Securities Exchange Commission (SEC) each year.
[b] Awards minus redemptions cumulated year on year.

It is known that business travellers are heavily influenced by their FFP membership in choosing the flights of a particular airline. A survey undertaken by the US General Accounting Office (1990) found more than half the responding travel agents reporting that travellers always or almost always choose their flights in order to build up FFP mileage points (Table 3.7), the GAO concluding that FFPs 'tilt the playing field on which carriers compete'. In a number of ways FFPs encourage travellers to choose the airline on which they are most likely to fly in the future. This is especially so for FFPs marketed by airlines dominating particular hubs. Frequent flyers in the hub city could become virtually 'captive' to the hub airline. Multiple membership of several different FFPs is always possible, but the rewards are usually structured in a non-linear fashion such that their marginal value increases as the passenger builds up more and more

Table 3.6 Membership of FFPs, selected airlines. *Source: www.webflyer.com*

	Est. no. of members	As at
Aer Lingus TAB USA	2 11 000	Aug 02
Aeromexico Club Premier	16 00 000	Jun 03
Air Canada Aeroplane	60 00 000	Nov 03
Air China Companion	24 00 000	Jul 05
Air France/KLM Flying Blue	1 00 00 000	Jun 05
Air-India Flying Returns	75 000	Aug 98
Air New Zealand Air Points	10 15 900	Mar 04
Alaska Airlines Mileage Plan	37 00 000	Aug 03
Alitalia MilleMiglia	18 00 000	Jun 03
All Nippon Mileage Club	1 00 00 000	Jul 03
America West Flight Fund	41 00 000	Aug 03
American AAdvantage	4 80 00 000	Jan 05
British Airways Executive Club	45 00 000	Jul 02
British Midland Diamond Club	1 75 000	Jul 99
Cathay Pacific Asia Miles	1 01 128	Aug 03
China Airlines Dynasty Flyer	–	–
China Southern Sky Pearl Club	24 00 000	Mar 04
Continental Airlines OnePass	1 90 00 000	Apr 01
CSA Czech Airlines OK Plus	9 40 000	Jun 03
Delta SkyMiles	3 50 00 000	Sep 04
Emirates Skywards	10 00 000	Sep 04
Finnair Plus	3 50 000	Jul 02
Frontier Early Returns	10 00 000	Sep 03
Gulf Air Falcon	1 30 000	Apr 02
HawaiianMiles	8 80 000	Aug 03
Iberia Plus	12 27 000	Aug 02
JAL Mileage Bank	1 40 00 000	Aug 03
Korean Air Skypass	97 00 000	Jun 03
LanChile LanPass	9 00 000	May 04
LOT Voyager	8 30 000	Apr 00
Lufthansa Miles & More	1 02 00 000	May 05
Malaysian Enrich	3 01 000	Jan 03
Mexicana Frequenta	8 24 500	Aug 03
Midwest Miles	16 54 000	Mar 04
Northwest WorldPerks	2 50 00 000	Aug 03
Portugalia Sky Club	15 000	Aug 98
Philippine Airlines Mabuhay Miles	27 500	–
Qantas Frequent Flyer	36 60 000	Jun 03
SAS EuroBonus	25 00 000	Sep 03
SAA Voyager	15 00 000	Nov 04
SIA KrisFlyer	16 00 000	Aug 03
Southwest Rapid Rewards	4 00 00 000	Dec 05
Swiss Travel Club	20 00 000	Sep 03
Thai Royal Orchid Plus	14 00 594	Jan 02
Tarom Smart Miles	25 000	Aug 03
United Mileage Plus	4 30 00 000	Dec 03
US Airways Dividend Miles	2 68 00 000	Apr 05
Virgin Atlantic Freeway/Flying Club	10 00 000	Aug 03

–Not available.

Table 3.7 The influence of FFPs. *Source*: US General Accounting Office

No. of times business travellers choose in order to build up mileage points	% of travel agents reporting
Always or almost always	57
More than half the time	24
About half the time	9
Less than half the time	4
Rarely if ever	2
Other	3
	100

points on a single airline. Indeed, some airlines have created 'elite' levels in their FFPs at which additional bonuses over and on top of any existing entitlements are awarded to members chalking up total mileages of 25 000 to 30 000, 40 000 or 60 000 or 70 000 to 90 000 within some specified period. These additional bonuses serve to increase passengers' switching costs still more.

Taking the Air France/KLM scheme as an illustration, the number of award miles needed to qualify for each elite status level at the time of writing are:

Silver   25 000 miles for residents outside France
            30 000   "   "   "   in   "

Gold   40 000 miles for residents outside France
          60 000   "   "   "   in   "

Platinum 70 000 miles for residents outside France
           90 000   "   "   "   in   "

The bonuses at each elite level are:

Silver   50 per cent additional miles

Gold   75 "   "   "   "

Platinum 100 "   "   "   "

There are also bonuses according to class of travel:

First   200 per cent additional miles

Business 100 "   "   "   "

Economy 50 "   "   "   "

As an example, a *Silver* member travelling first class on an Air France Paris – New York one-way flight earns:

3640 miles for the distance flown +
7280 as First class bonus +
1820 miles as *Silver* elite bonus
    = 12740 miles in total

And as examples of the rates at which award miles can be redeemed:

20000 miles	Paris-Nice	Economy class
25000 ..	Amsterdam – Rome	" "
50000 ..	Paris – New York	" "
80000 ..	Amsterdam – Tokyo	" "

Conditions applying to mileage points and rewards can often be rather complex, making it difficult to compare one FFP against another. European FFPs are often somewhat less generous than their counterparts in the US, insofar as they tend to award points only for travel at premium fares (first, business or full economy) whereas US FFPs allow points to be earned on all travel, albeit at different rates depending on the fare category. Where European and US carriers are in direct competition, as on transatlantic services, European FFPs have to be more generous to remain competitive and so they give special bonuses. The FFPs of European airlines are much more closely targeted at business travellers. Of European business travellers 86 per cent are members of at least one scheme; among those making more than 20 trips per year, the figure is as high as 97 per cent.

It is sometimes thought that airlines could possibly be storing up trouble for themselves in operating FFPs. What might happen if there were suddenly to be a 'run' on awards, a lot of passengers seeking to redeem accumulated mileage points all at one and the same time? Under ordinary circumstances only something between 15 and 30 per cent of accrued points is actually redeemed. Although the possibility exists of a surge in the take-up rate, as happened when in 1984 Pan American suddenly imposed a relatively short cut-off period for redemptions and the take-up rate soared to 85 per cent. But other airlines are now conscious of the dangers in doing something like that and most FFPs have standard cut-off dates set a long way in advance, sufficiently distant from the time mileage points are accrued to prevent redemptions coming in a rush. As shown in Table 3.5, in 2002 the number of FFP miles actually redeemed (403 billion) was just a quarter of those earned and awarded (1646 billion). But in this connection the more serious concern lies in the accumulated liability for unredeemed awards which is steadily mounting up year by year.

Another issue concerning FFPs is whether they generally have the effect of increasing airlines' total expenditure on marketing. Shenton (1993) points out that FFPs are only one form of marketing expense and that their growth has not been associated with increased marketing costs in total, because at the same time expenditure on media advertising has declined. Shenton cites data showing that US airline media advertising declined by 35 per cent between 1982 and 1992, while airline revenues more than doubled. In 1982 media advertising was equivalent to 1.15 per cent of revenues and dropped to 0.73 per cent by 1992, a 'saving' of $300 million, more than enough to pay for FFPs, Shenton argued. This may seem a reasonable argument and it is one apparently endorsed by the UK Civil Aviation Authority (1993b). But perhaps it needs more supporting evidence, since there could be other reasons to explain the fall in the advertising/revenue ratio, as a brief reference to economic theory might show. In economic theory, the advertising/revenue ratio is known as the 'advertising intensity' ratio and it has been demonstrated that the optimal (profit maximizing) advertising intensity is achieved when the ratio of advertising expenditure (A) to sales revenue, the product of price (P) times quantity sold (Q), is the same as the ratio of advertising elasticity of demand (E_a) to price elasticity of demand (E_p):

$$\text{advertising intensity} = \frac{\text{advertising expenditure}}{\text{sales revenue}} = \frac{A}{P \cdot Q} = \frac{E_a}{E_p}$$

where

$$E_a = \frac{dQ}{dA} \cdot \frac{A}{P} \text{ is the advertising elasticity of demand}$$

and

$$E_p = \frac{dQ}{dP} \cdot \frac{P}{Q} \text{ is the price elasticity of demand.}$$

It is commonly observed that $A/P \cdot Q$ tends to remain broadly constant over time for a particular firm or industry, but this is only the case where the magnitudes of E_a and E_p, and the relationship between them, also remain constant over time. Where there are significant changes in elasticity magnitudes, one rising relative to the other, then one should expect to see some change in the advertising intensity: if demand becomes relatively more price elastic and relatively less elastic with respect to advertising expenditure, the amount spent on advertising as a proportion of revenue will fall. This is quite possibly what has been happening in the deregulated US airline industry. With greater price competition and indeed, as discussed above, price wars, the magnitude of E_p must have been rising over time, if not for the industry as a whole, then certainly for the individual airline; and even if E_a remained constant, the value of the ratio would fall, leading to a fall in the advertising intensity, revealed by advertising expenditure falling as a percentage of revenue. It is quite likely that FFPs are partly substituting for media advertising, but just as likely that falls in advertising intensity are the result of price elasticities generally increasing.

Far from being just another heavy item of sunk costs FFPs can often be a lucrative source of income and profits. Interestingly, when United Airlines filed for bankruptcy in 2002, the only part of its business to be shown profitable was in fact its FFP (*The Economist*, 2006). An airline like United can build a marketing relationship between its FFP and a credit card company. The latter is charged for each FFP mile earned on the credit card and the income from this source has been estimated to be more than US $10 billion a year for the entire industry worldwide. The other advantage is that this income comes upfront, whereas the earned miles are not redeemed until later if at all. Even when they are redeemed, the marginal cost of a free seat for the FFP member works out only about US $25, this amount covering fuel, ticketing and in-flight catering. Grossing this up to the industry as a whole – and allowing for some loss of revenue from FFP passengers who might otherwise have paid a fare – the total cost of redemptions is probably not much more than US $1 billion per annum. That leaves a huge US $9 billion a year profit margin.

A more serious criticism is that FFPs put small airlines with relatively few routes, or routes just within one particular geographic area, at a big disadvantage when competing for the loyalty of premium fare passengers. This was recognized by airlines like British Midland and Virgin Atlantic. Neither have very extensive networks and so when they launched their respective FFPs, they sought to minimize their disadvantages in various ways. British Midland attached to its Diamond Club FFP the label 'Destinations', presumably in an attempt to distract passengers' attention away from the fact that its network is limited to short-haul domestic and European routes between large cities and has no long-haul services nor many flights to holiday resorts. And the rewards in Virgin Atlantic's 'Freeway' FFP initially concentrated on non-travel benefits (like golfing weekends) possibly seeking to offset the disadvantage of a network restricted to barely half a dozen long haul routes and appealing to those frequent travellers whose desire for further overseas travel had diminished or been sated by having flown on so many overseas trips already. Factors like this led the European Commission to the view that, a priori, FFPs may be considered a barrier to entry for new entrants with a small network' (Commission of the European Communities, 1993b).

It has been shown in theoretical terms that FFPs erect entry barriers on the demand side of the market by creating artificial linkages between different services, so that they deter entry by creating a need for airlines to establish from the outset a network of a certain size (Cairns and Galbraith, 1990). The only real way of offsetting the disadvantage of a small network is for the airline to link its FFP with those of other carriers. This is what many airlines with limited networks have done. British Midland for example, entered into reciprocal FFP arrangements with Air Canada, SAS and United, while Austrian Airlines had similar pacts with Delta and Swissair. But at the same time many of the larger airlines are also combining their FFPs, especially those grouped in one of the emerging global alliances. As the Chairman of Lufthansa, a member of the Star Alliance, put it:

> It [the combined FFP] is the glue to hold the alliance together.
> (Jurgen Webber, quoted in *Airline Business*, August 1997, p. 34)

And the six principal members of the Star Alliance have promoted the advantages of its combined FFP in the following terms:

> Be recognized as a frequent flyer on not one, but six airlines – SAS, Air Canada, Lufthansa, Thai, United Airlines and Varig. Apply mileage points from qualified flights on any of the six airlines towards your overall frequent flyer status . . . Redeem miles for reward travel on any of our six carriers, giving you more than 600 destinations around the world to choose from.
> (Advertisement placed in *The Economist*, 5 September 1998)

As two members of the oneworld Alliance, BA, and American Airlines want to combine the Air Miles and AAdvantage schemes to permit full reciprocity. So it is clear that alliances are attaching a great deal of importance to jointly marketed loyalty schemes. And it is not hard to see why: the more extensive the network to which the FFP applies, the greater the advantage large airlines which are members of a global alliance will have over smaller non-alliance carriers in competition for high-yield business travellers.

It has been argued (Levine, 1987) that, in targeting their FFPs primarily at business travellers, airlines are seeking to take advantage of the 'principal– agent' problem that arises when the traveller (the agent), monitored imperfectly by his or her fare-paying employer (the principal), makes inefficient choices between fares/travel times and additional FFP mileage points. It has been suggested that FFPs encourage unnecessary travel, or travel at higher fares than necessary, or travel over more circuitous routings, just so that the traveller, who does not meet the costs involved, can increase the number of FFP points he or she can thereby accumulate.

An advertisement taken out by the low-cost carrier easyJet reproduced a finding of a MORI survey that:

> some travelling executives were choosing flights, which earned maximum points, rather than sticking to airlines offering the most economic flights.
>
> (*Financial Times*, 7 October 1996)

And raised the question:

> Have you calculated the *real* cost of airline loyalty schemes to your company? (emphasis in the original)
>
> (*The Times*, 6 December 1996)

If this is perceived as a large problem – and as yet there is no evidence on the overall size of the problem, just anecdotal reports – then it is possible that employers will put a lot of pressure on airlines to direct the benefits from FFPs to them rather than to the individual traveller.

Corporate discounts

Some have been doing so already. Several large companies in Germany traced all the accumulated mileage bonuses outstanding to employees flying Lufthansa, as a first move towards asking for them to be handed over. In Sweden leading companies like Saab–Scania, Electrolux, and Volvo pressed SAS to award benefits from its 'Eurobonus' FFP directly to the companies and not to the travellers.

One airline that has already responded to the call is Virgin Atlantic. Virgin has given companies the option of taking the accumulated mileage credits as part of its 'Corporate Freeway' FFP; and some 250 companies have taken up this offer since it was introduced in 1994. In America almost 10 per cent of companies insist that business travellers hand back their benefits so that they can be used to obtain free or reduced price tickets for other staff. Companies that do this claim to have saved between 12 and 15 per cent on their air travel budgets. Among British companies, some have banned the use of FFPs altogether, while others take the view that the benefits should be shared by all employees and not just those who travel. Even some UK local authorities have taken an interest in FFP benefits: it was reported that Birmingham City Council, for example, demanded that all councillors making civic trips overseas hand over all mileage points so earned. Some organizations appreciate the positive effect FFP benefits have on travellers' morale and because of this are quite prepared to let their individual employees continue to enjoy them. But there are now so many FFPs in existence that their translation into some kind of corporate discount scheme would mean some significant savings for employers who spend a lot on air travel. Hence it might be expected that more and more employers will press for the loyalty bonuses to be earned on a corporate rather than an individual basis.

The corporate discount schemes that already exist tend to be cast in terms of ascending thresholds according to the number of journeys made, or the amount of money spent, on the services of a particular airline within a specified period of time. If purchases by a company or organization exceed these thresholds, then deeper discounts progressively apply, so that the discounts given rise in a non-linear fashion in a similar way that the benefits of FFPs do.

The deals are normally enshrined in formal and written contract documents signed both by the carrier (the airline or the airline alliance and by the firm). As such the contracts are legally binding, to the extent that any formal and written documents of this kind are. Each firm can have deals with several different carriers, and even separate deals with the same carrier in different countries or different regions of the world. The number of corporate deal contracts per company ranges from 5 to about 20, with the average tending to be 8 or 9. The majority of deals are offered by one single airline, although with the evolution of codesharing partnerships and airline alliances the deals increasingly cover travel by two or more airlines.

The form and detail can vary quite a lot both across airlines and from client to client. The main features and characteristics can be described as follows. The incentives in a deal may be specified as applying globally, by region, by country of destination, or by city-pair (or even by airport-pair). The discounts or rebates usually apply only to travel at premium fares (first, business or fully flexible economy class) but in some cases (e.g. often on domestic routes) travel at all fares qualifies. Also there is sometimes a difference between what counts towards a particular threshold and what qualifies for a discount or rebate: in some cases travel at all fares counts towards the threshold, with only travel premium fare qualifying for the discount or rebate.

Some contracts are couched in terms of retrospective rebates, some in terms of upfront discounts, some in terms of specific reductions on particular routes, and some involve a combination of all three. The structure of a corporate deal is often determined by the origin of the airline. US airlines have shown a preference for upfront discounts, whilst airlines in Europe traditionally have preferred rebates or a combination of rebates and upfront discounts (although this is changing).

Retrospective rebates

In rebate schemes the airline makes a refund to the client in accordance with the amount of business conducted between the two parties within some specified period, usually a year. During the year the client pays fares without any discounts and then at the end of the year the airlines returns a rebate cheque, the size of which depends on some 'trigger' threshold level reached by the client. This threshold is specified either in terms of the actual amount spent on fares or in terms of the number of sectors flown. The former is often specified in contracts as 'flown revenue' (or sometimes as 'net flown revenue' when a deduction is made for commission paid to travel agents).

An illustrative example can be given in the following terms.

Trigger Threshold (£ of flown revenue)	Rebates		
	%	£	Incremental (%)
1 400 000	3	42 000	>13.3
1 550 000	4	62 000	>20.5
1 650 000	5	82 500	>22.5
1 750 000	6	1 05 000	>24.5
1 850 000	7	1 29 500	

In this example all flown revenue, in addition to counting towards the trigger threshold, also qualifies for payment of rebates. Once the client reaches flown revenue of £1 400 000 a rebate of 3 per cent becomes payable. At the trigger threshold level itself, a 3 per cent rebate amounts to £42 000 which in effect means that the client is reimbursed for its expenditure on flown revenue from £1 358 000 to £1 400 000. The percentage rebates then rise from 3 up to 7 per cent as higher trigger thresholds are reached. Once the client reaches a particular threshold, the higher rebate is given not just on the incremental flown revenue beyond that point but on all flown revenue back to the beginning of the agreement period. Thus, once the £1 550 000 threshold is attained, the 4 per cent rebate applies to all flown revenue up to that point, so that the incremental rebate on the £150 000 of flown revenue between £1 400 000 and £1 550 000 is £62 000 minus £42 000 equals £20 000 or an incremental rebate of 13.3 per cent. Similarly, a further £100 000 of flown revenue yields an incremental rebate of 20.5 per cent. And the rebates rise in a graduated fashion, giving the client progressively greater and greater incentives to concentrate travel on the carrier concerned. Indeed, if the client's expenditure is just below the next threshold level up the list, the incremental percentage rebate can be extremely high (e.g. an addition of, say, £25 000 to flown revenue of £1 825 000 could generate an additional rebate of £20 000 an incremental rate of 80 per cent!)

Upfront Discounts

Upfront discounts come in a number of different guises. There are two basic forms in which they are paid, either as agreed percentage discounts or as net fares. An example of the former is given as follows:

Trigger Threshold (£) (£ of expenditure)	Upfront Discounts (%)	
	Long haul routes	Short haul routes
1 29 00 000	14	12
1 44 00 000	15	13
1 62 00 000	16	14
1 83 00 000	18	15
2 04 00 000	20	16

Once again there is a graduated structure, the percentage discounts rising with the trigger thresholds. Also the discounts often vary by routs (as retrospective rebates often do as well). The discounts are usually higher on long haul routes, although there are certain exceptions to this.

Net fares are fixed discounts which are offered on specific routes for particular classes of service. They are sometimes further discounted, as 'net net fares', when no commission is payable to travel agents (or even, less commonly, as 'net net net fares', when there is also no commission to credit card companies or to the hosts of CRSs). There is of course no graduated structure present in a net fares scheme. The fares are set at particular levels. Usually a net fare for economy class travel is set about 30 per cent above the cheapest excursion sold to leisure travellers.

As airlines extend their networks in the process of globalization, the more able they are to offer corporate bodies comprehensive travel packages, using not just their own online services but the services of alliance partners as well. Some alliance groupings may soon be able to offer companies worldwide service through the medium of codesharing and also through the use of franchise operators on regional routes. And if cross-border mergers take place on a significant scale, the scope for corporate deals will become very much greater.

TACOs

TACOs are to travel agents what FFPs are to individual travellers and corporate discounts are to companies. Airlines reward travel agents for directing more passengers to them, and TACOs are designed to encourage agents to concentrate bookings on a single carrier. TACOs are paid over and above standard rates of commission. The overrides may be paid, either in absolute or percentage terms, on an agent's sales for a particular airline, either in total or for a particular set of routes. They are triggered by reaching some target threshold level of sales determined in relation to the level of sales the agent achieved for the airline in the previous year. Once the threshold has been reached, the additional commission is paid not just on additional sales beyond that point but on those already made within the year in question as well. Hence the effective rate of commission on incremental sales beyond the threshold is well above the standard rate, depending on the volume of incremental sales and the proportion this bears to the threshold sales volume, usually set somewhat above the agent's sales for the previous years.

At first sight TACOs appear to tie agents to much the same extent that FFPs tie passengers and corporate discount tie firms. But there is a bit of a difference here. While FFPs and corporate discounts are offered to the airline's end-customers this is not the case with TACOs, which are deals with intermediaries. Deals with travel agents are less exclusive and have less direct influence on the travel decision. Agents can earn TACOs from a number of different airlines at the same time. And, as the Civil Aviation Authority (1994) has explained, agents may in the long run at least, have little to gain from boosting the sales of any one dominant airline. For if in 1 year the agent diverted as much traffic as possible to one particular carrier, this could have the effect of making the following year's override commissions that much harder to achieve.

Are airline loyalty schemes anticompetitive?

All three kinds of loyalty scheme create strategic advantages for airlines with high market shares and reduce the potential for competition. They go a long way towards making an extensive network almost a *sine qua non* for serious participation in the valuable premium fare market. The advantages of network size for a FFP are fairly clear. A large network gives passengers more opportunities both to earn the mileage points and to use them once they have earned them. An airline with relatively few routes is doubly disadvantaged here. The same applies, perhaps *a fortiori*, to corporate discount schemes. Corporate discounts may pose a threat to competition, possibly more so than FFPs if large airlines exploit the advantages of their networks in such a way that small competitors find it difficult, if not impossible, to respond. The UK Civil Aviation Authority (1994) has argued that discount incentives directly linked to overall use of an airline's global network are likely to be anticompetitive, against which effective action can only be mounted at a supra-national level, involving both the European Commission and the US authorities.

Virgin Atlantic made representations to the European Commission about BAs' corporate discount schemes, claiming that they are in breach of Article 86 of the Treaty of Rome which refers to an abuse of a dominant position.

BA responded that its discounting policies are standard practice, not just in the airline industry but also in hotels and car rental companies. Virgin countered that the mere fact of other firms following similar policies does not make the practice right and entered the specific complaint that BA unfairly persuades companies to use its services by offering a combination of discounts for different routes. Companies whose staff travel on routes on which BA faces little or no competition – such as from the UK to South America – are, it is said, offered additional discount if they also agree to use the airline to fly on routes served by many carriers. If true, this would be tantamount to a form of price discrimination, which can certainly have anticompetitive effects. Price discrimination is a topic discussed in Chapter 6.

Small airlines contend that they are also put at a disadvantage by the TACO schemes operated by their larger competitors. Once the initial override threshold has been reached some airlines allow the agent further overrides in exchange for still further growth in sales, on a sliding scale above the threshold level. The incremental commissions earned by the agent can become very high at particular points on this scale, on which there are significant discontinuations, known in the industry as 'spikes'. These spikes occur at sales levels at which the airline believes the agent will need the biggest incentive to further increase the sales of its tickets. As a result of this the agent's incremental commission can go up to something in excess of 50 per cent of an airline's additional sales revenue. In principle this should not necessarily be to the disadvantage of small airlines but sometimes it can be, depending on the formula used to calculate the TACOs. In particular small airlines have complained when large airlines have calibrated TACOs in relation to market shares, rewards to the travel agent being based on comparisons of sales between those for the airline paying the commission and those on other airlines the agent is dealing with. This issue was raised a few years ago in the US, when Morris Air complained to the Clinton Commission about the kind of TACOs that Delta was paying agents located in Salt Lake City. The complaint was that Delta's overrides were related to agents' percentage sales on Delta rather than simply sales growth. It might be argued that commission payments like this are in the nature of 'kickbacks' that have anticompetitive effects and thus justify intervention by the regulatory authorities.

Sales agents in other industries receive different rates of commission on different products or brands and so naturally tend to be biased towards the high-commission sale. The same might be expected of travel agents. There may be no general reason to regulate travel agents' commissions, but, since agents often hold themselves out to the public as unbiased conveyors of travel information, there may be a case for at least some controls over the way in which TACOs are structured. Otherwise there is some risk of the incentives to favour one airline over others becoming so great that, abandoning all sense of impartially, agents might increasingly lead unsuspecting travellers to sub-optimal choices between travel alternatives merely in order to meet override targets. But in any event this risk is just becoming very much less. The issues concerning TACOs are receding as airlines cut standard commission rates and achieve higher direct sales, with more and more passengers using the Internet to book online.

All loyalty schemes tend to reduce demand elasticities. That indeed is their underlying purpose. Perhaps the most serious implication for airline competition would be a general decline in the magnitude of cross-elasticities, including those with respect to the quality factors. If loyalty schemes succeed in rendering premium fare passengers more or less captive to particular airlines or to particular alliances, or to particular alliance groupings, other independent airlines are going to find it difficult to compete, not just in the premium fare segment of the market, but for promotional fare passengers as well. The non-linear incentive structures built into the schemes are designed to achieve just that.

Policy issues

If it is accepted that loyalty schemes have anticompetitive effects, what if anything should government competition authorities do about them? This question is becoming more and more pressing as time passes. Whether there are going to be two, three, or four main global alliances the future success, or even the future survival, of independent airlines remaining outside these grouping may depend crucially upon how much of the premium fare traffic becomes captive to the alliance carriers. The marketable networks of alliance carriers are set to expand greatly which will make their loyalty schemes very much more attractive to passengers; and this, together with the non-linear reward structures built into the loyalty schemes, could diminish cross-elasticity magnitudes still further. Hence independent airlines will find it extremely difficult to win the traffic back, and without the revenue from premium fare passengers many of these independent airlines may have to withdraw from some of the most important markets. Concerns of this kind have led to a number of suggestions being put forward for government policy on airline loyalty schemes; and some of the main ones are discussed briefly below.

Outright prohibition?

Some people have raised the question of whether loyalty schemes should be banned if they can be shown to be reducing competition. A total ban might seem a rather draconian measure and one likely to evince the response: why ban them in air transport, when they are in such common use in other industries?

Loyalty schemes are used a lot in retailing, by supermarket chains (in the UK, Sainsbury, Tesco, Asda, and Safeway) and a whole host of other retail outlets besides (in the UK, Boots the Chemist and W. H. Smith). The fact that firms in other industries market loyalty schemes is because they see the same competitive advantages in them as airlines do. Loyalty schemes marketed in other industries also have the effect of reducing price elasticities of demand. There is, for instance, some suggestion that supermarket chains in the UK have been able to use their purchasing power to squeeze discounts out of their suppliers but have not been passing on the cost savings to customers in the form of price cuts. Supermarkets' price-cut margins have been tending to rise. One possible explanation for this is that the widespread use of loyalty cards has reduced supermarket customers' price elasticities of demand, perhaps to such an extent that supermarkets' total revenue would fall if they cut prices. Hence the fact that loyalty schemes exist in other industries may not, in itself, be a good enough reason to justify their use in air transport.

Is it practicable for them to be banned outright? Is it not too late for this? Many air travellers have already clocked up mileage points which they have not yet redeemed. At best the schemes could only be phased out, perhaps over a fairly long period of time. But even if they were, would they not reappear in some other guise? And exactly how far would a ban go? Would it cover 'two for the price of one' offers and other similar promotions?

In short, an outright ban would be very difficult to apply and might smack of re-regulating an industry which is supposed to be in the course of deregulation. Banning FFPs in toto is not really a practical proportion. It is however more practical to apply partial bans (e.g. banning their use on certain routes). This is what two Scandinavian countries have done, Sweden in 2001 and Norway 1 year later. The Swedish Market Court banned the earning of mileage awards in SAS's Eurobonus FFP for those domestic routes on which SAS was in competition with other airlines. The ban imposed by the Norwegian Competition Authority was somewhat wider in applying to all domestic routes whether there was competition on them or not. The problem with partial bans like this is that they could be unduly disadvantaging SAS when similar bans do not apply to the FFPs of other major European airlines.

Government controls?

If it is not possible to prohibit loyalty schemes, is it possible to replace them in some way to remove, or at least reduce, their anticompetitive effects? As mentioned previously in relation to TACOs, some control over reward structures might do something to lessen the dominance of individual airlines of alliance groupings, but such controls would also amount to a fair degree of re-regulation, and as such may be considered unacceptable, not just by the airlines, but by the travelling public as well. The whole thing could easily become a regulatory mess. The successful application of 'codes of conduct' in the use of computer reservation systems (which are discussed in the next section) demonstrates that some government intervention can still be useful in an otherwise deregulated industry, but controlling things like FFPs and corporate discounts could turn out to be an administrative nightmare. Levine (1987) concluded that government control over loyalty schemes are likely to succeed only in creating other problems and would entangle regulatory authorities in a morass of complex marketing decisions about which they have little specialized knowledge and expertise.

Taxing rewards?

There is an argument that rewards from airline loyalty schemes, especially where they are received by passengers not paying their own fares, should be taxed as non-pecuniary income, a taxable benefit of employment in much the same way as the use of company cars often is. A number of governments have been considering this. It has at various times been seriously considered by the Internal Revenue Service in the US. But once again, there would be particular difficulties in implementation. The tax authorities would have to find some way of distinguishing between awards from personal travel (not to be taxed, since passengers pay their own fares) and those earned from business travel (when employers meet the cost of the tickets). Also, as Humphreys (1991) has pointed out, accruing FFP points is not the same as using them, and so there would be some tricky administrative problems in measuring the taxable benefit. What exactly would the value of the benefit be, when numerous restrictions apply to when and how awards can be redeemed; when the monetary evaluation of a free flight will vary according to the destination chosen and the fares structure applying at the time; and when redemption is subject to capacity controls, so that there will be a question of whether the valuation should be in relation to the fare the passenger would have had to pay to get the same seat on the flight, or the actual cost to the airline of carrying this additional passenger on a space-available basis (which would be much less)?

The idea of taxing rewards might be supported on equity grounds and is a response to the principal–agent problem, but it would require some intricate solution to some ticklish administrative problems, in income tax systems which are already over-burdened with complexities. On top of everything else, the fact that awards accrue to passengers from many different countries is bound to generate a lot of anomalies and possible distortions, unless there is going to be an unprecedented degree of tax harmonization across countries.

Third-party access?

To protect competition in markets for premium fare passengers, one policy option that is worthy of serious consideration is that of requiring each loyalty scheme to grant 'third-party access'. In essence what this means is giving other airlines the same arrangements that exist online or between alliance partners. This could reduce the tendency for high-fare passengers to become captive to particular airlines or to particular alliances, which in turn could reduce the tendency for cross-elasticities to fall.

The US General Accounting Office (1990) supported the idea of requiring mileage points to be transferable from one FFP to another. The view of the UK Civil Aviation Authority (1994) is that, if regulation of some kind proves necessary, it should take the form either of large airlines being required to accept small carriers as participants in their FFPs or of FFP awards being made transferable. The German Cartel Office (the Bundeskartellamt) has on one occasion actually ordered third-party access when, in 1997, it required Lufthansa to grant it to one of its small competitors, Eurowings. This followed a complaint from Eurowings that Lufthansa's Miles and More FFP violated the strict German competition laws by giving Lufthansa an 'unfair' advantage on German domestic routes, encouraging business travellers to choose Lufthansa rather than Eurowings simply on account of FFP bonuses rather than on the basis of price or service. When Lufthansa agreed to open its FFP to Eurowings, under 'fair and reasonable conditions', the Cartel Office stopped its proceedings. The European Commission has also used the third-party access condition as a kind of *quid pro quo* for approving airline mergers and acquisitions. It did so when approving Air France's equity stake in Sabena (a stake which has since been relinquished) and when approving BAs' investment in TAT European (Commission of the European Communities, 1992a; 1992b).

There are, however, a certain number of problems with third-party access. One of them is that the honouring of points earned on other carriers' services could seriously disadvantage airlines whose networks include many routes to desirable holiday destinations, routes on which many passengers might seek to redeem rewards in other carriers' schemes. This might be overcome by a suitable adjustment in inter-airline revenue prorating but a rather heavy burden of transactions cost is likely to be incurred. When one airline sells tickets on which FFP mileage points are earned and these points are then redeemed on the services of another carrier, a fairly complex form of inter-airline accounting has to be employed to arrive at an appropriate division of the relevant costs and revenues. There could often be great imbalances between sales and redemptions, from one airline to another. Government regulation to ensure that third-party access is in fact granted could also prove costly in administrative terms.

Secondary trading?

Loyalty schemes are by no means a new idea. They have been marketed by many firms in many industries for many years. One of the best-known schemes in the UK used to be the Green Shield trading stamps scheme, which was at its peak during the 1970s. Under this scheme customers collected stamps at a whole host of retail outlets, like grocery stores and petrol stations, and redeemed them for catalogued goods distributed through a separate chain of shops run by the Green Shield Company. The stamps were a kind of common currency bonus which could be earned in a great many different places. But collecting and redeeming them meant some fairly heavy transactions cost to the customer; and since they were not bespoke to particular companies, they did little to reduce cross-price elasticities demand for the products of individual firms. The Green Shield stamps scheme did not make customers 'captive' to particular businesses and consequently it did little to suppress price competition. It eventually died out because firms sought increased market shares by offering price reductions instead.

Airline loyalty schemes might also in the long-term die out, if they too led to rewards of a common currency kind, that is if the rewards could be redeemed on any carrier and were not bespoke to particular airlines or particular airline alliances. This could be achieved if passengers were able to buy and sell loyalty scheme rewards as traded goods, that is if a secondary trading market could be set up in which passengers were able to exchange rewards earned with one airline or alliance for those of another.

The idea seems more relevant to FFPs than to either corporate discounts or TACOs. A secondary market in FFP mileage point appears increasingly possible with increased use of the Internet. At present FFP mileage points can have different marginal values to different passengers, depending on their proximity to points thresholds that have to be reached to qualify for rewards. To passengers only a few points away from a threshold the marginal value of some extra points can be much greater than it is to passengers needing many more points to reach this threshold. Also, where the rewards structure is non-linear, passengers who have built up a large number of points in a particular FFP can benefit more from a few extra points than passengers whose points tally is much lower. So, because the marginal value of additional points can vary a lot between passengers, there is plenty of scope for profitable exchange, especially where some passengers are members of two or more FFPs and are closer to rewards thresholds in some FFPs than they are in others.

Consider a simple example. Suppose a passenger is a member of two FFPs, one marketed by Airline X, the other by Airline Y. To qualify for, say, a free holiday, the passenger needs 40 000 mileage points in the Airline X FFP or 30 000 points in the FFP of Airline Y. So far the passenger has collected 10 000 points in the Airline X FFP but 28 000 points in the Airline Y FFP. At the same time a second passenger, who is seeking an upgrade from economy to business class, for which the threshold is 8000 points on Airline X and 6000 points on Airline Y, has accumulated 5000 points in the

Airline X FFP and 2000 points in the Airline Y FFP. If the two passengers could trade with each other and exchange 3000 points in X for 2000 in Y, both could achieve their rewards without having to notch up further points on either FFP.

If it were possible to trade FFP mileage points in this way, passengers would feel more encouragement to collect points across a number of different FFPs rather than skew their travel decisions in favour of one airline merely because they are closer to a rewards threshold with that airline. They would make their choice of airline more on the basis of relative price and service qualities, and cross-elasticities of demand with respect to these factors would correspondingly increase.

It is true, as mentioned above, that quite a number of frequent flyers have multiple FFP memberships; but often this is more because they have to use the services of different airlines on account of the restrictions on traffic rights (which are discussed in Chapter 4) rather than due to passengers preferring to earn rewards in a number of different FFPs. One of the objectives in alliance formation is to overcome these restrictions on traffic rights; and the purpose of alliance members extending reciprocal FFP membership to each others' passengers is to promote loyalty to the alliance as a whole. Passengers are thus given a rewards incentive to concentrate their flying on carriers within a particular alliance and the more global the networks of the alliances become, the less need there will be for passengers to use non-alliance carriers. Hence cross-elasticities of demand, for the services of one alliance relative to the service of non-alliance carriers in general, could fall quite sharply. But if secondary trading in FFP rewards were to be permitted, with passengers able to exchange points earned on alliance FFPs for points earned on FFPs outside the alliance, the incentive for passengers to concentrate bookings within the alliance, purely because of FFP rewards, could be much reduced.

Some trade in FFP rewards has in fact taken place, especially in the US, where independent agents have provided a brokering service. Sometimes passengers have exchanged FFP rewards for cash. But it was all on a fairly small scale and airlines successfully took action against it through the courts (Braden, 1990). The airlines' case was that tickets are not transferable from one person to another and that this also applies to the FFP rewards earned by purchasing them. It was submitted that non-transferability is a condition of sale, and that airlines have the right in law to prevent secondary trading in both tickets and FFP rewards. Although courts might accept this as a correct legal interpretation, is there not a case for amending, laws here? There may be good operational and safety reasons for making tickets non-transferable, but it is difficult to see any compelling reasons why non-transferability should be extended to FFP rewards, and it is interesting that some airlines are beginning to relax restrictions on the transfer of FFP rewards. Witness the promotion currently being marketed by Air France under which members of its Frequence Plus FFP can nominate any person of their choosing to receive the 'Rewards' tickets earned within the FFP. There are of course certain qualifications to this offer, but it does at least demonstrate that it is not impossible for airlines to permit transferability in the matter of FFP rewards.

Although the airlines are likely to oppose its general introduction, secondary trading of FFP rewards is not only possible but also highly desirable on competition grounds. If it catches on in a big way, it might even mean the phasing out of FFPs altogether. However, it is less easy to see how secondary trading could apply in the case of corporate discount schemes. The same principle might apply, but the practical problems of arranging a market between firms might be huge. And it is likely that, if secondary trading causes FFPs to lose much of their function in blunting cross-elasticities of demand, airlines will increasingly turn to corporate discounts to achieve much the same effect.

Recent developments

Some innovations in e-commerce are permitting at least some forms of secondary trading to take place. *Points.com* is a web site devoted to expediting the exchange of mileage points for goods. A large number of suppliers and retailers take part, including mail order firms. Also the right to transfer FFP mileage points from one person to another seems to be gaining at least some partial acceptance. Mileage points are beginning to be recognised legally as assets that can be passed on in wills or form settlements in divorce cases. More generally in the ordinary course of events, some FFPs permit transferability between immediate family members, for example, between husbands and wives, parents and children.

Loyalty schemes are primarily associated with full-service airlines. They are not something normally expected from a low-cost airline. There might not seem a *prima facie* case for them in a low-cost business model. Neither Ryanair nor easyJet run one. On the other hand there has recently been quite an increase in other low-cost airlines running FFPs (Table 3.8). Southwest Airlines, the pioneer of the low-cost model, started one as long ago as 1987 and its 'Rapid Rewards' programme is now one of the largest in the world, with a total membership estimated at 40 million. Since 1998 10 low-cost airlines have introduced FFPs. This applies across North America, Europe, and the Asia-Pacific region. In the UK another low-cost airline, flybe has been seeking to position itself as, in the words of one of its advertisements, a 'low-fare airline with a business agenda' and it also lays claim to having the 'UK's most generous' FFP. The main reason for their interest is that they hope, like flybe, to attract increasing numbers of higher-yield business travellers to their services.

Table 3.8 Redemption of FFP awards, 10 US airlines, 2003. *Source: www.webflyer.com*[a]

	Free awards redeemed (number)	*Free awards as % of revenue passenger miles*	*Outstanding award liability (number)*
Alaska Mileage Plan	6 06 000	8.7	2 353 000
America West Flight Fund	–	2.6	–
American AAdvantage	2 500 000	7.8	9 300 000
Continental OnePass	1 505 848	7.6	–
Delta SkyMiles	2 800 000	9.0	14 300 000
Midwest Miles	64 000	5.0	178 000
Northwest WorldPerks	1 408 000	7.5	7 180 000
Southwest Rapid Rewards	2 500 000	7.5	1 400 000
United Mileage Plus	2 000 000	9.0	9 700 000
US Airways Dividend Miles	1 200 000	7.0	6 272 000

[a] Data derived from the 10-K reports that the airlines file with the US Securities Exchange Commission (SEC) each year.
– Not available.

3.4 Sales distribution

If government authorities have left matters like loyalty schemes very much to airlines' discretion, that has not been the case with business practices in the distribution of airline ticket sales. Concerns about possible abuses of market power led both the US Government and the European Commission to for a time issue some 'codes of conduct' for the operation of CRSs the precursor what are now known as global distribution systems (GDS).

When first developed in the 1960s and 1970s, CRSs were seen simply as devices for saving time and labour in handling large and growing amounts of flight reservations data. Airlines that invested in CRSs made their system publicly available and in the regulated era, when route entry and fares were tightly controlled, these airlines did not see any particular market power advantages from CRSs. All that changed with deregulation. In deregulated markets passengers had very many more options for their journeys, in terms of carrier, fares, routeing, etc. and they could no longer rely upon any one individual airline to provide them with a list of the available alternatives. For that they had to go to travel agents, the vast majority of whom were linked into one or other of the powerful CRSs owned or hosted by major carriers. By using CRSs agents could focus swiftly upon the multiplicity of flights, fares, and seat availabilities on any given route.

It was well known that around 80 per cent of all flight bookings were made through CRSs operated with the aid of visual display units (VDUs) located in travel agents' shops. Of these about three-quarters are made from the first screen page to appear on the VDU and about half from the first line of the first page. Access to the first screen page, and if possible to the top line, became an extremely important factor in airline competition. So how did an airline get its flights listed near the top of the first screen display? It did of course help if what the airline is offering was fairly close to what the passenger wanted to buy. But airlines owning or controlling CRSs soon realized it was possible to programme the computer so as to bias the selection of flights in favour of those they operated themselves. There was certainly a lot of this taking place in the 1980s, some clear examples being identified by Lyle (1988) and by the House of Commons Transport Committee (1988). A competitor's flights often appeared on a later screen page than the flights of the CRS owner, even when the competitor's flights were more convenient and less expensive. There were also fears that CRS owners were able to charge some very high prices for services provided to other airlines. These concerns led to calls for airlines to be divested of CRS ownership. But governments preferred to regulate them instead. Codes of Conduct were introduced by the US government, the European Commission, and the Civil Aviation Conference. These codes explicitly forbad display bias and required charges to be reasonable and non-discriminatory. It is fair to say that regulatory intervention removed most of the initial concerns, but it proved difficult to eliminate bias and discrimination altogether, once airlines owning or controlling CRSs became adept at finding loopholes in any set of rules. One development that presented a big challenge to the Codes of Conduct was the growth in codesharing, something which is discussed in the following chapter. One possible explanation for the proliferation of codesharing was that airlines were seeking display advantages by cluttering CRS screens with repetitive displays of the same service, pushing other airlines' services further down the screen page or onto the next page, a practice referred to as 'screen padding'. This practice was allowed under the US Codes of Conduct, but was restricted under the EC Code to two combinations of codesharing flights.

There were also concerns about CRS ownership and the trend towards higher concentration in the CRS industry. In the operation of CRSs there are some very high fixed costs, but marginal cost is close to zero. Hence there are some enormous economies of scale, with average cost declining continuously as the number of bookings handled increases. There may be no 'natural' monopoly in airline operations, but there were fears that there could be one in CRS operations. There appeared no technical reason why global demand for CRS services could not be met by one single megasystem, which system could be owned and controlled by one or more 'host' airlines which would then wield enormous market power. The particular fear was that the market would be completely dominated by one of the large CRSs in the US, American Airlines' Sabre CRS or Worldspan, the CRS company formed through the merger of Delta's Datas system and the

Pars system which used to be controlled by TWA and Northwest. To meet the threat of US dominance airlines in other parts of the world decided to group together to establish their own large systems, such as Galileo, and Amadeus in Europe and Axess and Abacus in the Far East. The four biggest – Sabre, Worldspan, Galileo and Amadeus – became known as 'super' CRSs and by the middle of the 1990s they accounted for 80–85 per cent of CRS operations around the world. This increased concentration and the close marketing and technical links that existed between the super CRSs raised fears about market power; and these fears eventually led to tighter regulation in the US and European codes of conduct.

It was not just government authorities that had concerns about GDSs. Many airlines did as well. In 1994 the European Commission received a formal complaint from a group of five UK airlines (British Midland, Loganair, Jersey European, Manx, and Air UK) about the pricing policies followed by Galileo International in Europe. The five UK airlines complained that Galileo was using its dominant position to increase its fees and that their distribution costs were rising by some 30 per cent a year. The carriers wanted their complaint against Galileo to be treated as a test case, promising further complaints against Amadeus, Sabre, and Worldspan as well (Humphreys, 1994). GDS fees are charged on a per booking basis irrespective of the fare paid. As such they are bound to have a relatively greater impact on airlines with high proportions of low-fare passengers (i.e. those operating short haul routes and those with relatively high percentages of excursion passengers travelling on discounted fares). One argument put forward is that they should vary by the value of the journey booked, if they

Table 3.9 Low-cost airlines with FFPs. *Source*: Airline Business

Airline	Launch date	No. of members
North America		
AirTran	1998	20 00 000
ATA	2002	7 00 000
JetBlue	2001	2 40 00 000
Southwest	1987	4 00 00 000[a]
Europe		
Air Berlin	1998	3 00 000
Germanwings	2006	–
HapagFly	2005	1 50 000
Virgin Express	2005	1 20 000
Asia-Pacific		
Cebu Pacific	2000	75 000[a]
Lion Air	2000	30 000[a]
Virgin Blue	2005	10 00 000[a]

[a] Carrier's own estimate.
– Not available.

Table 3.10 GDS in 2004[a]. *Source*: Airline Business

	No. of airline bookings (millions)	Market share (%)	Share of US bookings (%)	Online bookings (%)
Amadeus	381[b]	33	7	10
Sabre	343	29	40	10
Galileo	250	21	20	36
Worldspan	190[c]	16	33	50
Total	1164	100	100	22

[a]Booking figures as reported by leading GDSs.
[b]Excludes German Leisure business.
[c]Estimated from data covering nine months.

are not to prove discriminatory against some small airlines. But GDS costs do not vary with the value of the booking, the costs involved in processing a first class fare from London to Tokyo being much the same as those in processing an economy fare from London to Amsterdam. To avoid their fees impacting relatively more heavily on low-fare airlines GDS companies would have to discriminate positively in their favour.

As CRSs evolved, they diversified into other lines of business, so that to their original airline ticket booking function, they began to take bookings for hotels, car hires, train journeys, cruise holidays, etc. They also started selling airlines other professional services, such as IT for personnel and aircraft scheduling, and also for baggage handling. In the expansion of these activities they became known as GDS reflecting the increasingly international and diverse nature of their business. Since the mid-1990s airlines have sold their shares in GDSs. Sabre became an independent company, fully divested by AMR Corp., the parent company of American Airlines; Galileo became a subsidiary of Cendant Corp.; and both Worldspan and Amadeus have been sold to private investors. Thus ended the vertical interpretation between GDSs and the airlines. But the four largest GDSs are still very dominant in terms of the number of airline bookings handled (Table 3.10). Whilst many airlines having been making losses, the owners of GDSs have been enjoying some very healthy rates of return on invested capital (as illustrated in Chapter 2, Figure 2.21). In order to improve their financial situation airlines have been seeking to cut costs, including distribution costs. An IATA study (International Air Transport Association, 2006) revealed that distribution used to make up 17–18 per cent of distribution costs were incurred in paying travel agency commissions, a further 30 per cent or more on reservations and ticketing and still a further 7 per cent on GDS fees. With revenue yields declining because of keener inter-airline competition, it became ever more pressing to reduce costs, especially distribution costs.

Airlines have been approaching this in two main ways. The first has been to cut travel agency commission rates, something achieved progressively so that agents' standard rates are now about half, or less than half, what they were around 10 years ago. The role of agents has been undergoing a major change. There is now far more emphasis on them serving travellers in return for fees and much less on them acting on behalf of airlines in return for commissions. The second way has been to bypass traditional travel agents and sell direct to the travelling public. Airlines have been helped in this by the enormous growth in the use of the Internet. Air travel has become one of the most successful forms of e-commerce. It all started with the low-cost airlines encouraging – and in some cases requiring – their passengers to buy online. A passenger making a booking online is given a confirmation number, all that is needed for baggage handling and flight check-in. Flight check-in ordinarily takes place in the terminal, but on some airlines this can now be accomplished online too, before the passenger leaves home. There is on some airlines no seat allocation process, passengers boarding the aircraft in order of arrival at the gate. Not only can this substantially reduce queues and speed up boarding, it can also eliminate the cost of physically producing tickets in paper form, a saving of something in the order of US $20 per ticket.

Online bookings are rising rapidly. In the US they now represent between 40 and 50 per cent of total bookings. This growth has been accompanied by the establishment of large online travel agencies which compete actively with airlines' own web sites. The three biggest online travel agencies – Expedia, Travelocity, and Orbitz – attract up to twice as many web site visitors as the three most popular airline web sites, those of Southwest, American, and Delta. But the airlines score more highly when it comes to the 'visitor conversion rate', the proportion of visitors who actually go on to make a booking (Table 3.11).

Table 3.11 The top three airline web sites and the top three online agencies, April 2005. *Source*: Nielson//NetRatings

	Unique audience (thousands)	Visitor conversion rate (%)[a]
Airline web sites		
Southwest	8141	14
American	5663	9
Delta	4912	10
Online travel agencies		
Expedia	16 260	5
Travelocity	11 714	3
Orbitz	11 616	4

[a] The percentage of 'lookers' who ultimately become 'bookers'.

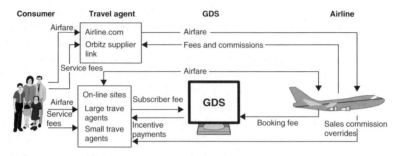

Figure 3.5   Distribution channels for airline sales (*Source*: US General Accounting Office)

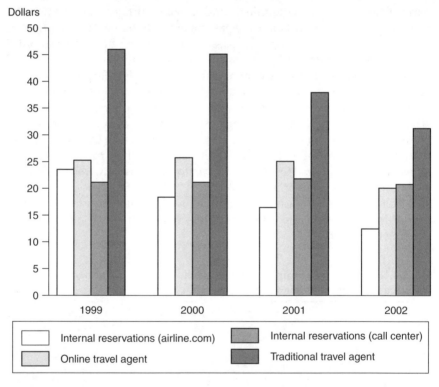

Figure 3.6   Average booking costs, US airlines, 1999–2002 (*Source*: US General Accounting Office)

Whilst the increased use of the Internet and the cuts in travel agency commissions has had the desired effect of reducing distribution costs, airlines still have to engage with GDSs. This is especially so in dealing with business travellers and their more complex itineraries. So, with small travel agents of the traditional kind, online travel agents like Orbitz, airline web sites, and GDSs there is now a wider variety of distribution channels. A summary flow chart depicting the various players and how they pay each other is depicted in Figure 3.5. How booking costs vary by distribution channel is shown in Figure 3.6. Costs via all four channels are in decline, but traditional travel agents remain much the most expensive, costing airlines in the US an average of US $31 per booking. This compares with only US $11.75 for a booking made via the airline's own web site (US Government Accountability Office, 2006). Airlines have been taking steps to encourage direct online bookings. Sometimes airlines reward passengers with additional FFP bonuses for booking online; but more often the incentive is in the form of a reduced fare. For booking online rather than making a reservation by telephone, BA rewards passengers flying the North Atlantic a saving of £30 on their return fares.

3.5 Increasing concentration

If liberalization is going to be carried further and include some relaxation of constraints on foreign ownership and control, thereby making it much more possible for cross-border mergers to take place, then one might expect the global airline industry to become more and more highly concentrated. It is interesting to speculate on just how many airlines will survive and on how far the industry will be dominated by some very large carriers. One way of looking at this is given in Figure 3.7. As discussed above, US deregulation initially led to lowering of concentration. But then, after a spate of bankruptcies and takeovers, the industry consolidated and became somewhat more oligopolistic than it was in the pre-deregulation era. A similar pattern of deregulation and consolidation was seen when airline competition was liberalized in other countries around the world, in Canada, in Australia, and in the European Union (all of which is discussed below in Chapter 7). Mergers and acquisitions then were limited to those that could be consummated within national boundaries, but they still meant that the share of world output performed by the top airlines increased further. The emergence of a lot of new low-cost airlines in the 1990s kept the large airlines' share of world output on something of a plateau, as did the troubles many of them experienced in the first few years of the new century. But if transnational airlines are to be formed from mergers between airlines in different parts of the world, then we could see industry concentration rising again, so that by the year 2020 the top airlines might be responsible for over 70 per cent of world output, as measured by passenger-kilometres performed.

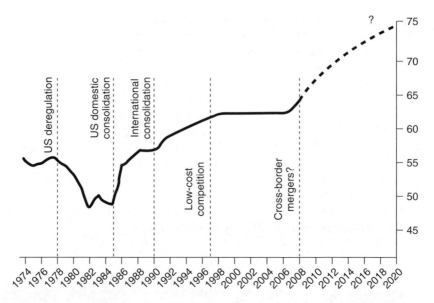

Figure 3.7   Approximate share of world passenger-kilometres performed by the top 20 airlines, 1974–2020

Increasing concentration raises the question of what will happen to inter-airline competition. Will it become more or less intense? Before addressing this issue it may be helpful to consider some theoretical points.

On one view high levels of concentration in any particular industry facilitate collusion and lead to higher prices for consumers and higher profits for firms. An opposing view is that a direct relationship between concentration and profits is more likely to reflect more efficient firms gaining market share and thereby becoming more profitable. Much depends on the relationship between concentration and prices. Even where increasing concentration is simply the result of efficient firms becoming more dominant, once they achieve this greater dominance they will enjoy a greater degree of monopoly market power, which they may then use to raise prices. Hence there may be a trade-off to consider, if increasing concentration leads both to greater efficiency and to some enhancement in the monopoly market power exercised by dominant firms.

In a frequently cited article the economist Oliver Williamson (1968) analysed this trade-off and showed how the balance between market power and efficiency effects depends crucially on the price elasticity of demand for the goods or service in question. Without entering too deeply into the technicalities of microeconomic theory, it is possible to summarize Williamson's arguments as follows. In theory the degree of monopoly market power exercised by a firm is shown by its price–cost margin, which is represented by the ratio:

$$\frac{\text{price} - \text{marginal cost}}{\text{price}}$$

A ratio of zero would apply to firms with no monopoly power at all; that is, to firms operating under conditions described in microeconomic theory as perfect competition, where all firms have to accept that they can charge no more than marginal cost. Under imperfect competition, firms do have some measure of monopoly market power, and the closer the ratio is to one, the greater that power is. The effect of a price–cost margin greater than zero is to reduce the profit-maximizing equilibrium output below the level it would be set under perfect competition. When output falls there is a loss of consumer benefits and the magnitude of this loss depends upon the elasticity of demand; the more elastic the demand, the greater the loss of benefits. But the overall effect of an increase in market power depends on how the event that gives rise to it (e.g. a merger or an alliance) affects the level of marginal cost. If the marginal cost level falls (e.g. as a result of economies of scale/scope) then it is possible for cost savings to the firm to outweigh the loss of benefits to consumers and the net overall outcome could be positive. Whether or not the outcome is positive depends on the size of the cost reduction relative to the magnitude of the demand elasticity. In this respect it is important to note that a much smaller proportionate reduction in cost is required to offset a given loss in consumer benefits, since the cost reduction applies to the whole of the firm's output whereas the loss in benefits only relates to the restriction from the competitive output level. Williamson demonstrated this by performing a number of simulations, at varying demand elasticities, to show the percentage cost reductions sufficient to offset given price–cost margins. For example, he found that, at a demand elasticity of -1, a 10 per cent margin would be offset by a cost reduction of only 0.5 per cent; and that, at an elasticity of -2, a cost reduction of just 4 per cent would be sufficient to offset a margin of as much as 20 per cent. The conclusion from this is that, if there are any non-trivial savings in costs, the margins from monopoly market power have to be rather substantial for the net overall effect to be negative.

The Williamson trade-off is illustrated in Figure 3.8 in terms of the standard price output diagram used in microeconomics. Under perfect competition the price–cost margin is zero with price, P_1, set at marginal cost, at which price the output level is Q_1. If as a result of concentration the firm gains market power, it can set a price, P_2, above marginal cost, which will have the effect of restricting output to Q_2. The losses from market power are then the reduction in consumer benefits, area P_2ABP_1 less the increase

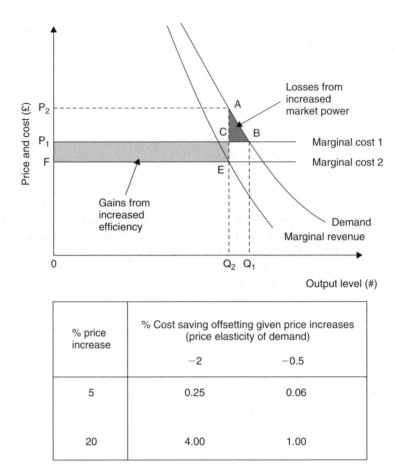

Figure 3.8   Theoretical model of potential trade-offs with increased concentration

in profits to the firm, area P_2ACP_1, or the triangle ABC. If at the same time increased concentration leads to increased efficiency, this will have the effect of lowering marginal cost (which is assumed in the diagram to be constant with respect to output level, so that it is equal to average cost and can be represented as a horizontal straight line). If the reduction is from marginal cost 1 to marginal cost 2 the total saving in cost is the fall in cost per unit times the number of units, which is represented by the rectangle P_1CEF. Whether area P_1CEF is greater or less than area ABC depends crucially on the slope of the demand curve, which in turn determines how large the restriction of output, Q_1–Q_2 is in relation to the original output level Q_1. Other things being equal, the steeper the demand curve, the smaller the output restriction and the more likely it is that the efficiency gains (area P_1CEF) will outweigh the losses from market power (area ABC).

The above analysis is subject to a number of important qualifications. First of all, no allowances are made for the relative timing of the market power and efficiency effects; and it can be quite important to consider the shapes of their respective time streams. For instance, the stream of consumer losses may start immediately once the firm gains an increase in market power, whereas the reduction in cost may take some years before it is fully achieved. In this case the relevant comparisons would be in terms of equivalent present values, with future effects on costs and benefits discounted at an appropriate rate of interest. The comparison may also require some adjustment where the cost saving accrues to just one firm, but where the market power effects carry over to other firms in the industry. Other firms may take advantage of the opportunity afforded by increased concentration to increase their prices as well, under a kind of 'umbrella' effect. When this occurs, there may be a whole series of losses from raised prices to be set against a saving to just one firm, and so some kind of weighting factor may have to be introduced to reflect this. There may also be questions about distributional equity. It may, for instance, be argued that losses in benefits to consumers should be weighted more heavily than cost reductions for the firm. In this case £x of consumer losses would no longer be regarded as being compensated for by £x of additional profits (i.e. the rectangle P_2ACP_1 in Figure 3.8 would no longer be regarded as a neutral 'transfer payment' in this respect). In other words in one of Williamson's simulations referred to above, if one were to weigh consumer losses at, say, twice the rate of the gains in profits, a 20 per cent rise in price at an elasticity of -2 would require a compensating cost saving, not of 4 per cent, but of 12 per cent.

All this is on the premise that the firm's cost level does actually fall when its market power increases. If instead it rises, then there would of course be no trade-off to consider at all, and the increase in cost should be added to the consumer losses in measuring the net outcome overall. The question of what happens to the cost level is crucial. So if increased concentration leads to greater market power, what does it do to the cost level?

So far as the airline industry is concerned there are grounds for believing that increased concentration does indeed lead to lower-cost levels, not through economies of scale but through economies of scope. In particular, in creating larger networks, increased concentration can result in greater market power on some routes, but at the same time can generate some significant economies. This can be illustrated in terms of the close relationship that exists between market concentration and the development of hub and spokes route networks. The development of hubbing is discussed in detail in Chapters 4 and 5 and only a brief discussion of the possible trade-offs is presented here.

The market power effects of hubs derive from the fact that for passengers with origins and destinations in hub cities there is often little choice but to travel on the airline based at the hub. Hub airlines are often very dominant in their hub cities partly because airport capacity constraints (especially at peak periods) seriously inhibit competition from new entrants. There is no doubt that they enjoy considerable market power and it has been very clearly demonstrated that they have been using this power to charge higher fares on routes to/from hubs compared to routes of similar distance elsewhere. A number of econometric studies found significant positive correlations between higher fares and the degree of concentration. Some of the market power hub airlines enjoy comes from having a larger presence in a given city, something that enhances the customer loyalty effects of their FFP and TACO strategies.

But hubbing can also lead to some significant reductions in costs. In funnelling traffic onto a smaller number of routes, hubbing has the effect of increasing route traffic density. It is well known that marginal cost declines with increases in route traffic density, as a number of empirical studies has shown (Caves, Christensen, and Tretheway, 1984). Hence there can be some cost savings to set against the losses from higher fares to/from hubs. However there is a further trade-off to consider. As explained in Chapter 5, the increased concentration on routes to/from hubs may be accompanied by reduced concentration in through markets served via the hubs. It is sometimes the case that when competition *at* hubs falls, that *between* hubs rises. And the significance of Williamson's analysis here is that often the price elasticity of demand is higher for travel in through markets than in point-to-point markets to/from hubs.

All these points tend to be concealed when comparisons are made of changes in aggregate industry concentration, such as for example in the graph in Figure 3.7, which shows the share of total industry output accounted for by the top 20 airlines. A rise in aggregate concentration does not necessarily imply a fall in the intensity of competition. In Chapter 2 it is noted that there are some 1200 scheduled airlines in the world, but because of restrictions on route entry, not many of these are in direct competition with each other. With route entry being liberalized, it is certainly possible for the total number of airlines to fall, for aggregate concentration to rise, and for competition intensities to increase, all at one and the same time.

Of more relevance than aggregate industry concentration is concentration in particular city-pair markets. Market concentration can be measured in a number of different ways. Two principal measures are the n-firm concentration ratio (CR_n) and the Hirschman–Herfindahl Index (HHI). These are illustrated in Figure 3.9. The CR_n is calculated as the sum of the market shares of the n largest firms, where n is chosen fairly arbitrarily. For example, in the diagram:

$CR_3 = 90\%$ in market A
$CR_4 = 60\%$ in market B
$CR_5 = 70\%$ in market C

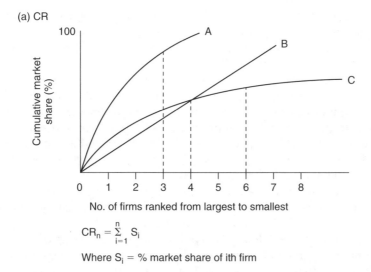

(a) CR

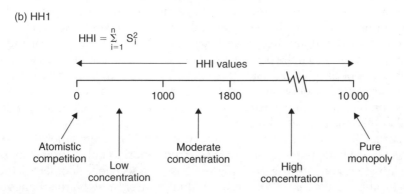

(b) HH1

Figure 3.9 Two measures of market concentration

Reading off the vertical axis on which market shares are cumulated. The CR_n is a popular measure because of its limited data requirements, all it needs being the total market sales and sales made by the n largest firms. The drawbacks are that it only considers the largest firms and takes no account of disparities in firm sizes. The greater the number of firms and the more uniform they are in size, the greater the degree of competition likely to be present. A measure of market concentration should ideally capture both these elements, the total number of firms *and* their size distribution. These are the advantages of the HHI measure, which is calculated as the sum of the squared market shares of all firms in the industry. The process of squaring gives greater weight to the larger firms, and the more unequal the size distribution of firms, the higher the value of the HHI. The HHI is zero when there is a very large number of equal-sized firms and it reaches its maximum value of 10 000 (or 100^2) under pure monopoly. Because it more appropriately reflects the intensity of competition, the US Department of Justice (DoJ) bases its antitrust policy on the HHI measure, which it uses as a screening criterion in deciding whether or not to challenge a proposed merger. If a merger would leave the relevant market with a HHI of less than 1000 (regarded as 'low' concentration) the DoJ will not challenge it; but where the post-merger market would have an HHI of more than 1800 ('high' concentration) all significant mergers will be challenged. In the 'grey' area in between, where $1000 < \text{HHI} < 1800$, the DoJ challenges mergers that have the effect of increasing the HHI by 100 or more.

The HHI has also been used in studies charting changes in concentration over time and changes following deregulation or liberalization. When used for this purpose it is important that the 'market' to which the HHI relates is properly defined. In air transport a market is made up of all passengers who want to travel from a specific origin to a specific destination, and of all airlines that provide service from that origin to that destination. In this respect there is an important distinction between a city-pair market and a route: a route is the physical path an aircraft takes between take-off at one airport and landing at another; whereas a market is the pairing of the airports at which the passenger's journey originates and terminates. In hub and spokes networks many passengers travel on several different routes but participate in only one market. The most relevant basis on which to measure concentration is the origin–destination (O–D) city-pair market rather than the individual route.

Earlier in this chapter it was observed that US deregulation had the effect of causing aggregate industry concentration to fall and then subsequently to rise again. The same pattern has been seen in econometric studies examining concentration on individual routes. But what happened to concentration in O–D city-pair markets? This was examined in a study by Belobaba and Van Acker (1994) who calculated average HHI values for the top 100 O–D city-pairs in the US domestic industry from 1979 to 1991 (Figure 3.10). What they found was that the average HHI fell from a level of 4920 in 1979 to 3360 in 1985 and subsequently increased again to 4020 by 1991, repeating the experience of aggregate industry and route concentration. But the 1991 level was 900 (or 18 per cent) below the 1979 level, indicating that concentration in O–D markets is still significantly less. About 70 per cent of the top 100 markets experienced an overall decrease in concentration between 1979 and 1991. Although the HHI values appear high in relation to the US DoJ merger guidelines, it should be noted that the sample of city-pairs to which the averages relate is not representative of the industry as a whole. The Belobaba and Van Acker study also found that concentration is higher in those O–D markets where at least one of the endpoints served as an airline hub. It also provided some evidence that

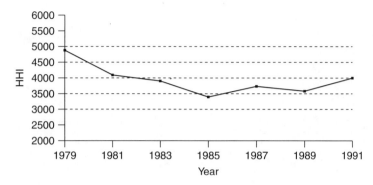

Figure 3.10 Values of the HHI for top 100 US domestic routes, 1979–91. (*Source*: Belobaba and Van Acker (1994))

concentration is higher in the large O–D markets and that the gap between these and the smaller markets appears to be widening over time. Had it been possible for Belobaba and Van Acker to consider other markets outside the top 100, it is likely that they would have found concentration in markets linking non-hub cities to be falling more.

What is emerging is that competition in through markets is becoming fiercer over time, a point that has relevance not just to hubbing but also to the questions raised by mergers and alliances, which are considered in Chapter 7. Depending on the relative magnitudes of price–cost margins and price elasticities of demand, the effects of increased competition for through traffic could offset, or more than offset, the effects of any reduction in competition on point-to-point routes. This is very largely an empirical question and is something that can vary quite a lot from one market situation to another.

4

Route networks

Most route patterns have an affinity to one or other of three or four basic types: line, grid, or hub and spokes/low-cost point to point. These are illustrated in Figure 4.1.

In a line network the aircraft sets out from its base airport and makes a number of intermediate stops en route through to its ultimate destination. The intermediate stops are made either to refuel or to pick up traffic. Without stops some long-haul services would not be operationally or economically viable. As aircraft range increases, or as the volume of long-haul traffic grows, the need for intermediate stops becomes that much less. Although there are still plenty of airlines around the world that operate route systems like this, the emphasis has shifted very much away from line networks. For they have disadvantages on both the cost and revenue sides. Costs tend to be high, because station expenses are spread over just a few flights using each airport, maybe just one or two a week. This also means that local marketing is difficult and rather expensive in terms of average cost. At the same time cockpit cabin crews often have to have long

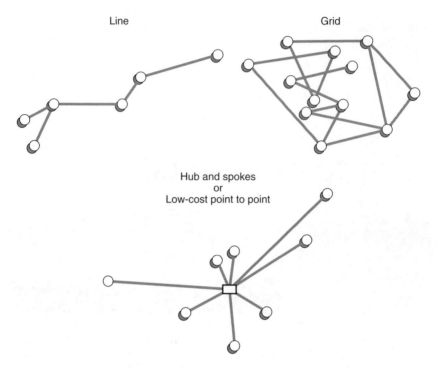

Figure 4.1   Network patterns

stopovers or alternatively have to be ferried to their next flights; and in some cases long-haul aircraft can be very inefficiently employed on relatively short sectors operated at low load factors at tail ends of the route. On the revenue side yields are often poor, because the low frequencies at which services on line routes tend to be operated do not appeal to business travellers paying the higher fares. Nor do the journey times on such multi-sector routes. The Scandinavian airline SAS used to serve no less than four intermediate stops (Lisbon, Rio de Janeiro, Sao Paulo, and Montevideo) on its service between Copenhagen and Buenos Aires; and the Brazilian carrier Varig made three intermediate stops (Sao Paulo, Johannesburg, and Bangkok) on its service between Rio de Janeiro and Hong Kong. But the most famous of all were the round-the-world services operated by the former Pan American and TWA.

Grid networks have often been a characteristic of domestic air transport. A prime example used to be the US where, before deregulation, many airlines operated grid networks, especially on the eastern seaboard. One of these was the former Eastern Airlines (Figure 4.2). A current example is India, where the domestic airline's network is very much in the pattern of

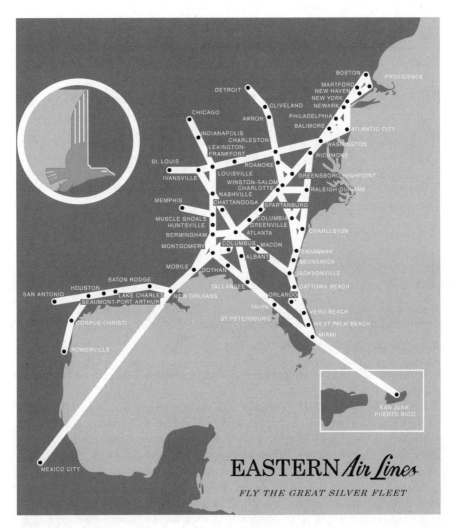

Figure 4.2   Network of the former Eastern Airlines (*Source*: US Government Accountability Office)

a grid, based as it is on the 'diamond rectangle' of Bombay/Delhi/Calcutta/ Madras. The main advantage of grid networks is that they make it easier to achieve high rates of utilization, of both aircraft and crews. Flights can be scheduled to operate on a number of different routes without back-tracking, which helps to minimize the time for which aircraft are idle on the ground and which also means that crew stopovers and slippage can be minimized. Traffic flows through stations are higher than they are in line networks, but the sales effort is still rather dispersed, a disadvantage that

Figure 4.3 Network of routes radiating out of United Airlines' hub at Chicago O'Hare (*Source*: US General Accounting Office)

becomes that much more serious in deregulated or liberalized air travel markets.

An important advantage in hub and spokes networks, in which routes radiate from a central hub airport to a number of outlying spoke airports, is the effect they have in multiplying by permutation the number of city pairs an airline can serve. When airports are linked via a hub, the number of available city pairs is much greater than when they are linked directly, as shown in Figure 4.3. If for example five direct services, each linking a single city pair are replaced by connecting services from the same group of cities via a hub, there is an eleven-fold increase in the number of linked city pairs from a mere doubling in the number of sectors operated. One additional spoke would raise the number of possible linkages by a further eleven city pairs. Mathematically, if there are n spokes, an airline can provide through connecting services for up to a theoretical maximum of $n(n-1)/2$ city pairs. When these are added to the n city pairs to/from the hub itself, the total possible city pair markets is $n(n+1)/2$; and the way in which total city pairs rise with the number of spokes is illustrated in Table 4.1. In practice, some city pairs may require too great a deviation to attract traffic, and some may not be served because they are already well supplied with direct services. But the leverage of hubs in generating city pair linkages was a prime motive for the thoroughgoing change from line and grid networks in the deregulated US domestic market. A prime example is

Table 4.1 Markets in a hub and spokes system

Number of spokes (n)	Maximum number of connecting markets (n(n−1)/2)	Number of local markets (n)	Maximum number of city-pair markets (n(n+1)/2)
5	10	5	15
10	45	10	55
25	300	25	325
50	1225	50	1275
100	4950	100	5050

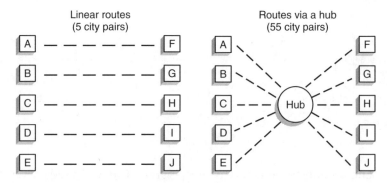

Figure 4.4 Leverage of a hub

United Airlines' network of routes emanating from its hub at Chicago O'Hare (Figure 4.4).

Figure 4.5 illustrates two main kinds of hub, the 'hourglass' hub and the 'hinterland' hub (Doganis and Dennis, 1989). Through an hourglass hub flights operate from one region to points broadly in the opposite direction; and through a hinterland hub, short-haul flights feed connecting traffic to the longer trunk routes. An hourglass hub usually only caters for connections in two directions, outbound and return, whereas a hinterland hub serves as a multi-directional distribution centre for air travel to and from its surrounding catchment area. Flights through an hourglass hub are usually operated by the same aircraft, whereas connections through a hinterland hub often require a change of gauge (e.g. from regional aircraft to long range jets). Both kinds of hub have become common in the deregulated US domestic market.

Hub and spokes networks may now be a familiar feature within the US, but they have in fact been the predominant pattern in international operations for some considerable time, although for different reasons. With

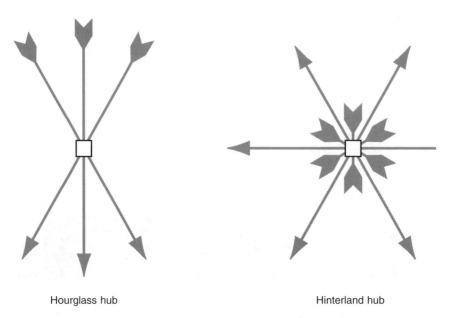

Hourglass hub   Hinterland hub

Figure 4.5   Two kinds of hub

each state claiming sovereignty over the services above its territory, international services can be flown only with the consent of the governments involved. In this matter governments negotiate with each other on a bilateral basis, one state with another; and governments draw up air service agreements specifying the routes that designated airlines from each of the two countries can fly. The way in which this has developed has meant that only airlines registered in the states involved are licensed to enter the routes. As a result national airlines have tended to operate the vast majority of their international routes to and from their home country, in and out of their main hubs, usually located in their capital or largest cities, for example London for British Airways (BA), Paris for Air France, Frankfurt for Lufthansa, and so on. But these primarily star-shaped networks often did not generate anything like the multiplier effects on city pairs linkages as the hub and spoke networks that developed in the US following deregulation. This was partly because of the way international services were operated, but mainly due to restrictions in inter-governmental bilateral agreements.

The networks operated by low-cost airlines bear a very close physical resemblance to hub and spokes systems, in that routes radiate out of a centrally located base airport. The essential difference is that arrivals and departures of low-cost flights are not co-ordinated to expedite transfer connections. It is possible of course for passengers to connect at the base airport from one low-cost flight to another, but the schedules – and in some cases the tariff polices – of the low-cost airline have not been designed with this in mind. A major example is Ryanair at London Stansted. In the Summer of 2006 Ryanair had 39 aircraft based at Stansted which it flew to no less than 86 destinations spread all over Europe. But Ryanair's flights were not banked into waves, with arrivals preceding departures in sufficient time to allow passengers to connect from inbound to outbound services. In a true hub and spokes system this is how flight schedules are drawn up. In addition to its base at Stansted Ryanair has a further 14 bases (including Dublin, Frankfurt Hahn, Stockholm Skavsta, Rome Ciampino, and Brussels Charleroi). At all these bases Ryanair's operations are in the same pattern as those at Stansted.

4.2 Freedoms of the air

Air service agreements are negotiated by governments within the framework of the five 'freedoms of the air' defined in the Chicago Convention. Governments negotiate the exchange of overflying rights, the first freedom; rights to land for technical reasons, the second freedom; rights to carry traffic to/from the home state, the third/fourth freedoms; and rights to carry traffic to/from third countries en route, the fifth freedom. Except where special political or military difficulties apply, mutual exchange of the first and second freedoms usually takes place as a matter of course. But in the exchange of the remaining three freedoms, governments bargain hard with each other.

In negotiating traffic rights all governments are concerned about the market shares secured by their own national carriers. In the past some protectionist governments have insisted upon a minimum share of 50 per cent whereas some more liberal governments have been willing, within limits, to let market shares be determined through airline competition. A traditional view has been that bilateral agreements should result in an 'equitable exchange of economic benefits' (Loy, 1968). But the question of what constitutes an equitable exchange has long been open to a number of interpretations, especially when a large country is negotiating an agreement with a small country. Market shares have been the cause of many disputes, and many bilateral agreements have included restrictions on airline capacity levels, especially in relation to fifth freedom services. The philosophical basis on which traffic rights are exchanged is essentially mercantilist. Governments expect reciprocity. This can be a problem for the government of a small country, with relatively little traffic-generating potential but with big ambitions for its national flag carrier. One way in which such a country might enhance its participation in air travel markets is to trade other benefits in exchange for traffic rights. Another is to engage in the carriage of what has become known as 'sixth freedom' traffic.

The sixth freedom of the air, which was neither recognized nor defined in the Chicago Convention, refers to the carriage of traffic between two foreign states via the state in which the airline is registered. As an example, if BA carries a passenger from New York to London, where the passenger transfers to another BA flight on which he travels to Mumbai, the airline is engaging in the carriage of sixth freedom traffic. The notion of a sixth freedom is one on which there has been considerable controversy. Some states have considered the sixth freedom to be a special form of the fifth freedom, because neither the origin nor the destination of the traffic concerned is in the state of registration. Accordingly these states have argued that sixth freedom traffic should be subject to the same restrictions that apply to fifth freedom traffic. This has been rejected by other states on the ground that the sixth freedom is implicit in the grant of a pair of third/fourth freedoms. Not surprisingly, the latter view was often taken by countries whose locations present their airlines with good opportunities to carry sixth freedom traffic; and the opposing view has tended to be held by countries which originate or attract large volumes of traffic, but which are not particularly well placed on the world's air routes so far as capturing sixth freedom traffic is concerned.

The main point at issue is illustrated in Figure 4.6. This shows the traffic rights enjoyed by an airline registered in State A whose government has negotiated the exchange of third and fourth freedoms with both States B and X, as well as fifth freedom rights between States C and D. By combining the pair of third/fourth freedoms, the airline of State A can carry traffic between States B and X. The question that has often been raised concerning

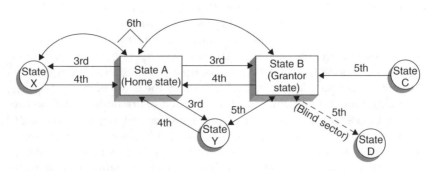

Figure 4.6   Freedoms of the air

this traffic is whether or not it should be classed as fifth freedom, to be negotiated for and restricted in the same way as fifth freedom rights to/from States C and D.

Negotiations on fifth freedom rights have often been very protracted, not least because there are always at least three countries involved. The fact that fifth freedom rights require the simultaneous agreement of three or more states has often in practice meant that only a small proportion of rights traded bilaterally can in fact be used. It is possible to distinguish – and in some bilateral agreements this distinction is in fact drawn – between three kinds of fifth freedom: intermediate-point, beyond-point, and behind-point which is shown below:

- The intermediate-point is exercised when an airline carries traffic between a grantor state and another foreign country located somewhere between the home and grantor states. In Figure 4.5, the airline of State A has intermediate-point rights between States B and Y.
- Beyond-point rights are enjoyed when the airline is allowed to carry traffic on routes beyond the grantor state, between State B and States C and D in Figure 4.5.
- Behind-point rights may be held to apply to the carriage of through traffic on routes behind the home state, for example between States A and X.

Whatever their kind, potential grantor states have tended to view fifth freedoms as encroachments upon their 'natural' third/fourth freedoms. But the economic viability of through services on long-haul routes on which traffic is thin often depends on the airline being able to carry traffic to/from foreign countries en route. Hence a compromise often had to be reached. Sometimes the fifth freedom carrier was restricted to carrying no more than a relatively small proportion – of the order of, say, 10–15 per cent – of the total capacity offered by third/fourth freedom carriers. And sometimes the compromise has involved the granting of so-called 'blind sector' rights. A blind sector is one on which the airline has fifth freedom rights only in respect of stopover traffic. That is, the airline of State A has blind sector rights between States B and D, if the only traffic it can pick up in B and set down in D (or, vice versa, pick up in D and set down in B) is traffic which originates in A (or in D) and is making a stopover in B en route.

Unless it wants something in return, the UK Government, like many other governments, usually turns down requests for fifth freedom rights. But there has recently been something of a policy shift on this recently. As part of a broader policy of liberalizing air transport, and in line with its own aviation White Paper (Department for Transport, 2003) the Government now says it will apply a general presumption in favour of granting fifth freedom rights on routes from regional airports. The Government wishes to encourage regional airports to take some of the pressure off the crowded

London airports system. Hence it is considering granting foreign airlines some additional fifth freedom rights, provided these are exercised at regional airports and away from London. It commissioned a report from the Civil Aviation Authority (2005a) which estimated that, overall, the benefits to the UK in terms of business and tourism would outweigh UK airline losses by a factor of more than 3:1 on long-haul routes other than those to the USA (on which benefits would exceed losses by only 1.4:1). The Civil Aviation Authority (CAA) undertook economic evaluations in the following sample case-studies:

1   Dubai–Manchester–Houston (Emirates)
2   Prague–Glasgow–Los Angeles (CSA)
3   Manchester–Stockholm–China (Air China)
4   Singapore–Manchester–Washington (SIA)
5   Bangkok–Delhi–Manchester (Thai International)
6   Toronto–Birmingham–India (Air Canada)
7   Pakistan–Manchester–New York/Chicago/Toronto/Houston (PIA)

In all but one of the studies the estimates yielded a positive net benefit for the UK. The exceptions was Study 4 where the fifth freedom sector would be in head-to-head competition with an existing airline and where the capacity available to UK passengers on the third/fourth freedom sectors would be reduced rather than increased because of the new fifth freedom rights. The CAA considered whether or not the UK should declare open fifth freedoms, always provided they are exercised outside the London airports system. But this could weaken the UK's negotiating hand by removing the Government's ability to secure something of value in exchange. Therefore the CAA concluded it is preferable to shift policy from the existing position in which the general presumption is that new fifth freedom rights should be refused to one that favours fifth freedoms.

From time to time there were attempts to use the question of stopovers to resolve disputes over sixth freedom traffic. One idea was to classify X to B via A traffic, or C to A via B traffic, as fifth freedom, if the length of time the passenger spends at the point of transit is less than some specified period (e.g. 12 or 24 hours), and as a combination of third/fourth freedoms if the stopover is longer than this (Hanlon, 1984). But no general agreement has ever been reached on the definition of stopover traffic; and the only restriction that individual countries have ever successfully placed on sixth freedom operations has been to prevent them being advertised as through services under a single flight number. In practice this restriction is often not a meaningful one. Flight numbers can be amended with letter suffixes, passengers can be transported to their final destinations on the same aircraft and, to all practical intents and purposes, advertisement of a through sixth freedom service can be both overt and widespread.

Two further freedoms, also not specified in the Chicago Convention, are the 'seventh' and the 'eighth'. An airline has the seventh when it is permitted to operate stand-alone services entirely outside the territory of its home state, to carry traffic between two foreign states. The seventh freedom is comparatively very rare because it is usually not in the commercial interests of the airlines of the two foreign states which would both have agree to grant it. For many years a US airline had such rights when operating a shuttle service between Tokyo and Seoul. A current example is the service flown by TACA, the national airline of El Salvador, between Canada/US and Cuba. The eighth freedom is where an airline is given the right to carry traffic between two points within the territory of a foreign state. This is more commonly known as 'cabotage', a term that originated in shipping (and derives from the French *caboter*, which means 'to sail around the coast'). In commercial air transport the term applies to traffic on domestic routes, or on routes between the grantor state and its overseas territories or former colonies (e.g. UK–Bermuda). Cabotage rights are usually reserved for national carriers and only very rarely granted to foreign airlines. But there have been some instances of foreign airlines operating on cabotage routes. For example, for many years Air France was granted cabotage rights on internal domestic routes in Morocco; and even the US has on occasion permitted cabotage, such as in 1979 on routes to/from Honolulu (although in this case only when US airlines were affected by a strike and by the temporary grounding of DC-10 aircraft). But these exceptional cases apart, sovereign states have steadfastly refused to trade cabotage rights and have insisted that domestic routes can be operated only by airlines registered in the home state. The result of this is that, for example, Swissair has no rights to domestic traffic between London and Manchester, just as BA has no rights to Geneva–Zurich traffic. But some of the restrictions on cabotage are now being lifted, at least at regional level.

One of the provisions in the establishment in 1996 of the Single Aviation Market (SAM) between Australia and New Zealand was the mutual exchange of eighth freedom or cabotage rights. Another example came with the 2001 Multilateral Agreement on the Liberalization of International Air Transport (MALIAT) signed by Brunei, Chile, Singapore, and New Zealand. The last-named has also exchanged cabotage rights with Ireland (in 1999) and the UK (in 2005) although, given the distance between the countries, the agreements might just as well be seen as reflecting political principle rather than an expectation that these rights will be taken up in the near future.

Where cabotage rights are always more likely to be taken up is within the European Union (EU) where air transport has been liberalized in three packages. One effect of the third package of liberalization measures, which came into effect in 1993, was to grant access to international routes to all EU airlines. Airlines registered in any member state became eligible for fifth and seventh freedom rights on international routes throughout the Union, except for a number of 'lifeline' routes on which public service obligations were imposed and some thinly trafficked routes on which new services had just been introduced. Cabotage eighth freedom routes were also fully liberalized, but this concession did not come into effect until 1997. Between 1993 and 1997 member states could still refuse cabotage to airlines of other EU states, unless it was 'consecutive' cabotage, with the domestic sector operated as an extension to an international route. A list of new freedoms taken up under these EU liberalization measures is given in Table 4.2. In most cases, new fifth or seventh freedom rights have led to new competitors entering routes dominated by national carriers, like Debonair's flights from Germany to Spain and Italy, and Virgin Express's Spain–Italy routes. But a few of the new routes are monopolies, such as Portugalia's service between Madrid and Turin and Regional Airlines' services on the Bilbao–Lisbon and Stuttgart–Venice routes. By December 1997 fifth and seventh freedom services within the EU accounted for 1195 international round trip flights a month, 2 per cent of the total (Civil Aviation Authority, 1998). Eighth freedom cabotage services are less significant – representing about 1 per cent of total domestic services within the EU – but they are increasing. There were 26 services in December 1997, 10 of which were on routes in Spain, although most were either on thin monopoly routes or provided only a small part of the total frequency on relatively dense routes.

The new freedoms may well become less exceptional in the future. It may, for instance be possible for seventh freedoms to be exercised on international routes. Under the so-called 'Heathrow Agreement' of 1991, in return for the UK government agreeing to United and American taking over rights previously held by TWA and Pan American, the US government granted UK airlines seventh freedom rights to operate stand-alone services to the USA direct from France, Germany, and several other European countries. This could, for example, mean BA being able to fly non-stop between Paris and New York or between Frankfurt and Chicago. At present these rights cannot be exercised, awaiting as they do the consent of the relevant European governments, just as rights to operate UK–USA services held for many years by certain European airlines still await the approval of the UK government. At the moment traffic rights between EU states and third countries outside Europe are still the subject of bilateral negotiations, although the European Commission (EC) would like to acquire sovereignty in this matter, something which is referred to as 'external competence'. Similar liberalization measures have been taken in other regional groups of states. The states of the Andean Pact agreed in 1991 to establish an 'open skies' area in which the five freedoms of the air are granted without restriction to airlines of member states. More recently in 1996, fourteen governments within the Caribbean Community concluded an agreement to provide a more liberal exchange of traffic rights between member countries. It is thought by some that, eventually, the entire system of bilaterally

Table 4.2 New freedoms taken up under EU liberalization measures by
December 1997.[a] *Source*: CAA

Airline (and country of registration)	Sector [origin/destination on through routes]	Freedom
Aero Lloyd	Lanzarote–Fuerteventura–Linz	7th
(Germany)	Linz–Tenerife	7th
	Linz–Las Palmas	7th
	Malaga–Vienna	7th
Alitalia	Malaga–Barcelona–[Milan]	8th
(Italy)	[Rome]–Barcelona–Seville	8th
British Airways	[Manchester]–Brussels–Rome	5th
(UK)	Helsinki–Stockholm–[London]	5th
British Midland (UK)	[London]–Cologne–Dresden	8th
Debonair	[London]–Dusseldorf–Munich–[Barcelona]	8th
(UK)	Dusseldorf–Munich–[Barcelona]	8th
	Dusseldorf–Munich–[Madrid]	8th
	[London]–Dusseldorf–Munich	8th
	Dusseldorf–Munich	8th
	Barcelona–Munich–[Dusseldorf]–[London]	7th
	Barcelona–Munich–[Dusseldorf]	7th
	Madrid–Munich–[Dusseldorf]	7th
	[London]–Munich–Rome	5th
	Munich–Rome	8th
EasyJet (UK)	Amsterdam–Nice	7th
Finnair	[Helsinki]–Barcelona–Madrid	8th
(Finland)	Amsterdam–Gothenburg–[Helsinki]	5th
	Barcelona–Dusseldorf–[Helsinki]	5th
	Berlin–Stockholm–[Helsinki]	5th
	London–Stockholm–[Helsinki]	5th
	Manchester–Stockholm–[Helsinki]	5th
	Brussels–Stockholm	7th
	Copenhagen–Stockholm	7th
	Dublin–Stockholm–[Helsinki]	5th
	Milan–Stockholm–[Helsinki]	5th
	Oslo–Stockholm	7th
	[Helsinki]–Stockholm–Vienna	5th
GB Airways	[London]–Valencia–Jerez	8th
(UK)	[London]–Murcia–Valencia–[London]	8th
Golden Air (Sweden)	Bergen–Skien	8th
Hamburg Airlines	[Hamburg]–Lyon–Toulouse	8th
(Germany)		
Hapag Lloyd	Lanzarote–Fuerteventura–Luxembourg	7th
(Germany)	Fuerteventura–Mulhouse	7th
Iberia	[Barcelona]–Hamburg–Helsinki	5th
(Spain)	[Madrid]–Hamburg–Oslo	5th
KLM	[Amsterdam]–Lisbon–Porto–[Amsterdam]	8th

Table 4.2 *Continued*

Airline (and country of registration)	Sector [origin/destination on through routes]	Freedom[a]
(The Netherlands)		
Lauda Air (Austria)	[Vienna]–Barcelona–Lisbon	7th
LTU	Salzburg–Lanzarote–Fuerteventura–Salzburg	7th
(Austria)	Salzburg–Las Palmas	7th
Luxair	Munich–Saarbrucken–[Luxembourg]	8th
(Luxembourg)	Lanzarote–Fuerteventura–[Luxembourg]	8th
Muk Air	[Copenhagen]–Kristianstad–Ronneby	8th
(Denmark)		
Portugalia	Barcelona–Bilbao–[Porto]–[Lisbon]	8th
(Portugal)	Palma–Valencia–[Lisbon]–[Porto]	8th
	Bilbao–Madrid–[Lisbon]–[Porto]	8th
	[Lisbon]–Las Palmas–Tenerife–[Lisbon]	8th
	Hanover–Madrid–[Lisbon]–[Porto]	7th
	Hanover–Mulhouse–[Lisbon]–[Porto]	7th
	[Porto]–[Lisbon]–Madrid–Mulhouse	7th
	[Lisbon]–Madrid–Turin	7th
Olympic (Greece)	Marseille–Naples–[Athens]	7th
Regional Airlines	Munster–Stuttgart–[Venice]	8th
(France)	[Munster]–Stuttgart–Venice	5th
	[Bordeaux]–Bilbao–Lisbon	5th
	[Toulouse]–Madrid–Porto	5th
Ryanair	London–Glasgow	8th
(Ireland)	London–Sandefjord	7th
	London–Stockholm	7th
Sun–Air (Denmark)	Geilo–Oslo–[Billund]	8th
TAP Air Portugal	[Lisbon]–Lyons–Nice–[Lisbon]	8th
(Portugal)	[Lisbon]–Berlin–Hamburg–[Lisbon]	8th
	Athens–Rome–[Lisbon]	5th
	[Funchal]–[Lisbon]–Copenhagen–Oslo	5th
	[Porto]–[Lisbon]–Copenhagen–Oslo	5th
	[Faro]–[Lisbon]–Copenhagen–Oslo	5th
	[Porto]–[Lisbon]–Munich–Vienna	5th
Tyrolean	[Vienna]–Gothenburg–Oslo	5th
(Austria)	Lanzarote–Mulhouse	7th
	Las Palmas–Mulhouse	7th
	Luxembourg–Tenerife	7th
	Mulhouse–Tenerife	7th
Virgin Express	Barcelona–Rome	7th
(Belgium)	Madrid–Rome	7th
VLM (Belgium)	London–Dusseldorf	7th

[a] The list does not include the traffic rights enjoyed by wholly owned subsidiaries (such as British Airways' subsidiaries Deutsche BA and Air Liberté).

agreed freedoms of the air may be replaced by some form of multilateral agreement, or at least a series of plurilateral agreements, under which traffic rights are increasingly traded on a regional rather than national basis. But the growth in global alliances, and the multinational ownership of privatized airlines, are likely in the end to prove to be more important developments than whether countries or regions will allow external airlines to carry traffic on routes previously reserved for national airlines. All this may take some time to change things. And nationalism in civil aviation will die hard. In the meantime the airlines likely to gain most from further liberalization of international routes will be those best placed to develop hub and spokes networks designed to capture sixth freedom traffic.

4.3 Accidents of geography

The countries whose airlines have relatively good opportunities for sixth freedom traffic are those in Europe, in the Middle East and in the Far East. Relatively few opportunities are afforded to airlines based in Australasia, in Southern Africa or in North and South America. An airline's sixth freedom opportunities depend to a very large extent upon the geographical position of its hub in relation to major flows of air traffic. This explains why opportunities are much greater in certain parts of the Northern Hemisphere than they generally are in the Southern Hemisphere.

Airlines in Europe for whom sixth freedom traffic is an important part of total traffic include KLM, SAS, Austrian, and TAP Air Portugal. These airlines operate out of small countries and consequently have comparatively little 'home grown' demand in terms of origin and destination traffic; but they are able to feed in traffic from other countries in close proximity that generate and attract large volumes of air traffic. Major sixth freedom carriers based in the Middle East are Emirates, Qatar Airways, Etihad, and Gulf Air. All these airlines have the advantages of bases sited midway along the 'silk road' between Europe and the East. In the Far East, the rapid rates of growth achieved by Cathay Pacific, Garuda, Malaysian (MAS), Philippine Airlines (PAL), Thai International and, most prominently, Singapore International Airlines (SIA) are due mainly to their participation in sixth freedom markets, especially for travel to and from Australia. For the Australian airline Qantas, for South African Airways and for airlines in South America, long-haul sixth freedom opportunities are very limited indeed. There are also relatively few opportunities in North America, although US carriers do of course have the advantage of high levels of cabotage traffic.

The advantages afforded by geography to some countries but not to others leads to situations in which the benefits derived from a bilateral agreement are noticeably imbalanced. If one country consistently gains more in terms of market share, then there is the danger of the other party to the agreement renouncing the pact, or at least demanding an ex post facto review, with the objective of redressing the balance. But the exploitation of geographical advantages to carry fifth and sixth freedom traffic inevitably involves relations with third countries elsewhere; and it may be difficult for the home state to offer the grantor state additional rights of any real value, without at the same time jeopardizing the operations of its own carriers. In this event the home state might bring to the negotiating table some non-aviation quid pro quo, or some agreement might be reached on the payments of royalties. Non-aviation quid pro quos are not usually documented in formal treaties but are covered by confidential 'memoranda of understanding'. It is often suggested that the Dutch Government did in the past make frequent use of this negotiating technique, on one occasion threatening to withhold contributions to NATO until the US granted specific concessions to KLM. Trade incentives have also been employed in the negotiations. For example, on one occasion the Malaysian Government insisted upon increased frequencies to/from London for MAS, in return for promising to purchase defence equipment from British manufacturers.

Where route traffic royalties are used as an alternative way of finding a balancing benefit, the form in which they are paid can vary. In some cases, the airline of the grantor state receives a certain percentage of the revenues (or net revenues); and in other cases the payment is set at a fixed amount per passenger, sometimes applying only when the number of passengers carried is in excess of a given number of 'free' passengers. The level at which royalties are charged also varies, both over time and from route to route. This is something influenced by the value that an aspiring fifth freedom carrier attaches to gaining access to the particular route involved.

To maximize its opportunities to carry connecting traffic, an airline needs a hub located along one of the main flows of traffic, ideally in a position suitable for routeings along both axes, north–south and east–west. This explains why many important hubs in the US are to be found towards the centre of the country, and why some airports along the eastern or western seaboards have not for the most part emerged as major hubs, their suitability for domestic linkages being limited largely to those on the north–south axis.

The classic example in the US is at Hartsfield Airport in Atlanta, where Delta Airlines operates what it can claim to be the busiest single-airline hub in the world, with some 600 daily departures. More than 20 000 Delta passengers change planes in Atlanta each day, giving rise to a joke amongst the American travelling public about a dying Southerner being told that, whether he was going to heaven or hell, he would have to change planes in Atlanta! Each of Delta's arriving and departing waves consists of over 50 aircraft, requiring all four runways to be used simultaneously for arrivals and then simultaneously for departures. Each pair of arriving and departing waves is known as a 'complex'. The scheduled duration of each complex – from the time the first aircraft lands to the time the last aircraft takes off – is no more than 90 minutes, and the minimum connecting time is a mere 35 minutes, a slick operation by any standard. Each complex in Atlanta generates a total of 2500 possible city pair linkages. North–south linkages predominate, but there are a great many routeings via Atlanta on the east–west axis as well.

On the other side of the globe, at Changi Airport in Singapore, flight activity is concentrated very much in the evenings, the time when SIA's flights to and from Europe link up with its services to and from Australasia. Services from Europe arrive in the early evening, in time to enable passengers to transfer to flights to Australia and New Zealand taking off two or three hours later. Just as flights to Australasia are leaving, those from that part of the world start arriving, to connect with European services scheduled to depart in the hours before and after midnight. In all, the airline handles the arrival and departure of about a dozen Boeing 747 'Kangaroo route' flights in its evening complex, this not counting connections with other points in the Orient arriving and departing at roughly the same time. With spokes emanating from its hub in diametrically opposite directions, SIA operates a classic example of an hourglass hub ideally suited for the carriage of sixth freedom traffic (Figure 4.7). This network shape also affords an advantage especially important in long-haul operations, insofar as it makes it easier for the airline to slot services into appropriate time 'windows', allowing for differences across time zones. SIA services depart from passengers' origins early in the evenings and arrive at their final destinations early in the mornings, something that passengers generally find more convenient than arrivals and departures at midday or in the middle of the

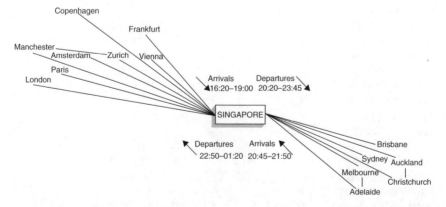

Figure 4.7   Connections through Singapore, SIA services, June 2004 (*Source*: Derived from Official Airline Guide)

night. Schedule windows are important, not just because of the desirability of providing popular departure and arrival times, but also because of the need to meet curfews at spoke airports. SIA has been most successful in exploiting these advantages in the Europe–Australasia travel market and is now turning its attention to other markets such as the North Atlantic. Other Asian carriers have also built up connecting complexes based on hub and spokes scheduling: Thai International in Bangkok, Cathay Pacific in Hong Kong, MAS in Kuala Lumpur, Garuda in Jakarta, and PAL in Manila. For their participation in London–Australia sixth freedom traffic, PAL, MAS, and Thai International used to pay royalties to the third/fourth freedom carriers, BA and Qantas. In Thai International's case the royalties were paid only in respect of passengers not spending at least a night in Thailand; and in PAL's agreement with BA, the level of royalties also depended on the value of interline traffic generated for BA's services (Doganis, 2002).

In the Middle East there are three main competitors for long-haul sixth freedom traffic: Emirates at Dubai, Qatar Airways at Doha, and Etihad Airways at Abu Dhabi. All three enjoy high rates of growth; and it looks as

Table 4.3 Aircraft fleets and orders, three main Middle East long-haul airlines. *Source: Airline Business*

	Current fleet	Orders	Projected deliveries						
			2005	2006	2007	2008	2009	2010	2011
Emirates									
Boeing 777-300ER	5	25	4	14	7				
Airbus A340-500/-600	9	19	1		2	4	11	1	
Airbus A380-800[a]		43			10	6	11	8	8
Other widebodied	59								
Total widebodied	73	87	5	14	19	10	22	9	8
Qatar Airways									
Airbus A330-200	11	8	1	4	2	1			
Airbus A330-300	4	8	2	3		1	2		
Airbus A340-600		4		2	2				
Airbus A380-800		2						2	
Other widebodied	9								
Total widebodied	24	22	3	9	4	2	2	2	
Etihad Airways									
Boeing 777-300ER		5	5						
Airbus A330-200	1	13	1	6	6				
Airbus A340-500/-600		8		4	2	2			
Airbus A380-800		4			4				
Other widebodied	7								
Total widebodied	8	30	6	10	12	2			

[a] Includes orders for three freighters.

though more growth is expected to come, judging by the orders these airlines have been placing for new aircraft (Table 4.3). Within six short years
the fleets of widebodied aircraft operated by these three airlines will more
than double (and this does not include commitments for other narrowbod-
ied types of aircraft). The most extraordinary story is that of Emirates – 'from
scratch into a global airline in 21 years' according to Maurice Flanagan, the
Emirates Executive Chairman. The airline has been exceedingly successful
in attracting sixth freedom traffic which in the future will be able to transit
in the ultra-modern six-runway Jebel Ali airport in Dubai. Emirates' route
network is extensive and now includes destinations right across the globe
(Figure 4.8). Dubai is both an hour glass hub for long-haul traffic and a hinterland hub for routes to other cities in the Middle East.

The Government of the United Arab Emirates has been most assiduous
in negotiating traffic rights for its airline, so much so that airlines from
other countries have sought to complain. One particular bone of contention
concerns Emirates' fifth freedom rights on trans-Tasman routes between
Australia and New Zealand. On these routes Emirates operates one daily
flight in each direction from several Australian cities to Auckland and
Christchurch, using aircraft which would otherwise stand idle on aprons

Figure 4.8   Network of Emirates Airline, June 2005 (*Source*: Emirates Airlines)

at Australian airports between their morning arrival from Dubai and (in the normal schedule window) their return to Dubai in the evening. Services like these are sometimes referred to in airline parlance as 'tail-end charlies'. Both third/fourth freedom carriers on the route, Air New Zealand and Qantas, have several times claimed that Emirates is, through these tail-end charlies, dumping capacity in the trans-Tasman market, seeking only to cover its marginal costs and in the process driving down fares to levels unprofitable for competitors. Another problem in aeronautical relations with Australia centres over the imbalance in benefits from the air service agreement, with the benefits so heavily slanted in favour of Emirates. Qantas has complained that the operations of sixth freedom carriers – SIA as well as Emirates – have been responsible for a sharp fall in its market share of international traffic to/from Australia. And in the future, with Emirates seeking to double flights into Australia, Qantas is going to feel its geographical disadvantage even more. Qantas states it is arguing for parity rather than protection; but the difficulty is what does 'parity' actually mean here. The UAE maintains an open skies policy and so it could offer Qantas the opportunity to set up a hub in Dubai. But this might well be something of an empty gesture (as it was regarding Singapore) given that Qantas would still need fifth freedom rights to operate beyond Dubai. As a third/fourth freedom carrier Qantas also complains that Emirates simply diverts traffic, but more than 80 per cent of the passengers Emirates currently carries in and out of Australia are flying to/from cities not served by Qantas, for example Paris, Zurich, and Vienna (*Airline Business*, 2006). But because a third/fourth freedom carrier cannot match the sixth freedom carrier's economies of route traffic density, it is bound to be at a competitive disadvantage, due to the geographical accident of its home country's location.

There are various kinds of hubs in Europe and liberalization is opening up many new opportunities for them. Most of the European services of TAP Air Portugal fly outbound in the morning and inbound in the evening, so that convenient connections are possible with the early morning arrivals and late evening departures of long-haul services between Lisbon and South America and between Lisbon and points in Southern Africa. Iberia, the national airline of Spain, has a similar focus on Latin America, not only developing connections through Madrid, but also establishing hubs on the other side of the Atlantic. TAP's hub in Lisbon and Iberia's in Madrid are both in the nature of hourglass hubs, located on the periphery of Europe but nevertheless in quite good positions to serve as gateways for long-haul traffic. In Copenhagen, SAS's hub is also very much of the hourglass variety and also on the periphery of Europe, not well placed in relation to the main flows of long-haul traffic but more suited to providing links between Scandinavia and the rest of Europe. Austrian Airlines also operates an hourglass hub and provides an interesting example of a predominantly short-haul operator exploiting its geographical position to develop high volumes of sixth freedom traffic between West and East Europe via Vienna.

The strongest hubs in Europe tend to be those of airlines based in more central locations: Lufthansa in Frankfurt, Swiss in Zurich, Air France in Paris, and KLM in Amsterdam. BA in London is at a geographical disadvantage for Europe-to-Europe connections (save for city pairs like London–Oslo). Nor is it particularly well placed to offer links between domestic points. But it is in a relatively good position for UK–Europe and also for Europe–North America, although not so well placed as its continental competitors for Europe–Africa, Europe–Middle East, Europe–Far East, etc. London, Paris, and Frankfurt all have the advantage of sheer scale, in terms of number of destinations and service frequencies. Clearly, the more destinations that are served the greater the chance of an intending passenger finding a suitable connection, and the odds shorten with every additional flight. In these respects, London ranks ahead of its continental competitors, but the lead it enjoys is diminished by the split of traffic between its two main airports. Heathrow is still the European airport with the greatest number of destinations, but Gatwick ranks alongside Rome as a relatively weak hub in the international context. There is less of an imbalance in Paris, which enjoys a more central location, but a traditional policy of route sectorization between Charles de Gaulle and Orly means that as individual airports both slip below Frankfurt in scale of departures and destinations. And of course there is now the question of the split between Paris and Amsterdam, now that the Air France-KLM merger has been consummated. The dual hub strategy being pursued by the combined airline is discussed below.

Liberalization of air services in the EU presents opportunities for airlines to overcome their geographical disadvantages by seeking hubs in other European countries. Any restrictions on cabotage, such as those limiting it to consecutive flights or to 50 per cent of the capacity operated on the primary international route, are likely to be less of a deterrent to airlines setting up a new hub. For the new hub can have a number of international routes feeding into a number of domestic sectors. In this way, an airline can establish 'mini hubs' in foreign countries. This is what Iberia is doing in Amsterdam, taking advantage of Amsterdam's central location. Flights from Madrid and Barcelona are routed via Amsterdam on their way to Copenhagen, Gothenburg, Helsinki, and Stockholm and timed so that passengers can make suitable connections between them in Amsterdam. It is possible that there are going to be many more mini hubs of this kind.

4.4 Europe compared with the US

There are a number of reasons why, even with cabotage completely unrestricted, the experience of the US will not be repeated on quite the same scale in Europe. One is airport congestion. If airport slots remain scarce, and if as a result it becomes increasingly difficult to co-ordinate flight schedules into waves of arrivals and departures, then the scope for developing effective hub and spokes systems will be that much less. The problems of airport capacity are discussed later, and there are other reasons why US-style hubbing will not become so prominent in Europe, at least so far as intra-European services are concerned.

For one thing, some immutable geographic and demographic factors mean that the proportion of passengers who can readily travel on an indirect routeing via an intermediate airport is considerably smaller. Population density is very much lower in the US, 26 per square kilometre as compared with 164 per square kilometre in the EU. At the same time the US population is much more widely dispersed geographically, leading to longer average journey lengths (approximately 1200 per kilometre as against circa 900 kilometre in the EU). In terms of total passenger-kilometres flown, the US domestic market is more than five times greater than the intra-European market so that, despite the wider population dispersion, the density of traffic is still very much higher in the US than it is in Europe.

In Europe most of the important travel-generating centres are fairly close to one another – especially those business centres within the so-called 'hot banana' (Figure 4.9) running across from Southeast England to Northern Italy. As a result most routes are too short to be susceptible to competition from indirect flights. Also a much higher proportion of travellers than in the US begin and end their journeys in a hub city. Hence, on many intra-European routes, cross elasticities of demand between direct and indirect flights are always likely to be fairly low. At the same time, on many routes, cross elasticities between air and surface transport are fairly high.

Cross elasticities are also high between hub airlines and their low-cost competitors. To a large extent the US experience with low-cost airlines is being repeated in Europe. Indeed, Ryanair, by some measures the largest low-cost airline in Europe, is modelled upon the US pioneer Southwest, as its Chief Executive, Michael O'Leary, has readily acknowledged. But here again, in relation to competition from low-cost airlines, there is still something of a difference between US hubs and hubs in Europe. In the US the spokes linked through a hub both tend to be short or medium hauls, whereas the European hubs tend predominantly to connect short/medium-haul services with long-haul intercontinental flights. The big city-pair markets in the US have sufficiently large traffic flows to justify direct point to point services by low-cost airlines bypassing hubs. But that is rarely the case in Europe, from where most long-haul traffic flows are too thin to be served point to point. This point has been made by the Deputy CEO of Air France-KLM (Gourgeon, 2005) who shows just how tiny is the proportion of long-haul city pairs that are served direct with point to point service: 6 per cent of 12 000 Europe–Asia city pairs, and 3 per cent of 21 000 Europe–North American city pairs. Overall, some 60 per cent of passengers travelling on long-haul intercontinental services

Enclosing areas with the highest
levels of economic activity

Figure 4.9   The European 'hot banana'

to/from Europe are connecting through a hub. It is possible that this may change in the future, if a somewhat larger number of thinner routes become economically viable when they can be operated with Boeing 787 Dreamliner aircraft, rather than bigger airliners such as the Boeing 747 or the forthcoming Airbus 380. In the meantime the future for many of the European hubs looks more secure than the future for US hubs.

The shorter distances in Europe mean that road and rail are much closer substitutes. In particular there is much greater competition from high-speed trains in Europe (see Figure 4.10). There has already been evidence of significant diversion from air to rail, 35 years ago on the London–Glasgow route following electrification, and 20 years or so ago on the Paris–Lyon route where air lost more than two-thirds of its traffic following the introduction of TGV (*Train à Grande Vitesse*) services. But perhaps of greater importance in the present context are the possibilities of rail services linking airports,

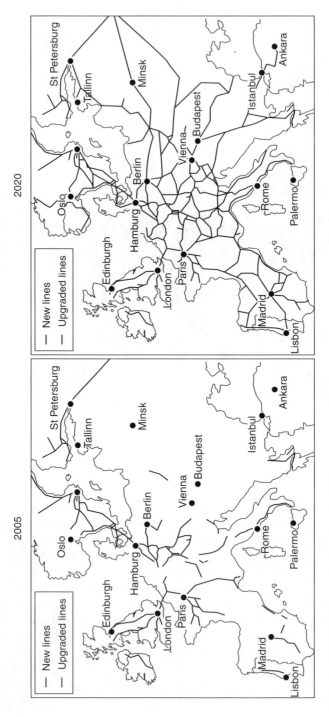

Figure 4.10 High-speed rail networks in Europe

replacing some short-haul feeder services. It is for short-haul journeys (including those to/from hub cities) that surface modes offer the most effective substitutes for air travel. Air transport is at a substantial disadvantage compared with rail on most short-haul routes because of the difficulty of getting between the airport and major business/residential areas. Air transport's speed advantage is often offset by long access and egress times to, from and at airports. In Europe the development of high-speed trains has extended rail's competitiveness for distances up to 300 miles; and the chief of Lufthansa has predicted that it will not be long before many short-haul services into Europe's major hubs are replaced by trains. For some years Lufthansa has been operating the airport express rail service between Frankfurt and Dusseldorf via the cities of Bonn and Cologne. The TGV services pioneered by the French are now spreading throughout Germany, Italy, Sweden, and Spain; and in the liberalized market they will provide some stiff competition for intra-European air services. The access/egress disadvantages of air services are diminished in the case of feeder links to hubs, when passengers are making onward connections. But nonetheless the progressive shortening of city-centre to city-centre journey times by rail, together with improved railheads at airports, is tilting the balance increasingly in favour of rail on many of the shorter routes. Further extensions to the high-speed rail network, including routes like London–Paris and London–Brussels (following the opening of the Channel Tunnel) and Paris–Frankfurt and Paris–Zurich, will further enhance rail's position in the short-haul market.

All this may not be totally unwelcome to the airlines. For short-haul services are not all that profitable in Europe, at least not for many full service carriers. In the accounts of BA for instance, it is often revealed that intra-European services in some years earn only a tiny surplus and in others actually sustain a loss, with virtually all the airline's operating surplus coming from operations outside Europe. It is on the long-haul routes that these airlines make money. Almost all major carriers in Europe have long-haul networks, and another major geographic difference between European and US air transport is in the relative importance of traffic flows to/from points outside the region. International passenger-kilometres flown on routes to/from the US amount to about 50 per cent of domestic passenger kilometres, whereas the number of passenger-kilometres flown on routes between EU and non-EU countries is some three times the number flown on routes entirely within the EU. This difference is largely explained by the relatively self-contained US economy and by the significance of former colonial links for EU countries. To many full service EU airlines, the real value of short-haul routes lies in their ability to feed high-yield passengers onto their long-haul networks. This is where the hub and spokes systems of the US find their closest parallel in Europe and why hub location is so crucial.

Large full service airlines in the US typically earn 75 per cent of their total revenue from domestic operations, the remaining 25 per cent coming from international long-haul routes. For their counterparts in Europe it is almost the other way around. An airline like BA gets about two-thirds of its revenue from long-haul intercontinental flights with just from one-third from short-haul intra-European services (Taneja, 2004). In some ways this puts the European carriers in a better position to meet competition from low-cost airlines which so far have concentrated on short and medium-haul intra-European markets. But the advantage of a strong long-haul network is now increasingly being recognised by US airlines which are eager to expand their revenue base through greater presence in markets like the North Atlantic.

4.5 Regional services

Another difference between Europe and the US is in the scale and importance of regional services, which have been expanding faster than the airline industry as a whole. This expansion has been particularly noticeable in Europe, although regional services are still far more prominent in the US, where they are a well-established part of the public transport scene, accepted and used by travellers more or less as airborne bus services. This much is reflected in the relative sizes of US regionals as compared to their counterparts in other parts of the world. When ranked by passenger numbers, US regionals occupy 9 of the top 10 positions (Table 4.4).

Table 4.4 The top 100 regional airlines in 2004 ranked by passenger numbers. *Source*: *Airline Business* (May 2005)

		Country	Passengers (thousands)	Total aircraft fleet
1	American Eagle	USA	14 869	255
2	ExpressJet	USA	13 739	249
3	SkyWest	USA	13 425	220
4	Comair	USA	12 632	164
5	Atlantic Southeast	USA	10 428	144
6	Mesa Air[a]	USA	10 240	180
7	Air Wisconsin	USA	7158	86
8	Lufthansa CityLine	Germany	6700	81
9	Pinnacle	USA	6340	121
10	Chautauqua	USA	6268	116
11	Horizon Air	USA	5930	65
12	Air Canada Jazz	Canada	5444	87
13	Mesaba	USA	5429	97
14	KLM Cityhopper[b]	The Netherlands	4950	52
15	British Airways CitiExpress	UK	4130	58

16	Piedmont[c]	USA	4048	64
17	Air Nostrum (Iberia Regional)	Spain	3827	53
18	UNI Airways	Taiwan	3606	26
19	SN Brussels	Belgium	3580	38
20	Aegean Airlines	Greece	3578	20
21	Trans States Airlines	USA	3463	75
22	Regional	France	3355	65
23	Austrian Arrows	Austria	3200	50
24	TransAsia	Taiwan	3130	18
25	BritAir	France	3102	40
26	Swiss Regional Ops	Switzerland	3093	30
27	Shandong Airlines	China	3009	22
28	Merpati Nusantara	Indonesia	3000	40
29	Eurowings	Germany	3000	33
30	Executive Airlines	USA	2796	41
31	Binter Canarias	Spain	2359	13
32	PSA Airlines	USA	2230	48
33	China Eastern Regional Ops	China	2158	22
34	Iran Aseman Airlines	Iran	2075	33
35	Alitalia Express	Italy	1968	35
36	Bangkok Airways	Thailand	1860	15
37	Wideroe's Flyveselskap	Norway	1791	29
38	Mandarin Airlines	Taiwan	1787	17
39	CityJet	Ireland	1408	17
40	Mount Cook Airlines	New Zealand	1400	12
41	Skyways	Sweden	1400	27
42	Eastern Australia	Australia	1375	21
43	Air Dolomiti	Italy	1282	21
44	CCM Airlines[d]	France	1195	12
45	Air Nelson	New Zealand	1186	17
46	Malmo Aviation	Sweden	1146	9
47	Blue 1	Finland	1139	14
48	Chicago Express Airlines	USA	1106	14
49	Aeroliteral	Mexico	1066	25
50	Regional Air Lines	Morocco	1050	7
51	Aerocaribe	Mexico	1032	12
52	PGA-Portugalia	Portugal	1001	14
53	MidAtlantic Airways[e]	USA	1000	22
54	Aer Arann	Ireland	977	10
55	Regional Express	Australia	938	29
56	EuroLot	Poland	932	13
57	Airlink	Australia	891	1
58	SAM Columbia	Colombia	874	4
59	Arkia Israeli Airlines	Israel	863	13
60	Augsburg Airways	Germany	803	11
61	South African Express	South Africa	800	13
62	Eagle Airways	New Zealand	742	16
63	Air Tahiti	French Polynesia	732	12
64	South African Airlink[f]	South Africa	732	20

Table 4.4 *continued*

		Country	Passengers (thousands)	Total aircraft fleet
65	Sunstate Airlines[g]	Australia	730	13
66	bmi Regional	UK	706	13
67	LIAT	Antigua	700	9
68	Midwest Connect	USA	680	22
69	Colgan Air	USA	667	30
70	Gulfstream Int'l	USA	650	34
71	Aires Colombia	Colombia	638	8
72	Aerosur	Bolivia	592	12
73	AirBaltic	Latvia	589	16
74	Aeromar	Mexico	578	15
75	Cimber Air	Denmark	570	19
76	Shuttle America	USA	570	20
77	West Caribbean	Colombia	568	15
78	TACV	Cape Verde	563	5
79	VLM Airlines	Belgium	554	13
80	Pelita Air Services	Indonesia	550	23
81	Golden Air	Sweden	526	13
82	Aurigny Air Services	UK	515	14
83	Air Nippon Network[d]	Japan	510	11
84	Great Lakes Aviation	USA	484	36
85	Loganair	UK	434	18
86	J-Air	Japan	430	6
87	Cape Air	USA	426	3
88	Island Air	USA	411	8
89	Eastern Airways	UK	394	25
90	SATA Air Acores	Portugal	390	5
91	Montenegro Airlines	Montenegro	365	2
91	Era Aviation	USA	365	14
93	Air Iceland	Iceland	333	11
94	CommutAir	USA	324	24
95	Rio-Sul S.A. Regionais	Brazil	323	11
96	Air Greenland	Greenland	320	11
97	Scenic Airlines	USA	300	14
98	Air Caledonie	New Caledonia	275	4
99	Carpatair	Romania	268	11
100	Air Alps Aviation	Austria	257	9

[a] To the year ended 30 September 2004.
[b] Includes KLM UK.
[c] Includes Allegheny up to 31 July 2004.
[d] To the year ended 31 March 2004.
[e] Started up in April 2004.
[f] To the year ended 31 August 2004.
[g] To the year ended 30 June 2004.

Regional airlines in the US today are the direct descendants of what in the regulated era used to be classed as 'commuter' airlines. Under regulation the US interstate industry developed on three levels. On the first level, 10 trunk airlines became the major domestic carriers, principally serving high-density, long-haul routes with jet aircraft. On the second level, local service airlines were licensed to expand services to small cities and to feed the trunk system. Just before deregulation 8 of these airlines were still in existence. But their role had changed to include greater provision of longer-haul, higher-density jet service, turning them into 'mini trunks', each with a distinctly regional focus. Finally, on the third level, the commuters, which began service after the Second World War, were restricted to flying piston-engined and turbo-prop aircraft on short-haul routes serving mainly small communities. Some services were operated under subsidy, under conditions that obliged airlines to provide adequate service, at specified minimum frequencies, to/from all points eligible for subsidy. There was no automatic freedom of exit and withdrawal from a route often entailed a long administrative process and the provision of a replacement carrier. As a result, before deregulation many points were served with equipment which was far too large to be economic.

In liberalizing route entry and exit, deregulation effectively shifted the opportunity and responsibility of serving small communities to third-level carriers. At the time many small communities feared that deregulation would result in them losing airline service altogether. Their argument was that, with open price competition, airlines would find it less easy to cross-subsidize loss-making services on low-density routes. There had already been some evidence of airlines seeking to pull out of subsidized services, where the subsidies paid did not cover the higher costs of operating larger aircraft. And to begin with, it looked as if their fears were going to be realized. In the early years of deregulation many small towns and cities did indeed lose service, although it has never been entirely clear just how far this was due to deregulation and how far to the contemporaneous events of fuel price increases and economic recession. But in any event it was not long before a high proportion of the routes abandoned by first- and second-level carriers were taken over by the regionals. After deregulation regional airline traffic continued to grow apace, total passengers enplaned increasing more than four-fold, with an even greater increase in revenue passenger-miles, reflecting a 60 per cent increase in average trip length per passenger. But the number of carriers operating on regional routes has fallen (by around 40 per cent). The Airline Deregulation Act provided for subsidies to communities that would otherwise lose service, under a new Essential Air Service (EAS) subsidy programme. Under the new arrangements the US Department of Transportation determines the level of EAS subsidy required to ensure continued access and then requests competitive bids from airlines willing to operate the route. To be eligible for an EAS subsidy, a community must be located at least 70 miles by highway from the nearest medium or large hub airport, 55 miles from the nearest small hub airport or 45 miles from the nearest non-hub airport that enplanes 100 passengers or more per day; and no community can receive a subsidy exceeding $200 per passenger. But some political representatives have complained about the apparent deterioration in services to small communities in their constituencies.

The effect on services to small communities is often presented as an adverse outcome of deregulation. One writer put it thus:

> While deregulation has a class of beneficiaries, consumers in small towns and rural communities are not amongst them...With the elimination of entry and exit regulation, airlines have been free to reduce their level of service to less lucrative communities and focus their energies and equipment on more profitable market opportunities. The result of airline deregulation is that many small communities have experienced a drastic reduction in air service.
> (Dempsey, 1990)

In the first 2 years of deregulation more than 100 communities lost service altogether, inducing a feature advertisement to be placed in the *Wall Street Journal* in 1980 exclaiming that 'Deregulation has shot down more planes than the Red Baron!' This resulted not so much from the reduction in subsidies, but more from the fact that, as carriers left thinly trafficked routes for denser markets elsewhere, regional airlines shifted their operations to take their place, exiting many routes previously ineligible for subsidy. But did this lead to the 'drastic reduction' in air service to small communities that writers like Dempsey claim? There are a number of aspects to consider here. Besides those communities that have lost scheduled service altogether, there are others which have experienced some reduction in the number of destinations served by direct flights or in the frequency of those flights. Also there are many more for whom destinations and frequencies have failed to increase at the same rate with secular increases in air services generally. The most relevant comparison is always with what might have been the case had regulation continued. But simply counting the number of flights may misrepresent some of the more important changes taking place, including the development of hub and spokes systems. Other things being equal, service to a hub is superior to service to a non-hub, because the former generates greater opportunities for connections; and a flight to a large hub is better still, especially if it arrives at the hub just prior to an outgoing bank of flights. What small communities tended to lose were flights to non-hubs, or to small hubs; what many of them gained was an increase in service to the larger hubs, often flights with vastly increased online connections. Taking all this into consideration it is highly possible for a small community to have come out of deregulation with a net gain in airline service. And some studies confirmed this. Butler and Huston (1990) for instance, in

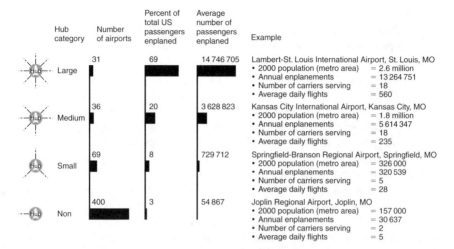

Hub category	Number of airports	Percent of total US passengers enplaned	Average number of passengers enplaned	Example
Large	31	69	14 746 705	Lambert-St. Louis International Airport, St. Louis, MO • 2000 population (metro area) = 2.6 million • Annual enplanements = 13 264 751 • Number of carriers serving = 18 • Average daily flights = 560
Medium	36	20	3 628 823	Kansas City International Airport, Kansas City, MO • 2000 population (metro area) = 1.8 million • Annual enplanements = 5 614 347 • Number of carriers serving = 18 • Average daily flights = 235
Small	69	8	729 712	Springfield-Branson Regional Airport, Springfield, MO • 2000 population (metro area) = 326 000 • Annual enplanements = 320 539 • Number of carriers serving = 5 • Average daily flights = 28
Non	400	3	54 867	Joplin Regional Airport, Joplin, MO • 2000 population (metro area) = 157 000 • Annual enplanements = 30 637 • Number of carriers serving = 2 • Average daily flights = 5

Figure 4.11   Differences among US airports offering commercial airline service, 2001 (*Source*: US General Accounting Office)

a study of 225 non-hub airports, found that even where the number of direct flights fell, this was swamped by a surge in possible connections, so that the average non-hub airport enjoyed a 55 per cent increase in airline service.

Nonetheless the provision of air service to small communities is still considered to be something of a problem. Airports served by commercial airlines in the US are categorized into four main groups based on the number of passenger enplanements: large hubs, medium hubs, small hubs, and non-hubs. These are illustrated with examples in Figure 4.11. In 2001, the 31 large hubs and the 36 medium hubs together accounted for the vast majority (89 per cent) of the more than 660 million air passengers emplaned at US airports. At the other end, those normally referred to small community airports, the 69 small hubs and the 400 non-hubs, enplaned only 8 per cent and 3 per cent of US passengers. Small community airports have long had a problem of limited air service, which stems quite clearly from their small population base. But recently this has got worse, both because of cutbacks by the major full service airlines and also because of the growing presence of low-cost airlines. The majors do not serve small communities themselves, but their cost cutting has had knock-on effects on the smaller regional airlines with whom they had agreements for feeder traffic. Nor do the low-cost airlines tend to serve small communities, but they have attracted significant numbers of passengers from there. The US General Accounting Office (2002) investigated the extent to which there was 'leakage' of passengers away from small community airports and found that half the non-hub airports are within 100 miles of a major airline hub; and that over half the small community airport officials surveyed said they believed local residents drove to another airport because of the availability of lower fares there. Apart from the remoter regions of Montana, Wyoming and the Dakotas, almost the whole of the country lies within a 100-mile radius of a major airline hub or airport served by a low-cost airline (Figure 4.12).

In the past few years the pattern of regional services in Europe has been undergoing radical change. It has for some time been the policy of the EC to promote air services to small communities in order to encourage regional economic growth. In one of its first steps towards liberalization the EC issued its Inter-Regional Air Services Directive in 1983. This was intended to give more or less automatic multilateral approval for airlines to provide international services on regional routes throughout the Community. But it was an agreement qualified in a number of important respects: the services could only be operated by aircraft up to 70 seats and only on routes of 400 kilometre or over; routes to/from airports classified as Category 1 airports – which included 25 of the busiest airports in Europe – were excluded; and protection was granted for indirect or parallel services to nearly all airports (and also for a group of more than 20 specified airports in Denmark, Greece, Italy, and Spain, which were made exempt). With all these limitations it was hardly surprising that the 1983 Directive did not result in any immediate upsurge in regional operations. The main

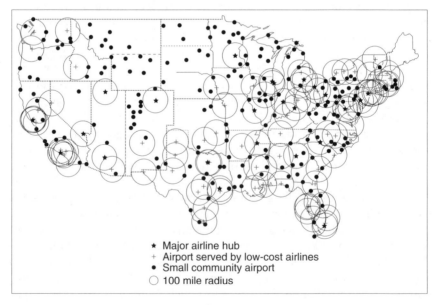

★ Major airline hub
+ Airport served by low-cost airlines
• Small community airport
○ 100 mile radius

Figure 4.12   Proximity of US small community airports to major hubs and airports served by low-cost airlines (*Source*: US General Accounting Office)

reason for this was the exclusion of Category 1 airports. These serve the main travel-generating centres and are almost without exception important hubs for the major carriers. So if the hope was to stimulate regional services, it was a mistake to exclude these airports, particularly since US experience had shown that the biggest growth area in regional air transport was in feeder traffic to the hubs. As it was, only 10 new services were authorized under the 1983 Directive, and in 1985 the market for regional airlines, limited as it was to non-Category 1 airports, covered only 115 city pairs or just 2.6 per cent of passengers on international air services in Europe (Wheatcroft and Lipman, 1986). Restrictions in the 1983 Directive were about to be relaxed when they were overtaken by the more wide-ranging measures to liberalize route licensing and market access leading up to the third package of reforms that came into effect in January 1993. The intention of EC liberalization is that there should be almost total freedom for EU-licensed airlines to fly anywhere within the Community, including regional routes. The only significant restriction in the EC's proposals concerns routes with a low traffic volume. The EC has been concerned to see that some essential but uneconomic 'lifeline' services to national development regions, and also services between regional airports, survive in the single market. Accordingly it protects public service routes with fewer than 30 000 seats per annum by limiting access for a period of up to 3 years. Otherwise, regional airlines are now free to operate to as many Category 1 airports as they please, provided that is, they can acquire the necessary take-off and landing slots.

The capacity constraints at European airports constitute a major impediment to development of regional services. The response of governments and of the EC has been to consider means of reforming the present system of allocating take-off and landing slots, so as to reduce the barriers facing new entrants and encourage competition. As discussed later, this is a very difficult matter and finding a solution acceptable to all concerned is no small problem. One suggestion is that slots be auctioned, a possibility that would have very serious consequences for regional airlines: 'A regional airline operating a Saab 340 on a 300 kilometre route would be in an impossible position against an airline operating a B747 across the Atlantic' (Wheatcroft and Lipman, 1990). What the EC has decided to do is to take all new and unused slots at congested airports, place them in a 'pool' and allocate anything up to 50 per cent of them to new-entrant airlines. The problem with this is that hardly any new slots are becoming available at congested airports and incumbent airlines are prepared to go to almost any lengths to keep the slots they already have, under the system of 'grandfather rights'.

In many cases a regional airline's best prospects for gaining access to congested airports lie in going into partnership with a major airline. The practice has for sometime been widespread in the US where the majors have grouped the services of their regional partners under single brand names: American Eagle/American Connection, United Express, Continental Connection, Northwest Airlink, Delta Connection, and US Airways Express. One main reason why major airlines enter into relationships with regionals is to gain market access, ensure traffic feed and extend their marketable networks at low cost.

4.6 Extending marketable networks

Where it is possible, one way of extending networks is to acquire the routes of other carriers. This was the main way in which the large US airlines which were previously restricted to domestic routes, American, Delta, and United, were able to move into international operations, purchasing the route authorities of Pan American and TWA, the two traditional US flag carriers, when these airlines got into financial difficulties (Table 4.5). Elsewhere it is mostly not possible to do this, given constraints in bilateral agreements on the designation of airlines to international routes. But a large part of the economies of scope associated with network size can in fact be reaped without the airline necessarily operating all services on all routes itself. Many of the marketing benefits from large network size, in advertising, customer loyalty devices, computer reservations systems, etc., can be achieved by close co-operation with other carriers serving

Table 4.5 International route sales between major US airlines (1985–1992). *Source:* US General Accounting Office

Buyer	Seller	Route(s)	Price[a] ($ million)
American	Eastern	Latin American system	471
American	TWA	3 US–London routes	445
Delta	Pan American	European routes	526
Delta	Pan American	New York–Mexico City	25
Northwest	America West	Honolulu–Nagoya	15
Northwest	Hawaiian	Pacific routes	9
US Air	TWA	2 US–London routes	50
United	Pan American	Pacific routes	716
United	Pan American	US–London routes	400
United	Pan American	Latin American system + Los Angeles–Mexico City	148

[a] In some cases the price included the transfer of related facilities.

complementary routes. Growth in such co-operation is a major feature of liberalized air travel markets. Three particular kinds are especially important in this regard:

- franchising,
- blocked spacing,
- code-sharing.

Franchising

This is the practice of one airline permitting another to use its name, aircraft livery, uniforms and brand image generally. One airline sells these privileges to another, often as part of an overall package in which the franchisor undertakes the franchisee's marketing and sales management as well. In return the franchisee pays royalty fees and often acts as a feeder carrier to the franchisor's main network.

A list of franchise agreements, current in October 2005, is given in Table 4.6. It is true to say that franchising has not become as widespread as once it was

Table 4.6 Franchise agreements, October 2005. *Sources*: Compiled by the author from airline websites

Franchisor	Brand name	Franchisee(s)
Air France	Air France	Brit Air City Jet Compagnie Corse Mediterranee Regional
Air New Zealand	Air NZ Link	Mount Cook Islands Eagle Airways Freedom Air Air Nelson Air Pacific
American Airlines	American Connection	Chautauqua Airlines Regions Air Trans States Airlines
British Airways	British Airways	British Mediterranean Comair (South Africa) GB Airways Loganair Regional Air Sun-Air (Denmark)

Table 4.6 *Continued*

Franchisor	Brand name	Franchisee(s)
Continental	Continental Express	Cape Air Colgan Air Commutair ExpressJet Gulfstreamair
Delta	Delta Connection	Atlantic Southeast Airlines Chautauqua Airlines Comair (USA) Freedom Airlines Shuttle America SkyWest
Iberia	Iberia Regional	Air Nostrum
Lufthansa	Lufthansa Regional	Air Dolomiti Augsburg Airways CityLine Contact Air Eurowings
Northwest	Northwest Airlink	Pinnacle Airlines Mesaba Airlines Pacific Islands Aviation
Qantas	QantasLink	Airlink Eastern Australia Airlines Sunstate Airlines
United	United Express	Air Wisconsin Chautauqua Airlines Mesa Airlines Shuttle America SkyWest Trans States Airlines
US Airways	US Airways Express	Air Midwest Air Wisconsin Chautauqua Airlines Colgan Air Mesa Airlines MidAtlantic Airways Piedmont Airlines PSA Airlines Republic Airlines Trans States Airlines

expected to be. Of the dozen airlines with well-established franchises, half of them are in the US and the rest in Europe and in British Commonwealth countries. It is true to say that quite a few former franchise agreements have disappeared simply because the regional partners have been taken over by franchisor and incorporated as fully or partly owned subsidiaries of the parent airline. An example of this is in Canada where Air Canada Jazz is now part owned by Air Canada for whom it operates feeder and commuter services. It was established in 2001 from the consolidation of *Air Canada Connector* carriers Air BC, Air Nova, Air Ontario, and Canadian Regional Airlines, all of which carriers were former Air Canada franchisees. It began operations shortly after the merger of Air Canada with Canadian Airlines International (CAIL).

BA was the pioneer of franchising in Europe. But even BA has fewer franchisees now than it had 10 years ago. In Feb 2002 BA published its *Future Size and Shape* proposals, policy changes designed to reverse the airline's decline in profitability and to respond to growing competition from low-cost airlines. These included some changes to BA's regional operations. It formed in March 2002 a new subsidiary, then known as BA CitiExpress, which absorbed the operations of former airlines BA Regional, Brymon, British Regional Airlines Group, CityFlyer Express and Manx Airlines. BA CitiExpress has since been rebranded as BA Connect. With this consolidation BA rationalised its regional routes and aircraft fleet, withdrawing some services and reducing the number of its regional aircraft types from nine to four. All this was done to bring unit costs down by around 30 per cent.

A franchising agreement can be beneficial for both franchisor and franchisee. The benefits for the franchisor include: the spreading of its name more widely; the transfer of some high-cost, low-yield routes to franchisee carriers, which are often more suited to operating such services cost effectively; and, most significant of all, increased traffic feed to its main network. The franchisee benefits from the value of the franchisor's brand; from being able to use the franchisor's marketing and distribution expertise; and from an increase in traffic over what it would otherwise be able to attract as an independent operator.

Generally speaking, franchising has been profitable for both parties. This has certainly been the case for the franchising arranged by BA (Civil Aviation Authority, 1998). But there are also the questions of what impact it has on passengers and how it affects the degree of competition on the routes affected. It is possible that passengers may benefit from the lower costs of franchise carriers, if these are passed on in reduced fares. Whether that will be the case may depend on whether the franchise increases the franchisee's market power relative to independent operators. Other possible benefits for passengers are that marginal routes are more likely to survive if they are operated under a strong brand name, that service of a particular standard is assured and that there may be improved linkages to connect with the franchisor's main network. On the other hand, franchising may cause confusion for passengers even though airlines are legally obliged to inform passengers which carrier is actually operating the flight; and another potential disadvantage for passengers will arise if franchising strengthens an airline's dominant position and results in the carrier charging excessive fares or engaging in predatory behaviour.

These points are discussed more fully by Plender (1999). In another study (Denton and Dennis, 2000) the general conclusions are that franchising produces positive net benefits for passengers, and that it is not usually harmful for competition, except possibly where it gives the franchisor an especially dominant position in one market area. One such area where a dominant airline employs franchising extensively is the Highlands and Islands of Scotland. In this area BA has been franchising services since 1993, to reduce the costs, and eliminate some mounting losses, it had incurred when operating the services itself. An investigation by Pagliari (2003) found that franchising had the effect of reducing service capacity levels but also that the franchisees were more adept at managing capacity, with improved scheduling, more direct services and some new routes. The only question that remains is whether the franchisees, in controlling virtually all routes in the area, are exercising monopoly market power through the setting of some excessively high fares, or whether the high fares simply reflect the high costs of operation.

It is possible that franchising will become more widespread in the future. There may be no global air transport market in the same sense that there is for cars, computers, food and drink, etc. For instance, the production of air services on domestic routes in Japan is not of direct relevance to passenger demand on the North Atlantic. Under the present system of traffic rights, negotiated in terms of freedoms of the air and with restrictions on cabotage, each country or region tends to be an individual market, with generally rather limited competition on routes between these markets. In order to be thought of as a 'global' carrier, an airline will need to be perceived as a major supplier in foreign markets, on domestic routes in other countries and also on all major international routes, not just those to and from its home country. This is presently precluded by lack of traffic rights, but franchising possibly represents a way in which an airline can tap into foreign markets using its own brand name.

Franchising has been used to great effect in some other industries, turning certain businesses into truly global operations. Two prominent examples are the Coca-Cola company and McDonald's hamburger restaurants, instances that provide good illustrations of two main forms of franchising working successfully. Coca-Cola is an example of a 'product' or 'trademark' franchise. Here the franchisor supplies its brand name plus some essential ingredient, like the Coca-Cola syrup, and the franchisees put in something else, for example carbonated water and bottling, and then distribute the product to final consumers. The case of McDonald's is an example of a 'business format' franchise. In this the franchisor supplies its brand name plus a blueprint for running a particular type of business and assists by providing training, monitoring, quality control, marketing and advice generally, all to a much greater extent than is typically the case with a product franchise. Both have led to truly global products, ensuring that a coke is a coke is a coke, wherever you happen to be in the world, or that the McDonald's hamburger, and the way it is delivered to the consumer, is essentially the same whether it is bought in Tokyo, Toronto or Tottenham. By supplying a standard product, slightly adapted if desired to local taste, and relying on a well-defined franchise concept for management control, McDonald's have actually been able to raise capital during its growth, rather than spending it, as some airlines have done, on mergers and acquisitions.

How far can the franchise concept be applied in airline operations? Both kinds of franchising are possible, but perhaps it is the business format kind that airlines are more likely to adopt. There is little doubt that the image projected by one airline can be more favourable in marketing terms than that projected by another; and that the brand name associated with one carrier is more saleable than that of another. Airline branding is a nebulous concept, but one that is becoming more and more crucial for success. On one definition, an airline's brand is the property it owns over and above the 'hard' and 'soft' values of the physical product in operating services (Simons, 1994). In this context hard values are the fundamental requirements for operating flights, in terms of aircraft, infrastructure, schedules, finance, managerial resources, sales outlets, etc., all the things an airline needs before it can even enter the market. Soft values on the other hand are the more tactile aspects of flying services, such as cabin staff, inflight catering, seat configuration, video systems, interior design and so on. And beyond these hard and soft values, brand values are those associated with the 'personality' of the airline, often deriving from its company or geographic heritage. Over time the relative importance of hard, soft, and brand values has been changing. In the past the most important things distinguishing one airlines from another were the hard values. For example, if one airline flew a new and improved aircraft type (e.g. a 'whisper' jet) whilst its competitors persevered with older aircraft, that gave it a distinct advantage in the eyes of passengers. But as flight equipment became more and more standardized amongst the major airlines, passengers began to take the hard values more or less for granted. The competitive struggle then switched to the soft values, with airlines attempting to out-do each other in inflight service and entertainment. But any competitive advantage won in soft values tends to be relatively short lived, as other airlines respond swiftly to any innovation finding favour with passengers. Expenditure on soft values is also subject to diminishing marginal returns: ultimately there must be some limit to the number of video channels passengers can view or the number of glasses of champagne they can drink or the amount of cordon bleu cooking they can enjoy, even on a long-haul flight!

The current focus on brand values is manifest in the various ways airlines market their services. In 1988 BA became the first airline to adopt a policy of branding individual classes of service: First, Club World, Club Europe, World Traveller, Euro Traveller, etc. The choice of the 'Traveller' label to replace 'economy' class is particularly significant in this regard. The promotion of brands is also evident in recent airline advertisements. Two such advertisements, seeking to associate brands with the personalities of company chairman taken out by Virgin Atlantic and British Midland in conjunction with American Express are illustrated in Figure 4.13.

For many years certain airlines derived competitive advantages from their positions as national flag carriers. Flag carriers typically display their nationalities on the fuselages of their aircraft, and the airlines of advanced industrial nations often gained from this relative to airlines from developing countries. The airlines of some countries are often perceived by passengers as being in some sense safer or more reliable than those of others. But with the standardization of hard values this is changing somewhat. It may still be the case that many passengers prefer, other things being equal, to fly on airlines from certain countries, but increasingly the brand value of flag carrier is giving way to brand values based on emotional or attitudinal factors more generally. In most other markets consumers go for brands that are perceived in one way or another as 'best', regardless of where they are produced and regardless of whether the producer is British, French, German, American, or Japanese. It is possible that the same will eventually emerge in markets for air travel, so that brand values based on the flag carrier concept may to some extent become passé. Also, those airlines whose nationalities are perceived as competitive disadvantages but which still possess valuable third, fourth, and fifth freedom traffic rights, may see a lot of benefit in becoming franchisees to airlines with strong brand names. The latter may also view the possibilities as attractive, insofar as it permits extension of their marketable networks without the requirement to finance heavy capital expenditure.

It is all very regrettable, but what might be considered a strong brand name may be undergoing some changes due to the current climate of fear engendered by terrorism or threats of terrorism. If for political reasons some airlines are perceived as more likely targets than others, and if perceptions of this kind persist for a considerable time, then passengers' choice of airline could be very significantly affected. If, whether through alliances or as a result of cross-border mergers, transnational global airlines are to emerge, then these entities might, for security reasons at least, prefer to drop all references to nationality in the name of the airline.

Figure 4.13 Advertisements taken out by Virgin Atlantic and British Midland (*Sources*: *The Times* and *The Sunday Times*)

Figure 4.13   (Continued)

On a more pleasant note, it is interesting to observe how far some airlines are prepared to go to promote brand awareness through sponsorship of high-profile events. The Middle Eastern airline Emirates has been going in for this in a big way, specializing in sponsoring sporting events. The airline's first major sports sponsorship was of the Australian cricket team in the 1999 World Cup, which Australia won and then 'even taxi drivers in Australia suddenly knew who we were' (Tim Clark, Emirates CEO). Emirates followed this with title sponsorship of the Melbourne Cup (Australia's premier horse race) and the America's Cup (the world premier sailing race). It was also heavily involved in sponsoring the FIFA World Cup and its soccer sponsorships continue with its purchase of the naming rights for the new London stadium of UK Premier club Arsenal. According to its CEO, Emirates seeks to be a premier global brand and that is why it is willing to spend more than other airlines on marketing. (Even so, one prized sponsorship has eluded them, flybe having got its brand name on the shirts of Birmingham City Football Club!)

Block spacing

Under a block space agreement one airline allocates to another a number of seats on some of its flights, a kind of partial 'wet' lease. The other airline then sells these seats to the travelling public through its own marketing and distribution system. This kind of agreement is used where the airline to whom the seats are allocated is unable for one reason or another to serve the city airport in question.

Block spacing is no simple matter, however. First the size of each block has to be agreed, and then the booking policy has to be decided. For instance, will the block be expanded if one airline happens to receive more bookings than it has space for? And how will each airline allocate seats within its block between different categories to be shared between the carriers when passengers travel on either of the partners beyond the sector to which block space agreement applies? All these are details that need to be ironed out satisfactorily before an agreement is reached.

Block space agreements known to be in operation in September 2005 are listed in Table 4.7. Two airlines that favour this approach more than others are Air France and Qantas. Air France has block space agreements with nine other airlines and Qantas with six; and other airlines with several agreements are Emirates (five), Thai International (five) and Japan Airlines (three). The advantage to the airline selling a block of seats is an expected increase in revenue when the purchasing airline markets its service across its distribution network. The increase in passengers might enable the selling airline to increase its frequency of service and thus gain from the generally well-established S-shaped relationship between frequency and market share. The purchasing airline can gain by being able to sell tickets on relatively thin routes that would be costly to operate itself.

Table 4.7 Block space agreements, September 2005. *Sources*: Compiled by the author from *Airline Business* and various press reports

Partner Airlines	Routes
Aeroflot/Austrian	Vienna–Moscow
Aeromexico/Air Europa	Madrid–Cancun
Aeromexico/Japan Airlines	Mexico City–Vancouver
AeroSvit/Malev	Budapest–Kiev
AeroSvit/Olympic	Athens–Kiev/Odessa
AeroSvit/Thai Int'l	Kiev–Bangkok
Air Canada/Avianca	Toronto–Bogota, Bogota–Medellin[a]
Air China/SAS	Copenhagen–Beijing
Air China/Thy Turkish	Istanbul–Beijing/Shanghai
Air France/Air-India	Paris–Delhi
Air France/Austrian	Paris–Vienna
Air France/China Southern	Paris–Guangzhou
Air France/Finnair	Paris–Helsinki
Air France/Korean	Paris–Seoul
Air France/Malev	Budapest–Paris/Lyon
Air France/Middle East Airlines	Paris–Beirut
Air France/TACA	Miami–Central America
Air France/Vietnam Airlines	Paris–Hanoi/Ho Chi Minh City
Air Mauritius/LTU	Frankfurt/Dusseldorf–Mauritius
Air Pacific/Qantas	Nadi–Sydney/Melbourne/Brisbane, Suva–Sydney
Air-India/Emirates	Dubai–Chennai–Cochin
Air India/Thai Int'l	Bangkok–Mumbai/Chennai/Bangalore
Austrian/Egyptair	Vienna–Cairo
Austrian/Royal Jordanian	Amman–Vienna
China Airlines/Thai Int'l	Kaohsiung–Bangkok
China Eastern/Qantas	Sydney/Melbourne–Shanghai
China Southern/Dragonair	Guangzhou–Hong Kong
Egyptair/Thai Int'l	Bangkok–Cairo
El Al/Thai Int'l	Tel Aviv–Bangkok
Emirates/Philippine Airlines	Dubai–Manila
Emirates/Japan Airlines	Osaka–Dubai, Ogaka–Tokyo/ Fukuoka[b]
Emirates/Royal Air Maroc	Casablanca–Dubai
Emirates/South African Airlines	Dubai–Johannesburg
Eva Air/Qantas	Sydney–Taipei
Garuda/Gulf Air	Jakarta–Surabaya/Denpasar, Jakarta–Abu Dhabi[c]
Garuda/Philippine Airlines	Manila–Jakarta[d]
Garuda/Qatar	Doha–Jakarta, Jakarta–Singapore[e]
Japan Airlines/Qantas	Tokyo–Cairns/Melbourne, Tokyo/Osaka–Brisbane
Lot/Pulkovo Aviation	Warsaw–St Petersburg

Qantas/South African Airlines	Johannesburg–Sydney/Perth[f]
Qantas/Vietnam Airlines	Ho Chi Minh City–Sydney/Melbourne
Qatar/Thai Int'l	Bangkok–Doha

[a] Air Canada operating Toronto–Bogota with Avianca operating Bogota–Medellin.
[b] Emirates operating Osaka–Dubai with JAL operating Osaka–Tokyo/Fukuoka.
[c] Garuda operating Jakarta–Surabaya/Denpasar with Gulf Air operating Jakarta–Abu Dhabi.
[d] Via Singapore, with Philippines Airlines operating.
[e] Qatar operating Doha–Jakarta with Garuda operating Jakarta–Singapore.
[f] Qantas operating to/from Sydney, with SAA to/from Perth.

While not all that common so far, block space agreements are, like franchising, likely to increase in the years ahead, as more and more airlines seek to break out of conditions attaching to bilateral air service agreements negotiated by national governments. Another means of doing this, far more frequently used, is the practice of code-sharing.

Code-sharing

This is a commercial agreement between two airlines under which an airline operating a service allows another airline to offer that service to the travelling public under its own flight designator code, even although it does not operate the service. The practice is now becoming widespread across the world, although as yet not so pervasive as it is in the US regional industry, where it has been extremely common for a long time (Chambers, 1993). It is normal for franchising and block space agreements to be accompanied by an agreement on code-sharing also; and code-sharing agreements often include provisions for revenue or profit sharing, co-ordination of schedules, baggage handling, etc.

Each monthly issue of the *OAG World Airways Guide* contains a detailed listing of shared designator codes, from which it can be determined which airlines are actually operating the relevant services. The *Guide* (in its September 2005 issue) shows that all flights under BA designator codes BA6003–BA6080 are in fact flown by Finnair and codes BA7553–BA7561 by America West. It also shows that bmi British Midland flies under the codes of Air Canada, Lufthansa, SAS and United. Lufthansa's code is used by as many as 32 different airlines, while the AF, DL and IB codes of Air France, Delta and Iberia are each carried by 20 to 30 different airlines. The KLM/Northwest alliance makes extensive use of code-sharing, both for through flights via KLM's hub in Amsterdam and Northwest's hubs in the US, and for non-stop services across the Atlantic. The same is true of the Star Alliance, centred around the services of Lufthansa and United. And reciprocal code-sharing is one of the things BA and American Airlines wish to introduce once its oneworld alliance gains full regulatory approval. An extensive list of code-sharing agreements involving major airlines is given in Table 4.8.

Table 4.8 Code-sharing agreements involving the largest airlines, September 2005.[a]
Sources: Compiled from *OAG Flight Guide, Airline Business* and various press reports

Air Canada (AC)

Air Creebec
Air Georgian
Air Jamaica
Air Wisconsin
Austrian
bmi British Midland
Calm Air
Central Mountain Air
EVA Airways
Lot Polish
Lufthansa
Lufthansa Cityline
Mexicana
Sky West
United

Air France (AF)

Air Caledonie
Aeroflot
Aeromexico
Air Europa
Air Mauritius
Air Seychelles
Air Tahiti Nui
Alitalia
Austrian
Brit Air
CCM Airlines
China Eastern
China Southern
City Jet
Continental
Croatia Airlines
Czech Airlines
Delta
Finnair
Flybe

Japan Airlines
JAT
KLM
Korean Air
Luxair
Maersk Air
Malev
Middle East Airlines
Portugalia
Regional Compagnie Aerienne
Royal Air Maroc
Styrian Spirit
Tarom
Tunis Air
Ukraine Int'l

All Nippon (NH)

Air Canada
Air Central
Air China
Air Japan
Air Nippon
Asiana
Austrian
Hokkaido Int'l
Ibex Airlines
Lufthansa
Malaysian
Qatar
Shanghai Airlines
SIA
Thai Int'l
United
Varig

Air China (CA)

Air Dolomiti
Air Macau
Alitalia

All Nippon
Asiana
Augsburg Airlines
Austrian
Contactair Flugdienst
Dragonair
Eurowings
China Eastern
China Southern
Finnair
Korean
Lufthansa
Qatar Airways
SAS
Shanghai Airlines
Shandong Airlines
Turkish Airlines
United

Alitalia (AZ)

Aeroflot
Air Alps Aviation
Air China
Air France
Alpi Eagles
China Airlines
City Airline
Croatia Airlines
Cyprus Airlines
Czech Airlines
Delta
Japan Airlines
Korean Air
Malev
Qatar Airways
SN Brussels
Tarom
Varig

American Airlines (AA)

Air Pacific
Alaskan
American Connection carriers
American Eagle carriers
British Airways
Cathay Pacific
China Eastern

EVA Air
Finnair
Iberia
Horizon Air
Japan Airlines
Lan Airlines
Mexicana
Qantas
Swiss
TACA
Tam Linhas Aereas
THY Turkish

British Airways (BA)

Aer Lingus
Air Nostrum
American
American Eagle carriers
America West
British Mediterranean
Comair (SA)
Finnair
GB Airways
Iberia
Lan Airlines
Loganair
Qantas
Japan Airlines
SN Brussels
Sun Air (Scandinavia)

Cathay Pacific (CX)

Aeroflot
American
American Eagle carriers
British Airways
Malaysian
South African Airways
Vietnam Airlines

Continental (CO)

Commutair
Continental Connection carriers
Continental Micronesia
Copa Airlines
EVA Airways
Expressjet

Table 4.8 *Continued*

Flybe
Horizon Air
KLM
Northwest
Virgin Atlantic

Delta (DL)

Aeromexico
Air France
Air Jamaica
Alaskan
Alitalia
Atlantic Southeast
Avianca
Chautauqua
China Airlines
China Southern
Comair (US)
Continental
Czech Airlines
Delta Connection carriers
El Al
Expressjet
Flybe
Freedom Airlines
Korean Air
Mesaba Aviation
Northwest
Pinnacle Airlink
Royal Air Maroc
Shuttle America
SkyWest
South African Airways

Iberia (IB)

Aer Lingus
Air Atlanta
Air Nostrum
Air Senegal
American
Audeli
Avianca
British Airways
Czech Airlines
El Al

Finnair
GB Airways
Lan Airlines
Lithuanian
Maersk Air
Royal Air Maroc
Royal Jordanian
SN Brussels
Swiss
Syrian Arab Airlines
TAP Air Portugal
Tarom
Ukraine Int'l

Japan Airlines (JL)

Air France
Air New Zealand
Air Tahiti Nui
Alitalia
American
Cathay Pacific
China Eastern
China Southern
Emirates
Korean Air
Hainan Airlines
Qantas
J-Air
Japan Transocean
Thai Int'l
THY Turkish
Swiss
Vietnam Airlines
Xiamen Airlines

KLM (KL)

Air France
Alaskan
Alitalia
China Southern
Cyprus Airways
Czech Airlines
Expressjet
Kenya Airways
Malaysian

Malev
Northwest
Portugalia
Regional Compagnie Aerienne
Ukraine Int'l

Korean Air (KE)

Aeroflot
Air China
Air France
Alitalia
China Airlines
China Eastern
China Southern
Japan Airlines
Malaysian
Shanghai Airlines
Vietnam Airlines

Lufthansa (LH)

Adria Airways
Air Canada
Air China
Air Dolomiti
Air India
Air One
All Nippon
Augsburg Airways
Austrian
bmi British Midland
Cimber Air
Cirrus Airlines
Contactair Flugdienst
Croatia Airlines
Czech Airlines
Eurowings
Lauda Air
Lot Polish
Lufthansa Cityline
Luxair
Maersk Air
Qatar Airways
SAS
SIA
South African Airways
Spanair
TAP Air Portugal

Thai Int'l
Tyrolean Airways
United
US Airways
Varig

Malaysian (MH)

Air Mauritius
Austrian
Cathay Pacific
Dragonair
Garuda
Lauda Air
KLM
Korean Air
Philippine Airlines
Qatar Airways
Royal Brunei
Sri Lankan
Thai Int'l
Uzbekistan Airlines
Vietnam Airlines

Northwest (NW)

Alaskan
Continental
Hawaiian
Horizon Air
KLM
Mesaba Aviation
Pinnacle Airlink

Qantas (QF)

Air Caledonie
Air Nauru
Air Niugini
Air Pacific
Air Tahiti
Air Vanuatu
Alaskan
Asiana
British Airways
China Eastern
EVA Airways
Finnair
Gulf Air

Table 4.8 *Continued*

Japan Airlines	Malaysian
Jetconnect	Myanmar Airways
Jetstar Airways	Qatar Airways
Lan Airlines	Royal Jordanian
Polynesian Airlines	Swiss
Qantaslink	United
South African Airways	
Swiss	**United (UA)**
Vietnam Airlines	
	Air Canada
	Air Canada Jazz
SIA (SQ)	Air China
	Air New Zealand
Air New Zealand	All Nippon
All Nippon	Asiana
Austrian	Austrian
Lufthansa	bmi British Midland
Malaysian	Gulfstream
Royal Brunei	Island Air
Silk Air	Lot Polish
	Lufthansa
Thai Int'l (TG)	SAS
	United Express carriers
Aerosvit Airlines	US Airways Express carriers
Air Madagascar	Varig
All Nippon	
Asiana	**US Airways (US)**
Austrian	
China Airlines	Bahamasair
Egyptair	British Midland
El Al	Caribbean Sun Airlines
Emirates	Lufthansa
Eurowings	United Airlines Express carriers
Japan Airlines	US Airways Express carriers
Lufthansa	

[a] The codes used are those of the airline in bold type, beneath which are listed the airlines actually operating the services.

One particular instance illustrates how code-sharing is practised. The bmi British Midland code-shares on the through route Glasgow–London Heathrow–Johannesburg with South African Airways. British Midland's designator code is BD and that for South African Airways is SA. An afternoon flight from Glasgow (departure 15:15) is shown in the *OAG Worldwide flight Guide* (September 2005 issue) as SA7613 to Heathrow (arrival: 16:35) and as SA235 from Heathrow (departure 19:30) to Johannesburg (arrival: 07:30, the following morning). British Midland operates the Glasgow–Heathrow sector and markets point-to-point service on the route under its own code BD009; and South African Airways is able to 'hold out' a through service to/from Glasgow as its own even although it does not fly there.

The above example can be referred to as 'complementary' code-sharing, where two carriers link up with each other to provide connecting services for an origin–destination city pair. Another kind is 'parallel' code-sharing, where two carriers operating on the same sector share codes. The main purpose of parallel code-sharing is to offer passengers a higher (co-ordinated) flight frequency than the carriers would be able to supply without code-sharing, in the hope that both would benefit from the L-shaped relationship between frequency and market share. For instance, Air Canada (whose designator code is AC) and Asiana (designator code OZ) code-share on the Vancouver–Seoul route, flight number OZ 6101 being operated by Air Canada which also markets the service under flight number AC063.

Some marketing agreements involve code-sharing of both kinds, as in that between KLM and Northwest. On the transatlantic sectors both airlines operate and the services of both have parallel codes entered into GDSs. Beyond the Amsterdam/Minneapolis hubs, KLM operates in Europe and Northwest on US domestic sectors, but both can market through services under their own codes.

Although it can be traced back 30 years or more code-sharing became a major marketing activity only relatively recently. The proliferation of code-sharing agreements reflects the growing emphasis on feeder traffic in hub and spokes networks. The contemporaneous development of sophisticated GDSs has given some further impetus to code-sharing. This is especially so where the display algorithms give preference to online over interline services, whether the 'online' services are genuinely online or only made to appear so through code-sharing. It is sometimes possible that code-sharing has affected competition through screen 'padding', when code-sharing airlines clutter the screen display with multiple entries of the same service, in this way pushing other airlines' service further down the screen, or onto the next screen page. But the Civil Aviation Authority (1994) concluded that, in overall terms, the rise of international code-sharing in recent years was unlikely to have been caused by attempts to gain GDS advantages.

Where both carriers operate on the same route, the fact that they code-share could have a substantial impact in lessening competition between them, particularly if the agreement covers revenue or profit sharing as well. Code-sharing implies close co-ordination between the partners and it may be difficult to ensure that this does not lead to collusion in other areas, such as capacities and fares on other routes. On the other hand code-sharing may have some pro-competitive effects, insofar as it enables carriers to enter or develop routes that would not otherwise be viable to operate. This was for example the justification, put to the US Department of

Table 4.9 Passenger traffic travelling Northwest/KLM between the US and Europe/Middle East.[a] *Source*: Hannegan and Mulvey (1995)

	1991	1992	1993	1994
Total passengers on all carriers	1 488 610	1 688 510	1 744 090	1 810 780
Passengers on Northwest/KLM	17 510	23 260	52 510	60 630
Northwest/KLM market share (%)	1.2	1.4	3.0	3.3

[a] Routes between 34 US cities and 30 cities across Europe and the Middle East.

Transportation, by Northwest and KLM in defence of code-sharing on the Amsterdam–Detroit and Amsterdam–Minneapolis routes (de Groot, 1994).

A number of studies have investigated the effects of code-sharing. One by the US General Accounting Office (1995) found that code-sharing often generates large gains for airline partners in terms of increased passenger numbers and enhanced revenues. But a paper by Hannegan and Mulvey (1995) shows that the gains achieved are largely zero-sum in that they come at the expense of competing airlines. The increased market shares achieved by the Northwest/KLM alliance (Table 4.9) can be attributed in large part to the code-sharing these airlines introduced in the first half of the 1990s.

Many factors other than code-sharing influence traffic development. An attempt to measure the net effects of code-sharing has been made by the International Civil Aviation Organization (1997a). The results of this study are summarized in Table 4.10. The International Civil Aviation Organization (ICAO) study analyses traffic data for a sample of transatlantic city pairs over a period of 10 years, to give an idea of the general pattern of traffic development. Using published information on airlines operating the services and on changes in market shares, comparisons were made of with/without code-sharing situations, due allowances being made for the effects of other factors on traffic growth and market shares. To the question of whether code-sharing resulted in strong increases in traffic, the evidence was mixed: the answer was negative in 45 per cent of cases and positive in 40 per cent (the remaining 15 per cent being cases in which it was too soon to tell). On the issue of the relationship between code-sharing and competition, the ICAO study suggested that in about three-quarters of the city pairs the competitive situation remained unchanged, but where it did change the effect was in the direction of reducing competition.

It should be noted that the ICAO results relate to parallel code-sharing in point-to-point city pairs, on direct non-stop routes between hubs. But, as explained in Chapter 3, it is entirely possible for competition to fall on direct routes to/from hubs while at the same time increasing in through markets served via the hubs. And in another study, this time of complementary code-sharing on transPacific routes, it was found that code-sharing caused the leading airlines to behave more competitively and led to overall increases in traffic (Oum, Park and Zhang, 1996).

Other issues concern the effects on passengers. On the positive side passengers may benefit insofar as code-sharing facilitates the provision of higher service quality in terms of more convenient connections, single check-ins, baggage transfers, transferable bonuses in frequent flyer programmes and so on. It may also have the effect of reducing through fares. All this may increase the value of the joint product to the passenger. And code-sharing agreements do not necessarily imply exclusivity. It is at least possible to connect from a non-affiliated flight to one of the code-sharing flights; but where schedules, marketing, etc. are not co-ordinated in quite the same way, it is much less likely that the passenger will be able to find a convenient connection. Hence airlines participating in code-sharing agreements often argue that passengers derive substantial benefits from them. But an alternative view, expressed by the UK Civil Aviation Authority (1994) is that all these benefits could be provided by airline alliances without the need to code-share. And it has also been argued that code-sharing results in passengers being deceived or misled, when the airline identity at the boarding gate is not the same as that printed on the passenger's ticket.

Despite rules requiring the operator of the flight to be properly identified, it is clear that many passengers are still not being given full information on this. The rules apply only to GDSs and to things like the *OAG World Airways Guide* and there is no guarantee that correct information is passed on by the travel agent to the traveller. In two telephone surveys, one conducted by the US Department of Transportation and one by the UK CAA sufficient information on the identity of the airline operating the flight was not given in a large number of cases (30 per cent in the US survey and as high as 60 per cent in the (preliminary) UK survey). Often the first time a passenger knows of a code-sharing arrangement is when he or she reports to the departure gate in the airport terminal (and in some cases perhaps even later than this). In particular business travellers not making their own reservations may be confronted with some unpleasant surprises! In this sort of situation passengers sometimes lodge complaints. The only real way of avoiding such complaints is to ensure greater disclosure at the time the passenger's booking is made. But so far as multisector journeys involving transfer connections at intermediate points are concerned, much of the purpose airlines have in code-sharing – and in franchising and block spacing as well – is to make interline connections appear so far as possible as online ones. Other things being equal, passengers prefer online to interline connections, in order to enjoy what is referred to as 'seamless' service right across their itineraries.

Table 4.10 Effects of transatlantic code-sharing agreements on traffic development: agreements between European and US airlines in effect as of 31 December 1994. *Source:* ICAO

Airlines	Route*	Context of traffic development^a	Positive effect on traffic development^b	Situation with code-sharing Change in competition^c	Situation with code-sharing Frequency of service^c	Airline benefiting from change in market share^d
Aeroflot/Delta	MOW–NYC	+	No	=	=	Delta
Alitalia/Continental	ROM–NYC	–	No	=	=	=
	MIL–NYC		(B)	=	=	
	ROM–HOU	(A)	(B)	=	+	Alitalia
Alitalia/US Air	ROM–BOS	–	Yes	–	–	Alitalia
Austrian/Delta	VIE–NYC	–	Yes	–	–	Austrian
	VIE–WAS	(A)	(B)	=	+	Austrian
BA/US Air	LON–BWI	+	Yes	=	=	BA
	LON–BOS	+	No	=	+	BA
	LON–CLT	=	Yes	=	=	–
	LON–LAX	=	No	=	=	BA
	LON–NYC	+	Yes	–	=	=
	LON–PHL	+	Yes	=	–	BA
	LON–PIT	=	Yes	=	=	
SAS/Continental	CPH–NYC	–	No	–	–	SAS
	OSL–NYL	–	No	–	–	SAS
	STO–NYC	–	No	–	–	SAS
Malev/Delta	BUD–NYC	+	Yes	–	–	Malev
Sabena/Delta	BRU–ALT	–	Yes	=	=	Delta
	BRU–BOS	–	(B)	=	=	=
	BRU–CHI	=	(B)	=	=	=
	BRU–NYC	–	No	–	–	Sabena
Swissair/Delta	ZRH–ATL	+	No	=	=	=
	ZRH–CVG	(A)	Yes	=	+	=
	ZRH–NYC	–	No	–	–	Swissair

Airlines	Route	[a]	[b]	[c,d]
Swissair/Delta	GVA-WAS	(A)	(B)	−
TAP/Delta	LIS-NYC	=	No	=
KLM/Northwest	AMS-ATL	+	No	=
	AMS-BOS	+	Yes	=
	AMS-CHI	=	No	=
	AMS-DTW	−	Yes	+
	AMS-HOU	+	No	=
	AMS-LAX	+	No	=
	AMS-MSP	−	Yes	+ Northwest
	AMS-NYP	+	No	− KLM
	AMS-ORL	+	Yes	=
	AMS-SFO	+	Yes	=
	AMS-WAS	+	Yes	=
Lufthansa/United	FRA-ATL	+	No	=
	FRA-CHI	+	No	=
	FRA-SFO	+	No	=
	FRA-WAS	+	Yes	=

[a] An indication of how traffic was developing without code-sharing. The + sign denotes a growing trend, the − sign a decreasing trend and the = sign a standstill. (A) means the service was non-existent before the code-sharing agreement.

[b] Shows whether code-sharing has produced a positive effect on traffic development, that is a growth superior to the normal trend described in the previous column, or a reverse trend in the case of declining traffic. (B) means code-sharing agreement concluded too recently to allow sufficient perspective.

[c] −: decreasing; +: increasing; =: no change.

[d] = signifies no change in market shares.

* Decoding as follows:

AMS	Amsterdam	CLT	Charlotte	LAX	Los Angeles	NYC	New York
ATL	Atlanta	CPH	Copenhagen	LIS	Lisbon	ORL	Orlando
BOS	Boston	CVG	Cincinnati	LON	London	OSL	Oslo
BRU	Brussels	DTW	Detroit	MIL	Milan	PHL	Philadelphia
BUD	Budapest	FRA	Frankfurt	MOW	Moscow	PIT	Pittsburgh
BWI	Baltimore	GVA	Geneva	MSP	Minneapolis	ROM	Rome
CHI	Chicago	HOU	Houston				

SFO	San Francisco		
STO	Stockholm		
VIE	Vienna		
WAS	Washington		
ZRH	Zurich		

'Seamless' networks

In marketing joint services airlines have paid some attention to advertising their alliances. The text of a press advertisement placed by the former Delta/Swissair/SIA alliance read as follows:

> Global Excellence: A Seamless Travel Experience around the World with Three Excellent Airlines. For you, the co-operation of Delta Air Lines, Singapore Airlines and Swissair has pleasant consequences on a global scale. The timetables of all three airlines are co-ordinated to give you smooth access to more than 300 destinations worldwide. En route, there are 400 city ticket offices ready to serve you. And on a trip around the globe, you can benefit from specially attractive (around-the-world) fares. All these benefits add up to the perfect fit: Global Excellence and you.

Similarly, Northwest and KLM have made the following points in their publicity:

> The partners' synchronised timetables and once-only passenger and luggage check-in have created a seamless network of connecting flights ... Hundreds of routes within North America have been opened up to UK travellers through feeder flights to KLM's home base at Amsterdam Schiphol Airport. The partners run joint venture services from there to 11 US gateway cities, of which three are major Northwest hubs offering dozens of onward connections.

The concept of a seamless network can be promoted when partner airlines adopt a common aircraft livery. This is what Northwest and KLM at one time decided to do in their international operations, combining different features of their separate logos. And sometimes aircraft have even been painted in the colours of both partner airlines, such as on an Alitalia/ Continental code-shared service between Newark and Rome, on which the aircraft carried the Alitalia livery on one side of the fuselage and that of Continental on the other. But a common livery, or a common uniform for cabin staff, is unlikely to disguise a change of aircraft type, something that can cause some consternation to passengers preparing to board flights, as the author David Lodge (1984) knows:

> Inside the Rummidge Airport terminal . . . the flight to Heathrow is called, and Morris follows the ground hostess out onto the tarmac apron. He frowns at the sight of the plane they are to board. It is a long time since he has flown in a plane with *propellers*.

The emphasis appears in the original (and in this work of fiction 'Rummidge' seems to serve as a thin cloak of anonymity for Birmingham, from where at the time of the hero's fictional journey, flights to Heathrow were flown in non-pressurized Short 330 turbo-props).

Props are generally perceived as being less comfortable than jets. A passenger's inflight experience is clearly affected by noise, vibration and pressurization to a far greater extent in propeller aircraft. These physical discomforts can sometimes, for marketing reasons, limit the length of route over which props can be deployed, in some cases imposing more severe constraints on maximum flying times than the technical payload-range characteristics of the aircraft itself. Typical cramped-at-the-shoulders seating configurations add to the general discomfort, as do the arrangements for boarding and disembarking the aircraft. Manufacturers of the latest turbo-props are making efforts to render their machines compatible with standard (jetway) airbridges in use at major airports, in the hope that this will help to eradicate the distinction in passengers' minds between jets they hardly see and props which they often have to brave the elements to board. But perhaps even more important is passenger' perception of propeller aircraft as being 'old' and relatively less safe. For all these reasons passengers tend to prefer jets. But on short-haul regional routes, and on feeder services to the hubs, props are very often cheaper for airlines to operate.

At the regional level the trade offs between jets and turbo-props can be described as follows: jets offer superior comfort, higher cruising speeds and greater productivity in terms of seat-miles per hour flown, whereas turbo-props offer better field performance and manoeuvrability, savings in fuel burn from greater propulsive efficiency and lower capital costs. The relative advantages of jets increase with sector distance. As a broad generalization, the break point occurs at a distance of around 250 miles. Below that turbo-props come out best in operating economics, their lower fuel costs outweighing jets' faster speeds. On the shorter routes there is often little appreciable difference in block (chocks off to chocks on) flight times, the higher performance of jets at cruising altitudes being, to varying degrees, offset by turbo-props' greater manoeuvrability at and near airports. For example, modern turbo-props, such as the ATR 42, Fokker 50 and British Aerospace ATP cruise at between 265 and 285 knots, considerably below the 425–450 knots offered by the British Aerospace 146, the new Canadair Regional Jet and the Fokker F28 and F100 aircraft. But the vast majority of regional routes are less than 250 miles. In an analysis of flight departures by jet and turbo-prop aircraft of less than 90 seats, across the Western world in 1988, it was found that over 80 per cent were operated on routes less than 250 miles, with only 7 per cent above 350 miles (Snow, 1990). In the USA the average distance per passenger travelled on regional airlines was 194 miles in 1992 (Regional Airline Association, 1993) while in Europe the mean sector distance flown by members of the European Regional Airlines Association in June 1991 was 225 miles (European Regional Airlines Association, 1991a). Sectors flown by the Swiss regional airline Crossair are typical, with 65 per cent of flights below 200 nautical miles. On sectors of this length the jets' higher speeds translate into a block-time advantage of just 5 to 10 minutes.

On longer routes jets retain more of their block time advantage, but the recent introduction of high-speed turbo-props, like the Dornier 328 and Saab 2000, cut into their speed advantage here as well. At the same time the block fuel consumed by jets can be up to 50 per cent greater than that burnt by turbo-props of equivalent size on the same route. This is partly because the proportion of block fuel used by a jet during taxing, take off, climb and descent rises to as much as 40 per cent on a 200 nautical mile sector.

On a great many routes turbo-props are more cost efficient and only marginally slower in terms of block time. They are also smaller, and in many cases more suited to the frequency sensitive business travel market served on regional routes than any of the jets currently in service. These factors should ensure that they have an important role to play for many years to come. But their relative lack of passenger appeal renders them vulnerable to competition from the new generation of regional jets in the markets for 45 to 70 seater aircraft. Substitution in the reverse direction, from jets to turbo-props, did of course take place on deregulation in the USA, but in that case the jets that were redeployed – to higher priorities on first- and second-level routes – were quite simply far too large to be in any sense economic on regional routes. Smaller jets are far closer substitutes for turbo-props.

The choice between jets and turbo-props is often influenced by the hub-based major airlines to which regionals feed traffic. With competition in through travel markets becoming keener all the time, increasing attention is being paid to the seamless product concept. More and more, the larger carriers are demanding that regionals employ aircraft types that will minimize any perceptible differences in service quality in the eyes of the through passenger. Service quality is often of prime importance to passengers paying full business or first class fares, and while such passengers may be relatively few in number on any particular flight, the fares they pay form a disproportionately large part of total revenue yield, especially for the trunk route airline to which the passengers connect. When there is fierce competition between hubs, and when a passenger in planning an itinerary has an effective choice between two or more hubs, this can be a very important consideration. The contributory revenue from high-yield passengers may compensate for the higher cost of operating jets and may be especially important in Europe, where many passengers on regional flights are using them as one leg on long-haul intercontinental journeys. These points were apparently not lost on the Italian authorities when at one time they refused Crossair permission to upgrade to British Aerospace 146 'Jumbolina' aircraft on the regional route between Lugano and Venice, on the ground that the aircraft is 'too comfortable' (Crossair, 1991)!

Passengers may be concerned not just with the type of aircraft they are to fly in but also with the name and reputation of the airline operating the service. Large, well known, profitable or flag carrying airlines are often more acceptable to passengers than small, financially strapped and not very well-known carriers from some remote or less developed regions of the world. Whether justified or not, passengers tend to associate airline names with varying degrees of safety, reliability and service quality. It was mainly recognition of this that led many airlines to fly under the banners of major carriers. There is a lot in a name, at least so far as marketing is concerned. Just as McDonald's or Coca-Cola sell a universally known product through a usually unknown local operator, airlines may seek to market a brand, by standardizing and, where necessary, upgrading safety, reliability and service quality generally. To an airline parenting a brand this can be a useful way of transcending the limitations of air service agreements and generating additional feeder traffic. To airlines operating under another airline's brand name it can offer some escape from the competitive disadvantages they might be at on account of their relatively small size, their lack of presence in main markets and their image generally.

Bringing networks together so that they appear seamless to the travelling public is not always easy. Ensuring that passengers perceive no material difference in standards when changing from one airline to another within the overall brand may require extensive staff training. There is also the possibility that problems with one of the airlines flying the brand can have disproportionately damaging effects on the parent company and also perhaps on other brand carriers. One example of where such a problem might arise is where one of the airlines is beset by a number of fatal crashes in fairly quick succession.

5

Scheduling through hubs

Traditionally full-service airline schedules were designed, either for the convenience of local point-to-point passengers, or to meet operational objectives such as maximizing aircraft/crew utilization, minimizing airport and station costs, etc. But the emphasis has now clearly changed. As markets become more competitive, more and more importance is attached to co-ordinating arrival and departure times to attract connecting traffic. An important part of this is to concentrate flight activity at the hub into a limited number of peaks, or waves, during the day. Services on the spokes are timed so that they connect at the hub, arrivals preceding departures in sufficient time to permit the transfer of baggage from inbound to outbound flights. Ideally a lot of inbound flights should arrive within a short space of time and then depart again as soon as some minimum connecting time (MCT) has elapsed. To maximize the potential benefits the amplitude of each wave should be as great as possible. The fewer the number of waves across the operating day, the greater the number of possible connections. The theoretical maximum is achieved only if all flights are scheduled into just one large wave; and in theory, if all flights to or from a particular airport are timed so that a passenger could connect between any two, the maximum number of possible connections would equal the square of the number of flights. The objective here is to maximize the number of *useful* connections. Not all connections are useful ones, however. Some are entirely useless ones to return flights and some involve so much backtracking as to be of little use to passengers. Some are unattractive because they entail lengthy waits at the hub. But careful network planning can minimize the number of redundant connections and ensure that most of the scheduled linkages are indeed useful ones. In practice the number of waves an airline can schedule is subject to a number of important considerations concerning airport and airspace capacities, flight safety, aircraft/crew rostering, etc. High waves place severe peak-load demands on airport capacity. The ideal kind of airport to operate as a high-capacity hub is one with a multi-runway airfield and just one large terminal building. Runway slots are often the most binding constraint, especially where there are restrictions limiting flexibility in their use. Peak-load capacity can sometimes be marginally increased, for example if in the first phase of a wave all runways could be used for arrivals and in the second all used for departures. This is not always possible, however. Sometimes it is inhibited by environmental controls.

Other things being equal, concentration of flight activity at certain airports at certain times of day, increases the danger of collisions, both in the air and on the ground, as compared with spreading the same level of activity across a number of airports and across the day. To some extent there is a compensating factor here, insofar as connecting flights tend to reduce conflicting movements between arriving and departing aircraft. But most aviation accidents occur in landing/take-off or in climb/descent and, to the extent that hub and spoke operations reduce average sector lengths and encourage multi-sector routeings against direct non-stop flights, the development is not entirely conducive to flight safety. Flight safety records indicate that the risk to passengers on a non-stop flight is virtually independent of its length. On that basis, flying from A to B via C, which entails two flights, may be considered twice as dangerous as flying from A to B non-stop. However, it is by no means necessarily the case that hub and spokes systems, once fully developed, will result in a reduction in non-stop travel. Experience in the deregulated US domestic market has been that connecting passengers as a percentage of total passengers has increased only marginally since 1978 (Boeing Commercial Airplane Company, 1986). The proportion of passengers changing planes in hub and spokes networks is only fractionally greater than it was in linear networks before deregulation.

What has changed with deregulation is the proportion of passengers changing airlines as well as planes: in deregulated markets online connections are now five or six times as numerous as interline connections, compared to the situation in regulated markets when they were both about the same. There is some evidence that non-stop point-to-point service, far from ubiquitous in the regulated era, has increased markedly in recent years. Much of this increase has no doubt been due to secular growth in US passenger demand, but an analysis of the years 1977 to 1989 (Barnett, Curtis, Goranson, and Patrick, 1992) has shown that airline hubbing probably did not retard this development and perhaps accelerated it.

But there may be other reasons for concern about safety. One is the critical importance of punctuality. A late arrival at the hub has a multiplicative effect on delays, and from time to time there have been some suggestions that safety has been compromised in the interest of protecting schedules. There have been reports in the US of 'near misses' and of maintenance checks and other procedures being rushed or simply overlooked in the rush to keep aircraft and crews in planned positions. In closely co-ordinated operations the pressure to maintain punctuality can be great. An initial delay can generate substantial widespread 'knock on' effects throughout the timetable. If in order to await a connection, a flight is held at the hub beyond its scheduled departure time, it is likely to be late again on its return to the hub leading to still further delays and missed connections. Late running may no longer be isolated to a particular flight but can be rapidly transmitted throughout the entire schedule. One of the drawbacks of hub and spokes networks is that inclement weather at the hub airport can delay or, in the worst eventuality, cause the cancellation of virtually all the airline's flights. Clearly, the prevalence of inclement weather is another important factor in hub location.

The problem of delays poses some difficult decisions. The principal dilemma lies between slightly delaying many passengers ready to board a flight departing the hub and severely delaying a few trying to connect to it. Some airlines take account of revenue yields from connecting passengers (i.e. first and business class exerting more influence than tourist or economy) and others consider the consequences of missed connections (the last service of the day being the one likely to be held the longest). At busy hubs delays can lead to difficulties in the allocation of runway and terminal slots, affecting other aircraft movements, and even where aircraft can absorb a delay, this may not be possible for its crew – especially the crew on the flight deck. When flight crews are approaching their duty-hours limit for the day, there is the additional complication and cost of finding fresh crew.

Despite all this there are airlines operating to demanding schedules that are consistently amongst the best in terms of on-time performance. In Europe for example, Swiss, SAS, and KLM all operate to very tight schedules and yet all maintain excellent punctuality records. It is of course rather a case

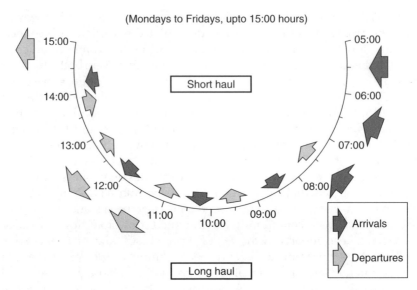

Figure 5.1   Typical connections scheduled at European hubs

of having to be punctual if the highly complexed hub operations of these airlines are to succeed. Connections through European hubs are typically scheduled as shown in Figure 5.1.

Considerations of crew rostering sometimes place limits on the number of complexes per day. On short- and medium-haul operations there is little demand for services during the night (when in any case most airports have curfews). So most of an airline's fleet is necessarily left idle overnight, and traditionally aircraft return to the airline's home base, where maintenance and 'deep' cleaning are undertaken during the small hours. If the home base is being operated as a hub, this has an adverse effect on total connection opportunities, since the first flights out in the morning and the last returns in the evening are without feeder links. In effect one of the complexes is broken overnight. This could be avoided, if instead aircraft were to be stabled overnight at spoke airports. In the example illustrated in Figure 5.2, stabling at spoke airports increases possible connections by one-third, with no change in the length of the operating day or in the number of flights. With stabling overnight at the hub, the airline can schedule only three connection complexes, whereas with stabling overnight on the spokes it can schedule four. Stabling on the spokes has been standard practice in US domestic networks for some time, but is still very much the exception in Europe. Stabling at the hub is far more common in Europe, partly because many long-haul flights arrive at European hubs very early in the morning, to connect with short-haul services starting out from the hub. But at the other end of the day there are not that many late-evening

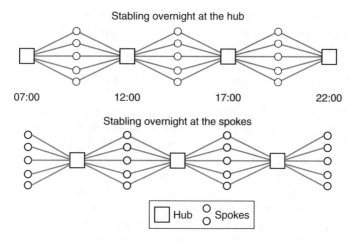

Figure 5.2   Effect of where stabling overnight takes place

departures from European airports (apart from a few intercontinental services to Africa and South America), so that when the short-haul aircraft return to the hub, they have little or nothing to connect with. Some European airlines, like Lufthansa, are beginning to stable away from the hub in their hinterland operations, in order to maximize connections in short-haul markets. There are however certain diseconomies in this. It is more difficult and expensive to make standby provision at spoke airports, and some economies of scale in aircraft maintenance are sacrificed when the fleet is scattered overnight across the network. It is always possible to schedule maintenance by withdrawing aircraft from service in rotation, but emergency work may often require less 'flying spanners', mechanics and engineers travelling out from the hub, and this can push up mainte-nance costs quite appreciably. Stabling on the spokes might be less popu-lar with crews. Unless crews are resident in spoke cities, extra lodging expenses will be incurred. These can amount to some not inconsiderable additions to costs, especially where the crew bringing in the aircraft on the last flight in the evening (perhaps landing as late as 23:00 hours) is unable to fly the first sector the following morning (taking off at 07:00 hours), so that two crews are required to night-stop in the spoke city. Stabling on the spokes can also be important to ensure the most appropriate schedules for the convenience of passengers. Passengers resident in spoke cities at both ends of a route through a hub can have vastly different requirements. More passengers in spoke City A may wish to travel to spoke City B than vice versa. For example, this may be the case, in some short-haul business markets, where A is a small city and B a large one or where A is an outlying city in the airline's home country and B a capital city or major business centre in a country abroad. Differences in originating demand generate directional imbalances in passenger flows, the predominant flows being from A to B in the mornings and back from B to A in the evenings. Clearly, this can be an important consideration in deciding where to stable the aircraft overnight.

Another aspect of hub scheduling that can be very important for the convenience of passengers is the pairing of connections for round-trip journeys. To the extent that passengers' choice of transfer point is influenced by the ability to fly the same routeing on both outbound and return journeys, it is often not all that useful to have fast connections in one direction without matching ones in the reverse direction. This has been a particular problem for British Airways (BA) in London, sometimes putting the airline at a serious competitive disadvantage in markets for connecting traffic. For example, in summer 1986, fast (within 90 minutes) connections to/from BA transatlantic flights were available in just five Europe–North America city-pair markets, a lot fewer than those to/from other airlines' transatlantic services. KLM for instance had over 50 paired connections.

5.2 Online and interline connections

Historically, BA's competitive position in through markets via London owed much to the advantage it derived from the sheer scale of flight activity at Heathrow, both in terms of service frequencies and in range of destinations served. London has always been an extremely important point on the international air services map. London's role as a leading political, commercial, and cultural centre generates an enormous demand for air travel, and from this there developed a vast set of possibilities for connecting traffic. But hitherto London's success as a transfer point has been in terms of interline connections and, when the emphasis changed to online connections, its airports system was not ready to accommodate the change, rather like the system in New York.

In this respect BA's ability to compete for online connecting traffic has been hampered in ways similar to the problems that beset the former Pan American airline in the US. Pan Am's main base was in New York which, like London, has been heavily congested for some time; and the operations of Pan Am in New York were split between two airports, just as BA's are split between Heathrow and Gatwick. Pan Am operated only a limited number of domestic routes and tended to rely on interline connections to supply feeder traffic from elsewhere in the US. But with the demise of interline arrangements, other airlines increasingly preferred to feed their own hubs rather than supply interline passengers to carriers like Pan Am, a trend reinforced by computer reservations systems giving priority to online over interline connections. BA has always operated a large number of routes to/from London, but its flight schedules for connecting traffic have not always been well co-ordinated, partly because of the difficulty of securing appropriate slots (especially at Heathrow) and partly because of the ready availability of interline traffic.

The latter point is illustrated in Tables 5.1 and 5.2, which contain some results of a representative sample survey undertaken by the Civil Aviation

Table 5.1 Traffic connecting through London.[a][b] *Source*: Derived from Civil Aviation Authority (1984) London Area Airports Study

Delivering carrier	Receiving carrier			Total for delivering carrier
	British Airways	British Caledonian	Other airlines	
BA	27	–	15	42
British Caledonian	1	6	3	10
Other airlines	17	4	26	48
Total for receiving carrier	45	10	45[c]	100

[a] Heathrow, Gatwick, and Stansted.
[b] All values are percentages.
[c] Numbers do not sum precisely because of rounding.
– Less than 1 per cent.

Table 5.2 Connections through Heathrow.[a] *Source*: Derived from Civil Aviation Authority (1984) London Area Airports Study

Delivering carrier	Receiving carrier					Total for delivering carrier
	BA short haul	BA long haul	Domestic UK[b]	Foreign short haul	Foreign long haul	
BA short haul	10	9	2	5	7	32
BA long haul	10	3	1	2	1	17
Domestic UK[b]	3	2	–	3	2	10
Foreign short haul	5	2	2	3	5	17
Foreign long haul	8	1	2	4	7	22
Total for receiving carrier	36	17	7	17	22	100[c]

[a] All values are percentages.
[b] Excluding BA domestic (included in BA short haul).
[c] Numbers do not sum precisely because of rounding.
– Less than 1 per cent.

Authority in 1984. The matrices here show distributions of connecting traffic by receiving and delivering carriers. Table 5.1 shows that just over a quarter of total connecting traffic was online to BA and 6 per cent online to British Caledonian, and that the now merged BA/BCAL was involved in just about half the connections either as delivering or as receiving carrier. These proportions were about double the proportions to be expected, if the numbers of connecting passengers simply mirrored the numbers of flights operated. So the British airlines did derive significant advantages from their hubs in London. But their position in London was not nearly so dominant as that enjoyed by some foreign airlines elsewhere. For example, KLM was involved in four out of every five connections in Amsterdam, compared with one in two for BA/BCAL. And roughly 60 per cent of Amsterdam's connecting traffic was online to KLM – more than twice the proportion of London transfers contributed by BA–BA transfers (27 per cent). A more detailed examination of transfers at Heathrow (Table 5.2) reveals some striking comparisons. It became apparent that BA fed more traffic to foreign carriers' long-haul departures than it received in return for its own intercontinental flights – a rather unusual situation to occur at a home carrier's main base. Not only was the total number of connecting passengers received by foreign carriers' long-haul services greater than the total received by BA's long-haul flights, but the number fed from BA short haul to foreign long haul was almost three times as great as the corresponding number fed the other way, from foreign short haul to BA long haul. (The same imbalance was seen in traffic moving in the reverse direction.) Of course part of the explanation for this lies in the pattern of services supplied, the preponderance of BA on short hauls, and the exceptionally wide range of foreign carriers on long hauls. But a relative dependence on interline transfers has often placed British airlines at something of a competitive disadvantage in some important markets, like the North Atlantic. It was clear that US airlines – at that time mainly Pan Am and TWA, now replaced by American and United – received the lion's share of interline feed. And survey data relating to London–USA routes (Figure 5.3) shows how US airlines dominated when the transfers took place in the USA and how they even had the edge for traffic connecting in London. It was difficult for UK airlines to attract passengers transferring in the USA, not only because the gateway airport was often a major hub for a US airline, but also because computer reservations systems have given advantages to online over interline connections. The ability to share flight codes with domestic carriers in the USA reinforced these advantages. Overcoming the competitive disadvantages they faced in the US transfer market was clearly a prime motive behind the various alliances that European carriers formed (at that time) with major airlines in the US: BA with USAir, Lufthansa with United, KLM with Northwest, Air France with Continental, Delta with Swissair and so on. In London the US airlines possessed 'combination

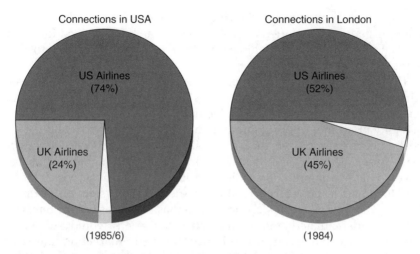

Figure 5.3 Connecting traffic on London–USA routes (*Source*: Derived from CAA, *London Area Airport Study* (1984) and Office of Population Censes and Surveys, *International Passenger Survey* (1985–86))

rights' permitting them to market through USA–European services under single flight numbers and this has enabled them to achieve shares of London transfer traffic that are high in relation to the number of services operated.

It is now clear that the traditional concept of a hub simply as an airport with a large volume of flight activity undertaken by a large number of airlines is not so appropriate in deregulated markets as it was under regulation. This is because airports can now serve as effective hubs only for particular airlines. The US experience of interline connections being replaced by online connections is being repeated in international markets. Even at Heathrow, with all its problems of congestion, online connections as a proportion of total connections have increased quite dramatically in the past 10 years: except where carriers have joint marketing or code-sharing agreements, it is highly likely that interlining will decline still further. Passengers always tend to prefer single-airline service, both for convenience and for reliability. In the past restrictions on route entry often meant that airlines operating in different city pairs did not see each other as direct competitors and so they were more than willing to devise mutually satisfactory schedules to facilitate interlining. But now that these restrictions are being lifted, airlines are able to enter city-pair markets previously closed to them and by routeing services through hubs can often provide online travel that is far superior to any interline alternative. For each airline the priority in scheduling is to complex flights at their own individual hubs. There may indeed be a strong motive for airlines to avoid timing services so that they connect with other airlines' services, because this could lead to a loss of through traffic. Also when airlines can enter through markets on their own, there is less incentive to offer joint interlinable fares. Interline fares are now often more expensive than fares charged for online travel. For all these reasons online travel via hubs can be expected to grow at the expense of interline travel.

It is possible that interlining might survive at some places. Manchester Airport for example has made an interesting attempt to bring different airlines together to create a multi-airline hub. At Manchester there is a large diversity of airlines offering international scheduled services and the airport authority recognized that, if the airport was to achieve the 'critical mass' to sustain hub operations, with more routes and higher frequencies, it would have to embrace interlining (Muirhead, 1993). Otherwise it would tend to remain a spoke airport in the two-tier airport system polarizing in Europe. The view taken by Manchester was that, so long as Europe remained only semi-deregulated, interlining between carriers would still be an important factor. So the airport authority launched a marketing campaign, 'Manchester Connects', to publicize connections between international flights and regional services to cities like Belfast, Norwich, and Cardiff. The connections to Norwich are listed in Table 5.3.

At first sight they represent an impressive array of interline linkages. Norwich is a fairly large city, with a population of around 128 000, but it is not well served by direct flights. The only significant ones are those to Amsterdam, operated by either Fokker 50 (turbo prop) or Fokker 70 (jet) aircraft, taking just under or just over an hour. Services to Manchester are operated with the use of Jetstream 41 (turbo prop) aircraft, taking 55 minutes, and these feed into morning and evening complexes to provide through passengers with a variety of connection possibilities. The airport authority was conscious of the desirability of providing good connections in both directions. The schedules have recently been increased from twice daily to three times daily, which is good. But these Norwich–Manchester feeder links are only operated on weekdays. So a passenger from Norwich who wishes to make either the outbound or return journey at the weekend faces the prospect of surface travel on the Norwich to Manchester leg. And another problem with these schedules is that they are always vulnerable to hub airlines adjusting their service timings. If for instance Lufthansa were to advance its morning departure to Hamburg by half an hour, or retard its arrival from Frankfurt by half an hour, some important linkages will immediately be lost. The Manchester interline hub was clearly a well thought out marketing exercise, but the problem with it lies in coping with capricious alterations to flight schedules by a host of largely independent airlines, including the airlines supplying the feeder links. Indeed, the feeder links originally featured in some of Manchester Airport's interlining publicity – and also used as an illustration in an earlier edition of this book – were those to and from Cardiff. But the airline operating these services, Air Kilroe, subsequently withdrew them when it decided to

Table 5.3 Interline connections through Manchester to/from Norwich, March 2004. *Source*: Derived from *Manchester Airport Timetables*

	Morning complex		*Weekly frequency*
Arrival			
0735	T3 401	Norwich	5
Departures			
0820	LH 5963	Hamburg	6
0820	KL 1074	Amsterdam	7
0825	NI 605	Lisbon	5
0830	BA 7603	Belfast	6
0830	BA 7732	Southampton	5
0830	LX 375	Basle	6
0835	LG 4981	Dublin	5
0835	BA 8741	Vienna	7
0845	BD 371	Aberdeen	5
0845	BA 1864	Edinburgh	6
0845	BA 4402	Isle of Man	7
0850	BD 391	Glasgow	5
0850	BA 1640	Madrid	6
0855	CF 002	Gothenburg	5
0905	BA 8246	Billund	6
0910	AF 1669	Paris	7
0910	GR 673	Guernsey	7
0930	QR 042	Doha	2
0930	PK 718/24	Islamabad	2
0930	PK 712/16/18/22/24	Karachi	5
0930	PK 716/18	Lahore	2
0945	WW 5513	Malaga	5
0945	SQ 345	Zurich/Singapore	2
1000	CO 21	Newark	7
1000	BA 1503	New York	7
1000	WW 5593	Geneva	5
1010	BA 7723	Knock	2
1020	BD 341	Toulouse	5
1025	LG 4982	Luxembourg	5
1025	BA 7911	Lyons	6
1025	VS 075	Orlando	6
1025	SN 2174	Brussels	7
1030	AA 55	Chicago	7

Table 5.3 *Continued*

| 1030 | AY 934 | Helsinki | 5 |
| 1030 | BA 7915 | Nice | 7 |

Arrivals

0545	JN 32	Malta	1
0550	MH 12	Kuala Lumpur	4
0550	BD 702	Washington	6
0555	BA 1502	New York	7
0640	PK 701/13	Islamabad	2
0645	QR 041	Doha	2
0725	FR 552	Dublin	6
0725	KL 1071	Amsterdam	7
0725	VS 076	Orlando	6
0725	LG 7981	Luxembourg	5
0730	LH 5980	Dusseldorf	6
0730	BW 990	Barbados/Port of Spain/Tobago	2
0740	LH 5932	Hamburg	6

Departure

| 0825 | T3 402 | Norwich | 5 |

| | *Afternoon complex* | | *Weekly frequency* |

Arrival

| 1615 | T3 405 | Norwich | 5 |

Departures

1700	LX 381	Zurich	7
1705	BA 7835	Copenhagen	6
1710	BA 7925	Hanover	5
1715	FR 557	Dublin	6
1715	BA 7607	Belfast	7
1715	LH 5995	Munich	7
1715	VZ 7033	Murcia	4
1725	BA 4147	Aberdeen	6
1725	BA 1688	Dusseldorf	6
1725	AF 2569	Paris	7
1730	SN 5426	Brussels	6
1730	BA 1846	Glasgow	6
1735	AY 938	Stockholm/Helsinki	6
1750	KL 1090	Amsterdam	7
1800	BA 8969	Luxembourg	3
1810/1815	LH 4855	Frankfurt	7

1815	BA 8248	Billund	7
1815	BA 7845	Cork	6
1820	NI 609	Lisbon	5
1830	PK 710	Islamabad/Lahore	1
1850	X3 3521	Cologne	5
1855	LX 379	Basle	6
1900	CF 006	Gothenburg	6
1900	GR 679	Guernsey	7
1900	NI 603	Oporto	1
1915	BA 1711	Edinburgh	6

Arrivals

1350	EI 212	Dublin	6
1350	AF 2268	Paris	7
1400	LH 5987	Dusseldorf	6
1405	JM 005	Kingston/Montego Bay	3
1410	BA 1673	Geneva	6
1415	LH 5998	Munich	7
1420	BA 7632	Shannon	5
1420	BA 7891	Pisa	4
1430	BA 8742	Venice	7
1440	BA 1692	Glasgow	5
1440	BA 4146	Aberdeen	6
1440	ZB 575	Malaga	7
1440	BA 7792	Vienna	1
1455	BD 344	Toulouse	5
1500	BA 7912	Lyons	7
1500	BA 1655	Rome	7
1505	LH 4851	Frankfurt	7
1510	SK 154	Copenhagen	7
1515	SN 2177	Brussels	6
1515	BA 7842	Cork	6
1540	BA 7726	Knock	1
1550	BA 1627	Amsterdam	1
1600	WW 5524	Alicante	1
1605	BA 1867	Edinburgh	6

Departure

1645	T3 408	Norwich	5

	Evening complex		*Weekly frequency*

Arrival

1915	T3 407	Norwich	5

Table 5.3 *Continued*

Departures			
1955	BD 389	Edinburgh	5
2000	AF 1169	Paris	7
2000	JZ 1966	Stockholm	1
2000	BA 1677	Glasgow	6
2005	WW 507	Belfast	5
2005	LH 5941	Hamburg	6
2025	EI 217	Dublin	5
2040	BA 4417	Isle of Man	1
2055	KM 147	Malta	5
2110	RE 518	Galway	7

Arrivals			
1645	BA 1607	Paris	7
1650	AY 937	Helsinki	6
1650	FR 556	Dublin	6
1655	BA 7765	Jersey	6
1710	JZ 1965	Stockholm	5
1710	BD 376	Aberdeen	5
1710	BA 1629	Amsterdam	6
1730	SN 5425	Brussels	5
1745	BA 1680	Edinburgh	5
1745	BA 8247	Billund	7
1815	SK 541	Copenhagen	6
1815	QR 043	Doha	2
1815	EK 019	Dubai	7
1815	WW 5506	Belfast	5
1820	CF 005	Gothenburg	6
1825	NI 600	Lisbon/Oporto	1
1825	LX 378	Basel	6
1825	X3 3524	Cologne	5
1830	LH 5992	Dusseldorf	6
1830	GR 678	Guernsey	7
1840	BA 1711	Frankfurt	6
1840	BA 1677	Geneva	7
1840	BA 1714	Glasgow	5
1855	WW 5534	Barcelona	5
1905	BA 4409	Isle of Man	7

Departure			
1940	T3 408	Norwich	5

concentrate more exclusively on executive air charters. And so there are now no direct scheduled services between Manchester and Cardiff, and hence no interlining possibilities. Manchester has also lost some long haul services to which connections used to be possible. Qantas and South African Airways withdrew their Manchester services because the proportions of lucrative business passengers on these flights were rather low, 2.8 and 3.9 per cent, respectively, as compared with 23 and 35 per cent from London Heathrow (House of Commons Environment, Transport and Regional Affairs Committee, 1998).

5.3 Quality of connections

Ian Botham, the former England test cricketer, in a television interview once declared Heathrow to be the 'best airport in the world', adding quickly as an after-thought, 'on the way in!' But as a UK resident Botham is unlikely ever to want to change planes there. Passengers making transfer connections might describe it in somewhat less complimentary terms.

One of the most important factors in the competition for connecting passengers is transfer quality, a factor embracing not just the interval of time required to change from one aircraft to another but also the simplicity and convenience of the connections process. Here single-airport, single-terminal systems operating some way below full capacity (e.g. Amsterdam) are at a distinct advantage. London however, is a multi-airport, multi-terminal system now heavily congested.

MCTs for a selected number of airports are shown in Table 5.4. These refer to the minimum interval that must elapse between an arrival and a departure in order for a passenger to book a connection. Their length clearly depends on a number of factors. At busy congested airports (e.g. New York) the MCTs are longer than at places where the pressure on facilities is relatively less (e.g. at some of the smaller airports in the US, where online connections can in some cases be made in as short a time as 10 minutes). Connections to/from long-haul flights often require greater MCTs, because of longer loading and unloading times. Where the linkage is between domestic and international services, the requirement for passengers to pass through customs and immigration control also lengthens MCTs. Shorter MCTs apply where the transfer can be made entirely within the same airport terminal (e.g. in Amsterdam) especially if the terminal is a modern purpose-built facility (such as Birmingham's Eurohub and the new airport in Munich). Some of the longest MCTs occur where a domestic ↔ international connection involves an inter-terminal transfer (as at Chicago O'Hare, London Heathrow or, in an extreme case, Mumbai). At Heathrow

Table 5.4 MCTs at selected airports, September 2004.[a] *Source: OAG Flight Guide*

Amsterdam	0:25	Domestic ↔ Domestic
	0:40	Domestic ↔ Europe
	0:50	Otherwise
Atlanta	0:55	Domestic ↔ Domestic
	1:00	Domestic → International
	1:30	International → Domestic
	1:30	International ↔ International
Birmingham	0:30	Domestic ↔ Domestic
	0:45	Otherwise
Chicago O-Hare	0:50	Domestic ↔ Domestic
	1:15	Domestic → International
	1:30	International → Domestic
Copenhagen	0:30	Domestic ↔ Domestic
	0:45	Otherwise
Denver	0:50	Domestic ↔ Domestic
	1:00	Otherwise
Frankfurt	0:45	
Hong Kong	1:00	
London Heathrow	0:45	Within Terminals 1 and 4
	1:00	Within Terminals 2 and 3
	1:00	Terminal 1 → Terminal 4
	1:00	Terminal 4 → Terminal 1, International ↔ International
	1:10	Terminal 1 → Terminal 2, Domestic → International
	1:15	Terminal 1 → Terminal 2, International → Domestic
	1:15	Terminal 1 → Terminal 2, International ↔ International
	1:15	Terminal 1 ↔ Terminal 3
	1:15	Terminal 2 ↔ Terminal 3
	1:30	Terminal 2 ↔ Terminal 4
	1:30	Terminal 3 ↔ Terminal 4
London Gatwick	0:40	Domestic ↔ Domestic, South Terminal
	0:45	Domestic → International, South Terminal
	0:45	Within North Terminal
	0:50	Channel Islands → Domestic, South Terminal
	0:55	International ↔ International, South Terminal
	1:00	International → Domestic, South Terminal
	1:15	South Terminal ↔ North Terminal
Los Angeles	1:10	Domestic ↔ Domestic
	1:30	International ↔ International
	2:00	International → Domestic
	2:00	International ↔ International
Madrid	0:45	Domestic ↔ Domestic
	0:45	International ↔ International
	1:00	Domestic ↔ International

Mumbai (Bombay)	0:30	Domestic ↔ Domestic
	1:30	International ↔ International
	2:30	Domestic → International
	3:00	International → Domestic
Munich	0:30	within Terminal 2
	0:35	within Terminal 1
	0:45	between Terminals
New York Kennedy	1:00	Domestic ↔ Domestic
	1:45	Domestic ↔ International
	2:00	International ↔ International
New York Guardia	0:45	Domestic ↔ Domestic
	1:00	Domestic ↔ International
	1:00	International ↔ International
New York Newark	1:00	Domestic ↔ Domestic
	1:00	International ↔ International
	1:15	Domestic → International
	1:30	International → Domestic
Paris Charles de Gaulle	1:00	within Terminals Domestic ↔ Domestic
	1:30	within Terminals Domestic ↔ International
	1:15	between Terminals Domestic ↔ Domestic
	2:00	between Terminals Domestic ↔ International
Paris Orly	0:45	within Terminals Domestic ↔ Domestic
	1:00	within Terminals Domestic ↔ International
	1:00	between Terminals Domestic ↔ Domestic
	1:15	between Terminals Domestic ↔ International
Rome Ciampino	0:25	Domestic ↔ Domestic
Rome Fiumicino	0:45	Domestic ↔ Domestic, International ↔ International
	1:00	Domestic ↔ International
San Francisco	0:50	Domestic ↔ Domestic
	1:00	Domestic → International
	1:45	Internal → Domestic, International ↔ International
Vienna	0:30	
Zurich	0:40	

[a] There are numerous exceptions and variations by individual airlines.

70 per cent of transfer passengers spend 2 hours or more making their connections, with 45 per cent of them taking over 3 hours.

A serious disadvantage at Heathrow is that ground facilities are divided between no less than four distinct terminals (and in the future five, once Terminal 5 is opened to traffic). What is more, unlike at some multi-terminal airports, the allocation of facilities is made with little attempt to minimize the number of inter-terminal transfers required. This situation is without a close parallel at any other major airport in the world and arises at Heathrow because of the traditional importance of interline connections and the sectorization of services between terminals in such a way that routes serving a similar geographical region leave from the same location. Generally passengers wish to connect between regions, not within them. There is for instance negligible demand for domestic ↔ domestic or Europe ↔ Europe transfers at Heathrow, and yet those are just those most likely to be accomplished within the same terminal building. This is illustrated in Figure 5.4, from which it can be seen that the proportion of Heathrow transfers involving a change of terminal is as high as two-thirds, and that just over 40 per cent of them require relatively difficult journeys, across one of the two main runways, between the central complex and Terminal 4. A possible alternative division between terminals is by airline, a system that operates well in other

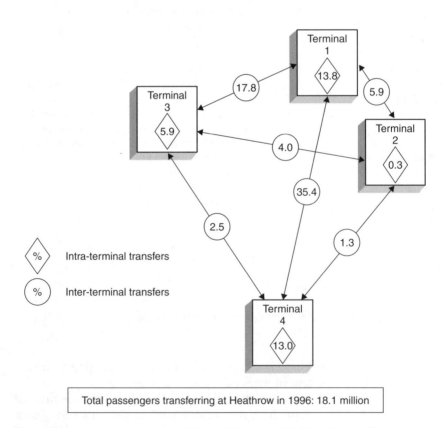

Total passengers transferring at Heathrow in 1996: 18.1 million

Figure 5.4   Intra- and inter-terminal transfers at London Heathrow (*Source*: Derived from 1996 CAA airports survey)

places where online connections predominate. Such an arrangement gives the locally based airline a useful advantage over competitors. For example, connections between the entire range of Air France's services can all be made within the same terminal at Charles de Gaulle (CDG) airport in Paris.

And now, by concentrating all its own services and those of its partner airlines in the North Terminal, BA is seeking to do much the same thing at Gatwick – and with some considerable success. Gatwick's North Terminal is potentially capable of disembarking passengers from one service and embarking them upon another within 30 minutes, although the MCT is still (at the time of writing) scheduled at 45 minutes. And swifter connections between more highly co-ordinated arrivals and departures is already reflected in a dramatic increase in the number of transfer passengers handled by BA at Gatwick, up from 1.7 million (9 per cent of total passengers) in 1991 to 4.2 million in 1996 (17 per cent of total passengers). But it is not so easy for BA to achieve a similar result where the bulk of its transfer traffic connects, namely at Heathrow. At least, not just now.

The opportunities for BA to attract connecting traffic will be much enhanced when the airline moves more than 90 per cent of its operations to a new terminal at Heathrow, Terminal 5. This move is scheduled to take place in March 2008, when all services will be transferred out of Terminals 1 and 4. Henceforth all services will be operated from Terminal 5, except services to Australia, Italy, and Spain which will transfer to Terminal 3. Flights to Spain and Italy will be operated by Boeing 757 aircraft so that keeping these aircrafts out of the new terminal will reduce complexity and, it is hoped, increase efficiency. The other aspect to this is that BA's oneworld alliance partners have signed an agreement to consolidate all their services – currently spread across all four terminals – in Terminal 3. Hence BA's Spanish and Australian services will be operated alongside those of alliance partners Iberia and Qantas.

Terminal 5 is going to be truly massive in size. It will be five times the size of Terminal 4, BA's current main long-haul base. There will be five levels in the main building, each the size of 10 full-sized football pitches! The baggage system will be able to handle up to 12 000 bags per hour, using no less than 18 kilometres of baggage belts to transport the luggage around the terminal. This is especially important for transfer connecting traffic; and the problems BA has had with onward connections because of the complexities associated with the underground transfers between Terminal 1 and Terminal 4 will become things of the past.

Passengers changing planes at Heathrow and Gatwick travel over a whole variety of different itineraries, and the major routeings they follow are illustrated in Table 5.5. The single most important routeing, especially for those passengers making airside connections, is between continental Europe and North America, which reflects the positions of both airports as gateways into Europe. This is reflected in the composition of passengers

Table 5.5 Major routeings taken by transfer connecting passengers at London Gatwick and London Heathrow, 1996 (two-way flow in thousands of passengers and percentages of totals). *Source*: Civil Aviation Authority (1997)

(a) Gatwick

Airside

	Europe	Africa	Asia/ Oceania	C&S America and Caribbean	Middle and Near East	Total
Europe	190 9.6%					
Africa	115 5.8%					
Asia/Oceania	58 2.9%	0 0.0%				
C&S America and Caribbean	164 8.3%	1 0.0%	1 0.1%			
Middle and Near East	15 0.7%	0 0.0%	0 0.0%	2 0.1%		
North America	1226 62.1%	85 4.3%	12 0.6%	0 0.0%	107 5.4%	1976 100%

Landside

	UK	Europe	Africa	Asia/ Oceania	C&S America and Caribbean	Middle and Near East	Total
UK	23 1.1%						
Europe	596 27.7%	210 9.8%					
Africa	91 4.2%	43 2.0%					
Asia/Oceania	52 2.4%	47 2.2%	3 0.1%				
C&S America and Caribbean	134 6.3%	54 2.5%	2 0.1%	1 0.0%			
Middle and Near East	31 1.5%	12 0.6%	0 0.0%	0 0.0%	0 0.0%		
North America	482 22.4%	279 13.0%	52 2.4%	11 0.5%	0 0.0%	24 1.1%	2147 100%

(b) Heathrow

Airside

	Europe	Africa	Asia/ Oceania	C&S America and Caribbean	Middle and Near East	Total
Europe	288 3.8%					
Africa	357 4.7%					
Asia/Oceania	2074 27.1%	41 0.5%				
C&S America and Caribbean	327 4.3%	4 0.1%	38 0.5%			
Middle and Near East	152 2.0%	2 0.0%	21 0.3%	8 0.1%		
North America	3310 43.2%	194 2.5%	411 5.4%	0 0.0%	434 5.7%	7661 100%

Landside

	UK	Europe	Africa	Asia/ Oceania	C&S America and Caribbean	Middle and Near East	Total
UK	63 0.6%						
Europe	2518 24.2%	895 8.6%					
Africa	223 2.1%	215 2.1%					
Asia/Oceania	1123 10.8%	959 9.2%	24 0.2%				
C&S America and Caribbean	61 0.6%	106 1.0%	2 0.0%	10 0.1%			
Middle and Near East	344 3.3%	171 1.6%	0 0.0%	0 0.0%	11 0.1%		
North America	1398 13.4%	1711 16.4%	104 1.0%	193 1.9%	0 0.0%	274 2.6%	10 405 100%

on board BAs' transatlantic flights. See, for example, Figure 5.5, which shows that on one BA flight from Gatwick to Dallas no more than 30 per cent of passengers began their journeys in the UK. But this is certainly not unique to BA. Of all Air France passengers flying to and from Canada and the US in 2004, only 28 per cent were actually resident in France (Figure 5.6).

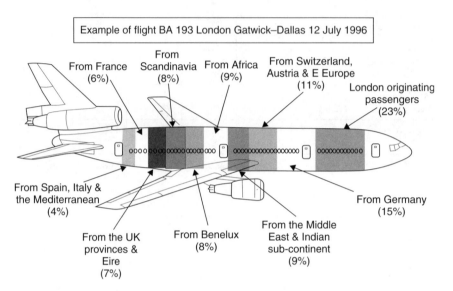

Figure 5.5 Composition of passengers on BA transatlantic flights (*Source*: BA)

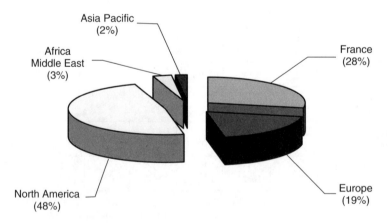

Figure 5.6 Composition of passengers on Air France North Atlantic services (Place of resident of AF passengers on flights to and from Canada and the US, 2004) (*Source*: Air France)

Table 5.6 Balance in international ↔ international connections made by passengers using UK airports, 1994–95/96[a]. *Source*: House of Commons Environment, Transport and Regional Affairs Committee (1998)

Airport	Estimated no. of passenger connections[b]	
	Out of the UK	Over the UK
Belfast International	9000	0
Bristol	32 000	0
Cardiff	32 000	0
Humberside	34 000	0
Teeside	1 80 000	0
Newcastle	79 000	1000
Norwich	36 000	0
Southampton	14 000	0
Aberdeen	84 000	0
Birmingham	2 32 000	18 000
Edinburgh	1 45 000	0
Glasgow	1 93 000	2000
London City	13 000	3000
Gatwick	2 86 000	16 07 000
Heathrow	38 95 000	64 13 000
Luton	2000	4000
Manchester	632 000	40 000
Stansted	60 000	33 000
Total	57 96 000	81 21 000

[a] Data for Belfast, Bristol, Cardiff, Humberside, Teeside, Newcastle, Norwich, and Southampton taken from the Civil Aviation Authority's Origin and Destination Survey for 1994–95. Data for Aberdeen, Birmingham, Edinburgh, Glasgow, London City, Gatwick, Heathrow, Luton, Manchester and Stansted is taken from the CAA's O and D Survey for 1996.
[b] Not including passengers travelling from a UK airport to a foreign hub and then transferring to a domestic flight in that country. (On routes to the USA such passengers can often form the majority of the on-board total.)

Due to the congestion in London increasing numbers of UK origin-and-destination passengers are making connections at continental European hubs. *It is still* the case that more connections are made by foreign origin-and-destination passengers connecting at a UK airport (Table 5.6) but the gap is narrowing rapidly. Direct international flights from regional airports are now much more of an alternative to services from London. The number of international destinations served with a frequent direct service from regional airports has risen manyfold over the past 15 years or so

Table 5.7 International destinations[a] with a frequent scheduled service from UK regional airports: 1990 and 2004. *Source*: Civil Aviation Authority

Top 10 regional airports	International destinations	
	1990	*2004*
Manchester	15	60
Birmingham	13	36
Bristol	5	21
Nottingham East Midlands	3	17
Liverpool	1	15
Newcastle	4	15
Glasgow Prestwick	0	12
Edinburgh	3	10
Glasgow Abbotsinch	5	10
Leeds Bradford	4	10

[a] With a minimum frequency of service broadly equating to a daily round-trip service each weekday.

(Table 5.7). Most of the international services from regional airports are short hauls, Amsterdam now being served from 17 regional airports in the UK, Dublin from 16 and Paris from ten. These developments have meant that only 55 per cent of passengers on international scheduled air services whose journeys originate or terminate in the regions actually travel via London airports, compared with 69 per cent in 1987 (and charter traffic is even better served from regional airports, only 14 per cent travelling via London). Nonetheless it is unrealistic to expect all regional demand to be met locally by services from regional airports, since they have a much smaller passenger base than the London airports, which in turn means that on many routes demand is insufficient to support a regular service, or at least a service at high enough a frequency to attract business travellers. For example, over 3 million passengers a year travel by surface transport from the West Midlands to board international flights at London airports rather than flying out of Birmingham International Airport. Although the pattern of services is changing in favour of direct flights from regional airports, it may be a very long time before regional airports can cater for the whole range of local passengers' demand. In the meantime many passengers from UK regions are flying via hubs on the continent. A ranking by percentage of transfer traffic (Table 5.8) shows Frankfurt heading the list at 54 per cent followed by Copenhagen and Amsterdam with just over 40 per cent each. Paris airports are not included in the list because of lack of data, but CDG is vying with Heathrow, Zurich, Madrid, Vienna, and Munich for the next place down the list. For historical, political, and

Table 5.8 Transfer traffic at airports in the European Economic Area, 2003.
Sources: Airports Council International and International Air Transport
Association

Rank[a] Airport[b]		Code	% of transfer passengers	Transfer passengers (thousands)	Total passengers (thousands)
1	Frankfurt	FRA	54	25 908	48 352
2	Copenhagen	CPH	42	7401	17 644
3	Amsterdam	AMS	41	16 342	39 960
4	London Heathrow	LHR	36	22 342	63 487
5	Zurich	ZRH	35	5885	16 977
6	Madrid	MAD	35	12 493	35 694
7	Vienna	VIE	34	4313	12 785
8	Munich	MUC	31	7450	24 193
9	Athens	ATH	27	3308	12 252
10	Bodoe	BOO	26	329	1243
11	Ljubkjana	LJU	22	201	921
12	Kirkenes	KKN	22	44	205
13	Oslo	OSL	20	2700	13 647
14	Trorasoe	TOS	19	261	1349
15	Caen	CFR	17	17	100
16	London Gatwick	LGW	16	4783	30 007
17	Milan Malpensa	MXP	14	2511	17 622
18	London Stansted	STN	13	2433	18 717
19	Trondheim	TRD	13	344	2614
20	Lorient	LRT	13	27	208
21	Barcelona	BCN	12	2730	22 749
22	Helsinki	HEL	11	1025	9708
23	Budapest	BUD	11	530	5010
24	Manchester[c]	MAN	11	2185	19 551
25	Prague	PRG	10	741	7456
26	Aberdeen	ABZ	10	252	2522
27	Brussels	BRU	9	1408	151 66
28	Stockholm	ARN	9	1356	152 06
29	Hammerfest	HFT	9	11	119
30	Bergen	BGO	6	202	3588

[a] Ranked by the percentage of transfer traffic.
[b] Statistics are not available for Paris airports, neither CDG nor Orly (ORY). Paris CDG is
estimated to rank among the top transfer airports.
[c] Data relate to 2001.

geographical reasons, Western and Central Europe is perhaps a little
crowded when it comes to hubs. And we have already seen the beginnings
of a shakeout, the demise of two main hub airlines Sabena in Brussels and
Swissair in Zurich.

5.4 Effects on airline operating costs

Is airline hubbing a good thing? It may have big advantages for individual carriers in particular city-pair markets. But is it good for the industry as a whole? Here this general question is addressed by considering in turn the effects of hubbing on airlines, airports and passengers, starting with airlines.

To begin with, what effect does hubbing have on airline operating costs? Compared with direct flights, hubbing involves additional passenger handling, places greater peak-load pressure on the hub airport, and may have the effect of reducing the average sector distance flown. Passengers routed via a hub are involved in two boardings and disembarkations; and their baggage has to be transferred from one aircraft to another. The concentration of flight activity means that this has to be accomplished within a short interval of time which in turn means that extra staff and more sophisticated handling equipment are needed to cope with sharp surges in the flow of traffic. To a certain extent some of these costs are a burden, not just on the airline, but on the airport authority as well. But if hubbing reduces sector lengths, then the cost penalties from this fall on the airline alone, given that such a high proportion of its direct operating cost is incurred in take-off, landing, climb, and descent. All these points are prima facie indications of a positive relationship between hubbing and unit cost – but that is far too simplistic a view.

One of the main determinants of unit cost is route traffic density. In this context density can be measured as the ratio of traffic to network size, for example passenger-miles divided by unduplicated route mileage, or passenger-miles divided by the number of cities served. It is well known that there are some significant economies in route traffic density (Bailey, Graham, and Kaplan, 1985). These economies arise because greater density enables the airline to use larger, more efficient aircraft with lower costs per seat-mile and/or to operate at higher service frequencies and consequently at higher seat-load factors, which lead to lower costs per passenger-mile. An increase in density may also permit more intensive utilization of aircraft and crews, operating more flight hours per day. For all these reasons unit cost falls as traffic density in the airline's network rises, and hubbing has a major effect in increasing density.

Hubbing increases density by enabling the airline to consolidate traffic from many different origin–destination markets onto a much smaller number of links in the network. It makes it possible for the airline to carry, on a single spoke, passengers with the same origin but different destinations or, the other way around, passengers with different origins but the same destination. In this way hubbing reduces the number of round-trips necessary to transport a given number of passengers over a given set of itineraries. Total passenger-miles flown may or may not increase (depending on the extent to which passengers fly 'dog-legs'), but the main effects in reducing unit cost come from a reduction in sectors flown, an increase in aircraft size and/or a rise in service frequency and load factor. But to what extent does hubbing reduce unit cost in this way?

Some empirical studies have been made using US data. Caves, Christensen, and Tretheway (1984) provide some empirical evidence on the magnitude of economies of density. They estimated a statistical cost function for airlines that included both network size (cities served) and output (revenue passenger-miles) and found that, holding network size constant, total costs increase less rapidly than output, with the associated elasticity equal to 0.8. McShane and Windle (1989) found that for each 1 per cent increase in hubbing, unit cost fell by 0.11 per cent which, when related to airline output, implies that US airlines saved some $2 billion as a result of expanding their hub and spokes networks. And support for the hypothesis that hubbing reduces unit cost came also in another study (Brueckner, Dyer, and Spiller, 1992), where it was found that mergers leading to a concentrated hub (between TWA and Ozark at St Louis and between Northwest and Republic at Minneapolis) generated significant gains in efficiency by creating larger networks. There have been other studies (e.g. Hansen and Kanafani, 1989) in which a more agnostic view was taken. The matter is quite complex. The indications that hubbing has some effect in reducing unit cost of airline operations are fairly convincing, but the evidence is not yet entirely conclusive. But the reduction referred to here is a reduction from full service cost levels without a hub and spokes system. Hubbing may certainly yield some efficiency gains over pre-deregulation grid-type networks, but it is still very much more costly than the star-shaped point-to-point networks of the low-cost airlines (Lawton, 2002). And in order to cover their full costs, hub-based full service airlines have traditionally relied on discriminatory pricing, charging price-inelastic business passengers more than price-elastic leisure passengers. Indeed the monopoly market power that some airlines were able to exercise on routes to/from their 'fortress' hubs became a serious concern for competition authorities, as discussed below. But once low-cost airlines began to operate at sufficient frequency of service to attract business passengers the pricing power previously enjoyed by hub-based full-service airlines began to decline. Pricing power is discussed at greater length in the following chapter. All that is noted at this point is that the competitive environment in the industry has become such that it will not support price discrimination on the scale on which hub airlines exercised it in the past (Tretheway, 2004). Full-service airlines being restructured under the protection of Chapter 11 are having to consider how far they should adjust their hubbing strategies to meet the challenges of increased competition.

There is a view (Taneja, 2004) that full-service airlines have created too many hubs and have made them too complex. One airline which may well have set up too many is US Airways (now merged with America West). To a passenger in a city on the eastern seaboard wanting to travel to a city in the mid-west US Airways offered a choice of no less than four different hubs: Baltimore, Philadelphia, Pittsburg, and Charlotte. This carried with it the chance that the hubs would compete, not merely against the hubs of other airlines, but also amongst themselves. And some hubs are quite simply too close to others. In South-East Asia, Malaysian's hub in Kuala Lumpur is very much in the shadow of the major hub in Singapore operated by SIA. In the Middle East, the hubs of the three main long-haul airlines are comparatively speaking almost on top of each other, with Emirates in Dubai, Qatar Airways in Doha and Etihad in Abu Dhabi. In Europe, as alluded to before, Swissair's hub at Zurich was rather close to major hubs at Frankfurt and Munich; and the hub of another failed carrier, Sabena in Brussels, also had two major hubs as near-neighbours in Amsterdam and Paris. Interestingly, following their merger, Air France and KLM adopted what they call a 'dual-hub' strategy, scheduling through connections via each hub at different times of the day. A very clear example of this is depicted in Figure 5.7. In addition to avoiding Paris-versus-Amsterdam competition for the through Madrid–Shanghai traffic, the schedule produces two good pairs

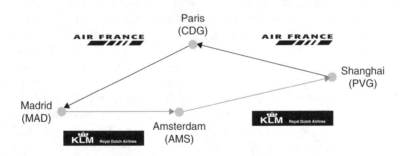

Outward Madrid–Shanghai

(1) AF2001	MAD-CDG	20:25	22:30
AF112	CDG-PVG	23:15	16:25+1
(2) KL1702	MAD-AMS	12:50	15:35
KL895	AMS-PVG	17:10	09:45+1

Return Shanghai–Madrid

(1) KL896	PVG-AMS	12:15	17:40
KL1707	AMS-MAD	19:40	22:15
(2) AF117	PVG-CDG	23:55	06:00+1
AF1000	CDG-MAD	07:15+1	09:20+1

(+1 signifies the following day, in local time)

Note: Paris drawn to the north of Amsterdam in the original issued by the airline

Figure 5.7   Illustration of the 'dual-hub' strategy of Air France-KLM (*Source*: Air France-KLM)

of outward and return connections, the importance of which was high-lighted earlier in this chapter.

In support of the argument that airlines have made their hub opera-tions too complex, Taneja suggests that many hubs are far too big from a systems point of view: they require very complicated revenue manage-ment procedures to make them effective; they place severe strains on the available infrastructure capacity; and they become more than usually vulnerable to extremes of weather. Much of the complexity, and much of the reason why so many different hubs emerged, stems from airlines being more focussed on high market shares than on high rates of profitability. The same basic point has been made by the CEO of the International Air Transport Association who expressed it in the following terms:

> Sometimes we have been our own worst enemy – chasing growth instead of profitability.
>
> Bisignani (2006)

With so many airlines incurring financial deficits in a more fiercely com-petitive environment, that must change.

5.5 Effects on airports

Airport economics

Hubbing is not entirely without its diseconomies, although these are largely external to the airline. In generating large volumes of transfer passengers, and requiring them to be handled swiftly, the hub airline contributes adversely to the peak-load capacity problem at the airport, not only on the runways but on the aprons and in the terminals as well. Its demand for facil-ities at the hub, such as baggage transfer equipment, can be very peaked indeed. Flight complexing leads to some severe peaking in arrivals and departures and this is necessary to ensure a large number of usable connec-tions. But at the same time it can reduce efficiency in the utilization of airport facilities which might only be maximized when demand is spread evenly across the operating day. In this regard there can be a conflict between the interests of hub airlines and profit-motivated airport authorities. In many ways the economics of transfer traffic are not so attractive to airport opera-tors as those of origin–destination traffic. In some cases fierce competition for 'footloose' transfer traffic, traffic that can choose between a number of different hubs, has induced some airports – like Amsterdam, Dublin and airports in Spain and Italy – to waive their passenger charges for connecting traffic. Income from aeronautical activities is often not so great as the revenue airports earn from their non-aeronautical commercial activities. But here too connecting traffic may often not be all that remunerative to the airport on a per-passenger basis. While at the hub transfer passengers do provide something of a captive market for retailers, but good connections mean less opportunity to spend money in airport shops. When passengers have barely half an hour to change planes, they have little time to patronize restaurants or the duty-free shop. Nor of course do they require car hire, parking, and other things on which the airport earns income from concessions. Also there are no 'meeters and greeters' to provide an additional source of revenue, as there often are for travellers beginning or ending their journeys at the airport. For all these reasons privately owned airports subject to capacity constraints may, other things being equal, prefer to cater for origin–destination traffic, rather than connecting passengers.

For airports with spare capacity and for airports in public ownership, it may be a different matter. In the US, airports are mainly owned by city and county authorities; and they actually vie with one another to become hubs. A clear motive is the huge potential for traffic growth, not just growth in transfer traffic, but in local origin–destination passengers as well. Demand from the latter can be greatly stimulated by the high level of service operated at a hub. Dennis (1993) illustrates this by comparing the 1977–91 growth of six medium-sized US airports, between three that developed as hubs and three that remained as non-hubs: the three hub airports (Salt Lake City, Minneapolis, and St Louis) saw their traffic levels treble, while traffic at the three non-hub airports (Kansas City, New Orleans, and Cleveland) tended to stagnate. The faster growth at a hub does have to be accommodated however, which often means that the airport authority has to invest in additional runway and terminal capacity, especially when peaks in traffic flows are exaggerated through flight complexing. But the growth in peak-load traffic will not generate the same proportionate increase in surface access and egress requirements, when a large part of the increased traffic is merely travelling through the airport to connect from one flight to another.

Scheduling through hubs can create peaks, not just at the hubs themselves, but also at spoke airports. When aircraft are stabled overnight on the spokes, services to various hubs all start from the spoke airport in the early morning and return there in the late evening. So there are at least two localized peaks at the spoke airport, a departures peak at around 07:00 and an arrivals peak after about 22:00. And there can be a number of other peaks during the day, depending upon how many round-trip repeat cycles are made and on the distribution of route lengths from the spoke to various different hubs. If flying times between a given spoke and a number of different hubs are broadly similar, aircraft will be arriving and departing the spoke in waves just as they do at the hubs. But even if the flying times to the different hubs vary quite a lot, there can still be some peak problems at the spoke, if synchronization of activity at the hubs requires some variation in turn-around times at the spokes (i.e. lengthening those for the shorter flights). This can add to peak-load pressure on gate availability at the spoke. Given that virtually all traffic at spoke airports is origin–destination traffic, any accentuation of peaks in flight activity carries over to peaks in demand for surface access and egress facilities. The extent of this peak-load problem clearly depends on the level of traffic at the spoke. At some of the larger spoke airports in the US, for example Norfolk, Virginia and Orange County, California, there can often be some very sharp peaks indeed.

Development benefits

The fundamental reason why local authorities are so keen to see their airports develop as hubs is the boost this gives to the local economy, both the direct impact on incomes from increased employment and the indirect multiplier effects from increased spending generally in the local area. In addition hubs play a role in attracting tourism, conferences and, most important of all, new industrial and commercial businesses, all of which can give further fresh impetus to the local economy. Various surveys of factors affecting industrial location have found that the presence of a comprehensive network of air services disproportionately strengthens the attractiveness of a particular city or region. Examples abound of firms' locational decisions being tipped in favour of one city rather than another because of its airport's function as a hub. Sony's decision to locate a large components factory in Pittsburgh mainly rested on the expansion of USAir's hub there. In 1991 United Parcels Service decided to move its headquarters from Connecticut (because of high housing and staff costs in that locality) and the final shortlist of alternative locations included Kansas City, Dallas, and Atlanta. Kansas City was eliminated because of its comparatively low level of air services; and UPS eventually plumped for Atlanta, having calculated that the company would save the equivalent of over two man years of travel time on the 18 000 air journeys made by its headquarters staff each year by locating in Atlanta as compared with Dallas. Since 1976, the year in which Atlanta received its first transatlantic service, over 1000 foreign-based firms have located enterprises in the Atlanta metropolitan region. Another place where hub development has led to a dramatic increase in the number of firms locating there is Nashville. In 1991 Nashville attracted Caterpillar's finance division, a medical technology manufacturer, the brokerage headquarters of a British insurance company employing over 1000 people, the US headquarters of Bridgestone/Firestone Inc., the Canadian group Northern Telecom, the administrative centre of the National Federation of Small

Businesses, and so on. Over 3000 new jobs were created from corporate relocations in 1 year alone (Small, 1993). The kind of businesses for which air service is an important locational consideration are: those whose operations are widely dispersed geographically, for example a large multinational organization; those whose highly specialized and technology- or knowledge-based activities require a diverse network of suppliers, clients and associates; and those manufacturing low-bulk, high-value products incorporating a high degree of added value. The highly skilled and highly paid employment generated by businesses like these enhance the multiplier effects on the local economy, when high disposable incomes are spent on locally produced goods and services, and when similar kinds of businesses are attracted in a kind of ripple effect.

None of this is lost on 'city fathers' and other local government officials. The economic development benefits flowing from hubs are such as to justify public investment in airports and expenditure on various inducements to airlines – in the form of tax breaks, low-cost loans, and subsidies. Indeed there have been several notable instances of local authorities in the US affording domestic airlines much the same thing as countries have supplied to national carriers as state aids. In the recent recession several hub cities have taken steps to support their incumbent hub airlines with financial packages that the press have come to label 'hubsidies'. For instance, in December 1991, an alliance between the State of Minnesota and the Minneapolis–St Paul city authorities put together a package of grant aid and loan guarantees for Northwest worth a total of $838 million, in exchange for promises from the airline that it would maintain service levels and thereby safeguard local employment (*The Economist*, 1992). In 1992 a similar arrangement between the State of Arizona and the city of Phoenix raised $70 million to keep its hub airline America West from bankruptcy. And now there are reports that American Airlines is being courted by the State of North Carolina regarding its hub at Raleigh–Durham, a conurbation which used to be heavily dependent upon the steel industry and which without its aviation-related employment would once again become a depressed area. The hub at Raleigh–Durham has never made much money for American, but its closure would have very serious repercussions on the overall level of economic activity in the area.

The importance of local authorities place on hubs is reflected in some of the investments they make. Pittsburgh spent $870 million on a new terminal complex to strengthen its role as a principal hub for USAir. In April 1993 Nashville agreed to buy USAir's Charlotte–London route licence for $5 million, so that it could be transferred to Nashville and then operated by American. But the most ambitious investment was made by Denver, where an entirely new airport is being built on a greenfield site of 53 square miles, consisting of 5 runways and 80 gates with expansion potential for 12 runways and 260 gates. The total cost of this project is estimated at $2.7 billion, expenditure justified on economic development grounds to the electorate of the State of Colorado, where as much as 10 per cent of total employment has been attributed to Denver's original Stapleton Airport. Investments like this show a lot of faith in the power of hubs to generate external effects on incomes and employment. But the strategy is not without risks. Airport facilities cannot move in the same way as airlines can. And there have already been cases of cities losing their hubs (e.g. Dayton, Ohio). Nonetheless the attractions of hubs appear to be very great, at least to publicly owned airports – and not just within the US. In Paris, the French have for a long time been developing plans to turn CDG Airport into a 'golden hub', with proposals for five runways, new terminals, and improved surface access.

The comparative lack of any similar plans in Britain led *The Times* (1 December 1989) to comment that the 'contrast between French dynamism and British pettifogging in the field of transport planning is glaring'. This may seem a somewhat harsh criticism, given the formidable environmental problems to be overcome if there is to be any significant expansion at Heathrow or, for that matter, at Gatwick. The French were able to select a greenfield site for CDG in 1964, in a tract of featureless and empty agricultural land, which gave room for almost any development that might be needed. Similar greenfield sites in South-East England have proved very difficult to find, the main possibilities for entirely new airports being offshore locations somewhere in the Thames Estuary. But one large airport can offer a much wider range of hubbing services than two or three airports of the same total capacity. This would indicate the further development of Heathrow. Without this there is a risk of the UK being set at an increasing disadvantage in competition with other European countries for the activities of multinational companies and international organizations. In particular, there could even be a serious challenge to London's position as a leading centre for financial services. The external benefits from expansion of Heathrow are clear enough, but so too are the external costs, since it would mean increasing air traffic in one of the most environmentally damaging locations in the country. The question is whether the external benefits exceed the external costs; and also whether the total net benefit to the economy (the net difference between positive and negative externalities plus any net revenue from the increase in air traffic) is greater or less than the net benefit that could be gained by devoting the same amount of resources elsewhere.

Capacity shortages

London Heathrow is, by passenger numbers, the largest airport in Europe and the third largest in the world, after Atlanta and Chicago O'Hare (Table 5.9). But its pre-eminence is being seriously challenged by other airports in Europe, notably Frankfurt, Paris CDG, and Amsterdam. Heathrow may still occupy a high position in the passenger numbers league table, but in

Table 5.9 The top 100 airports ranked by passenger numbers in 2004. Source: Airline Business (June 2005)

Airport-code	Passengers[a] (thousands)	Av. capacity per flight (seats)	Leading carrier	Flights by leading carrier (%)
1 Atlanta-ATL	83 579	124	Delta	74.8
2 Chicago-ORD	75 374	105	United	47.5
3 London-LHR	67 344	194	BA	42.3
4 Tokyo-HND	62 321	262	Japan Airlines	45.0
5 Los Angeles-LAX	60 711	136	United	28.7
6 Dallas/Ft. Worth-DFW	59 412	111	American	83.2
7 Frankfurt-FRA	51 098	160	Lufthansa	60.1
8 Paris-CDG	50 861	152	Air France	57.9
9 Amsterdam-AMS	42 541	157	KLM	50.7
10 Denver-DEN	42 394	103	United	54.9
11 Las Vegas-LAS	41 437	143	Southwest	36.0
12 Phoenix-PHX	39 494	122	America West	50.3
13 Madrid-MAD	38 526	148\	Iberia	56.7
14 Bangkok-BKK	37 960	218	Thai Int'l	29.4
15 New York-JFK	37 362	165	Delta	24.1
16 Minneapolis-MSP	36 749	105	Northwest	79.8
17 Hong Kong-HKG	36 713	258	Cathay Pacific	25.6
18 Houston-IAH	36 491	95	Continental	85.7
19 Detroit-DTW	35 199	101	Northwest	80.3
20 Beijing-PEK	34 883	176	Air China	35.8
21 San Francisco-SFO	33 497	138	United	56.1
22 Newark-EWR	31 847	111	Continental	66.2
23 London-LGW	31 462	151	BA	43.5
24 Orlando-MCO	31 111	135	Delta	27.7
25 Tokyo-NRT	31 106	291	Japan Airlines	22.1
26 Singapore-SIN	30 354	260	Singapore Airlines	36.1
27 Miami-MIA	30 157	151	American	53.1
28 Seattle-SEA	28 703	116	Alaskan	57.9
29 Toronto-YYZ	28 656	109	Air Canada	63.3
30 Philadelphia-PHL	28 509	102	US Airways	70.4
31 Rome-FCO	28 119	139	Alitalia	45.3
32 Sydney-SYD	28 066	155	Qantas	44.5
33 Munich-MUC	26 815	109	Lufthansa	64.0
34 Boston-BOS	26 141	102	American	21.1
35 Jakarta-CEK	25 676	148	Garuda Indonesia	30.8
36 Charlotte-CLT	24 732	96	US Airways	84.0
37 Barcelona-BCN	24 550	134	Iberia	46.4
38 New York-LGA	24 360	96	US Airways	32.9
39 Seoul-ICN	24 235	264	Korean	36.0

40	Paris-ORY	24 032	150	Air France	61.3
41	Mexico City-MEX	22 994	125	Aeromexico	30.2
42	Washington-IAD	22 660	82	United	46.7
43	Cincinnati-CVG	22 063	76	Delta	86.7
44	Dubai-DXB	21 712	217	Emirates	36.4
45	Manchester-MAN	21 548	118	BA	31.0
46	Shanghai-PVG	21 124	207	China Eastern	34.2
47	Kuala Lumpur-KUL	21 057	197	Malaysian	52.8
48	Fort Lauderdale-FLL	20 973	116	Delta	19.7
49	Honolulu-HNL	20 948	159	Aloha	25.7
50	London-STN	20 908	171	Ryanair	56.8
51	Baltimore-BWI	20 726	126	Southwest	42.7
52	Palma-PMI	20 411	158	Air Berlin	23.9
53	Guangzhou-CAN	20 353	168	China Southern	53.8
54	Melbourne-MEL	20 267	157	Qantas	41.5
55	Taipei-TPE	20 084	264	China Airlines	31.2
56	Chicago-MDW	19 771	140	Southwest	64.0
57	Osaka-ITM	19 317	193	All Nippon	49.8
58	Copenhagen-CPH	18 966	113	SAS	47.4
59	Milan-MXP	18 554	120	Alitalia	59.1
60	Fukuoka-FUK	18 526	225	All Nippon	42.1
61	Salt Lake-SLC	18 349	86	Delta	78.9
62	Sapporo-CTS	17 601	233	All Nippon	44.5
63	Tampa-TPA	17 397	119	Southwest	22.5
64	Istanbul-IST	17 367	158	THY Turkish	63.6
65	Zurich-ZRH	17 215	111	Swiss Int'l	50.9
66	Dublin-DUB	17 138	137	Aer Lingus	31.3
67	San Diego-SAN	16 377	120	Southwest	31.3
68	Stockholm-ARN	16 364	109	SAS	42.5
69	Vancouver-YVR	16 065	100	Air Canada	44.2
70	Washington-DCA	15 932	97	US Airways	45.2
71	Brussels–BRU	15 584	108	SN Brussels	29.7
72	Brisbane-BNE	15 480	146	Qantas	44.5
73	Dusseldorf-DUS	15 257	121	Lufthansa	38.6
74	Manila-MNL	15 187	163	Philippine Airlines	29.5
75	Mumbai-BOM	15 179	160	Jet Airways	31.7
76	Osaka-KIX	15 090	240	Japan Airlines	25.6
77	Shanghai-SHA	14 880	155	China Eastern	39.4
78	Oslo-OSL	14 865	122	SAS	53.6
79	Seoul-GMP	14 843	198	Korean	52.5
80	Vienna-VIE	14 786	103	Austrian	58.5
81	Johannesburg-JNB	14 310	127	South African	54.7
82	Shenzhen-SZX	14 244	152	China Southern	29.0
83	Oakland-OAK	14 098	134	Southwest	60.1
84	Antalya-AYT	13 770	193	THY Turkish	21.4
85	Sao Paulo-GRU	13 728	181	Varig	39.2

Table 5.9 *Continued*

Airport-code		Passengers[a] (thousands)	Av. capacity per flight (seats)	Leading carrier	Flights by leading carrier (%)
86	Sao Paulo-CGH	13 648	128	TAM	44.5
87	Athens-ATH	13 641	125	Olympic	46.1
88	Pittsburgh-PIT	13 272	74	US Airways	66.4
89	Portland-PDX	13 037	98	Alaskan	47.2
90	Moscow-SVO	12 865	139	Aeroflot	56.7
91	St Louis-STL	12 803	81	American	56.9
92	Naha-OKA	12 733	208	All Nippon	45.7
93	Jeddah-JED	12 391	231	Saudi Arabian	70.1
94	Delhi-DEL	12 210	158	Indian Airlines	30.0
95	Moscow-DME	12 095	138	Siberia Airlines	24.7
96	Malaga-AGP	12 028	143	Iberia	23.5
97	Chengdu-CTU	11 690	141	Air China	39.2
98	Cleveland-CLE	11 247	70	Continental	64.9
99	Jeju-CJU	11 116	210	Korean	54.7
100	Berlin-TXL	11 048	122	Lufthansa	34.7

[a] Passenger numbers include both those originating or terminating their journeys at the airport in question and those making a transfer connection there. In these statistics each transfer passenger is counted twice, once on arrival and once on departure.

other league tables it is rapidly slipping down the list. One such table is by destinations served non-stop, in which Heathrow is now (in the Summer of 2006) down to fifth place:

	Non-stop routes
Frankfurt	262
Paris CDG	223
Amsterdam	222
Munich	204
London Heathrow	180

There is no necessary merit in maximising destinations, especially if this were to mean the inclusion of a lot of routes on which traffic is relatively thin. Even so, the gap opening up between Heathrow and its three main challengers is becoming very significant. To be able to describe itself as a global hub, or maybe as the 'aviation capital of Europe', an airport really must hold a leading position so far as the range of destinations served is concerned. The gap is widening, and the main reason for that is that Heathrow is more handicapped by shortages in airport slots, which in turn is due to the fact that it has fewer main runways than its rivals:

	Runways	Maximum flights per hour
Amsterdam	5	120
Paris CDG	4	120
Madrid	4	120
Frankfurt	3/4*	100/120*
London Heathrow	2	85

If the Heathrow hub is not to fall further behind hubs on the continent, some extra capacity must be found.

Finding suitable sites for additional airport capacity presents some very great difficulties. There is often little prospect of any immediate relief from new construction. The timescale for planning and building new runway and terminal capacity is long, typically up to 10 years. In the meantime congestion is a serious and growing problem. There are already many airports around the world, approximately 150 of them, that are subject to scheduling constraints of one kind or another, and the number might rise sharply in the years ahead. The pressures on airport capacities are increasing all the time. In liberalized air travel markets even more importance is attached to the S-shaped relationship between service frequency and market share. In order to maintain or increase their frequencies in more competitive markets, many airlines have been reducing the size of aircraft they fly. It used to be thought that the problem of airport capacity shortages might be ameliorated to some extent by an upsizing over time in aircraft types flown. But the increased emphasis on high frequencies (and also the introduction of smaller twin-engined long range aircraft) has meant that aircraft size has stopped growing, and there has been something of a reversal in trend, from upsizing in the 1960s and 1970s to downsizing in the 1980s and early 1990s. This same point is illustrated, for the world as a whole, in Figure 5.8. From 1960 to 1980 average aircraft size just about tripled from 60 to 180 seats, but since then it has remained fairly constant. Average-load factors have been on an upward trend rising from 60 to 70 per cent over the past 20 years. Some comparisons between frequency and aircraft size at the main US and European hubs (Table 5.10) show very clearly the effect that the increased emphasis on frequency competition has had on the average number of seats per flight departure over the past decade or so. The two London airports were the only two to experience a significant increase in aircraft size, this reflecting the need for airlines to operate larger aircraft because of the extreme scarcity of runway slots in London.

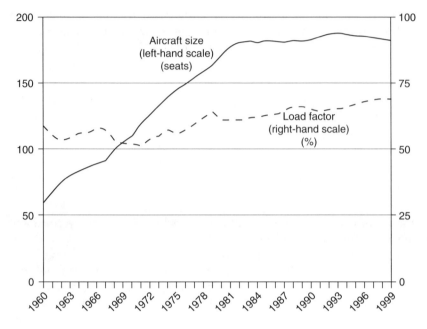

Figure 5.8   Average aircraft size and load factor, passenger aircraft on scheduled schemes, 1960–99 (*Source*: International Civil Aviation Organization)

The introduction in the 1980s of mid-size, high-technology aircraft, like the B-757, B-767, MD-80, and A-310 was an important factor in slowing down and then halting the upward trend in average aircraft size. In particular the use of B-767s on the North Atlantic, and to a lesser extent on transpacific routes, opened up many new airport-pair markets served with point-to-point flights. The next major aircraft innovations will be the arrival in a few years' time of the Airbus A-380 and the Boeing B-787 'Dreamliner'. The Airbus A-380 will become the largest airliner ever to enter commercial airline service. In a standard configuration of three cabins, the A-380 will have seats for 555 passengers, although in an all-economy configuration the absolute maximum could in principle rise to 850. These numbers can be compared with the 400 to 450 seats of the B-747s currently flying. The Boeing B-787 will be much smaller, with a maximum seating capacity of nearly 300 seats and a standard configuration of around 225 seats. One possible scenario is that the A-380s will be deployed on densely trafficked routes to/from congested hubs, whilst the B-787s continue and extend the role played up to now by B-757s and B-767s and operate in thinner markets with point-to-point services. What the net overall effect of these two developments will be on average aircraft size is difficult to say. The use of A-380s will, in itself, help to reduce the scarcity of slots problem at congested hubs; but this positive effect may

Table 5.10 Departures and seats per departure at main US and European hubs, July 1985 and July 1997. *Source: Airline Business*

Hub	Carrier	Departures per week			Seats per departure		
		1985	1997	% change	1985	1997	% change
Washington Dulles	United	103	1722	1572	200	67	−67
London Gatwick	BA	86	1163	1252	116	125	8
Los Angeles	United	520	1990	283	203	113	−44
Minneapolis	Northwest	940	3400	262	159	111	−30
Amsterdam	KLM	426	1416	232	178	129	−27
Brussels	Sabena	330	948	187	118	103	−13
San Francisco	United	894	2392	168	156	131	−16
Munich	Lufthansa	471	1206	156	128	105	−18
Vienna	Austrian	219	494	126	126	125	−1
Chicago O'Hare	American	1543	3327	117	165	117	−29
Dallas–Fort Worth	American	2584	5394	109	142	115	−19
Frankfurt	Lufthansa	936	1913	104	163	165	2
Zurich	Swissair	543	1109	104	148	130	−12
Atlanta	Delta	3219	5543	72	136	139	2
Chicago O'Hare	United	2263	3738	65	168	131	−22
London Heathrow	BA	1125	1642	46	178	212	19

be counterbalanced by an increase in congestion in the air, as a result of the much greater 'wake vortices' generated by air fanning out behind the A-380s wingtips. Safety may require other aircraft to fly as much as three times the normal distance behind it. This could significantly affect flight schedules at heavily congested airports such as Heathrow.

To meet increased traffic demand some airport expansion is taking place. A few new airports are being built, or have recently been built, notably those in Denver, Sydney, Hong Kong, Munich, Osaka, and Dubai; but for the most part the extra capacity is being provided by expansion of existing airports. In Europe, where some of the most serious capacity constraints apply, new runways have been opened, or are being planned, at Amsterdam, Madrid, Frankfurt, Paris CDG, Helsinki, Manchester, Oslo, Rotterdam, and Stockholm; but those cases apart, the plans are generally for more terminal or gate capacity.

Expansion of UK airports has been considered by the UK Department of Transport. The Department carried out a major consultation exercise following which it published its White Paper *The Future of Air Transport* in December 2003. This started from a prediction of future demand. The number of passengers using UK airports – which had increased five-fold over the previous 30 years – was predicted to almost treble over the next 30 years. To meet this demand the Department concluded that new runways would probably be required at Stansted, Heathrow, Edinburgh and Birmingham, and possibly in the longer term Gatwick and Glasgow as well. All new runways would be controversial proposals, but none more so than a third (main) runway at Heathrow. The White Paper supports the development at Heathrow but only on condition that some stringent environmental limits are adhered to as regards air pollution. The third runway at Heathrow is envisaged as one to be used by short-haul aircraft; and the Department of Transport would not expect it to be built until the 2015–20 period, after a new runway has been provided at Stansted (in 2011 or 2012).

With new runways at best some years off, is there anything else that could be done to relieve congestion at London airports? It is sometimes suggested that there should be a major diversion of traffic away from London and towards regional airports. There are a number of underlying problems in this. First, propensities to fly are much higher in London and the South East than in other regions of the country (as shown above in Figure 2.10). For a great many of air passengers an airport in the London area is their local choice and their most convenient. Second, apart from the relatively small airports at Bristol, Southampton, Cardiff and Exeter, most regional airports lie to the north of London. But most air routes out of the UK go in a southerly (south-easterly or south-westerly) direction, so that much additional travel, both air and surface, would be generated. If a lot of passengers resident in London and the South East were to be induced to fly from, say, Birmingham or from Nottingham East Midlands or from (one of the alternatives studied in the Department for Transport's consultation) a new four-runway airport situated outside Rugby, then a lot of extra resources are going to be used up in passengers travelling up to these airports. This would not fit in well with environmental objectives. Also, there must be serious questions about the capacity of surface transport to carry the extra traffic, given that road and rail links (e.g. the M1 motorway and the West Coast Main Line on the railways) are already very heavily used and operate close to capacity limits.

A policy of encouraging diversion might stand a greater chance of success if it focused, not so much on passengers in London and the South East, but more on passengers resident in the regions. Consider the Midlands region. Amongst the wealth of facts and figures presented in the Department for Transport's documents pertaining to Midlands airports, one stood out: almost half (49 per cent) of air journeys undertaken by passengers with origins/destinations in the Midlands are made using airports in other regions, predominantly the South East, but also other places, like Manchester. In other words the Midlands 'exports' much of its air travel to other regions. And a 'fly local' campaign promoted by the Department for Transport could do much to address this, especially if regional airports receive a more extensive range of services flown at higher frequencies.

To a large extent this policy is already underway. As already shown in Table 5.7, regional airports now receive a much increased level of frequent international services. This is also reflected in statistics on passenger throughputs (Table 5.11). Regional airports are now growing much faster, especially the likes of Liverpool, Bournemouth, Prestwick, Bristol, Southampton, etc. Regional airports now cater for a greater percentage of all passengers, with the two main London airports' share falling from 59 per cent in 1995 to 44 per cent in 2005. It is true that a great deal of the expansion at regional airlines is as an accompaniment to the growth in low-cost airlines; but it is also the case that foreign airlines with hubs on the continent have been stepping up services on what for them are spokes to the UK. Indeed it is now possible to fly to more UK regional airports from Amsterdam (21) and Paris (19) than from London Heathrow (9). Some domestic services from Heathrow have been withdrawn because of slot shortages.

Slot allocation

Pressure on existing airport capacities has led to slots being rationed. Take-off and landing slots are typically rationed in one of two ways, by 'traffic distribution rules' or by scheduling committees. Under the former, government authorities prevent certain types of air traffic (e.g. freight, general aviation) from using the busiest airports in peak periods, except on a highly restrictive 'prior permission' basis; and in scheduling committees,

Table 5.11 Passenger throughput at UK airports, 1995 and 2005[a]
Source: UK Civil Aviation Authority

		←2005→		←1995→		% change 1995–2005
		Passengers (thousands)	% of passengers at all UK airports	Passengers (thousands)	% of passengers at all UK airports	
1	London Heathrow	67 683	29.7	54 132	41.8	25
2	London Gatwick	32 693	14.3	22 383	17.3	46
3	Manchester	22 083	9.7	14 533	11.2	52
4	London Stansted	21 992	9.6	3890	3.0	465
5	Birmingham	9311	4.1	5193	4.0	79
6	Luton	9135	4.0	1810	1.4	404
7	Glasgow	8775	3.8	5423	4.2	61
8	Edinburgh	8449	3.7	3275	2.5	25
9	Bristol	5199	2.3	1431	1.1	263
10	Newcastle	5187	2.3	2486	1.9	108
11	Belfast International	4820	2.1	2346	1.8	105
12	Liverpool	4409	1.9	503	0.4	776
13	Nottingham East Midlands[b]	4182	1.8	1879	1.5	122
14	Aberdeen	2852	1.2	2243	1.7	27
15	Leeds/Bradford	2609	1.1	925	0.7	182
16	Prestwick	2405	1.1	313	0.2	668
17	Belfast City	2237	1.0	1281	1.0	74
18	London City	1996	0.9	554	0.4	260
19	Southampton	1835	0.8	511	0.4	259
20	Cardiff Wales	1765	0.8	1038	0.8	70
21	Durham Tees Valley[c]	898	0.4	428	0.3	109
22	Exeter	842	0.4	181	0.1	365
23	Bournemouth	829	0.4	99	0.1	737
24	Isle of Man	801	0.4	533	0.4	50
25	Coventry	719	0.3	4	<0.1	>10 000
	•	•	•	•	•	•
	•	•	•	•	•	•
	•	•	•	•	•	•
	Total all UK airports	228 214	100.0	129 586	100.0	76

[a] Passenger numbers include both those originating or terminating their journeys at the airport in question and those making a transfer connection there. In these statistics each transfer passenger is counted twice, once on arrival and once on departure.
[b] Formerly known simply as East Midlands.
[c] Formerly known as Teeside.

airlines bargain with each other for use of particular slots, with existing users having first entitlement, under a system of 'grandfather' rights, subject to a 'use it or lose it' rule (whereby if an airline was allocated the slot last year but used it less than a certain proportion (usually 80 per cent) of the time, the slot would be allocated to some other airline this year). Methods used to allocate airport slots form one of the most controversial topics in the whole field of air transport economics. Scheduling committees command wide support amongst airlines but have attracted criticism from competition authorities (e.g. Monopolies and Mergers Commission, 1990).

The way in which scheduling committees work is as follows. Each airline submits its application for slots about 6 months before the start of each travel season. The scheduling committee allocates the slots according to grandfather rights, the 'use it or lose it' rule and various operational criteria such as giving priority to regular year-round services and precedence to rescheduling to accommodate larger aircraft, rescheduling due to differences in daylight saving time, etc. Because of capacity constraints, not all airlines receive all the slots they ask for at the required times and, once the scheduling committee's allocation is announced, a process of trading takes place and airlines start swapping slots in order to improve their respective positions, with the committee acting as a kind of broker and only authorizing slot trades once it has checked there is sufficient terminal and apron capacity. This is the procedure that applies at most capacity constrained airports across the world, but in the US there are four airports where slots for domestic flights can be bought and sold for money, rather than merely swapped for other slots. The airports in question are Chicago O'Hare, New York Kennedy, New York La Guardia, and Washington National. At these heavily congested airports slots regularly fetch some high prices, anything up to $3 million depending on the time of day. It has been argued that monetarized slot trading is preferable to swapping for the following reasons: it makes trading more likely; it enables new airlines to enter the market without having to have existing slots to swap; it facilitates the leasing of slots; it should give airlines a legal title to slots and so permit mortgages to be taken out on them; it allows airlines in difficulties to sell out in whole or in part; and it offers airlines the option of selling or leasing out a slot rather than deliberately running loss-making services so as to avoid application of the 'use it or lose it' rule (Jones, Viehoff, and Marks, 1993). All this has proved possible at the four US airports where monetarized buy-and-sell trading takes place at present. The experience there has been somewhat mixed and there are clearly some major difficulties to be overcome in operating a free buy-and-sell market in airport slots. One is the problem of airlines acquiring matching slots. In order to operate a working timetable an airline does of course need both a landing and a take-off slot, both at the airport in question and at an airport at the other end of the route. The complexities involved in bidding for combinations of slots render any simple auctions rather difficult to conduct. For, in a free market, slot prices can vary quite a lot, not just by time of day but also from airport to airport. Nevertheless US experience suggests that a dynamic and fluid market can operate, and some airlines, like BA, are known to favour the introduction of a similar market in Europe (Starkie, 1994). Other airlines may go further. Richard Branson, the Chairman of Virgin Atlantic, has called for grandfather rights to be 'exterminated', as he put it. But that is certainly unlikely to find favour with incumbent airlines and unlikely to gain international acceptance. More recently, Virgin Atlantic that grandfather rights should at least be limited to a fixed period of time, for example 10 or 15 years (Humphreys, 2003). But such a restriction implies that slots are not in fact 'owned' by the airlines that use them. As Humphreys notes, airlines tend not to include any book value for its slots in its annual accounts (British Airways has in recent years included values for slots for which it has made a cash payment, although it assigns no value to the vast majority of the slots it historically acquired for nothing). Non-ownership of slots is also a logical implication of the 'use it or lose it' rule under which a slot can, under the EU Slot Regulation, be confiscated if the airline fails to make sufficiently intensive use of it.

Monetarized slot trading at the four US airports mentioned above has been taking place for more than 10 years. So, what can be learnt from it? For one thing slot trading should not in itself be expected to reduce the dominance of established airlines, perhaps the reverse. A study by the US General Accounting Office (1996) found that the established airlines' share of slots rose sharply in all four cases: between 1986 and 1996, American and United's share at Chicago O'Hare rose from 66 to 87 per cent; at Washington National the percentage held by American, Delta, and USAir went up from 25 to 43; the same three airlines saw their combined share rise from 27 to 64 per cent at New York La Guardia; and combined share of American, United, and TWA at New York Kennedy increased from 43 per cent in 1986 to 75 per cent in 1996. Some concern has been expressed about all this. Are substantial increases in slot holdings reinforcing the established airlines' dominance? In particular, is there anything to suggest that the established airlines have been buying up as many slots as possible in order to deter or drive out competitors? The possibility of established airlines doing something like this has been discussed by McGowan and Seabright (1989) who took the view that it is more likely for established airlines to direct any entry deterring or predatory behaviour to the services they operate rather than to the hoarding of slots. This may be a reasonable point in general terms but, as Starkie (1998) has argued, it is less convincing where the share of slots held by dominant airlines is already very high, as at Chicago O'Hare where over 85 per cent of slots is in the hands of American and United. When slot holdings are as high as this, the number of additional slots needed to forestall entry or pursue a predatory strategy could be rather small. However, if the established airlines acquire extra slots mainly to prevent them being used by competitors this might be reflected in lower slot utilization rates for the established airlines. But there is no evidence of this. For example, Kleit and Kobayashi (1996) examined the situation at O'Hare and found that American and United actually had higher slot utilization rates than their competitors (in respect of both the slots for which they had grandfather rights and slots they had leased).

In order to make room for new entrants to compete effectively – at peak periods and on roughly equal terms as regards frequency – slots might have to be confiscated from existing holders. But confiscation might cause a lot of dislocation and would very likely be strongly resisted by existing slot holders, some of whom might decide to close some of their services down rather than move them elsewhere. In February 1993 the European Commission introduced a regulation on slot allocation (Commission of the European Communities, 1993a), under which new entrants are offered up to 50 per cent of slots becoming available at congested airports, out of a pool containing new and unused slots. But the trouble is not all that many slots are in fact becoming available and incumbent airlines go to any lengths to hold on to those they have got. The UK Civil Aviation Authority (1993b) has argued that the EC regulation should be changed so that *all* newly created or unused slots are earmarked for new competitors and also that they be concentrated in such a way that effective 'third forces' can be established on as many routes as possible. In a review of how this appeared to work at Heathrow and Gatwick in summer 1994 and winter 1994/5 (Civil Aviation Authority, 1995) it was found that the regulation had little effect in encouraging competition from new entrants. This was partly because many of the slots allocated under the regulation were at different times of day to those requested by the new entrants: more than two-thirds of them were either before 07:00 or after 21:00, and many of these were simply returned to the slot co-ordinator. Another reason has been the limitation placed on the definition of a 'new entrant', this applying only to the airlines holding no more than 3 per cent of slots at the particular airport. As a result some established small- and medium-sized airlines remained ineligible, including for example British Midland at Heathrow despite its having been a most effective competitor on the routes for which it has been able to obtain sufficient usable slots. The regulation also excluded airlines such as Air UK, CityFlyer Express, and Jersey European from additional slots at Gatwick. Recognizing these points the CAA proposed a revised definition of a new entrant and came up with some detailed recommendations designed to ensure that as many of the newly created or unused slots go to airlines most capable of mounting effective competition to hub airlines at congested airports.

The UK Civil Aviation Authority and Office of Fair Trading recently issued a joint paper entitled *Competition issues associated with the trading of airport slots* (Civil Aviation Authority/Office of Fair Trading, 2005). In this paper strong support is given to the idea of slot trading. Some of the advantages the CAA/OFT see in slot trading are as follows. First, if airlines are able to buy, sell and lease slots, this will sharpen up the opportunity cost of holding slots. This should give airlines greater incentives to see slots to other carriers, which could use them more efficiently. It should also reduce rigidities in the current system of slot allocations and increase the opportunities to obtain slots. Another benefit concerns mergers or alliances. As argued below in Chapter 7, mergers and alliances can have both pro-and anti-competitive effects. To eliminate or reduce the anti-competitive effects, competition authorities have sometimes required divestiture of slots as a means of allowing an otherwise pro-competitive merger or alliance to proceed. With slot trading, airlines would be able to sell slots to meet the competition authority's conditions rather than simply give them away. It is possible that this will encourage some mergers and alliances.

The reason why so much attention is being given to slot allocation is that airport capacity constraints can confer on hub airlines some considerable market power. Once an airline is established at a particular hub, it often becomes very difficult for another airline to challenge it there, especially at peak times during the inbound and outbound waves in the hub airline's flight complexes. It is for this reason that the term 'fortress hub' has sometimes been used to describe an airport dominated by a single carrier. And when an airport is dominated there is always concern for the effects this might have on passengers.

5.6 Effects on passengers

The success of a hub and spokes system depends crucially on the airline's ability to control its traffic flows (and revenue yields) via the connecting bank of flights at the hub. Quite simply, hubbing will not work effectively without a major element of concentration.

The problem with concentration at hubs is that it tends to create a number of local monopolies, conferring upon the hub-based airline the ability to raise fares on routes to and from the hub itself. For passengers whose origin or destination is the hub city, there is often little competition. But the dominance of the hub-based carrier is often overstated, especially when comparisons of concentration are drawn in terms of enplanement data. The latter refers to the number of passengers boarding aircraft; and the

Table 5.12 Market shares of enplanements at highly concentrated US hubs, 1978, 1993, and 1999/2000. *Sources*: Button et al. (1998) and US General Accounting Office

Hub	1978		1993		1999/2000	
	Carrier	*Market share (%)*	*Carrier*	*Market share (%)*	*Carrier*	*Market share (%)*
Atlanta	Delta	49.7	Delta	83.5	Delta	74.3
Charlotte	Eastern	74.8	USAir	94.6	US Airways	90.0
Cincinnati	Delta	35.1	Delta	89.8	Delta	94.3
Dayton	TWA	35.3	USAir	40.5	–	–
Denver	United	32.0	United	51.8	United	69.5
Detroit	American	21.7	Northwest	74.8	Northwest	77.0
Minneapolis	Northwest	31.7	Northwest	80.6	Northwest	79.5
Nashville	American	28.5	American	69.8	–	–
Pittsburgh	Allegheny	46.7	USAir	88.9	US Airways	85.8
Raleigh–Durham	Eastern	74.2	American	80.4	–	–
St Louis	TWA	39.4	TWA	60.4	TWA	71.7
Salt Lake City	Western	39.6	Delta	71.4	Delta	71.7

hub-based carrier's share of total enplanements does of course include all connecting passengers. The dominant airline's share of total enplanements at its hub – in many cases between 60 and 90 per cent (see Table 5.12) – is often very much greater than its share of local originating/terminating traffic. Jensen (1990) cites the example of American Airlines at Raleigh–Durham in 1988: American's share of total enplanements was 69 per cent, but when connecting passengers are removed from the comparison, its share of originating/terminating traffic was just 39 per cent. Shares of total enplanements can be very misleading as indicators of the intensity of competition. The hub-based airline's share can go up simply when it adds new services (or spokes) to its existing schedules, or just because other carriers decide to withdraw from the airport in order to redeploy aircraft over their own hubs. In the US, hub and spokes networks have evolved to the point where one airline will generally fly to another airline's hub only from its own hub.

Despite these qualifications, there is no doubt that hub airlines enjoy considerable market power on local routes to/from the hub and, as shown in Table 5.12, the impetus given to hubbing by deregulation has greatly increased this market power. It has been argued that they have been using this power to charge average fares on routes to/from the hub that are significantly higher than average fares on other routes. A number of econometric studies (Borenstein, 1989; US General Accounting Office, 1990; US Department of Transportation, 1990; Berry, 1990) have all found significant positive correlations between the premium charged on fares to/from the hub (over average fares for routes of similar distance elsewhere) and the degree to which local markets are concentrated. Borenstein (1992) has illustrated this by comparing the extent of 'hubness' (represented by the percentage of passengers changing planes at the hub) with both the Hirschman–Herfindahl Index (HHI) of concentration and fares premia, in local markets to/from the hub. For the 30 largest US airports these comparisons are shown in Table 5.13. In this sample the zero-order correlation coefficient between the measure of hubness and the HHI is 0.74 and that between the HHI and the fares premium much weaker at 0.44. But once allowance is made for other factors, such as the mix of business and non-business

Table 5.13 Hubbing, concentration, and premium fares (30 largest US airports, second quarter of 1990). *Source*: Borenstein (1992)

Airport	Percentage changing planes	HHI	Average percentage premium	Rank by size
Charlotte	75.7	5790	18.8	20
Atlanta	69.0	3470	17.2	3
Memphis	67.7	3550	27.4	29
Dallas	65.8	3860	20.5	2
Pittsburgh	62.1	5290	15.9	16
Salt Lake City	61.3	4300	19.1	28
St Louis	56.2	3540	−4.0	13
Chicago O'Hare	55.7	2700	14.8	1
Denver	54.1	2720	15.3	7
Minneapolis/St Paul	51.0	4180	31.5	15
Houston International	49.5	4230	15.6	19
New York Kennedy	47.3	2020	2.9	6
Detroit	43.6	2960	−0.7	11
Baltimore	40.5	2990	9.1	26
Phoenix	33.1	2050	−28.4	9
Miami	31.0	1710	−14.3	14
Seattle	27.3	1450	−8.7	24
San Francisco	25.3	1450	−1.5	5
Los Angeles	25.2	1100	−5.3	4
Philadelphia	24.9	2170	11.2	22
Honolulu	22.4	1990	−20.8	17
Newark	19.6	2920	11.5	12
Las Vegas	18.9	1770	−27.8	23
Houston Hobby	17.5	4810	−23.4	30
Orlando	16.8	1800	−15.6	21
Boston	13.8	1200	9.0	10
Washington DC Nat'l	11.1	1250	10.7	18
Tampa	11.0	1810	−12.4	27
San Diego	6.0	1380	−18.1	25
New York La Guardia	6.2	1180	9.5	8

passengers in route traffic, the partial correlation between fares premiums and the HHI was found to be very much higher.

It is not only from airport capacity constraints that hub airlines derive market power. There are other factors involved as well. An airline with a large presence in a given city gains some important customer loyalty advantages from frequent flyer programmes (FFPs) and travel agency commission overrides (TACOs). Borenstein (1989) found FFPs and TACOs to be highly significant factors in explaining why dominant airlines can charge higher fares to/from the hub than other airlines serving the same route. The effect of FFPs and TACOs are especially important on business routes; and they increase market power by increasing the costs of switching from one airline to another, lowering cross-elasticities of demand, and reducing incentives for competitive price cutting. US experience has shown that airlines are following FFP and TACO strategies in areas where they have large market shares, such as on routes to/from dominated hubs.

Critics of US deregulation (e.g. Dempsey and Goetz, 1992) have stressed the adverse effects upon competition of increased market concentration to/from congested hubs. But at the same time it is clear that the development of hub and spokes networks induced by deregulation has enabled more airlines to provide through connecting services in city-pair markets that could not be served non-stop on a financially viable basis. So while competition *at* hubs has been falling, that *between* hubs has been rising. Later evidence (Belobaba and Van Acker, 1994) suggests that deregulation has had a positive effect in the top 100 (origin–destination) city-pair markets, about 70 per cent of which experienced an overall decrease in concentration between 1979 and 1991. Also, while reduced competition has led to higher fares on routes to/from hubs, increased competition between hubs has resulted in lower fares in through connecting markets.

One illustration is provided in the case of fares and service levels on routes to/from Akron, Ohio. Before deregulation Akron received only a few flights, mostly those operated by the old commuter airlines; but now, following deregulation, Akron is connected to no less than six or seven major hubs and, although each spoke from these hubs tends to be operated as a point-to-point monopoly, passengers boarding in Akron and travelling beyond the hubs are presented with an enormous choice of alternative routeings. Airlines can exert monopoly market power on local routes between Akron and each of the different hubs; but in markets for through journeys between Akron and the rest of the US, competition is fierce and fares have fallen substantially in real terms.

So, where hubbing results in increased market power on local routes to/from hubs and at the same time leads to greater competition in through markets via the hubs, how should the net result be weighed? Some through passengers may gain whilst other passengers on local routes lose; but do the pro-competitive effects outweigh the anti-competitive ones overall? There are reasons to believe that in many instances they do.

Many routes to/from hubs on which the anti-competitive effects of market power are likely to be most marked are relatively short hauls, whereas many of the through markets most likely to benefit from greater competition are relatively long hauls. If scheduling through hubs causes fares in through (long haul) markets to fall and fares in local (short haul) markets to rise, this can result in the structure of fares by distance reflecting more closely the manner in which average costs vary by route length. Cost per seat-mile bears a pronounced L-shaped relationship with route length, the cost per seat-mile on a flight of 300 miles often being around twice what it is on a flight of 1500 miles, for example. Fares per passenger-mile also taper with distance, but not in anything like as sharp a manner as cost per seat-mile does. Consequently price–cost margins are often much wider on long hauls than on short hauls. Hence, to the extent that hubbing reduces margins on long hauls, there could be some significant consumer gains to offset losses suffered on short hauls. Clearly the net balance will depend in particular cases on the relative volumes of traffic carried on long and short haul routes. It will also depend on price elasticities of demand. It is for short haul journeys that surface modes offer the most effective substitutes for air travel – especially rail travel in continental Europe, for example – so that there are at least some limits to the exploitation of market power in short haul markets. For this reason cross–price elasticities of demand are likely to be higher on short hauls, other things being equal. But at the same time aggregate own-price elasticities are likely to be higher on long hauls, given that business travellers, whose demand is known to be relatively price inelastic, tend to make up a larger proportion of total passengers on short hauls than on long hauls. So across the airline's entire network demand might rise overall. Also, if it is legitimate to consider the distribution of gains and losses in this context, the net balance between pro- and anti-competitive effects is likely to be 'progressive' in its impact. Most of the passengers gaining from the more competitive fares for through journeys will be those travelling on holiday or to visit friends and relatives. These are passengers who pay their own fares and who tend, other things being equal, to have lower average incomes than business travellers flying on short services to/from hub cities.

Given that hubbing can generate pro-competitive as well as anti-competitive effects, given that losses to some short-haul passengers might be offset, or more than offset, by gains to passengers making long-haul journeys, and given that hubbing may result in some significant density economies, there is no case per se for government authorities to deter airlines from forming and operating hubs. In many cases the positive effects may exceed the negative ones. But there may still be reasons for the authorities to be concerned about hubs. There may be some concern over the impact of hubs on the economics of direct flights and some concern about the environmental diseconomies associated with busy hub airports.

The presence of close competition from low fare airlines obviously influenced the pricing policies of hub airlines. Table 5.14 illustrates the effect by comparing markets in which dominant hub airlines faced competition from low-cost airlines with markets of similar distance in which the hub airline faces no competition from low-cost airlines. For instance, passengers travelling from Philadelphia to Atlanta appeared to benefit from AirTran's competition against US Airways, when the fares charged were very nearly the same; but passengers paid an average of $110 more to fly basically the same distance on US Airways from Philadelphia to Chicago, a market with no competition from low-cost airlines.

Table 5.14 Comparisons of selected hub markets in which dominant airlines face competition from low cost airlines with those in which no low-cost competition exists. *Source*: US General Accounting Office

Origin	Destination	Distance (miles)	Passengers per day (one way)	Average fare[a] (airline)
Atlanta	Boston	945	1130	$104.67 (Air Tran)
				$153.85 (Delta)
	Providence	902	82	$207.05 (Delta)
Dallas	Chicago[b]	795	576	$137.11 (ATA)
				$177.28 (American)
	Indianapolis	756	135	$254.04 (American)
Denver	Omaha	470	225	$141.95 (Frontier)
				$171.30 (United)
	Oklahoma City	493	79	$244.46 (United)
Detroit	Tampa	985	549	$103.92 (Spirit)
				$130.77 (Northwest)
	Dallas	981	434	$234.56 (Northwest)
Houston[c]	Baltimore	1232	392	$141.10 (Southwest)
				$215.01 (Continental)
	Pittsburgh	1124	117	$328.20 (Continental)
Philadelphia	Atlanta	666	1164	$92.71 (AirTran)
				$105.64 (US Airways)
	Chicago[d]	676	910	$216.18 (US Airways)

[a] Data for passengers and fares are for the period from the fourth quarter of 1999 to the third quarter of 2000.
[b] Fares and passenger totals shown are for ATA (American Trans Air) and American's service to Chicago Midway airport. American carried most of its Dallas–Chicago passengers to Chicago O'Hare airport.
[c] Fares and passenger totals shown are for Southwest's service from Houston Hobby airport and for Continental's from Houston's Bush International airport.
[d] Fares and passenger totals shown are for US Airway's service to Chicago O'Hare airport.

5.7 The future of hubbing

The success of low-cost airlines with their point-to-point networks, and the problems faced by full-service airline with their hub and spokes networks, has led some people to question the overall merit of hubbing. Are hubs doomed? That was a question posed to himself by Robert Crandall, the well-known former CEO of American Airlines, addressing the *Wings Club* in September 2004. His answer was: no, hubs are essential. Crandall admits that hubs are playing a smaller role than they did in the past, and that their role may become even less in the future. Only about 20 per cent of US domestic passengers now travel in city pairs that have no direct non-stop service. But the proportion of all city pairs which lack non-stop service is still very large; and many thousands of city pairs, both inside and out of the US, will never have point-to-point service. Therefore hubs, as connecting points, are and will remain the only way for many small cities to tie into national and international aviation systems.

In the past, when connecting times and service frequencies tended to be the most important factors, airlines ran their hubs so as to meet these desiderata. But now, the most important factor often seems to be the fare. In response to this some airlines are adjusting their hub operations in order to minimize costs rather than to maximize convenience. American Airlines, the airline that Crandall used to run, is leading the way here, with the introduction of its 'continuous' or 'rolling' hub concept.

In its long-established hub operations at Chicago O'Hare American Airlines used to schedule banks of 20 to 50 aircrafts to arrive and depart within minutes of each other. But the airline has 'de-peaked' its arrivals and departures, which now come and go in a steady stream across the operating day. The main advantage of a continuous or rolling hub is that it increases aircraft utilization rates, the number of hours flown each day, enabling the aircraft to be used on more services from which more revenue might be earned. Whilst the amount of time that aircraft spend on the ground at the hub does not change all that much, time is saved at the spoke airport, since the aircraft can be turned around and depart again as quickly as it can be reloaded. In the old hub and spokes operation, aircraft sometimes had to remain at spoke airports for relatively long periods. This was to ensure that their return to the hub was timed so as to be part of a bank of arrivals. This can be more of a problem when route lengths on the spokes are highly variable. The big disadvantage of a continuous hub is that it could impair the attractiveness of the airline's service to passengers who value convenience highly; and these are the passengers who pay premium fares whilst travelling on business. As mentioned before, revenues earned from premium fare passengers often represent a disproportionately large part of total revenues. So anything which endangers this could have serious repercussions on a full service airline's profit and loss account.

The continuous hub concept is not exactly something new. Essentially it is the same thing (under a different name) that some of the larger low-cost airlines in the US have been doing for years. Indeed a continuous hub can often make good sense for a low-cost airline. Southwest has been using them to carry one-third of its traffic as through transfer-connecting passengers (Dennis, 2005). A low-cost airline can often offer sufficiently large reductions in fares to persuade sufficient numbers of passengers to put up with longer transfers at the hub.

Low-cost airlines certainly pose a great threat to hub airlines, especially in short- and medium-haul markets. They are proving to be a more effective limit on hub airlines ability to earn monopoly profits than any action taken by the competition authorities. But hub airlines can still sometimes find themselves in a position to undermine the economics of point-to-point flights. When rival airlines seek to compete with a hub airline by meeting passengers' normal preference for direct non-stop flights, the hub airline might respond by (temporarily) undercutting fares in the affected markets, possibly financing reductions in revenues in the more competitive city pairs by higher revenues from elsewhere on the network. An airline operating a strong hub can often exercise fairly close control over tariffs. In a price sensitive market A–B it might be fairly easy to divert traffic via an intermediate hub X by discounting fares, something that might be done without affecting the primary justification traffic and without diluting revenues in the local A–X and X–B markets. An airline based at X and operating to both A and B need not impair its revenue yields in the A–X and X–B markets by reducing its fare for A–X–B travel in order to undercut a carrier that flies A–B direct. A hub airline relates costs to revenues across its network as a whole. Revenues might be maximized by reducing fares where its competitive position is relatively weak (in connecting markets) and raising them where it is relatively strong (on routes to/from the hub).

The main problem for the hub airline is to control the amount of capacity to be sold at discounts. Some close monitoring of sales is needed to ensure that the most lucrative traffic is carried, and it is here that CRSs perform a valuable secondary function in the management of revenue yields. In hub and spokes systems it is inevitable that some flights load more heavily than others and some passengers may have to be turned away because the flight on one sector of their required journey is full. For instance, spokes A–X and X–B may load rather heavily; and so selling one A–B ticket may be at the expense of selling two tickets A–C and B–D. The airline may therefore seek to control ticket sales for A–B, A–X, and X–B. The hub airline may find it profitable to leave empty seats on some spokes in order to accommodate extra passengers on others. At the same time it may be commercially attractive to offer deep discounts for through journeys on the lightly loaded spokes. The stronger the airline's position at the hub, the more scope it will have for discriminating in this way. The ability to exercise price discrimination carries with it the ability to engage in predatory pricing. The same point applies to another competitive weapon, service frequency; and the twin weapons of pricing and frequency provide powerful means by which airlines can defend their hubs against point-to-point operators who do not have the same network strength to draw upon. This is clearly something the government authorities should guard against. The issues involved are discussed further in Chapter 6.

Government authorities may also be concerned about the environmental diseconomies of hubs. If the objective is to minimize these, then the concept of 'wayports' may be worthy of further consideration. Wayports are basically airports constructed in remote, sparsely populated areas, with almost no origin and destination traffic, and dedicated more or less exclusively to handling transfer traffic; a kind of 'hub in the desert'. Wayports could be relatively cheap to build, costing around a third to a half the cost of a new airport in a metropolitan area. There might be little if any demolition involved, land would be much cheaper and the airport would require much less in the way of landside facilities such as check-in desks, car parks, surface transport links and so on. Wayports could be developed at some presently underused sites: a military airfield due for closure perhaps, or possibly a civil airport whose role has diminished due to some other change (e.g. three possibilities in Europe might be Shannon, Prestwick and Porto, all of which were once used as refuelling stops for transatlantic flights but which are now left with considerable spare capacity). Compared with airports close to densely populated residential areas, wayports would be somewhat safer locations for highly complexed hub operations.

However, creating a wayport at some remote location would raise a number of questions. (Who would staff the facility? Which airlines would want to operate there?) The local population might not be sufficient to run a large airport in an isolated community (e.g. in the interior of Nebraska, where it has been suggested a wayport could be sited in order to relieve congestion in Chicago). Also, there may be few airlines interested in serving connecting traffic on its own, since much of the scope and route traffic density economies airlines reap from hub operations derive from combining connecting traffic with local origin–destination traffic. On the other hand competition authorities should welcome wayports, insofar as multi-runway hubs away from major cities need not be dominated by individual airlines and could at least in principle cater for the flight complexes of several different carriers at different times of the operating day. At wayports there should be ample access for new entrants and also for feeder carriers.

Wayports might entail some huge financial risks but, as a means of relieving pressures on airports-serving metropolitan areas, perhaps they should not be dismissed out of hand. They would be long-term investments to meet the ever-increasing problem of airport capacities. But there would always be the danger of some of them turning out to be 'white elephants'. In the end the fundamental issue might be who is to finance and plan them: central government, local authorities, the airlines themselves, or some combination of all three.

The idea of a wayport as quite literally a hub in the desert can seem somewhat far fetched. If a wayport hub turns out to be successful, the place will not be a desert for very long, since a whole town, city, or even metropolis will spring up to service it. Take Emirates' hub in Dubai. This was not exactly set up in a desert, but before the airline started the city was much smaller than it is now. It has grown *pari passu* along with the airline. The same could happen in other places.

One result of terrorism and threats of terrorism is that security checks are becoming more rigorous and time consuming. This affects all flights; but an airline's hub operations could be more severely affected, if the authorities prohibit thorough check-in of baggage and if they also require through searches of passengers before they board each flight. The latter is likely to mean that MCTs will have to be increased. That will both push up costs and suppress demand. Hence, if the disturbances caused by terrorists continue, there could be serious repercussions for the economics of hubs.

6

Pricing power

Anyone who has bought an airline ticket will know it is possible to pay any one of a large number of different prices to fly a given route. Fares vary with time of travel, whether peak or off-peak; with class of travel, whether first, business, or economy; with the length of stay at the destination, whether it exceeds a certain number of days or weeks, or whether it includes a Saturday night; with where and when the ticket is purchased and paid for; whether the booking is made online, by telephone to the airline or via a travel agent; and with a whole host of other factors such as the size of the travelling group and the ages of any children involved. The multiplicity of fare categories is often so great that for scheduled service by a particular airline on a particular route – across the North Atlantic, for instance – there can be as many as 50 to 60 separate fares published in airline tariff manuals. The variation between fares can be such that it is possible for two passengers sitting next to each other on the same flight, and enjoying exactly the same quality of inflight service, to find that one is paying very much more than the other, in some extreme cases even more than double.

There is also extensive variation across routes. There are often marked differences in fare levels from route to route, even when the distance flown is roughly the same. Fare levels taper with distance, so that the fare per kilometre is often much lower on a long route than it is on a short one. But even allowing for this, in comparisons of routes of the same or similar length, some considerable differences remain. There are some wide differences by region. Table 6.1 draws some comparisons between International Civil Aviation Organization (ICAO) route groups. What stands out from this is that average fares – proxied by average revenue per passenger kilometre – were much higher in Europe than elsewhere. In interpreting these comparisons, two important qualifications should be made. First, no adjustment was made to allow for the taper in fares with distance. Given that there is a preponderance of short-haul routes in Europe, average revenue or fare per kilometre was always likely to be higher there. But even if some adjustments for this were made – as they were when ICAO fares data was available by route distance as well as by route group – the comparisons would still have shown European fares greater than fares in other route groups. The second qualification concerns the fact that the average revenues in Table 6.1 relate to the year 1999. A lot has happened since that time. Report

Table 6.1 Estimated average revenues per passenger kilometre by international route group.[a] *Source*: International Civil Aviation Organization (2003)

Route group	Revenue per passenger-kilometre (US only)
Between North America and Central America/Caribbean	7.5
Between Canada, Mexico and the US	7.4
Between North America and South America	7.8
Local South America	10.6
Local Europe	15.8
Between Europe and the Middle East	9.6
Between Europe/Middle East and Africa	7.3
North Atlantic	6.1
Mid-Atlantic	5.0
South Atlantic	6.3
Local Asia/Pacific	7.8
Between Europe/Middle East/ Africa and Asia/Pacific	6.0
North/Mid-Pacific	5.1
South Pacific	5.4

[a] On scheduled services in 1999.

after report, from bodies like the House of Lords Select Committee on the European Communities and the Air Transport Users' Council, levelled some strong criticisms at European fare levels. The general view was that European fares were very high. But not anymore.

Following liberalization, and following the arrival of the low cost airlines, the traditional full service airlines were forced to compete in terms of price. Some did so quite aggressively, including British Airways (BA). It launched its own website and began to take bookings online. It changed its fares structure to give passengers more flexibility and removed a lot of restrictions from its lower European fares, like the Saturday night stay. Other airlines did the same, and with the low cost airlines expanding rapidly and offering cheaper and cheaper deals to the passenger, European air fares have fallen sharply, especially since the Third Package of Liberalization Measures was introduced by the European Commission (EC) in 1997.

A study by Davies et al. (2004) examined changes in European air fares since 1992. Data was collected from the Galileo Computer Reservation System for 9 international and 3 domestic routes, all from London, for three fares categories (lowest business, lowest fully flexible, and lowest economy) which were then compared with the maximum fares agreed at International Air Transport Association (IATA) conferences and also with the UK's Retail Prices Index as a measure of inflation. The fares data was limited to full service airlines operating at least a daily weekday service or the routes concerned. The fares of low cost airlines were not included, not only because of lack of data but also because hardly any of them existed in 1992. The results are illustrated in Figure 6.1. The histograms show that the most remarkable changes took place in the level of the lowest economy fare. This had fallen 36 per cent by 1997 and 66 per cent by 2002. And these falls were purely in nominal terms. In real terms, after allowing for inflation, represented in Figure 6.1 by the height of the Retail Prices Index column, the falls are even greater.

Before too much is read into these comparisons it should perhaps be recognized that whilst air fares per se have been falling, other costs associated with air travel have been going on the opposite direction. The Davies et al. study only covered fares actually paid to the airline; it did not include the additional taxes, fees and charges (TFCs) that passengers often have to pay. These things were taken into account in another study, by the Air Transport Users' Council (2004) the results of which are summarized in Tables 6.2–6.5. The range of fares was found to be much wider for a full service airline like BA than for low cost airlines like Ryanair, easyJet. flybe or bmi. The cheapest fares tended to be offered, as expected, by the low cost airlines; but BA's fares for advance purchase often came close to matching those of the low cost airlines. The AUC study also consider the TFCs quoted by the airlines to cover items such as Air Passenger Duty, airport departure taxes, passenger service charges, and surcharges for fuel, security, insurance, etc. When added together these additional costs can often make up more than

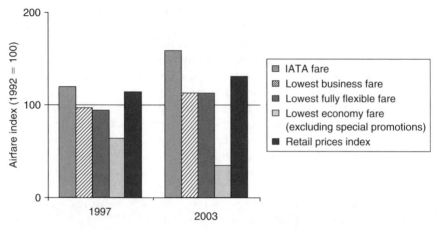

Note: See text for an explanation of coverage

Figure 6.1   Changes in indices of European air fares: 1992, 1997, and 2003 (*Source*: Davies et al., 2004)

half the total price paid by the passenger; and they vary widely from airline to airline even for travel over the same route.

The picture of air fare+TFCs can be a most confusing one; and some of the advertisements taken out by airlines can be very misleading on this account. Ultimately what the passenger is most concerned about is the total outlay for the round trip. In order to clarify this, the following is a breakdown of all the expenses incurred by the author on a Birmingham–Madrid round trip in April 2006:

	£UK
Return air fare (booked online)	69
Taxes, fees and charges	41
Credit card surcharge	2
	112
Hotel accommodation (3 nights)	225
Restaurant bills	100
Taxis to/from airports (4 rides)	50
Incidental expenses	13
Total outlay	500

Table 6.2 Comparisons of ranges in average return fares (£), 2003 and 2004.[a]
Source: Air Transport Users Council

Edinburgh–Birmingham[b]	
British Airways	55–269
flybe	59–252
Glasgow–Paris[c]	
British Airways	66–406
Ryanair	70–204
London–Berlin[b]	
British Airways	90–448
Ryanair	42–154
easyJet	44–132
London–Frankfurt[d]	
British Airways	82–526
Ryanair	35–234
London–Geneva[c]	
British Airways	80–488
easyJet	46–121
London–Glasgow[c]	
British Airways	47–290
Ryanair	45–330
easyJet	21–173
London–Paris[e]	
Bmi	49–259
easyJet	7–97
London–Stockholm[b]	
British Airways	119–486
Ryanair	40–156
London–Venice[f]	
British Airways	89–305
Ryanair	31–160
easyJet	53–135

[a] Fares were recorded for the cheapest and most expensive flights available to be booked on each airline for given lengths of stay at the destination (1 night or 1 week) and for different periods of advanced booking (1 day, 1–13 weeks).
[b] Fares recorded 1–8 November 2004.
[c] Fares recorded 19–25 May 2003.
[d] Fares recorded 28 April–4 May 2003.
[e] Fares recorded 28 April–5 May 2003.
[f] Fares recorded 27 September–4 October 2004.

As can be seen what was paid in fare amounted to slightly less 14 per cent of the total outlay for the round trip. The author recollects making exactly the same trip some 15 years previously and estimated that then the proportion the fare made up of total outlay was more in the region of 60 per cent. (In those days, there being no direct flights, the author had to make connections

Table 6.3 Variations in fares by duration of stay and by period of advance booking, 2003. *Source*: Air Transport Users Council

Average return fare (£) for travel	Next day	1 week later	4 weeks later	13 weeks later	Next day
Staying	1 week	1 week	1 week	1 week	1 night
London–Glasgow[a]					
BA cheapest	219	96	47	52	290
BA most expensive	223	161	80	73	290
Ryanair cheapest	117	51	51	45	290
Ryanair most expensive	199	145	121	105	330
easyJet cheapest	100	55	28	21	123
easyJet most expensive	162	95	63	48	173
London–Venice[b]					
BA cheapest	194	136	89	92	206
BA most expensive	245	239	203	135	305
Ryanair cheapest	56	31	33	41	81
Ryanair most expensive	160	58	58	88	257
easyJet cheapest	82	58	53	80	97
easyJet most expensive	112	66	81	106	135

[a] Fares recorded 19–25 May 2003.
[b] Fares recorded 28 April–5 May 2003.

Table 6.4 TFCs paid by passengers, selected routes and fares, November 2004. *Source*: Air Transport Users Council

Airline	Route	Total price	TFC	%TFC
KLM	Bristol–Amsterdam	£94.70	£52.70	56
BA	London[a]–Paris[b]	68.20	43.20	64
Bmi	London[a]–Paris[b]	55.90	39.90	71
easyJet	Luton–Glasgow	36.00	10.00	28
Ryanair	London[c]–Berlin[d]	41.00	25.00	61

[a] Heathrow.
[b] Charles de Gaulle.
[c] Stansted.
[d] Schonefeld.

via Heathrow. It wasn't possible to purchase the fare online; and travel arrangements precluded Pex/Apex/Saver tickets because of the 'Saturday night' rule. Also TFCs were insignificant.)

Although there must be a question about what is happening to total trip outlays, there can be little doubt that air fares have been coming down, not just in Europe but right across the world. But there is often still quite a wide variation in fares for a given route, for example from £290 down to £47

Table 6.5 Comparisons of TFC levels across different airlines, selected routes, November 2004. *Source*: Air Transport Users Council

Departure airport	Destination airport	Airline	TFC (£)
Southampton	Edinburgh	BA	35.70
		flybe	40.60
Glasgow	Bristol	easyJet	10.00
		BA	39.10
London[a]	Geneva	easyJet	14.00
		BA	33.90
London[a]	Barcelona	easyJet	9.50
		BA	28.90
London[a]	Amsterdam	easyJet	10.00
		BA	41.00
London[a]	Nice	easyJet	14.50
		BA	38.50
London[a]	Inverness	easyJet	16.50
		BA	34.50
London[a]	Dublin	Ryanair	28.16
		BA	37.70
London[b]	Valencia	Ryanair	22.02
		easyJet	9.50

[a] Gatwick.
[b] Stansted.

for a BA London–Glasgow return depending on how far in advance it is purchased (Table 6.3). Some quite dramatic comparisons can be drawn when the variation in fares for individual routes is combined with variation across routes. As one example, if one sets the cheapest economy return for London–New York against a business class return for a route like London–Rome, it is possible to find that the latter is more than double the former, leading to a question of why it should be more than twice as expensive to fly from London to Rome (1445 kilometre) than to New York (5565 kilometre). A comparison like this is not exactly on a like-for-like basis. The economy fare to New York is available on certain flights in off-peak periods, is valid for travel only on the airline taking the booking, has to be booked a long time in advance, is subject to minimum limits on how long the passenger has to stay before making the return journey, and does not permit stopovers nor any changes in reservations. The business fare to Rome on the other hand is fully flexible, available on demand for all flights, offers interlining facilities, imposes no restrictions on length of stay, permits any number of stopovers and affords the passenger complete freedom to alter reservations. There is also a vast difference in route lengths, with a significant tapering in fares per kilometre. Nonetheless, with all this said, the gap in fare levels is so wide as to suggest that airlines are able to discriminate against business class passengers on the London–Rome route and in favour of some economy class passengers on the London–New York route, charging in accordance with what passengers in each of the two markets will bear.

But before considering this further, it may be helpful to clarify exactly what is meant by discriminatory pricing.

6.2 Price discrimination

Doctors in private practice sometimes charge rich patients more than poor patients. Cinemas charge lower admission prices for children. Publishers of academic journals sometimes charge higher subscription rates to libraries and institutions than to individuals. And British universities levy higher tuition fees to students from non-EU countries than they do on home students. All these are instances of price discrimination, some being purer examples of it than others.

In economic theory price discrimination is held to be taking place when a producer charges different prices for different units of the same commodity, for reasons not associated with differences in the costs of supply. It occurs where price differentials do not directly correspond to differentials in cost. Price differentials often do correspond to differentials in cost. Differentials between peak and off-peak prices for instance are not in this sense discriminatory, insofar as they merely reflect the additional capacity costs incurred in catering for peak demand. Nor are such things as discounts for quantity purchases, to the extent that they reflect economies reaped by selling in bulk. Discrimination is being exercised whenever prices differ more than costs or, in what amounts to the same thing, whenever costs differ more than prices. The charging of uniform prices where costs differ significantly is just as much discriminatory as charging differential prices where costs are the same. It is only by comparing price–cost margins that one can asses whether prices for different customers are discriminatory. When price–cost margins vary, some customers are being discriminated against. More commonly customers paying higher prices are the ones discriminated against. But this is not always the case. It all depends on the size of the price differential relative to the size of the cost differential. Sometimes the discrimination is against customers paying lower prices, when the price differential is less than the cost differential.

In most cases of discrimination the greater influence is exerted, not by cost differentials, but by differences in demand elasticity. On the 'inverse elasticity rule', optimal pricing requires the firm to charge more where elasticity is low and less where it is high. If demand is inelastic, with price elasticity lying between zero and -1, a rise in price would increase the firm's total revenue; conversely, if demand is elastic, with price elasticity

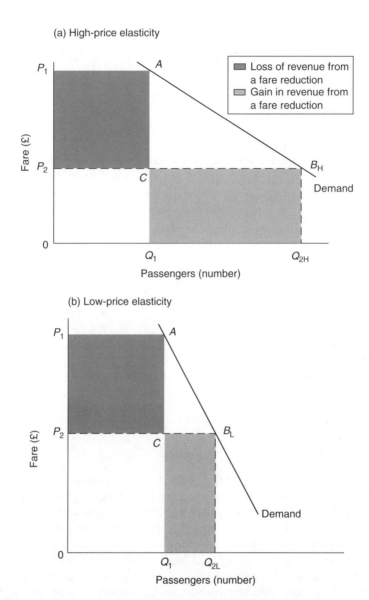

Figure 6.2 Pricing under high and low price elasticities of demand

less than −1, a fall in price would increase total revenue. It is customary to refer to a price elasticity between zero and −1 as 'low'-price elasticity and to a price elasticity less than −1 as 'high' price elasticity; and the effects of price changes under high- and low-price elasticities are illustrated in Figure 6.2. If from an initial situation (point *A*) in which price is P_1 and quantity Q_1, price is reduced to P_2, quantity will increase to Q_{2H} (point B_H) under high-price elasticity but only to Q_{21} (point $B_{L>}$) under low price elasticity. The impact on the firm's revenue will be favourable in the case of high price elasticity because the additional revenue from the $Q_{2H}-Q_1$ increment in quantity (area Q_1CBHQ_{2H}) will be greater than the loss on existing quantity caused by the P_1-P_2 reduction in price (area P_1ACP_2). The opposite will be the case with low price elasticity, the additional revenue from the $Q_{2L}-Q_1$ increment in quantity (area $Q_1CB_LQ_{2L}$) being less than the loss in revenue on existing quantity.

It is explained in many economics textbooks how a firm seeking to maximize profits sets price (P) at the point at which the marginal revenue (MR) earned from the last unit sold is equal to the marginal cost (MC) incurred in producing that unit. It is further shown that MR is a function of price elasticity of demand (E_p) via the relation:

$$MR = P\left(1 + 1/E_p\right)$$

when

$$E_p = \frac{dQ}{dP} \cdot \frac{P}{Q} < 0$$

where Q denotes the number of units sold.
Thus maximum profit requires that:

$$MC = P + P/E_p$$

or

$$(P - MC)/P = -1/E_p$$

The expression on the left-hand side is the (proportionate) price–cost margin, and profit maximization requires this margin to be higher where demand is inelastic and lower where it is elastic. This is shown in Table 6.6. If the price elasticity is -0.25, which implies that a 10 per cent increase (decrease) in price leads to a 2.5 per cent reduction (rise) in sales quantity, the profit-maximizing markup is as high as 400 per cent; and if the price elasticity is -5, which means that a 10 per cent increase (decrease) in price leads to a 50 per cent reduction (rise) in sales quantity, the profit-maximizing markup is only 20 per cent.

To vary the price–cost margin a firm must be able to distinguish between customers by magnitude of E_p, to inhibit those whose demand is relatively inelastic buying at prices intended for those whose demand is relatively elastic, and to prevent customers charged low prices re-selling to those who would otherwise be charged high prices. These requirements mean it is much easier to exercise discrimination in service industries, like air transport, than in markets for manufactured goods.

Table 6.6 Profit-maximizing markups of price over MC at varying price elasticities of demand

Price elasticity E_p	*Profit-maximizing markup (%)* $\dfrac{(P - MC)\ 100}{P}$
−0.25	400
−0.5	200
−1	100
−1.25	80
−1.5	67
−2	50
−2.5	40
−5	20

6.3 How airlines do it: yield management

Airlines prevent customers re-selling to each other by making tickets non-transferable. The customer's name is entered on the ticket and, for international travel, proof of identity in the form of a passport needs to be provided at check-in. Thus the process of arbitrage, which would be normal in markets for goods, cannot take place in the market for air travel. It is not possible for some customers to buy cheap tickets sometime in advance with the intention of selling them to other customers with a more inelastic demand closer to the time of departure.

From their market research, airlines know that high-income travellers, business travellers and those travelling for urgent personal reasons (e.g. to attend a funeral) have relatively price-inelastic demand. At the same time the airlines are aware that holidaymakers, those visiting friends and relations, students on vacation, etc. are all very sensitive in their demand to the fares charged. The price-inelastic travellers tend not to be able to book very far in advance, need fast and ready access to a seat on the flight or flights of their choice, want the flexibility to alter reservations at short notice, are generally subject to strict limitations on the time they can stay away at their destinations, and in some cases place a high value on the status or prestige afforded by travelling in relative luxury. The price-elastic travellers on the other hand are prepared to subordinate any preferences they might have so far as booking, seat access, reservations, length of stay and status are concerned to the benefit of being able to travel at lower fares. Differences between elastic and inelastic travellers in these respects are often rather wide and present airlines with good opportunities to segment

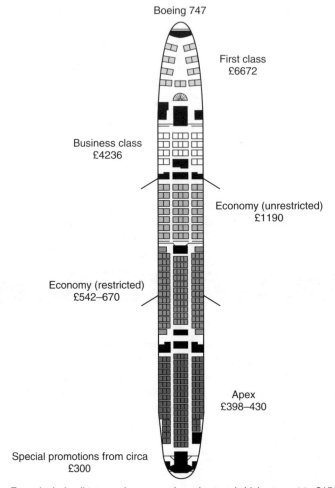

Boeing 747

First class
£6672

Business class
£4236

Economy (unrestricted)
£1190

Economy (restricted)
£542–670

Apex
£398–430

Special promotions from circa
£300

Note: Fares include all taxes, charges and surcharges (which amount to £156.50 for first,
club and unrestricted economy, and to £136.50 for restricted economy and apex).
Rates quoted are for online bookings (slightly higher fares applying for telephone
and other sales). If purchased using credit card, a further fee of £3.00 is incurred.

Figure 6.3 London–New York return fares, BA, November 2006 (*Source*:
ba.com)

the overall market by reason for travel and to use this as the basis for price
discrimination.

Discriminatory pricing is clearly evident in the structure of fares for individual routes, as illustrated in Figure 6.3 by BA London–New York fares.
There is an enormous range, from the first class return at one extreme down
to the cheapest special promotion at the other, a twenty-fold difference.

There are clearly some cost differentials between the various classes of travel, between first, business class and economy class. But it is doubtful that if cost differences can on their own explain, for example, the 350 per cent fare differential between business class and the most expensive fare for economy class. Passengers travelling business class have seats of greater width and pitch and receive a higher standard of catering than their counterparts further back in the aircraft; and so, on a fully allocated cost basis, seats in business class are clearly more expensive to provide than seats in economy class, due allowance being made for all the differences in capacity costs. Also, the average load factor is often lower in first and business, so that the cost differential widens when considered on a per-passenger basis. Airlines generally plan for an average load factor of around 60 per cent in business class as against 85–90 per cent in or economy class. Business class passengers can be regarded as paying for seats on demand, right down to a few hours before take-off. For that kind of service they are, as it were, also paying for the empty seats around them. Nonetheless the fare differentials are so huge – £2436 per passenger between first and business, and £3046 per passenger between business and the most expensive economy fare – that they can hardly be wholly justified by corresponding differentials in cost. The point applies more forcefully to fare differentials within economy class. Apart from some surcharges and discounts applying to fares for travel at peak and off-peak times, there is little prima facie reason in terms of airline costs to explain why passengers buying Apex tickets can fly for much less than half the full economy class fare. By far the greater part of the variation in economy class fares is due to discriminatory pricing.

Just to show that the London–New York fares in Figure 6.3 do not represent a isolated or special case, and also to illustrate how refined an airline's fares structure based on willingness to pay can be, Table 6.7 presents fares for the London–Johannesburg route. Note that the airline is now exercising discrimination within both first and business class, with the sale of first Apex, business Apex, and so on. And the graduations within economy class are becoming even more refined and precise.

Willingness to pay varies between passengers because of differences in 'consumer surplus'. In economic theory consumer surplus refers to the difference between what a passenger is prepared to pay for the service (rather than not be able to use it at all) and what he or she actually does pay when the fare is set by the airline. In a conventional price-and-cost against output diagram (Figure 6.4) points along the demand curve show what passengers are prepared to pay, and their consumer surplus is represented by the area between the demand schedule DD' and the appropriate price line. The airline may set its fully flexible fare for economy or traveller class to maximize profits at P_1, that is where MC = MR. At this price the number of seats sold is Q_1, leaving $Q_m - Q_1$ seats unsold. If the MC of an extra passenger

Table 6.7 London–Johannesburg return fares, BA, January 2006.[a] *Sources*: Airline Tariff Publishing Company and Worldspan GDS

Fare type	Fare level (£)	Bookings flexible?	Minimum stay	Advance purchase (days)
First	8194	Yes[b]	–	–
First Apex	3996	No	7 days	42
Business	5265	Yes[b]	–	–
Business Apex	3311[c]	No	–	7
.. ..	2876[c]	No	Saturday night	28
.. ..	2476[c]	No	Saturday night	42
Premium Economy	3416	Yes[b]	–	–
Premium Economy Apex[c]	1367	No	Saturday night	21
•	•	•	•	•
•	•	•	•	•
•	•	•	•	•
Premium Economy Apex[c]	991	No	Saturday night	21
Economy semi-flexible	1167[c]	No	Saturday night	–
•	•	•	•	–
•	•	•	•	–
•	•	•	•	–
Economy semi-flexible	591[c]	No	Saturday night	–
Economy seat sale[d]	456	No	Saturday night	–

[a] Fares include insurance/security/fuel surcharges and UK passenger service charge, but exclude government taxes.
[b] Reservations changeable; tickets refundable without penalty.
[c] A limited number of seats available at these fares, controlled by booking class (H, K, M, N, R, or V).
[d] Travel on selected dates only, for sales before 31 January 2006.

is constant up to the full capacity of the flight Q_m (at which point it rises vertically reflecting the additional costs incurred in putting on a second flight) then the airline may seek to sell the remaining seats and increase its load factor by reducing fares selectively, selling some at P_2, some at P_3, and so on. Different passengers enter the market at different fare levels. Those who are able to book a long way in advance, but have a relatively low willingness to pay, may be charged P_4; and if the airline has any seats remaining on the day of departure, it may sell these off as standby tickets (i.e. at MC). By discriminating between passengers the objective of the airline is to expropriate as much as possible of what would otherwise be passenger consumer surplus if all seats were sold at MC (the shaded areas in Figure 6.4). The purpose of restricting the availability of the cheaper fares is to inhibit passengers trading down from more expensive fares, or to limit what in airline parlance is called 'revenue dilution'. From experience airlines know

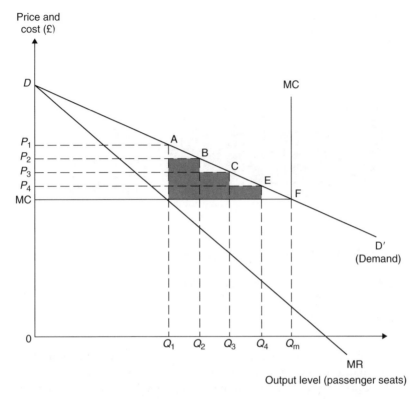

Figure 6.4 Price discrimination and consumer surplus

approximately how many seats to assign to passengers paying different fares and can vary the number of seats sold at each fare from flight to flight, and even on the same flight at different points in time up to departure. They also know how passengers purchasing different categories of fares tend to make their bookings, in particular how far in advance they book, as illustrated in Figure 6.5. Passengers buying business class accommodation often make their reservations only a few days in advance, whereas those travelling on advance purchase excursions and the lowest economy tickets are often able (or required) to book some weeks in advance. In some ways it would be easier for airlines to discriminate if it were the other way round, with the higher-fare passengers booking first. But the use of sophisticated computer reservations systems (CRSs), with finely tuned algorithms in 'yield management' programs, has greatly increased the facility for airlines to forecast the most revenue-enhancing seat allocation. And some airlines do this for each and every flight they operate.

Is it desirable for airlines to exercise discrimination and charge according to willingness to pay? The answer to this might vary with whose interest is

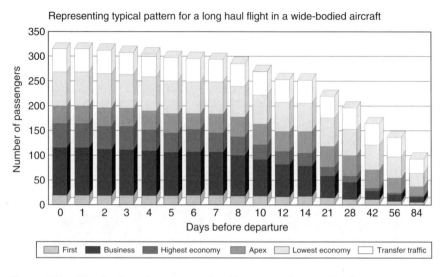

Figure 6.5   Distribution of passenger bookings over time and by fare category (*Source*: British Airways)

being considered, whether it is that of the airline, that of passengers with elastic demand who would not have travelled unless the fares structure discriminated in their favour, or that of passengers with inelastic demand who find themselves discriminated against. The airline must gain from discriminatory pricing. Otherwise it would not engage in it (except by mistake). Indeed, whenever it is possible, price discrimination is a necessary condition for the airline to maximize its profits. But compared with uniform pricing, discrimination is clearly seen as undesirable by passengers for whom price is raised and desirable by passengers for whom price is reduced.

Is it fair?

To the general public discriminatory pricing can sometimes appear rather unfair. But not always. Discounts for the young or for the old are generally approved of, even where price–cost margins are very low or perhaps even negative. Children's fares are often offered at discounts, when the child occupies a seat and receives the same (if not more) attention from cabin staff as adult passengers do. (And a further point is that children do not of course make inflight purchases of duty-free tobacco, alcohol and perfume, on all of which the airline may make a small profit.) On most scheduled services the discount for which children between the ages of two and twelve are eligible is 50 per cent of the applicable fare, whether business, full economy or excursion. Infants under two and not occupying separate seats are

charged 10 per cent. To a certain extent these are discounts for quantity purchases, in that children mostly travel in the company of their parents. But
to a more significant extent they reflect the greater elasticity in family
demand. Even so public opinion is rarely if ever against lower fares for
children.

Similarly, public opinion is not so much offended if the discrimination is
'progressive' in its effects, in the sense of impacting adversely upon the
relatively rich and tending to benefit passengers less well off. In the air
travel context this is often not so great an issue as it is when discrimination
is practised by other modes. For air travellers all tend to come from the
higher-income groups anyway (see Figure 2.8). There is some variation by
income within the population of air travellers: income levels vary with
country of residence; the average incomes of international passengers are
higher than those of passengers flying domestic routes; and business travellers tend to have higher incomes than leisure travellers. To the extent that
demand elasticities vary in much the same way, that is lower in rich countries, on international routes and for business travellers, discriminatory air
fares do indeed have something of a progressive impact.

Business fares

Business travellers often complain about the degree to which airlines discriminate against them. There is some justification for business travellers
paying higher fares, when they get almost instant access to seats, have
greater flexibility in making and changing reservations and enjoy higher
standards of comfort and inflight service. But business travellers sometimes argue that the additional amounts they have to pay for these privileges are excessive. Why, they ask, should people who have to travel in
the course of work have to pay so much more than people going away on
holiday, simply because their travel requirements preclude them meeting
the length-of-stay and advance-booking eligibility criteria for the lower
fares? A business class fare can often be some multiple of an Apex fare and
this, they argue, is inequitable. But differences between fare categories can
appear somewhat wider than differences in their real burden on different
groups of travellers. To begin with, business fares are mostly paid, not by
the travellers themselves, but by their companies, for whom expenditure
on air travel is a pre-tax item, whereas excursion fares are usually paid per-
sonally by holiday travellers out of post-tax incomes. This of course is a
general point that applies to all kinds of expenditure by firms and individuals. But the fact that air travel is a pre-tax expense for many companies
was one of the reasons why airlines originally identified businessmen as a
market segment capable of bearing higher fares; and comparisons of the
impact of different fares upon different kinds of traveller might well take
the tax effect into account. If for instance this is done by deflating business

fares at the appropriate marginal rate of tax on company profits, the difference between business and excursion fares narrows quite considerably. The importance of the tax factor obviously varies from company to company. Some companies do not make sufficient profits to be liable to company tax anyway, especially when they have substantial allowances to set against their tax liability. Also the significance of differences in direct taxation is declining over time, as governments pursue policies of shifting the burden of financing public expenditure from direct to indirect forms of taxation, that is from company and income tax to value-added tax, excise duties, etc. Rates of company and income tax have fallen quite appreciably over recent years and this could partly explain why sales of first and business class fares have been so slow to recover from the economic recession and why more and more companies are requiring their business travellers to trade down to economy class.

Business travel tends to be concentrated rather heavily among executives employed by large multinational companies and it is known that most of these organizations adopt fairly specific policies on things like class of travel, fare types, etc. (see Table 6.8). Among the more important factors are the seniority of the traveller and the length of the journey. Considerations of comfort and the need to be fresh enough to be able to conduct business at the destination mean that more of the executives qualify for first or business class as the distance to be flown increases. And passengers occasionally have other, sometimes more compelling, reasons for choosing first or business class. (Kenneth Galbraith, the late Emeritus Professor of Economics at Harvard University used to be is a prime example: at 6 foot 8 inches tall, and in his eighties, Galbraith insisted on travelling first or business when going on lecture tours, explaining that he found it difficult to squeeze into economy class accommodation!) The greater importance of comfort and fatigue

Table 6.8 Class of travel for company executives. *Source: The Times*

	Board directors	Senior managers	Middle/junior managers
Short-haul flights			
First	12	1	–
Business	40	30	14
Economy	42	62	77
Varies	6	7	9
Long-haul flights			
First	19	3	1
Business	49	46	26
Economy	17	34	53
Varies	15	17	20

All values are percentages.

factors on long journeys has some effect in lowering price elasticities of demand on the longer routes, especially when there are fears that long-haul air travel might be closely associated with the illness of deep vein thrombosis (DVT). This is reflected in wider differentials between fares on the longer routes. But the ability of airlines to exploit low price elasticities of demand has been curbed recently by many companies tightening up on their travel policies, in a new era of cost-conscious austerity. Some years ago a survey by the Civil Aviation Authority (1988) indicated that, in the matter of travel policies, UK companies divided into two broad groups: those for whom price was a relatively minor consideration, with quality of service being the paramount consideration; and those for whom price was a more significant factor. Recent indications are that the number of companies in the second group is growing rapidly. To cite just a few examples: GKN has eliminated all entitlements to first service; IBM has adopted an economy-only ruling for transatlantic flights to the US East Coast, even for the chief executive; and ICI is implementing a policy of buying discounted economy class fares for the outward leg of an executive's journey, only permitting the purchase of fully flexible fares, business or economy, for the return journey. Studies by ICI showed that 80 per cent of changes to their executives' reservations, if a trip has to be extended or cut short, occur on the return leg. ICI's top executives still travel business class on long-haul flights, but the company's other representatives travel out a day early and take a day off to recuperate, and the company finds this cheaper than booking them business class. More and more companies are doing something similar, all looking for ways of reducing the size of their travel budgets, not simply as a result of the harsher economic climate they face generally, but also perhaps because of the declining significance of the tax 'cushion'.

It is when they have to purchase fully flexible tickets that business passengers may feel most discriminated against. These tickets have always been aimed at passengers who may have to change their bookings after the ticket has been purchased. Such passengers have long exhibited price-inelastic demand, stemming from the fact that they often had no choice but to pay a business class or full economy fare. No choice that is, until the low cost airlines began to offer something different. Low cost airlines in Europe have achieved a great deal of success in attracting business passengers (Mason, 2001) and they have now developed a means by which passengers can pay for changes in bookings as and when they need them. Business passengers don't need to change their bookings all that often – on only one out of three short-haul trips to Europe (Mason, 2006) – but their problem is they don't always know in advance when they need to change. Many low cost airlines sell only one-way tickets, and offer only one fare for a particular flight at any one point in time. The lowest fare is offered when the flight first becomes available and the fare increases step-by-step as the departure date draws near. What some low cost airlines now offer business travellers is a kind of 'pay-as-you-go' flexibility: the passenger can change flights by paying the difference between the fare for the flight to which he or she wishes to transfer and the fare paid at the time of booking *plus* an administration charge (usually around £UK10).

Will something similar be developed for passengers on long-haul routes? Some entirely new business class only airlines have started up in the last 2 or 3 years. Air France was first, with its 'Dedicate' services marketed as a specialist operation for executives in the oil industry. Then came an airline known as Privatair which operates business class only services on behalf of other airlines: Amsterdam–Houston on behalf of KLM; Dusseldorf/Munich–Newark and Dusseldorf–Chicago for Lufthansa; and Zurich–Newark for Swiss. But perhaps the most relevant development in the present context are the services introduced between London and New York by Eos, MAXjet and SilverJet. Eos is offering an up-market Stansted–Kennedy luxurious service tailored specifically for business passengers, possibly seeking to resurrect a 'Concorde-like' passenger experience of exclusivity. By contrast MAXjet, which also flies between Stansted and Kennedy, is directing its attentions to the lower end of the business class market, offering return fares at around £800 plus TFCs. The third airline, the most recent new entrant SilverJet appears to be positioning itself midway between the first two, offering 'flat-bed' business class seats on its Luton–Newark service for £999 + TFCs return. But will business class only services become more widely available? One problem in launching business class only service is that, in order to attract business passengers, they ought to be offered at fairly high frequency, at least once, and preferably twice, a day in each direction. There are not that many city-pair markets, like London–New York, which can support several business class only airlines at that frequency. But there are some; and it would not be surprising if business class only services start appearing on more of the most densely trafficked routes in the future.

When might all passengers gain?

The question of whether price discrimination is fair or unfair involves making value judgements. Do the gains to those charged less outweigh the losses suffered by those charged more? There is no unambivalent way of resolving that issue on economic analysis alone. It is possible however to envisage circumstances under which, at least in theory, everyone gains from discriminatory pricing.

One special situation in which all passengers gain when the airline practises price discrimination is where demand is too weak to permit profitable operation of the service under uniform pricing. The added revenue gained through price discrimination may be sufficient to make the difference in whether or not a service is supplied at all. If without discrimination nobody is given the opportunity of using the service, then all passengers must gain when discriminatory fares are charged, including the passengers paying the higher fares, since they can exercise a choice which would not be open to them if the airline could only charge uniform prices. This kind of situation might occasionally arise on thinly trafficked routes to remote areas.

It has been argued that this can be a more general effect; that where discrimination results in seats being sold in an elastic market in which none would be sold by an airline charging a uniform fare, all passengers benefit from lower fares. One line of reasoning used to support this proposition is that the price to passengers paying the higher business or full economy fares would have to be even higher, if more seats in the aircraft were left unoccupied rather than filled by passengers stimulated to travel by the lower excursion fares. This was essentially the view expressed some years ago by British Airways (1977) when it defended its fares structure on European routes against some criticism from the Airline Users Committee (1976), arguing as follows:

> The economics of scheduled airline operation have been greatly improved by the traffic expansion lower fares have generated . . . Paradoxical though it may seem, promotional fares are helping to hold normal fares down.

It is worth considering this argument in some detail. On any given flight the cost per passenger is lower, the lower the proportion of unoccupied seats. This may be so, but why would so many seats be left unoccupied in the first place? The proportion of unoccupied seats, the reciprocal of the load factor, is a measure of the degree to which capacity is in excess of demand. To reduce this proportion, to raise the load factor, there are basically two courses of action open to the airline: either it can reduce capacity or it can attract more passengers by reducing fares. Reducing capacity can take one of two forms, a reduction in service frequency or a downsizing in the type of aircraft operated. Both of these things have their disadvantages: under competitive conditions a cut in frequency could seriously damage an airline's market share, and a smaller aircraft has a higher-cost per seat mile. So the alternative of promoting passenger demand through lower fares aimed specifically at the more elastic segments of the market can have some cost justification here. It permits the operation of a larger aircraft and/or a higher frequency of service than would be warranted for the carriage of the less elastic passengers alone. Take for example an airline currently operating a particular route with a Boeing B737 which is considering upsizing its aircraft type to an Airbus A320. The A320 has 150 seats compared to 110 in the B737. Clearly it would cost more per hour to fly the A320, but because of the A320's greater capacity, cost per seat-mile would fall by about 17 per cent or so (Doganis, 2002). Passenger demand currently justifies four B737 flights a day but, at the same load factors, only three if the A320 is flown. Service frequency can be a very important factor in attracting the first/business/full economy passengers, for whom schedule convenience can often be a more significant factor in choice of airline than the level of the fare. So replacing the B737 by the A320 and operating one less flight a day could threaten the loss of some high-yield traffic. But if the airline stimulates total demand by introducing a wider range of low fares for price elastic excursion passengers, this may still make it possible to take advantage of the A320's reduction in cost per seat-mile without sacrificing daily frequency. But an increase in excursion passengers would reduce the average fare paid and would raise the load factor at which the airline would break even on the service. If the breakeven load factor rises above the actual load factor, the airline would lose money on the service. In that event the airline would need to find some way of increasing revenue, the burden of which would likely bear more heavily on the first/business/full economy passengers, since any significant increases in fares charged to the more elastic excursion passengers would price many of them off the aircraft. If the demand of first/business/full economy passengers is less elastic with respect to fares than it is with respect to service frequency, the airline could choose to increase the fares these passengers pay rather than reduce the A320 frequency.

Hence the argument that business/full economy class passengers gain from the carriage of excursion passengers at discounted fares is a difficult one to sustain as a general principle. There is certainly a lot in the suggestion that discounted fares used to fill up aircraft already committed to a service improve the economics of scheduled operation. But whether they serve to hold down business/full economy fares in the long run is doubtful and this is something that would need to be demonstrated.

6.4 Discrimination and competition

To many people the most important consideration in deciding whether discrimination is good or bad is what it does to the level or intensity of competition. Does it help or hinder competition? Are its effects pro- or anticompetitive?

In its effects upon competition discrimination is something of a two-edged sword. It fosters competition by making it easier for firms to experiment in their pricing. Firms are less reluctant to change prices, if the changes do not have to be implemented across the board in each and every market served but can be applied selectively in a restricted number of test markets. Discrimination can also undermine pricing discipline in oligopolistic situations, removing price rigidity and causing firms to lose confidence in any form of collusive pricing. In order to utilize capacity more fully, some firms may offer secret concessions to selected customers usually through an intermediary (such as, in the airline context, a travel agent or consolidator). Sooner or later other firms find out and match or undercut the concessions. As the concessions spread, published prices become increasingly unrealistic, so that eventually they are formally reduced, benefiting all customers, not just the favoured few. It is possible to argue that the practice of airlines channelling sales of heavily discounted fares through unofficial travel agencies – often referred to pejoratively as 'bucket shops' – have in these respects had some positive effects on the intensity of competition. The same is also borne out by experience of deregulation in the US, but this shows that, if one reverses the question – what effect does the intensity of competition have on the prevalence of discriminatory pricing? – the relationship is very much a two-way simultaneous one. In the regulated era up to 1978, discriminatory air fares were effectively banned on US domestic routes (Civil Aeronautics Board, 1973); but since then there has been a veritable explosion in the number of passengers travelling on discounted fares, and the size of the discounts has increased sharply too.

The other side to the discrimination–competition relationship is where dominant firms with high market shares seek to weaken their competitors, by focusing price cuts on markets in which they face relatively fierce competition, whilst maintaining, or perhaps even increasing, prices in other markets in which they enjoy a greater degree of market power. This was what Laker Airways claimed IATA airlines on North Atlantic routes were doing in the late 1970s and early 1980s. In a price war for excursion passengers the IATA airlines made deep cuts to the levels of their Apex and other promotional fares, but only on routes on which Laker Airways operated its Skytrain service. According to Virgin Atlantic Airways much the same kind of thing is happening again now. In Europe the operators of non-scheduled services often used to complain that scheduled airlines cross-subsidized low fares on routes on which they competed with charters (e.g. to the Iberian peninsula) by higher fares on routes where there was no charter competition (e.g. to Scandinavia).

Discrimination between markets based on the existence of competitive alternatives is also evident when direct and indirect operators serve the same city pair over different routes. When for instance hub airlines compete with point-to-point operators they often seek to match, or undercut, each other's fares, even when there are wide differences in their respective operating costs. In the deregulated US domestic market it was not unknown for discrimination between markets based on the existence of competitors to be carried to the extent that a hub airline would charge less for a journey beyond the hub than for one terminating there. (For example, passengers flying from Washington to Cleveland via Detroit sometimes paid less than passengers only flying the Washington–Detroit sector.) But despite the cost disparity, if direct and indirect operators did not seek to match each other's fares, effective competition would be impaired. The same phenomenon is often present in international markets, when sixth freedom airlines compete against the services of third and fourth freedom airlines. In a bilaterally constrained situation, a sixth freedom operator can only compete with third/fourth freedom airlines, for the same traffic from the same catchment area to the same destination, by carrying passengers via an intermediate stop en route. To overcome the marketing disadvantage of the additional journey time, the sixth freedom operator may have to discount its through fares heavily in order to attract traffic. The sixth freedom operator may still find this worth doing, if the additional traffic enhances the profitability of the two sectors involved. Under these circumstances competition might well be diminished if the sixth freedom operator were to be denied the right to undercut the fares of third/fourth freedom airlines, even if its costs are higher. In any case it is by no means always the case that the sixth freedom operator's cost are higher. In some situations they might even be lower, especially if the carriage of through traffic leads to significant density economies.

In one sense, what Laker, Virgin Atlantic and the charter operators have complained about is no less than one would expect from the inverse elasticity rule. The most fundamental determinant of elasticity magnitude is the availability of close substitutes. Where airlines face competition, passengers have close substitutes; where passengers have close substitutes, their price elasticity – or more especially their cross-price elasticity – is high; and where elasticity is high, airlines will set fares at relatively low markups over cost. Nothing in this seems any different from the normal process of competition. Firms in other industries do exactly the same. But the complaints of Laker, Virgin Atlantic et al. went somewhat further in suggesting that what the IATA airlines were doing amounted to predatory pricing.

6.5 Predatory pricing

Broadly defined, predatory behaviour is conduct by a dominant firm designed to eliminate, restrict or deter competition. In relation to pricing it has often been described as the practice of temporarily selling at prices below cost, with the intention of driving a competitor from the market, so that in the future prices can be raised and higher profits made.

Is it rational?

It has sometimes been argued that predatory pricing is not a rational policy for a dominant firm to pursue, and that therefore it is unlikely to occur.

On this view predatory price cutting may not be all that sensible because it is typically more expensive for the predator than for the prey. By cutting prices to a level below cost and forcing its victim (or victims) to do the same, the predator forces everyone into a loss-making situation. So if the predator's market share is, say, four times that of its victim its losses from this may also be four times as great. But the predator expects to reap gains from the exercise once its victim has disappeared from the scene. And whether or not predation is economically worthwhile from the predator's point of view depends on the net present value (NPV) of the exercise.

Mathematically this can be expressed in the following way. Where the predator suffers losses of Λ_p in each period in which it is engaged in a price war with its competitor, but gains extra profits of π_p as a result of killing its rival off, if it takes t periods to drive the rival from the market, then at an interest rate of r representing the predator's opportunity cost of capital funds:

$$
\begin{aligned}
\text{NPV (predation)} = {} & -\Lambda_p - \Lambda_p (1 + r)^{-1} - \Lambda_p (1 + r)^{-2} \\
& - \cdots \cdots - \Lambda_p (1 + r)^{-t} + \pi_p (1 + r)^{-t+1} \\
& + \pi_p (1 + r)^{-t+2} + \pi_p (1 + r)^{-t+3} + \cdots \cdots
\end{aligned}
$$

If the NPV is positive, predation is economically worthwhile and therefore rational, even although the Λ_p losses suffered by the predator are of much greater magnitude than the losses suffered by the prey. Predation is only irrational if the NPV is negative. In other words it is only irrational if, in present value terms, the firm's losses outweigh its gains.

It may take rather a long time (t periods) for the predatory scheme to work and in the meantime the Λ_p losses may mount up to some considerable sums. Hence it has been suggested that a cheaper route to the π_p gains may be through purchasing the rival firm, although a tightening in government merger controls may effectively rule that out.

Where the competition authorities are prepared to sanction a takeover (e.g. to protect jobs) this may be a more profitable course for the dominant firm to adopt. For driving out a competitor by predatory pricing does not ensure the removal of capacity from the industry, given that the assets of the firm driven off can be sold and used by another firm to enter the market. In the airline context, assets most likely to be transferred to a new entrant include aircraft, aircrew, managerial expertise and, most crucially of all in some cases, take-off and landing slots at congested hub airports. The π_p gains following the exit of the prey are expected to come through the predator being able to increase its price–cost margin. But the scope for this may well be less, when the demise of one competitor is simply followed by the emergence of another.

It may be that the objectives of the dominant firm are better served by out-right purchase or merger than by predatory pricing. But this alone does not make predation an irrational policy. Predation can produce some important strategic benefits for the predator. It may for instance serve the purpose of 'softening up' the rival firm causing it to revise downwards its expectations of future profits, making it willing to sell out at a lower price. Predation is of course only one means of preventing or limiting competition; and a dominant firm may use it only when it is less costly than some other means of raising entry barriers. The scope for raising entry barriers, including those related to predation, may be enhanced by takeovers or mergers, if this increases the market power of the remaining firms.

How can it be detected?

Predatory pricing is notoriously difficult to prove and this makes it difficult to police. It is very difficult to distinguish between a reduction in price with predatory intent (made in order to force out a competitor) and one which represents competition 'on its merits' (rendered possible by savings in cost or by revenue-enhancing yield management).

In an influential paper Areeda and Turner (1975) proposed a test based on cost. The Areeda–Turner test, which has been embraced by the US courts in a number of antitrust cases, holds that a price is predatory if it is set below a firm's short-run MC. But what exactly is the firm's short-run MC? Formally, MC is the addition to total cost resulting from the last unit of output. It refers to those elements of cost that can be avoided or escaped if the last unit is not produced. This very much depends on the time frame considered. So how short is the 'short run' in this respect? In the very short run, MC may be negligible or close to zero, especially in a service industry like air transport.

Airline output is an instantly perishable commodity which cannot be stored if demand is less than supply. Once the aircraft door is closed, a seat which may have been on the market at a fare of several hundred pounds suddenly becomes worthless. Empty seats represent a waste of resources. The additional costs incurred in carrying an extra passenger on a flight that is going to be flown anyway may amount to little more than an airport passenger's charge, the cost of any food or drink consumed in flight plus a fractional increase in fuel burn due to the extra weight on board. In those circumstances it would pay the airline to get whatever it can from the sale of the seat rather than fly it empty. There is often excess capacity in times of economic recession. Thus it is no accident that these are just the times when complaints of airlines pricing below cost tend to be most frequent (e.g. in the early 1980s and then again in the early 1990s). But many of the low fares sold during these times are designed to attract passengers to otherwise unoccupied seats. Whilst low they are usually above – well above – the relevant short-run MC.

There are always problems in determining MC, both in defining the marginal unit and in identifying the costs that can be attributed to it; but these problems are particularly difficult in air transport. The most

fundamental problem is that the marginal unit of demand (a passenger journey) is not the same as the smallest unit by which supply can be varied at
the margin (in most circumstances, an aircraft journey). Except where seats
are sold in blocks (e.g. on a part-charter basis to tour operators and travel
agencies) it is the marginal unit of demand which has to be used as the pricing unit, but it is the marginal unit of supply to which the costs relate.

Recognizing this kind of difficulty Areeda and Turner suggested the use
of average variable cost (AVC) as a proxy for short-run MC; and they argued
that a price ⩾AVC should be regarded as competition on its merits, but
that a price <AVC should be condemned as predatory. They qualified this
basic rule by allowing prices <AVC in periods of weak demand or excess
capacity. Areeda and Turner would not therefore regard as predatory temporary reductions during times of economic recession, nor standby fares
and other fares sold on a space-available basis, like some of those sold
through bucket shops. They would also sanction promotional fares <AVC
sold by firms without market power. This could mean that a new entrant
could charge <AVC without being accused of predatory pricing, but if an
established carrier with a certain degree of market power were to do so,
that would be classed as predation.

How then is AVC to be measured? Variable costs are those that would be
escaped if a flight or series of flights (i.e. a service) were to be discontinued.
This includes all costs specific to individual flights: fuel, crew expenses,
passenger service costs, airport and en route charges, aircraft handling costs,
travel agency commissions, some allocation of engineering and maintenance costs, and so on. Items such as these are escapable more or less immediately once flight activity is scaled down. But over a longer term, many
other costs became escapable too, if the withdrawal of the flights is permanent and aircraft can be disposed of, staff numbers cut, sales offices shut, etc.
Given that airlines do not have to make infrastructure investments in navigation facilities, runways or terminals, the air transport industry is one in
which the ratio of fixed to variable costs is fairly low and 'as much as 90 per
cent of total costs can be varied in the medium term by discontinuing all
operations or by a partial withdrawal of certain operations' (Doganis, 1991).

Notwithstanding the problems involved in dealing with temporal dimensions in cost escapability, it is relatively easy to assess the AVC of a particular service. A far more difficult problem is how to allocate this between the
various different categories of fares, first, business, full economy, Apex, etc.
A great many of the costs incurred in operating a flight are incurred jointly
on behalf of all fare categories. It is possible for these joint costs to be
allocated to categories in accordance with space requirements (i.e. seating
densities) and load factors. But if the Areeda–Turner test is to be applied to
particular fares, the question that really needs to be answered is what costs
would be escaped if there were no sales at all in the category concerned. The
most difficult issue concerns the treatment of capacity costs. It can be argued

that a disproportionately high share of capacity costs should be allocated to the first/business/full economy categories since, as illustrated before in the A320 versus B737 example, the airline needs to schedule high services at high frequencies in order to sell these fares. To a certain extent the higher frequency requirements of the first/business/full economy categories are reflected in higher space requirements and lower load factors, but the frequency–space–load factor inter-relationships are not all that close and may vary quite a lot between airlines, aircraft types and routes.

Where it proves difficult to arrive at an unequivocal allocation of costs between fare categories, it will be simpler to test if the revenue generated by all fare categories is greater or less than the variable costs incurred. In other words, is the average fare paid greater or less than AVC? If the average fare is less than AVC, then this might be considered by the competition authorities as prima facie evidence of predation taking place. But one problem with this is that it could induce an airline wishing to avoid being accused of predatory pricing, to discriminate still further against price inelastic passengers and to raise its more expensive fares beyond their otherwise most profitable levels, merely in order to disguise some predatory intent in a lowering of its cheaper fares.

Another problem arises in how the revenue is assessed, in particular that earned from fares sold to connecting passengers. Because of the taper in fares with the length of a passenger's journey, the through fare paid by the passenger is normally less than the sum of the separate fares for each flight sector involved. Hence the carrier on each sector has to accept something less than its local point-to-point fare. Where the passenger makes an inter-line connection, the IATA pro-rating method shares out the revenue in proportion to the distance of each sector, with shorter distances given greater weight to allow for higher operating costs per seat mile. But where the passenger makes an online connection, the value of the revenue earned by the shorter sector may be much greater than the weighted distance in the IATA method would suggest. If the route plays an important role in feeding (possibly high-yield) traffic to other (possibly long haul) routes in the airline's network, its effective contribution to the airline's total revenue can be much greater than the pro-rated division of through fares. The increasing emphasis on hub and spokes networks means that differences in this respect are becoming more and more important.

The problems of identifying the precise costs and revenues associated with particular fares mean that it is always going to be difficult to apply a criterion like the Areeda–Turner test, to determine whether an airline is engaging in predation by pricing below cost. This might partly explain why the US antitrust authorities, which have pursued cases of predation against firms in other industries, have yet to take a single airline to court on a charge of predation. The heavy burden of producing proof may also have deterred a number of civil suits, despite the possibility award of triple damages under US law. Proving anything is bound to be difficult, when an airline's short-run MC is close to zero, or when the airline can use its computerized yield management systems to cut fares selectively whilst ensuring that revenue still covers AVC for the service as a whole. But the burden of proof would become heavier still, if it were admitted that fares *above* costs can sometimes be predatory too.

Can a fare above cost be predatory?

As a number of academic economists have argued (Joskow and Klevorick, 1979; Vickers, 1985; Tirole, 1988) pricing below cost is a sufficient condition for predation to be taking place, but not a necessary one. A price can still have predatory intent even when set above short-run MC or above AVC. In the formula for NPV (predation) given above, all that is necessary for predation to be rational is that the predator's sacrifice of current profits (the Λ_p losses) is less than the expected increase in future profits (the π_p gains). The Λ_p losses need not be accounting losses but only a reduction in profits from what they would have been, had the firm not sought to set a predatory price. Hence a more comprehensive definition of predatory pricing might omit any reference to cost, as in the one put forward by Joskow and Klevorick (1979):

> *Predatory price behaviour involves a reduction of price in the short run so as to drive competing firms out of the market or to discourage entry of new firms in an effort to gain larger profits via higher prices in the long run than would have been earned if the price reduction had not occurred.*

In other words an airline need not actually lose money on the service for its fares to be predatory: it only has to earn less profit on it, accepting a lower $(P - MC)/P$ margin than it earns on other services elsewhere.

A dominant airline that can make selective price cuts in a small segment of its market will aim to do so in such a way that they inflict maximum damage upon its competitor(s) at minimum cost to itself. The low fares may thus apply only over a limited number of seats (possibly some within each class) and not over the whole of the dominant airline's market share. Selective cuts in fares may also have an important 'demonstration effect' on potential entrants. Although the fares may never fall below short-run MC or AVC, the dominant airline may still be able to deter entrants by setting its fares at something less than profit-maximizing levels, as part of a policy of 'limit pricing'. Limit pricing means keeping fares low enough to ensure that entry by new airlines (or expansion by existing carriers) is not profitable. A new entrant airline may not have the same scope for selective pricing and therefore its low fares may have to apply across a large part of its market share. Hence it is possible for some low fares to be profitable for the dominant airline (albeit rather less profitable than before they were reduced) but unprofitable for the new entrant.

Thus predation can involve fares above or below costs. The signal conveyed to the prey about its future profitability matters as much as the predator's sacrifice of current profit (Milgrom and Roberts, 1982). If anything, predation with fares above costs is the more likely scenario.

Allegations of predatory pricing

It has been argued that predation is both a feasible and viable strategy for some airlines to adopt (Dodgson et al., 1990). The Organisation for Economic Co-operation and Development (1988) holds the same view, arguing that, when airlines operate in many different city-pair markets, predatory pricing in one market can be financed through cross-subsidization out of revenues earned in other markets, especially if entry to the other markets is restricted in some way. A former chairman of the US Civil Aeronautics Board, considering predatory pricing to be a likely and rational response by incumbent airlines to the arrival of low cost new entrants, characterized as a 'lamentable failure of the administration' the fact that no action had been taken against a single case of predation (Kahn, 1988). So far there have not been that many formal inquiries into allegations of predatory pricing by airlines. In a survey of cases in Organisation for Economic Co-operation and Development (OECD) member countries, none of the investigations related to the airline industry (Organisation for Economic Co-operation and Development, 1989).

One notable case in the US concerned the reaction of Northwest to the arrival of People Express on the route between Newark and Minneapolis/St Paul in 1983. Before People Express came onto the route, Northwest offered an unrestricted one-way economy class fare of $263 and a number of restricted fares, the lowest of which was set at $149. People Express charged just two fares, initially set at $99 (on weekdays) and $79 (for evening and weekend travel). Northwest responded by introducing two new restricted fares, just below those of People Express, at $95 and $75, announcing them in full-page advertisements in the press. At the same time Northwest stepped up its service frequency, from 10 to 13 flights a day. And when People Express reduced its fares to $79 and $59, Northwest matched them. People Express then felt it necessary to cut frequency, from 6 to 5 daily flights; but Northwest maintained its number of flights at 13 a day. In this case the new entrant offered the low fares on all seats, whereas the incumbent's low fares only applied to a limited number of seats. The competition authorities may have felt that Northwest's objective was to drive People Express off the route, but apparently feared that any intervention on their part would only make matters worse.

In a case that went before an antitrust court in 1993 the plaintiffs were Continental and Northwest and the defendant American. Continental and Northwest alleged that American was pursuing a predatory policy by introducing a 'Value Pricing' plan under which full coach fares were cut by 38 per cent and advance purchase excursions by 50 per cent. Continental and Northwest argued that American was trying to drive competitors from the market by pricing below cost with the intention of raising fares to supracompetitive levels to recoup losses once competitors had been eliminated. American responded by saying that its Value Pricing plan was merely an attempt to simplify consumer choice in a highly competitive market. The airline also made the point that, in such a competitive market, any attempt at predatory pricing was, in its view, doomed from the outset. In the event the court found in favour of American Airlines, the verdict accompanied by the opinion that the predatory scheme suggested by the plaintiffs would have been extraordinarily expensive and would have had no realistic chance of success. The court case proved to be rather expensive itself, something in the region of $20–30 million being spent on legal fees. The Chairman of American, Robert Crandall, complained that the large amount of resources which had to be devoted to a defence against the suit 'threatened the very existence of the company' (McKenna, 1993). And both the costs of the case and the ultimate verdict must have some effect on the readiness of airlines to bring such suits in the future. If the costs are forbidding for major carriers like Continental and Northwest, then they certainly must deter many of the low-cost airlines from taking legal action (Clouatre, 1995).

American Airlines found itself in court again in 1999, this time defending itself against a suit alleging predation brought by the US Department of Justice (DoJ) in the District Court of Kansas. As the judge wrote, the case

> . . . arises from competition between American Airlines and several smaller low cost carriers [Vanguard, Western Pacific, and SunJet] on various airline routes centered on Dallas-Fort Worth from 1995 to 1997. During this period, these low cost carriers created a new market dynamic, charging markedly lower fares on certain routes. For a certain period of time (of differing length in each market) consumers of air travel on these routes enjoyed lower prices. The number of passengers also substantially increased. American responded to the low cost carriers by reducing some of its own fares, and increasing the number of flights serving the routes. In each instance, the low fare carrier failed to establish itself as a durable market presence, and eventually moved its operations, or eased its separate existence entirely. After the low fare carriers ceased operations, American generally resumed its prior marketing strategy, and in certain markets reduced the number of flights and raised its prices, roughly to levels comparable to those prior to the period of low fare competition.

The plaintiff alleged that American monopolized or attempted to monopolize, through predatory pricing, seven airport-pair markets radiating out of Dallas Fort Worth, namely those to Kansas City, Wichita, Colorado Springs, Long Beach, Phoenix, Tampa, and Oakland. In addition the charge included a further 40 or so other airport-pair markets which American was accused of attempting to monopolize through its reputation for predatory pricing, a reputation it sought to enhance through its action in the seven market specified above.

The DoJ argued that American's response to the entry of the low cost airlines was over-aggressive; and that its fare reductions and capacity expansion made no business sense except for their effect in driving new entrants off the routes concerned. It was thought that American's aggression was due to its fear that the low cost airlines might establish a mini-hub at Dallas Fort Worth, similar to that established a little earlier in Atlanta by ValueJet, something which had reputedly led to a hub carrier there, Delta Airlines, to lose revenue to the tune of US $232 million (Edlin and Farrell, 2002; Gillen and Lall, 2005). With a potential loss of this sort of magnitude at stake, American was thought to have a strong incentive to sacrifice some current profits. The DoJ estimated this sacrifice at US $41 million, a sum there was a reasonable expectation of American recouping once there was less competition in the seven markets, and once the airline started to benefit from an enhanced reputation for predation elsewhere. Nonetheless, the District Court found for the defence, practically on the ground that American had not actually undercut its competitors' fares, merely matched them. The Court rejected the counter argument that if quality of service differences between American and the low cost airlines were taken into account, then acquiescing in American charging the same fare as the low cost airlines would be tantamount to allowing it to effectively undercut its competitors. That, the Court said, would require it to make a series of price comparisons based on intangible values. In delivering its verdict the Court noted that (in mid-2000) there were seven low cost airlines serving Dallas-Fort Worth, more than any other hub airport. It was relevant that at least 31 of the top 50 destinations from Dallas-Fort Worth were served by low cost airlines.

American Airlines was by no means the only major airline to be accused of predatory pricing. In 1995, Vanguard Airlines complained to the Department of Transportation (DoT) about what it claimed were the anticompetitive activities of Northwest. As shown in Figure 6.6, Northwest responded sharply and swiftly to Vanguard's entry into the Minneapolis–Des Moines market. By the third quarter of 1995 Northwest's average one-way fare on the route had fallen 68 per cent compared to what it was a year previously. Once Vanguard had withdrawn from the market, Northwest's fare rose to levels higher than it had been before. By the second quarter of 1997 it had risen to US $244, five times greater than the US $48 fare Northwest charged during Vanguard's brief time on the route (Dempsey, 2002).

A number of low-cost airlines in the US, feeling that they have been targeted for predatory action by the majors, formed themselves into a group, the Air Carrier Association of America (ACAA) to lobby for government support. The original members of the group included Air Tran Airways,

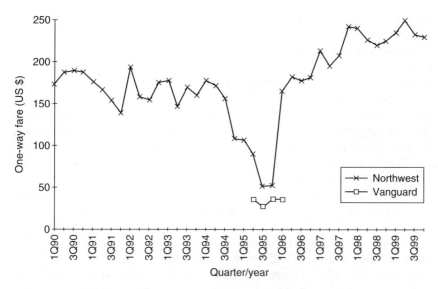

Figure 6.6 Average one-way fares on the Minneapolis–Des Moines route, 1990–2000 (*Source*: US Department of Transportation)

Arrow Air, Carnival Air Lines, Frontier Airlines, Sun Jet, Spirit Airlines, and ValueJet. Their main concern has been the majors' targeting of their low cost services from small cities into the major hubs. One extreme case frequently cited was that of the Atlanta–Mobile route, on which Delta raised its fares more than 500 per cent once ValueJet had withdrawn its service (Walker, 1997). Another case (US Department of Transportation, 1998) concerned Northwest's response to the entry (and subsequent exit) of Spirit Airlines to the Boston–Detroit route. In the first quarter of 1996, just before Spirit began offering service on the route, Northwest's average fare was $258.83. Following Spirit's entry with fares in the $69–159 range, Northwest's average fare fell to $106.05 in the second quarter of 1996 and $100.01 in the third quarter, a decline of 61 per cent. Spirit left the route at the end of the third quarter, claiming that it was driven out by Northwest's sharp cuts in fares. Northwest then raised its average fare to $189.52 in the fourth quarter and $267.54 in the first quarter of 1997. A very similar sequence of events apparently took place on the Denver–Billings route, on which Frontier Airlines challenged United and ended up being driven out after United had dropped its average fare by almost 50 per cent; and following Frontier's exit United's average fare rose to a level some 23 per cent above the level prevailing before Frontier entered. Cases like these, plus an increasing number of bankruptcies among low-cost airlines, including the failures of Air South WestPac and Pan Am, produced greater Congressional pressure for something to be done about the reactions of majors to the entry of low cost competitors.

Similar issues have been raised by low-cost airlines in Europe. In 1994, the EC investigated complaints from Ryanair that Aer Lingus had responded to its entry to the Dublin–Birmingham route by cutting fares to below costs. The EC made what was referred to in the press as a 'dawn raid' upon the head office of Aer Lingus, presumably in an attempt to obtain documentary evidence of Aer Lingus's intent. In submitting its complaint Ryanair argued that Aer Lingus was only able to match its new low fares by financing price cuts out of the IR£175 million of state aid that the EC had approved some months earlier.

Two cases have been raised by easyJet. One concerned the reaction of KLM to its entry to the Stansted–Amsterdam route. In a submission to the EC in 1997 easyJet claimed that KLM was trying to price it out of the market and cited as evidence an internal KLM memorandum which spoke of the need 'to stop the growth and development of easyJet and to make sure that this newcomer will not be able to secure a solid position in the Dutch market' (Skapinker, 1997). KLM did not deny the existence of the memo but said that it was not an official document. Nonetheless easyJet argued that KLM had contravened Article 86 of the Treaty of Rome, which prohibits abuse of a dominant market position. Then in a further case, in February 1998, easyJet took BA to a UK High Court seeking an injunction to prevent BA operating its own low cost subsidiary, Go. The ground on which easyJet sought an injunction was that BA was preparing to cross-subsidize Go out of profits earned on its main network, thus enabling Go to compete in the low-cost market on an unfair basis. Part of the case easyJet made was that Go had 'been given permission by BA to lose £29 million and then close in 3 years having put its rivals out of business' (Cassani, 2003). The injunction was not granted. But later in the same year easyJet applied to the EC asking for Go's lowest one-way fare on the Stansted–Edinburgh route, a fare of £15 (or £25 including airports tax), to be barred. There is a certain irony in reporting these cases now. For, just those 3 years later, BA sold Go to none other than easyJet – for a sum of £374 million.

Another airline to register a complaint with the EC was Air Liberté in France. Early in 1995 a fierce price war broke out on the Paris Orly–Toulouse route. This route used to be one of the most profitable routes in France, until the monopoly previously enjoyed by Air Inter was broken by liberalization of route licensing and the entry of two airlines, Air Liberté and Euralair. Air Inter responded to the new entry by launching a Fr540 'super leisure' return fare, at less than a third of its own standard fare and undercutting Air Liberté's inaugural promotional fare by Fr100. Air Liberté replied with a fare of Fr360, which was immediately met by Air Inter with a further cut in its super leisure return to Fr280. The complaint Air Liberté made to the EC demanded the immediate termination of the Fr20 billion of state aid to Air

France, which now owns Air Inter, on the ground that the condition applying to the EC's approval of it, namely that French domestic routes should be opened up to competition, was still not in effect being realized. And Air Liberté also made a second formal complaint, this time to the French Government, demanding that Air Inter should be required to offer similar cuts in fares on its other domestic routes, where it did not face such competition. Air Inter rejected Air Liberté's viewpoint and argued that it should be left free to offer promotional fares where and when it wishes. In the event Air Liberté got into financial difficulties and its owners decided to put the airline up for sale. It was eventually bought by BA which merged it with its other French subsidiary TAT European Airlines. The fact that Air Liberté's slots, aircraft, route licences, etc., remained in use lends at least some support to the argument that, even if successful in causing the original airline to exit, predation does not remove capacity from the industry. So if indeed Air Inter's policy was to drive Air Liberté from the market, this may have only resulted ultimately in one competitor being replaced by another (more formidable) competitor in the shape of a BA subsidiary.

If when hearing the American Airlines case the District Court of Kansas was reluctant to get involved in assessing service quality differences, this was not something to disconcert the Bundeskartellamt, the German Cartel Office, one of the strictest of competition authorities. In 2002 the Bundeskartellamt charged Lufthansa with predatory pricing on the Berlin Tegel–Frankfurt Main route. After Germania, a new competitor, entered this airport-pair market with a fully flexible fare of €198, Lufthansa reduced its fully flexible fare from €485 to €200, a drop of almost 60 per cent. This could be seen as a price-matching response, but the Bundeskartellamt took the view that Lufthansa was setting its fare below its average operating cost per passenger and stated that 'the only rational explanation for this pricing strategy is that it is an attempt to force Germania from [the] route and to recoup resulting losses at a later stage by discontinuing this price tariff and resorting to previous ones' (Bundeskartellamt, 2002). The Cartel Office also felt that Lufthansa's lower fare stripped Germania of its only competitive advantage; and it ordered that to Lufthansa's fare there was to be added a premium of €35, which premium to remain in effect for 2 years. This premium was to allow for the competitive advantages Lufthansa had which were not enjoyed by Germania; and it was determined by the following calculation:

allowance for drink + *newspaper supplied on a Lufthansa flight*	€3
value of frequent flyer programme (FFP) mileage points on a Lufthansa flight	€12
estimated value of Lufthansa's higher frequency of service	€25
ad hoc deduction for the sale of a conservative estimate overall	−€5
	€35

The relative precision of these estimates has attracted some criticism (Morrison, 2004). There are also some questions about the 2-year time period. The rationale for this appears to be a kind of 'infant industry', or 'infant airline', argument. The Bundeskartellamt said that within 2 years Germania should have established a sufficient base of regular passenger so that it would no longer need protection against predatory conduct. This suggests that the decision was more about protecting *competitors* rather than protecting *competition*; and there is a subtle but nonetheless important difference between the two.

A case in Canada involved a charter airline seeking to break into the scheduled market. Nationair entered three domestic routes out of Toronto (to Montreal, Ottawa, and Halifax) and competed against the two established carriers, Air Canada and Canadian Airlines International (CAIL). Its entry proved to be very short lived, however. Not long after commencing scheduled operations, Nationair was forced to seek bankruptcy protection in March 1993. At the same time it filed a complaint with Canada's Bureau of Competition Policy, alleging that the responses of Air Canada and CAIL to its deep discount fares on the three routes in question constituted predatory pricing.

Of the relatively rare cases where direct action has been taken to remedy a suspected instance of predatory pricing, one occurred in South Africa in 1993. The South African Competition Board found the domestic services of South African Airways (SAA) apparently being run at a substantial loss. The Competition Board suspected the airline was cross-subsidizing these losses out of net revenues earned on international services. After investigating, the Board concluded that SAA was pricing below cost on domestic trunk routes, forcing two rival airlines, Flitestar and Comair, to follow suit. The Board ordered SAA to restore fares to 1991 levels in real terms and to ensure that its discount fares were at the same (real) levels as those in place when one of the rivals, Comair, entered the routes.

Another case, this time concerning air freight services, was decided in Australia in 1994. Four years previously a small company, Discount Freight Express, complained to the Australian Trade Practices Commission that predatory pricing was widespread. There were also allegations of systematic price fixing, poaching of clients and various other anticompetitive practices. Two companies, Ansett Airlines and its parent TNT International Aviation Services were fined a total of A$5 million and were ordered to pay A$1.07 million in legal costs, equivalent to around 20 times the previous highest fines imposed for breaches of the Australian Trade Practices Act. Ansett and TNT had withdrawn their defence, without admitting liability, in order, as the TNT chairman explained, to limit the companies' legal expenses (which by the time an agreement was concluded had summed to A$11 million, but which were expected to reach A$17 million, if the case had gone the full distance in the courts).

In 1981, Laker Airways went into liquidation and then brought an antitrust suit alleging that a number of IATA airlines had conspired to force it out of business by predatory price cutting. The case never came to court. In 1984 an out-of-court settlement was reached, under which a total of $69 million was paid by a group of 10 North Atlantic airlines. Just less than half, $33 million, was met by BA, with Pan American and TWA each contributing $9 million, with five European carriers (KLM, Lufthansa, Sabena, SAS, and Swissair) each paying $2.8 million and with the remainder coming from British Caledonian ($3.9 million) and UTA ($0.1 million). All these payments were made with no admissions of liability. So far as BA was concerned there was a desire to reach a swift resolution of the dispute in the run-up to its privatization. The case was quite a complex one. The reasons why Laker Airways collapsed were many, most of them related to the airline's over-expansion. The airline's finances were highly geared, with an extremely high debt-to-equity ratio; and this made it vulnerable to hikes in interest rates. Much of the debt capital used to finance aircraft acquisitions was denominated in US dollars, whilst a high proportion of passenger revenues on the Skytrain North Atlantic services was earned in pounds sterling; and this exposed the airline to adverse movements in foreign exchange rates. When interest rates rose and sterling depreciated against the dollar, the airline got into some very serious financial difficulties. It would in all probability have gone bankrupt, whether it was involved in a fares war or not. At the time the fares war broke out, in the autumn of 1981, all the North Atlantic carriers were experiencing a downturn in traffic due to the economic recession of the time. One airline suffering from the effects of the recession as much as any other airline, if not more, was Pan American, and this airline matched Laker's Skytrain fares from the very beginning, obliging BA, TWA and the other transatlantic carriers to follow suit. So far as Pan American was concerned, matching Laker's fares was probably wholly defensive, a kind of 'knee-jerk' response to a fairly desperate situation. Ever since the Bermuda II agreement the North Atlantic has been an open market in which downward movements in any fare (except supersonic and perhaps also first class fares) tend to be matched more or less instantly. Hence, when Laker introduced a new 'Regency' class fare aimed at high-yield business travellers, it could have been fully expected that the other carriers would seek to match it. The main antitrust issue was whether the matching of fare cuts was concerted, something on which no final conclusion was reached since the matter never came to trial. But the matching did not need to be concerted to produce the same result: once Pan American matched, the others had to follow whether they wanted to or not.

Whatever the merits of the Laker Airways case, there was a further antitrust suit, this time brought by Virgin Atlantic. This alleged that BA used its monopoly power at London Heathrow to try to squeeze out competition from Virgin on transatlantic routes. The lawsuit was not so much concerned with predatory pricing as with other forms of predation involving things like 'switch selling', called 'bait and switch' in America, corporate discounts and travel agency commissions. Virgin sued for triple damages which, if awarded, could have amounted to an estimated $1 billion.

Generally speaking airlines have been somewhat reluctant to take legal action against alleged predators. A number of reasons have been identified for this (Dodgson et al., 1990). One is all the time and expense involved. Another may be an unwillingness to offend large airlines on whose good-will smaller airlines often rely for co-operation in aircraft maintenance, use of CRSs, through ticketing, etc. Also, it is possible that taking another airline to court could be bad for publicity: many of the victims of alleged predatory pricing may be new airlines whose owners or managers may have been amongst the most vocal in extolling the virtues of free competition and in calling for the abolition of regulation; and now it might appear as if, as plaintiffs, they are asking competition authorities to step in and raise fares. Then there is the attitude likely to be struck by the courts. In the US courts have generally been rather unsympathetic to allegations of predatory pricing, partly because of the traditional view that predation can never be a rational strategy. Also airlines are rather unlikely to succeed in litigation, so long as the US Department of Justice uses the Areeda–Turner rules as the main yardstick for detecting predation.

Non-price forms of predation

Airlines can use a variety of weapons as predatory devices. One of the most common involves the scheduling of capacity. Incumbent airlines have sometimes been accused of responding to the entry of a competitor by starting 'frequency wars', flooding the route with such extra capacity that the new entrant finds it difficult to launch its new service and make it pay. This was the kind of complaint lodged by British Midland against BAs' Shuttle service on the London–Glasgow route. Incumbent airlines may also try to undermine a competitor's service by following the practice of 'bracketing', scheduling departures to take off just before and just after the competitor's flights. Airline schedules are of course published, making data on frequencies, timings, size of aircraft used, etc. readily available. So it is relatively easy to observe what airlines are doing and to chart the sequence of events. But the central problem still remains: how to distinguish between predatory behaviour and competition on its merits. An incumbent airline is likely to argue that, since schedule frequencies and timings are powerful weapons in competition for market share, why should it be denied using them; whereas a new entrant is likely to claim that the incumbent does not intend the increase in capacity to be permanent, but to last only so long as it takes to drive the new entrant off the route.

The sort of dilemma that this presents to a regulatory authority can be seen in an application by Loganair (which, as it happened, was the incumbent airline with the greater market share in this case) to vary the air service licence held by BA on the Edinburgh–Manchester route (Civil Aviation Authority, 1992). Loganair used to operate the route with four daily frequencies as against one by BA. The route used to be profitable for Loganair, but that changed when BA decided to match Loganair's frequency. Loganair argued that, at eight flights a day, the frequency had become quite excessive in relation to demand and that, if it continued to incur losses, it would consider withdrawing from the route altogether. Loganair claimed that BA had predatory intent and sought to restrict its frequency back to just one a day. BA replied that in matching frequencies it was only acting in a normal competitive manner. As regulator, the Civil Aviation Authority (CAA) did not wish to be seen to be curbing competition, but saw a real risk that Loganair would withdraw and accepted that, unless there was some reduction in capacity, the route was likely to end up as a monopoly for BA. So the CAA compromised and decided to restrict BA's frequency, not to just one a day but two.

Increased frequencies can be a form of pre-emptive action (Beesley, 1986). In regulated markets incumbents might use this weapon to forestall the entry of potential competitors. Abbott and Thompson (1989) have suggested that the increased frequencies incumbents operated on the London–Milan route at the time of some protracted negotiations to provide for the entry of British Caledonian as a new competitor on the route represent a good example of such pre-emptive action.

A quite extreme example of an attempt at non-price predation occurred in the US. It involved Northwest's response to Reno Air's entry into the Reno–Minneapolis city-pair market in 1993. Not only did Northwest institute service of its own on this route, a route which it had previously abandoned, it also opened a new mini-hub in Reno that overlaid much of Reno Air's hub operation. It was only after the US DoT intervened that Northwest decided to abandon its overlay of Reno Air's network.

Another powerful weapon is advertising. In the debates on deregulation and contestable markets the significance of advertising for airline competition was rather underestimated. Expenditure on advertising, once made, is a sunk cost; and sunk costs act as entry barriers inhibiting contestability (Borenstein, 1992). Incumbent airlines usually have much deeper pockets out of which to finance a war in advertising expenditure.

CRSs and FFPs are also weapons that can be used in a predatory or anti-competitive manner. Before intervention by regulatory authorities, CRSs could be used to bias the information on flights, in such a way that the services and/or fares of certain airlines were displayed less prominently than those of the carriers owning the system. Although this practice has now been largely eliminated, there is still some concern that small airlines are at a disadvantage, both in relation to CRS fees and in relation to the role of CRSs as an increasingly important source of market information. So far as the latter is concerned, whilst all participating airlines have equal access to the huge quantities of booking data which CRSs produce, only the large airlines have the resources to make full use of it. This was something given much publicity in the row between BA and Virgin Atlantic (Gregory, 1994).

Another aspect to CRSs is the facility they afford airlines to signal threats to their competitors, either to deter entry or to discourage cuts in fares. One way in which a threat like this might be played out is as follows: Carrier A, a small airline, attempts to boost its market share by cutting fares on routes served by Carrier B, a larger airline, in order to market its new fares. Carrier A enters them in the CRS used by Carrier B; Carrier B responds, not only by matching Carrier A's new fares but also by 'pre-announcing' lower fares in other markets served by Carrier A, signalling its intention (often by code) to subject the smaller airline to a form of 'discipline pricing'; and then Carrier A, receiving the message, withdraws its lower fares, before Carrier B agrees to cancel its threatened reductions. What Carrier B appears to be signalling to Carrier A is that it should cease competing on the route in question or else face a damaging price war on a number of other routes as well. Two US airlines said to have been victims of this sort of predatory behaviour are Midway Airlines and America West.

Small airlines can also be at a disadvantage in relation to FFPs. There is some evidence that FFPs have become a significant barrier to entry, especially in the US (Humphreys, 1991). Airlines can utilize their FFPs in a predatory or anticompetitive manner by calibrating the rewards so that mileage and other bonuses are temporarily increased on routes on which they face new competition. In the marketing of FFPs airlines tend to target first/business class passengers. Although these passengers typically represent only around 20 per cent of total traffic, their contribution to total revenue is often much higher, about 50 per cent or so. Hence the potential gains from predation can be rather large here, especially if the FFP succeeds in securing the loyalty of high-yield passengers, whose demand becomes even less cross-price elastic than it was before.

6.6 Exclusionary behaviour

What, if anything, should government regulatory authorities – like for example the US DoT in Washington or the EC in Brussels – do about predatory behaviour? Their role in airline competition policy is one of identifying the point at which carriers cross the threshold between acceptable and desirable competitive action and destructive anticompetitive behaviour. In this, their position is analogous to that of a referee in a soccer match. The referee has to decide when a tackle is fair and when it is a foul, when to let a goal stand and when to disallow it for one reason or another. Much depends on the referee's discretion and judgement, but at least there are some basic rules. The regulatory authority's task is a little more difficult, in that the basic rules themselves are still a matter of some debate.

Any rule that condemns reductions in fares not only courts unpopularity with the travelling public, it may also have a chilling effect upon competition. A rule that makes it difficult to prove predation – like one requiring it to be shown that a fare is below an airline's cost – could make it more likely that predation is indeed attempted. Conversely, a rule under which it is relatively easy to claim predation could encourage a number of frivolous accusations from airlines seeking to frustrate the normal process of competition.

The crux of the matter is to find the dividing line between genuine revenue-enhancing yield-management techniques and practices aimed directly at undermining the economics of a competitor's operation. This is never going to be easy. It is not something that can be reduced to a simple criterion. A more pragmatic approach is required.

The UK Civil Aviation Authority (1993b) approached the problem by tracking fare developments and trends over time on a selected number of routes, in order to focus on cases where unusually low, and therefore potentially predatory, fares are being offered. Ideally such monitoring should include accessing the GDSs through which the fares are distributed. It is important to note not just the levels of the fares, but also the numbers of seats being sold in each fare category. Further, because of the time it can take to investigate complaints of predatory behaviour, the authorities should if necessary have the power to suspend the practice subject to complaint whilst these investigations are being carried out.

In 1998, the US DoT went so far as to proposed a definitive set of rules for dealing with predation. If enacted these would have put limits on how far incumbent airlines could go in reacting to the entry of new competitors. The rules proposed would have gone beyond the Areeda–Turner test in identifying as objectionable pricing and capacity additions by incumbents that have the result of producing 'lower local revenue than would a reasonable alternative response' (US Department of Transportation, 1999). Under the DoT rules predation would require not necessarily the acceptance of actual, out of pocket, losses but merely a sacrifice of profits that could have been achieved by some alternative policy, such as one involving lesser price reductions or the offer of a few additional discount fares or a refraining from adding capacity (Kahn, 1999). The terms used were rather vague and imprecise, but what they meant in practical terms was that the DoT would commence enforcement proceedings if it sees an incumbent carrier adding a very large number of seats at very low fares.

In the event the DoT's proposals were not proceeded with. They were seen in some quarters as an attempt to re-regulate airline competition. In the words of one commentator they 'would have created a regulatory swamp from which deregulation would not have returned alive' (Levine, 2006). But behind the proposals there was the underlying notion of a 'sacrifice' test and, if this could in some sense replace the Areeda–Turner test, it could have much to commend it (Edlin and Farrell, 2002). It may need to be accompanied by a further test, what Vickers (2005) terms the 'as-efficient competitor' test. When designing policy on exclusionary behaviour, a basic question needs to be asked: whose exclusion is the policy seeking to prevent? It would not be sensible to say competitors in general, because that might result in the policy protecting competitors, however inefficient they may be, rather than safeguarding competition itself.

Many cases involving predatory behaviour arise on international routes and thus may fall partly outside the jurisdiction of national regulatory authorities like the Bundeskartellamt, the CAA or the DoT. On routes within the EU responsibility for dealing with anticompetitive practices ultimately rests with the EC, under Articles 85 and 86 of the Treaty of Rome. The EC has been searching for meaningful criteria to adopt in identifying predation and seeking remedies for it. The Commission has been considering a criterion based on short-run variable costs: fares assessed as 'likely to be predatory', if the revenue they yield is less than 90 per cent of the total (fully allocated) operating cost of the service concerned (Commission of the European Communities, 1992c). This is very much like the Areeda–Turner test. For reasons given earlier, a criterion based only on cost is likely to founder on the burden of proof and will not encompass cases of predation where revenue from fares does in fact cover costs. Experience with the Areeda–Turner test in the US suggests that a per se policy of this kind might actually make it rather difficult to take any action against predatory behaviour in air transport.

However strongly it is suspected, it is always going to be difficult to *prove* predation. And cost-based rules like the Areeda–Turner test are not really adequate to cope with those possibly more serious cases of predation that involve limit and/or discipline pricing together with other non-price strategies designed to have similar effects.

There are some possible alternative policies in which direct recognition could be given to the dynamic and strategic nature of predatory behaviour. One of the more relevant in the present context is a policy of leaving incumbent airlines entirely free to respond to new entry by cutting fares, but, where predation is suspected, placing restrictions on the subsequent raising of those fares in the event of the new entrant airline exiting the route in question. This could reduce incumbent airlines' incentives to engage in predatory pricing, by reducing (if not eliminating altogether) the expected gains from it (the π gains). A policy measure of this kind would have certain advantages over other possible proposals insofar as it would place the emphasis more on ex ante deterrence than on ex post prosecution. But the precise modus operandi of any such policy would need to be very carefully thought out. For exactly how long would any constraints on incumbent airlines' freedom to reverse cuts in fares need to be maintained? (i.e. for how many periods after period *t*?) And to which kinds of fares should the controls apply – only those published in airline tariffs manuals or those marketed through consolidators and bucket shops as well? The latter would be difficult to police, but if they are not covered by the policy, then the possibility would exist of incumbent airlines channelling most (if not all) of their predatory fares through 'unofficial' travel agencies, rendering any constraints over published fares that much less effective. Some discount fares sold through unofficial travel agencies are advertised in the press (as shown in Figure 6.7) but many are not. Also, there is the problem of deciding what allowances should be made for general price inflation and for changes in factors outside the airline's control, like increases in fuel prices, increases in airport charges or an upsurge in market demand? Clearly, there would be much to think about in implementing a policy of this kind. But the main problem would still be in deciding when a cut in fares has predatory intent. When a new competitor enters a route, it attracts traffic away from the incumbent airline; and so the residual demand left for the incumbent is less than before, something that may call for lower fares independent of any predatory intent. Conversely, if the incumbent does not respond to entry by lowering fares, this may not necessarily mean that it has no predatory objective, since it may (before entry) have been practising limit pricing and sees no need to cut its fares further. It would be the task of the regulatory authority's monitoring exercise to distinguish between cases like these, possibly by close examination of the path that the incumbent airline's fares take over time.

Similar approaches might be adopted towards non-price forms of predation. For example, incumbent airlines could be required to maintain schedules following the withdrawal of a competitor, and rules could be devised to inhibit incumbents bracketing a new entrant's services. Something along the lines of the first of these things has been suggested by Starkie (2005) who puts forward a 'capacity lock-in rule' under which, in the event of a new entrant subsequently exiting the market, the post-entry capacity (although not the fares) would be temporarily frozen. This has the advantage of providing some ex ante deterrence, but it has just as many technical difficulties in implementation as the freezing of price reductions proposal.

In any event, the issues surrounding predatory behaviour have in recent years been of less immediate concern than the financial difficulties of airlines traditionally seen as the predators. For reasons discussed earlier, full service airlines have lost much of their pricing power, much of their ability to discriminate, and much of their hold on the valuable business travel

Figure 6.7   Advertisements of discount fares sold through unofficial travel agencies. (*Sources: The Times* and *The Sunday Times*)

Figure 6.7   Continued

Figure 6.7 Continued

market. Indeed, there may now even be a question of who the likely predators are. From time to time it has been mooted (e.g. by Ben-Yosef, 2005)
that low cost new entrants enjoy a 'honeymoon' period during which they
charge some extremely low 'penetration' fares, below average operating
costs, in order to get established in the market. Could this be regarded as
predatory? A literal interpretation of the following press report

> We're going to destroy the airline business as we know it [Ryanair]
> Chief Executive officer Michael O'leary told Reuters as he initiated more fare
> cutting to spur growth
>
> (Reuters, 3 June 2003)

might incline some people to say yes! But it is difficult to imagine any
competition authority even contemplating the prosecution of a case
against low cost airlines whilst passengers are enjoying very low prices to
fly in relatively new aircraft.

7

Mergers and alliances

One of the most striking results of deregulation is the impetus it gave to the level of activity in airline mergers and acquisitions. The constraints imposed in inter-governmental air service agreements, and the restrictions placed on ownership, had meant that so far most of this activity has taken place within national boundaries.

The highest level of activity has been in the US where, as discussed in Chapter 3, deregulation led to some considerable restructuring of the industry. Deregulation first appeared to encourage a lot of new entry, but later a wave of mergers and acquisitions left the industry somewhat more concentrated than it was before. Then the emergence of some new, strong, and fast growing low-cost airlines brought the rise in industry concentration to an end, at least for the time being.

The history of merger activity in the deregulated US industry is charted in Table 7.1. The flurry of activity in the early years of deregulation did cause some concern over increases in market

Table 7.1 Mergers and acquisitions in the deregulated US airline industry

1979	July	Republic formed from merger of North Central and Southern
1980	Jan	National merged with Pan American
	Oct	Republic and Hughes Airwest merged
1982	June	Eastern purchased Braniff's South American routes
	Oct	Continental acquired by Texas International
1985	Apr	United purchased Pan American's Pacific Division
	July	Midway acquired Air Florida
	July	Southwest acquired Muse Air
	Aug	Continental acquired New York Air
	Nov	People Express acquired Frontier
1986	Feb	Piedmont acquired Empire
	Feb	People Express acquired Britt
	May	Continental acquired Rocky Mountain
	Aug	Northwest acquired Republic
	Sep	TWA acquired Ozark
	Nov	Eastern became a wholly owned subsidiary of Texas Air
	Dec	Delta acquired Western
	Dec	Texas Air acquired People Express
	Dec	Alaska acquired Horizon
1987	Feb	Continental became a wholly owned subsidiary of Texas Air
	Apr	Delta absorbed Western Airlines
	Apr	Continental, People Express, and New York Air merged
	May	USAir acquired Pacific Southwest
	Aug	American purchased Air California
	Oct	Alaska and Jet America merged
	Nov	USAir acquired Piedmont
1988	Mar	Delta acquired 20% of Sky West
1989	June	Trump purchased Eastern's Shuttle services
	June	Midway purchased assets from Eastern
1990	Aug	American purchased Eastern's Latin American routes
	Oct	USAir purchased Midway's Philadelphia operations
	Nov	Northwest took 25% stake in Hawaiian and purchased Hawaiian's Pacific routes
	Nov	United purchased Pan American's London routes
1991	Jan	American purchased Seattle–Tokyo route from Continental
	May	American purchased three of TWA's London routes
	Aug	Delta purchased Pan American's European routes and shuttle services
	Dec	USAir reached an agreement to operate Trump Shuttle services
1992	Jan	United acquired Air Wisconsin
1993	Jan	TWA ownership acquired by employees and creditors
	Apr	Continental acquired by an investor group including Air Canada
1994	July	Employees took 55% in United
1998	Oct	Northwest acquired 14% of share capital of Continental
1999	Feb	American purchased Reno Air
1999	Mar	American Eagle took over Business Express
1999	Nov	Delta acquired Comair
2001	Apr	American purchased the remaining assets of TWA
2005	Sep	US Airways and America West merge (retaining separate operating certificates for the next 2 to 3 years)

power, but it was thought then that the impact was likely to be rather small. While responsibility for merger control remained with the Civil Aeronautics Board and the Department of Justice (DoJ) a fairly cautious approach was adopted; and in the late 1970s the competition authorities did in fact block a number of proposed mergers (such as that between Eastern and National and that between Continental and Western) because of the potential harm to competition. But then there was a substantial wave of mergers in the middle of the 1980s, leading to a sharp increase in industry concentration. In 1984 15 carriers accounted for 90 per cent of the total domestic air travel market; and by 1989 this share of the market was held by just 8 carriers. Between 1984 and 1988 it was the Department of Transportation (DoT) which had the ultimate say in merger references involving the airline industry; and the DoT had strong faith in contestable markets and so permitted to be consummated each and every merger submitted to it. The DoT has been heavily criticized for this (Kahn, 1988) although it should be recognized that the DoT's pro-merger stance probably saved the industry from even more bankruptcies than those that actually took place. What attracted the most criticism was the approval of mergers between airlines based at the same airport (Bailey and Williams, 1988). The issues involved can be seen quite clearly in two mergers in 1986, that between Northwest and Republic and that between TWA and Ozark.

Before their merger Northwest focused on long- and medium-haul routes while Republic offered mainly short- and medium-haul services. In 1985 they had a combined share of 8 per cent of the total US domestic market. The carriers argued that a merger would produce efficiency gains, on the ground that their fleets and networks were complementary. However, many of the routes served were duopolies and both airlines used the airport at Minneapolis/St Paul as their main hub. Because of this the DoJ recommended that the merger be rejected, but the DoT, convinced of the efficiency advantages and of the underlying contestability of the markets, approved it. By 1993 the merged airline had built up a market share of 81 per cent at Minneapolis where Northwest's market share had been only 32 per cent in 1978 (Table 5.12). A similar criticism was leveled at the TWA–Ozark merger, which led to TWA dominating the St Louis hub (Hurdle, Johnson, Joskow, Werden, and Williams, 1989). Not long after the merger TWA increased fares on formerly competitive routes emanating from St Louis by between 13 and 18 per cent.

A lot has been made of the adverse effects of local monopolies on consumers, but sometimes with no acknowledgement of the beneficial effects from increased competition on through routes via hubs. Both Northwest at Minneapolis and TWA at St Louis have been in keen competition for connecting traffic, not just between themselves but also with United and American operating out of the Chicago O'Hare hub.

From time to time there are threats of further waves of mergers taking place in the US domestic industry. One such threat came in the latter part of 1998. Northwest attempted to secure a controlling 51 per cent stake in the share capital of Continental; American began making overtures to US Airways about a possible merger; and United and Delta planned a marketing alliance so comprehensive it was being described as a 'virtual' merger, a merger in everything but name. None of these proposals came to (full) fruition. Northwest did acquire a stake in Continental, but only 1 of 14 per cent; the talks between American and US Airways did lead to an alliance involving a tie-up between the two carriers' frequent flyer programmes, but stopped well short of a full merger; and the virtual merger between United and Delta was abandoned once it was clear it would meet with stiff opposition from both the DoT and the DoJ. But when the authorities discourage mergers between the majors, this does not necessarily mean that majors will not merge with smaller (regional) airlines. And indeed there has been a rash of small airline acquisitions and attempted takeovers by majors trying to strengthen key hub positions. American has taken over Reno Air, and its subsidiary, American Eagle, has taken over the commuter airline Business Express. Ensuring traffic feed ahead of the next economic downturn was a clear motive in all these moves, although the majors were also encountering some resistance from pilots' unions which suspected another motive to be the transfer of capacity to a cheaper form of service operation.

Two merger proposals involving US Airways had two very different outcomes. In 2001 US Airways and United gave notice of their intention; but after the DoJ said it would take legal action to block it, the airlines called the merger off. The Justice Department said that the merger would give the combined airline a monopoly for non-stop service on more than 30 routes and would also substantially lessen competition on other routes. United was the second largest US airline and US Airways sixth; and the Justice Department expressed a lot of concern about passenger choice in hub-to-hub non-stop markets like Philadelphia–Los Angeles, San Francisco–Denver, and Pittsburgh–Washington, when United was the dominant hub airline at one end of the route and US Airways the dominant hub airline at the other. The DoJ also worried about competition in many markets along the East Coast, because United and US Airways were often the only two airlines offering connecting services between cities up and down the coast.

Four years later and it was a different story. This time the merger was between US Airways and America West, between a carrier with much of its operations in the East and an airline based in the West, and between a full-service airline and a low-cost airline. An important factor influencing the decision to merge was that both airlines operated large fleets of the same aircraft type, namely the Airbus A320. Although it was America West which was actually purchasing US Airways, it was decided to continue to fly under the latter's banner. The competition authorities saw no impediment to the merger which was duly consummated in July 2005.

Mergers are often discussed as a possible means of improving airline industry fortunes. There is often speculation about the next pairing. Will it be Hawaiian with Aloha Airlines, given that these two carriers have considered merging several times in the past? Or will United finally manage to find a marriage partner, in the shape of Continental perhaps? United Airlines CEO Glenn Tilton has on many different occasions urged relaxation of restrictions on foreign investment in airlines. This is discussed again later, but if the restrictions were to be lifted, are we going to see tie-ups like the following: United with Lufthansa (LH), American with British Airways (BA), Delta with the Air France-KLM Group, and so on?

The trend towards mergers only emerged some time after deregulation in the US. In Canada mergers had a somewhat longer tradition. Under the Canadian regulatory regime mergers were one means of solving the financial difficulties airlines got into when prevented by regulation from exiting loss-making routes. But when domestic deregulation effectively began in Canada, around 1983 or 1984, the nature of mergers changed and the major airlines took advantage of relaxation in government control to bring about a substantial reorganization of the industry. Under regulation domestic services were provided mainly by two transcontinental airlines, Air Canada and CP Air, and by five fairly large regional airlines (Eastern Provincial Airways, Nordair, Quebecair, Pacific Western Airlines, and Transair). The chronological path that mergers and acquisitions took in the deregulated environment is set out in Table 7.2. Both CP Air and Air Canada began by acquiring sizeable stakes in the large regionals, until CP Air was taken over by Pacific Western (which, up to then, had been very much the smaller of the two airlines) to form Canadian Airlines International (CAIL) in 1987. One year earlier the former all-charter carrier Wardair was allowed to start scheduled services on domestic routes and this airline mounted something of a challenge to Air Canada and CAIL, but not for long. By 1988 it was losing substantial amounts of money and in January 1989 was sold to CAIL. The end result was that Canada had a duopoly in scheduled airline services, with just over 50 per cent going to Air Canada and correspondingly just less than 50 per cent to CAIL. In addition to sharing the trunk routes, the duopolists also controlled most of the feeder carriers in Canada, under their respective brandnames Air Canada Connector and Canadian Partner. In the early 1990s Air Canada and CAIL both incurred some heavy deficits (losing a combined total of more than US $1 billion over the 2 years 1991 and 1992). Compared to the major US airlines, Air Canada and CAIL were still relatively small airlines and likely to remain so, given the size of Canada's population. In view of their poor financial performance serious consideration had over a number of years been given to merger. And it was almost agreed to do so in 1992. But concerns about market power arising from an Air Canada/CAIL near-monopoly in domestic air transport caused a change of mind. A further 8 years on and the financial difficulties

Table 7.2 Mergers and acquisitions in the deregulated Canadian airline industry

1983	Pacific Western acquired 42% of Time Air
1984	CP Air acquired Eastern Provincial
1985	Air Canada and Pacific Western each acquired 24.5% of Air Ontario
1986	CP Air acquired Nordair
	Air Canada acquired 49% of Air Nova
1987	Pacific Western and CP Air merged to form CAIL
	Air Canada acquired 75% of both Air Ontario and Austin
	Air Canada acquired 87% of Air BC
	Time Air acquired North Canada Air
	Pacific Western established Ontario Express with 49.5% stake
	Merger of Quebecair, Nordair Metro, and Quebec Aviation
	Pacific Western acquired 45% stake in Calm Air
	CAIL increased stake in Air Atlantic to 45%
1988	Air Canada helped to create Air Alliance with 75% stake
	Air Canada acquired 90% of Northwest Territorial
1989	CAIL acquired Wardair
1991	Canadian Regional Airlines formed as the holding company for Time Air, Ontario Express (both 100%), Inter-Canadian (70%), and Calm Air (45%) and as the name of the CAIL regional network
1996	Time Air and Ontario Express completely amalgamated and began operating as Canadian Regional Airlines
1997	First Air took over Northwest Territorial
1999	Air Canada took over CAIL
2000	Canadian Regional Airlines amalgamated with Air Canada Regional together with other regional airlines to form what is now known as Air Canada Jazz

continued, especially for CAIL. Numerous proposals were put forward for CAIL's survival, including a takeover bid led by American Airlines. But none of these came to fruition and so ultimately an Air Canada/CAIL merger took place in 2000. The combined firm still suffered from relatively high costs and, to aid its restructuring, in April 2003 it sought and gained bankruptcy protection, from which it emerged in September 2004. Under its new parent company ACE Aviation Holdings the reorganized Air Canada ran a number of subsidiaries each specializing in competing against a particular competitive threat. Regional operations were put into the hands of Air Canada Jazz, into which the carriers Air BC, Air Nova, Air Ontario, and Canadian Regional Airlines were consolidated. Another subsidiary, Air Canada Jetz, was launched as a charter operator specializing in the carriage of sports teams and professionals. In 2001, Air Canada launched itself into the low-cost sector with Air Canada Tango (with aircraft painted in purple). But this was dissolved in 2004. Another foray into low-cost operations began with a further subsidiary known as Zip (whose aircraft were also brightly painted) but this also failed to last very long. Thus the reorganized Air Canada acquired a position of dominance in full-service operations on the trunk routes and also for many regional services, but withdrew from competing in the low cost sector where the rapidly growing WestJet (founded in 1996) provided passengers with some kind of alternative in the lucrative Toronto–Ottowa Montreal triangle. The situation was described in the press as a 'David versus Goliath story, with 'David WestJet' needing help to defended passengers from the monopoly power of 'Goliath Air Canada' (Levine, 2006). The Canadian Government decided it was best to curb the possibility of monopoly by re-regulating fares on Canadian domestic routes.

For many years a duopoly had been the official government policy for domestic air transport in Australia. In the past, domestic interstate routes were served by the state-owned Trans Australian Airlines, renameda Australian Airlines in 1986, and the privately owned Ansett Airlines. All international routes were reserved for the state-owned flag carrier Qantas. This arrangement endured for over 30 years. The only other airlines operating scheduled passenger services were some fairly small regional airlines, most of which were acquired by Ansett, for example East West Airlines and Kendell Airlines. In 1987 the Australian government gave formal notice of its intention to terminate its 'two airline policy' for domestic routes; and domestic deregulation effectively took place in 1990.

A new entrant appeared in the shape of Compass Airlines. This independent carrier entered the most densely trafficked trunk routes, offering single class service in relatively large aircraft and charging relatively low fares. Compass achieved some early success in capturing market share but its existence was rather short lived: it was declared bankrupt in December 1991, after just over 1 year in business. In August 1992 a new airline under the name of Compass (but not directly related to its predecessor) was launched and once again concentrated on the dense routes with low fares. But this too suffered from some severe financial difficulties and ceased trading after only 9 months. In the meantime Australian Airlines was privatized and then taken over by Qantas, which is now completely privatized. Qantas integrated its international service with Australian's domestic network, so that domestic routes are still mainly operated as duopolies, although the intensity of competition, between Qantas and Ansett, is significantly greater than when Ansett operated alongside the former Trans Australian Airlines. In being able to feed traffic between international and domestic services Qantas became a considerable competitive threat to Ansett, which itself sought to expand into international markets and to forge links with foreign airlines. It did not last all that long. It was taken over by Air New Zealand (previously a 50 per cent shareholder) and then went into voluntary liquidation. This left Qantas with a near-monopoly in the Australian domestic air travel market, until, that is, Virgin Blue (originally owned by Sir Richard Branson) was introduced as a low-cost airline. Qantas responded to this new entrant by creating its own low-cost subsidiary named Jetstar.

Many other countries used to follow the practice of designating separate national airlines for domestic and international routes. As in Australia the trend towards mergers and takeovers has tended to bring them together. For example, in New Zealand domestic trunk routes used to be operated exclusively by the National Airways Corporation, while international routes were the preserve of Air New Zealand. The two were merged in 1978 when still in state ownership. In Thailand the domestic operator Thai Airways was merged with Thai International in 1987. For both these mergers a strong motive was network integration to ensure traffic feed. The same consideration might be an important factor in plans to merge the two large public corporations in India. At present Air-India is responsible mainly for long-haul international routes, while Indian Airlines operates a vast domestic network as well as some short-haul international routes to neighbouring countries. There could be some extensive economies of scope in merging them. There has recently been some renewed speculation about an Air-India/Indian Airlines amalgamation.

The model for airline industry organization in countries of the British Commonwealth was of course the original distinction the UK drew between its two main national airlines, British European Airways (BEA) and British Overseas Airways Corporation (BOAC). BEA served the domestic and European markets and BOAC served the Middle East and long-haul intercontinental routes. Their merger in 1974 resulted in BA having the most comprehensive route network in the world, extending half a million miles with 200 destinations in 84 countries. The BEA/BOAC merger was the first example in Europe of national airlines with different spheres of influence being amalgamated; and it was some while before something similar occurred in other European countries (Table 7.3). Before Air France had taken over UTA and gained control of Air Inter in 1990, and before LH had absorbed Interflug in 1991, following the re-unification of Germany, BA had in 1987 bought the largest independent UK airline British Caledonian.

The acquisition of British Caledonian by BA raised concerns regarding its impact on competition. Over half BCAL's net revenue from scheduled services was earned on routes on which it was in competition with BA. There was also concern lest the takeover would leave BA in a position to dominate both of London's two main airports, Gatwick as well as Heathrow. The matter was referred to the UK Monopolies and Mergers Commission. It was clear that BCAL could not continue as it was and that its financial position was so serious as to preclude its survival as a slimmed down niche carrier. The only other alternatives were a takeover by a smaller UK airline or a merger of one kind or another with a foreign airline. The only other UK airline to express an interest in bidding for BCAL was Air Europe, a former

Table 7.3 Airline mergers and acquisitions in European countries

1974	BEA and BOAC fully merged to form BA
1975	Svensk Flygtjanst and Crownair merged to form Swedair
1985	Aeromediterranea incorporated into ATI (a subsidiary of Alitalia)
1986	Air UK created from merger of Air Anglia, Air Wales, Air West, and British Island Airways
1987	BA took over British Caledonian
1988	Air Littoral merged with Compagnie Aerienne Languedoc
	KLM took over NLM which became KLM CityHopper
1990	Air France took over UTA and thereby acquired a controlling interest (75%) in Air Inter
1991	LH took over Interflug
	KLM acquired a controlling interest (80%) in Transavia
	KLM CityHopper took over Netherlines
1992	BA took over Dan-Air
	Air Outre-Mer merged with Minerve to form AOM French Airlines
	SAS acquired a controlling interest (57%) in Linjeflyg
	British Airways formed Deutsche BA which took over Delta Air
	British Airways took a 49.5 stake in TAT European
	LH took over DLT and renamed it LH CityLine
1993	BA took over Brymon Airways
	Maersk Air took over Birmingham European Airlines
1996	TAT became wholly owned subsidiary of BA
1997	KLM took over Air UK (subsequently renamed KLM UK)
	Air Inter fully integrated into Air France
	BA acquired a controlling 67% stake in Air Liberté
	Braathens took over Transwede
	SAS took 29% in Wideroe's
1998	Aviaco became wholly owned subsidiary of Iberia
	KLM took a 50% stake in Martinair
	SAS purchased Air Botnia
	KLM took 30% stake in Braathens
	BA purchased CityFlyer Express
	easyJet purchased a 40% stake in TEA, later renaming it easyJet Switzerland
2001	Sabena liquidated: group of investors managed to take over Delta Air Transport (a Sabena subsidiary) and transformed it into SN Brussels Airlines
2002	easyJet acquired Go (a subsidiary of BA
2003	Ryanair acquired Buzz (a subsidiary of KLM)
2004	Alitalia acquired Gandalf Airlines
	Air France and KLM merged, each airline retaining its own brand
2005	LH took over Swiss Air Lines (the remnant of Swissair)
	SAS acquired Braathens
2006	Austrian Airlines merged with Lauda Air

charter airline with ambitions to enter the scheduled sector. But this airline had neither the financial resources, nor the synergy benefits, to rescue BCAL and went into liquidation itself some years later. There were several draw-backs in a merger with a foreign airline: if a stake large enough to support

BCAL was taken by a foreign company, this might have been held to constitute the passing of control out of British hands, which might have led to BCAL's designation as a UK airline under bilateral air service agreements being challenged and its route licences possibly being revoked. Nonetheless, after BA had sharply reduced their offer price following the October 1987 stock market crash, BCAL actively considered a number of proposals from the Scandinavian airline SAS (Thomson, 1990). What can be described as an auction then took place, at the end of which BA finally purchased BCAL for the sum of £250 million. To assuage the MMC's fears over the effects of competition, BA gave a number of undertakings (Monopolies and Mergers Commission, 1987). These included surrendering at least 5000 slots at Gatwick and returning quite a few of BCAL's route licences (all domestic, plus those to Paris, Brussels, and Nice). The merger was then investigated by the European Commission (EC), who imposed further conditions on BA: limiting it to no more than 25 per cent of total slots available at Gatwick; increasing the number of BCAL route licences it was required to give up; and requiring it to acquiesce in Air Europe being designated as the UK operator on the Gatwick–Rome route.

Thus the MMC and EC approved the BA/BCAL merger, but only on terms designed to encourage competition from other airlines. A similar view was taken by the EC in respect of the Air France/UTA/Air Inter merger 3 years later. The conditions under which the French merger was approved were: first, that 8 domestic and 50 international route licences be transferred to other airlines; second, that Air France divest itself of the 35 per cent stake it had in TAT European Airlines, the next largest French airline; and third, that slots be made available at Paris Charles de Gaulle for independent operators to use on domestic routes.

At first sight the conditions applied to the BA/BCAL and Air France/ UTA/Air Inter mergers seemed reasonable safeguards for the maintenance of competition. This has not, however, been altogether vindicated by subsequent experience: there has been little or no new entry and also a decline in the number of competitors on many point-to-point routes (Doganis, 1994). In the UK two of the independent airlines expected to provide competition for BA both failed financially, Air Europe in 1991 and Dan-Air in 1992. In France, many of the busiest domestic routes have remained virtual monopolies for the Air France Group, partly because of the stipulation that new entrants should fly from Paris Charles de Gaulle rather than from the congested Paris Orly (the more popular airport for domestic passengers). For example, the two main charter airlines in France, Minerve and Air Liberté, both bid for licences from Orly, where they might have reaped some economies of scope by combining their charter operations with some scheduled services; but the French government declared that, because of congestion, both carriers could only operate new scheduled services from Charles de Gaulle. And elsewhere in Europe national airlines have been able to consolidate their home markets, with the acquisitions of Transavia by KLM and Linjeflyg by SAS, and with the collapse of other independent airlines like Air Holland, Trans European Airways in Belgium, and the German airline Wings. EC approval for KLM's acquisition of Transavia is difficult to justify on competitive terms, there being no other significant competitors in the Dutch home market. But the EC would have had some difficulty in applying a similar remedy to that in the BA and Air France cases, that is, the release of slots at the airline's main airport, because there was space capacity and thus no great slot problem at Schiphol Airport in Amsterdam.

Mergers within national boundaries have always been a cause for concern, whenever the possibility exists of the merged airline attaining a position of unassailable dominance in home markets. For this reason, two mergers in 1998 were referred to competition authorities, KLM's stake in Martinair and BA's takeover of CityFlyer Express. The KLM acquisition was referred to the EC and the BA takeover to the Monopolies and Mergers Commission. In both cases the main concern was the increased presence that the mergers would give the acquirers at busy airports, KLM at Schiphol and BA at Gatwick. In the latter case, if the MMC ruled against the takeover, there was another British airline willing to acquire CityFlyer Express and that was Virgin Atlantic. Virgin was willing to match BA's £75 million bid for CityFlyer, its Chairman, Richard Branson, at the time stating that he regarded the acquisition as the last chance to create a 'second force' airline in the UK capable of competing effectively against BA. The objective of encouraging a second force to compete against BA used to be part of official UK government policy (Committee of Inquiry into Civil Air Transport, 1969) and led to the formation and development of British Caledonian. But the question now is whether there is less reason for a specifically *British* second force, if airlines are to be permitted greater freedom to merge with carriers from other countries.

Before leaving the subject of domestic mergers, mention should perhaps be made of one of the most important airline mergers to be made in recent years, that between Japan Air Lines (JAL) and Japan Air System (JAS) in 2001. This was a marriage between an international carrier, JAL, and a domestic one, JAS; and the division of responsibilities remains much as it was before in pre-merger days, with JAL changing its name to Japan Airlines International and JAS to Japan Airlines Domestic. At the time of the merger the combined airline became the sixth largest in the world in terms of the number of passengers carried and the third largest when measured by revenue. Bringing them together fits in with the long established policy of successive Japanese governments to permit mergers between indigenous companies in the hope that their larger size will enable them to compete better with foreign competition. An interesting question is whether the combined airline will remain aloof from membership of a global alliance, now that the other main airline in Japan, All Nippon Airways, has become a member of the Star alliance.

7.2 Cross-border acquisitions

As pointed out in Chapter 2 the idea of airlines making investments in foreign carriers is not a new one and can in fact be traced back quite a long time. There have also been some instances of fully fledged mergers creating multinational airlines. So far these have been limited to airlines from neighbouring countries agreeing to pool their resources and form consortia on regional bases: SAS in Scandinavia, Gulf Air in the Middle East, LIAT in the West Indies, Air Afrique in francophone West Africa plus some other consortia no longer in existence (Table 7.4). But neither these mergers nor the trade investments airlines used to make in the past are quite the same thing as the kind of acquisition airlines are most interested in making now. In the past, cross-border acquisitions were made by state-owned airlines and were promoted by national governments; their success or failure depended almost entirely upon political considerations; and their overriding objective was to save operating costs, especially in the procurement and maintenance of aircraft. The main interest in cross-border acquisitions today is shown by privatized airlines seeking to break free from intergovernmental air service agreements and extend their marketable networks by taking equity stakes in carriers operating complementary services, not just in neighbouring countries but, increasingly, in regions at the other ends of long-haul routes.

In the airline context the ability to acquire shares in foreign companies is heavily constrained by governments, which so far still largely adhere to the principle that air carriers should be 'substantially owned and effectively controlled' by nationals of the state in which the carrier is registered. For example, when BA was privatized in 1987, its prospectus declared that not more than 22 per cent of its share capital would be allocated to investors outside the UK, although it was accepted that foreign holdings might subsequently rise to almost double that figure. In its initial flotation some 17 per cent of BA shares were purchased by foreign nationals, but 6 years later the proportion had grown to somewhere between 35 and 45 per cent. BA now (in 2006) has around 233000 shareholders, amongst whom the nationality spread covers more than 100 countries worldwide, although the majority of foreign shareholders reside in the US (British Airways, 2006). A year after the BA privatization, when SAS attempted to acquire British Caledonian, the

Table 7.4 Multinational state-owned airline consortia[a]

Name	Year established	Participating countries	Share held[b]
Air Afrique[c]	1961 (ceased 2003)	Benin	7.3
		Burkina Faso	7.3
		Central African Republic	7.3
		Chad	7.3
		Congo	7.3
		Ivory Coast	7.3
		Mali	7.3
		Mauritania	7.3
		Niger	7.3
		Senegal	7.3
East African Airways Corporation (EAAC)	1946 (ceased 1977)	Kenya	68
		Uganda	23
		Tanzania	9
Gulf Air[d]	1973	Bahrain	50
		Oman	50
Leeward Islands Air Transport Services (LIAT)[e]	1956	Barbados	10
		Trinidad and Tobago	10
		Antigua	5
		Grenada	5
		St Lucia	5
		Guyana	2
		Jamaica	2
		Montserrat	2
		St Kitts	2
		Nevis	2
Malaysia–Singapore Airlines	1966 (ceased 1972)	Malaysia	–
		Singapore	–
Scandinavian Airlines System (SAS)[f]	1946	Sweden	21.4
		Denmark	14.3
		Norway	14.3

[a] In addition to those named here there has for many years been a planned consortium between several North African countries (Algeria, Libya, Morocco, and Tunisia) to form a multinational airline to be known as Air Maghreb. But so far this consortium has not come to fruition.

[b] The percentage shares do not always sum to 100, because other organizations sometimes hold shares as well.

[c] Two of the original member countries dropped their participation, Cameroun in 1971 and Gabon in 1977.

[d] Originally there were four countries involved, but recently two have withdrawn, Qatar in 2002 and Abu Dhabi in 2005.

[e] The company was subsequently reorganized and became known as LIAT (1974). In 1995 the airline BWIA (of Trinidad and Tobago) took a 29% stake in LIAT (1974).

[f] The ownership structure changed in 2001 following partial (50%) privatization. (Previously the state shares were Sweden 42.8%, Denmark 28.6%, and Norway 28.6%.)

UK government made it clear that a foreign airline would not be allowed to achieve overall control of a British airline. In the US there is a statutory limit on foreign ownership of airline stock: foreign airlines can hold only up to 25 per cent of voting shares, and the president and two-thirds of the board of directors must be US citizens. The Chinese government has placed a ceiling of 35 per cent on foreign investments in domestic airlines. And similar, if not more restrictive, limitations used to apply in Europe, until the EU implemented its Third Liberalization Package on 1 January 1993, since when ownership of any EU airline has (at least in principle) been opened up to nationals of any member state. However, there are still the restrictions implied by the ownership clauses in inter-governmental air service agreements (e.g. if BA were to buy, say, 40 per cent of Olympic Airways, the Greek national carrier, some non-EU countries might no longer accept Olympic as the designated Greek carrier on international routes to/from Greece).

There are some indications of government beginning to think of relaxing restrictions on foreign investment. Some airlines have been able to take sizable stakes in foreign carriers (Table 7.5). LH owns 30 per cent of the share capital of bmi British Midland; and another 20 per cent of bmi is taken by SAS, which airline has a 49 per cent holding in Estonian Air. But as yet very few foreign holdings are as large as this. Air France appears in Table 7.5 with the longest list of shareholdings in foreign airlines but more than half these are in relatively small carriers from countries with which France has historical or colonial links. Other notable investments include Emirates' 43 to 44 per cent holding in SriLankan Airlines, SIA's stake of 49 per cent in Virgin Atlantic, and Virgin's own holding of 49 per cent in Virgin Nigeria.

What are the advantages and disadvantages of holding shares in another airline? One possible advantage is that the act of purchasing shares demonstrates commitment, and this assures the other airline of a serious interest in long-term collaboration. Alliances struck without either partner purchasing shares might be relatively short lived or rather ineffectual. The BA/United marketing agreement, for instance, did not survive the failure of BA's bid to participate in the buyout of United; and the co-operation agreement between Air France and LH, which involved no exchange of shares, did not materialize into a closer relationship. Where alliances are accompanied by share purchases they might, it is sometimes suggested, prove to be more durable. But share purchases are neither a necessary nor sufficient condition for alliance durability. For instance, when it was in an alliance with USAir (now US Airways) BA took a 24.6 per cent share in that airline; but when it changed course and struck an agreement with American Airlines in the oneworld global alliance it moved swiftly to sell the USAir shareholding. Then, the other way around, when BA sold its 25 per cent stake in the equity of Qantas, this did not materially affect the relationship between the two airlines in the oneworld alliance.

Table 7.5 Equity stakes in foreign airlines, August 2006. *Sources*: Compiled from data published in *Airline Business* and in various press reports

Held by	Held in	% of share capital
Aer Lingus	Futura International	20.0
Air France[a]	Air Madagascar	3.2
	Air Mauritius	2.8
	Air Tahiti	7.5
	Alitalia	2.0
	Austrian Airlines	1.5
	Cameroun Airlines	3.6
	Royal Air Maroc	2.9
	Tunisair	5.6
Air New Zealand	Air Pacific	3.7
Air-India	Air Mauritius	2.6
American Airlines	Iberia	1.0
Austrian Airlines	Slovak Airlines	62.0
	Ukraine International	22.5
British Airways	Air Mauritius	3.8
	Comair (South Africa)	18.0
	Iberia	9.0
Continental Airlines	Copa Airlines	10.0
Emirates	SriLankan Airlines	43.6
Iberia	Royal Air Maroc	1.0
KLM	Kenya Airways	26.0
LH[b]	bmi	30.0
	bmi regional	30.0
	Luxair	13.0
Qantas	Air Pacific	46.3
	Thai Air cargo	49.0
Royal Air Maroc	Air Gabon	51.0
	Air Senegal	51.0
SAS	bmi British Midland	20.0
	Estonian Air	49.0
Singapore Airlines	Virgin Atlantic	49.0
South African Airways	Air Tanzania	49.0
Taca	Aviateca	30.0
	Islena Airlines	20.0
	Lacsa	10.0
	Taca peru	49.0
Tap Air Portugal	Air Macao	20.0
Virgin Atlantic	Virgin Nigeria	49.0

[a] This does not include Air France's takeover of KLM.
[b] This does not include LH's takeover of Swiss International Air Lines.

An equity stake is not a riskless investment, of course. If the partner airline gets into financial difficulties this will obviously reduce the market value of the stake and, in the extreme circumstances of the partner entering bankruptcy and ceasing operations, the investment may have to be written off altogether. The experience of three European airlines investing in US domestic carriers – SAS in Continental, KLM in Northwest, and BA's past stake in USAir – is testimony to the nature of the risks involved. SAS has perhaps lost the most in this respect, because when Continental entered Chapter 11 bankruptcy, it had to write off an investment of $100 million. Both KLM and BA saw the value of their shares fall, but of course any losses sustained in share values have to be set against the value of the additional traffic that the alliance generates.

Neither the Air France/KLM nor the LH/Swiss mergers are covered by the information presented in Table 7.5. But they both represent important steps in the consolidation of the industry. For almost the first time we have seen major airlines from different countries coming together to form a single entity. Until the matter of the nationality clauses in our service agreements is resolved it will be necessary for each of the merged parties to continue operating under their own specific brandnames. Otherwise traffic rights on international routes outside Europe could be placed in jeopardy. The marriage of Air France with KLM brings the latter within the SkyTeam alliance along with its partner for many years in the so-called 'Wings' alliance, Northwest. The merger between LH and Swiss was one between members of the same global alliance, Star. It is pretty clear that a central objective in both mergers is to extend marketable networks; and it has been shown in Chapter 5 how Air France and KLM have been developing their dual hub strategy for intercontinental traffic. It is also clear that in both cases the need to achieve synergies leading to cost reductions is a more immediate concern. For both of the airlines being taken over—if that is a strictly correct way of putting it – had been in serious financial difficulties, Swiss more so than KLM, but both suffering greatly from the financial vicissitudes of the 2001–03 period. Allowing for both revenue benefits and cost savings, synergies from the Air France-KLM merger have been estimated to reach about €440 million per annum by year 5 of the merger (Doganis, 2006).

7.3 Alliance patterns

Many alliances struck between airlines involve no investments in equity at all. Many are limited to marketing agreements and technical co-operation. In the mid-1990s there was an absolute frenzy in alliance formation, both the number of pacts and the number of airlines involved in them rising rapidly. At the time airline executives must have felt a growing sense of urgency to

Table 7.6 Passenger traffic and revenue of members of the oneworld global alliance, 2005. *Source: Airline Business*

Member	Date joined	Passenger traffic		Passenger revenues
		RPK (millions)	Passengers (millions)	(US $) (millions)
Aer Lingus	Jun 00	12 563	8	1093
American	Sep 98	222 412	98	20 712
BA	Sep 98	111 859	36	15 122
Cathay Pacific	Sep 98	65 110	15	6548
Finnair	Sep 00	16 735	9	2317
Iberia	Sep 00	49 060	28	6073
LAN Airlines	Jun 00	17 491	8	2506
Qantas	Sep 98	86 986	33	9524
Alliance total		582 216	234	63 895
Share of world total		14.7%	11.3%	14.2%
Japan Airlines		100 345	58	19 346
Malev		4406	3603	
Royal Jordanian		5504	2	772
Share if above carriers join		17.5%	14.4%	18.6%

get their consortia together before the best partners were spoken for, so to speak. Over the past 6 or 7 years airline managers' attention has been drawn to other, more pressing, problems and the question of alliance strategies was rather pushed into the background. But once again the topic of alliances is receiving a lot of attention, especially global alliances.

Most alliances tend to be between just one airline and another. The annual survey conducted by *Airline Business* magazine uncovered many hundreds of agreements, the vast majority on a bilateral basis. There are, by contrast, just three global alliances: oneworld, SkyTeam, and Star. Details of each of these, in terms of membership, joining date, passenger traffic, and passenger revenues are given in Tables 7.6–7.8. By all three measures – revenue passenger kilometres, number of passengers, passenger revenue – Star is the largest, its members currently representing 20 to 25 per cent shares of world totals. More than half the world totals are accounted for when all three global alliances are put together, leaving the rest to carriers that remain as yet non-aligned. Within the next year or so the oneworld alliance is expecting to welcome Japan Airlines, Malev, and Royal Jordanian into the fold; SkyTeam is looking forward to a group of seven associate/regional members signing up; and Star's membership will be bolstered with the addition of Air China and Shanghai Airlines (which carriers are developing a 'dual hub' strategy similar to that of Air France-KLM, except on the other side of the world). With all these extra carriers involved the three global alliances together will account for just over two-thirds of world passenger revenue.

Table 7.7 Passenger traffic and revenue of members of the SkyTeam global alliance, 2005. *Source*: *Airline Business*

Member	Date joined	Passenger traffic		Passenger revenues
		RPK (millions)	Passengers (millions)	(US $) (millions)
Aeroflot	Apr 06	20 750	7	2 540
Aeromexico	Jun 00	14 500	9	3 604
Air France-KLM	Jun 00	189 253	70	26 036
Alitalia	Jul 00	37 969	24	5 940
Continental	Sep 04	114 659	45	11 208
CSA Czech	Mar 01	7784	5	922
Delta	Jun 00	193 006	119	16 191
Korean	Jun 00	49 046	22	7 424
Northwest	Sep 04	121 994	56	12 286
Alliance total		748 961	357	86 152
Share of world total		19.0%	17.3%	19.1%
Air Europa[a]		13 442	8	1 124
Copa[a]		5 209	2	609
China Southern[a]		61 923	44	4 682
Kenya Airways[a]		6 635	2	694
Middle East Airlines[a]		2 191	1	382
Portugalia[a]		945	1	–
Taron[a]		1 448	1	281
Share if above carriers join		21.3%	20.2%	20.9%

[a] Associate/regional member.
– Not available.

Some comparisons between the alliance groupings are shown in Tables 7.9 and 7.10. In financial terms oneworld appears to be strongest, the only one to return a positive overall result for net profit in 2005. In network terms the Star alliance has an appreciable lead, but this lead is likely to be eaten into when JAL joins oneworld.

It is interesting to observe the position of some prominent airlines that as yet remain non-aligned. One of them, THY Turkish Airlines has recently opened negotiations to join Star and so it might not remain non-aligned for long. Another of the non-aligned, Malaysian Airlines is linked with the SkyTeam alliance. Virgin Atlantic may value its independence, but 49 per cent of its share capital is held by Singapore Airlines, which is a member of Star. At the same time Virgin is heavily involved in code-sharing agreements with Continental and that might suggest membership of SkyTeam. Then there is Emirates, which so far has shown very little interest in alliances, apart from a few bilateral block space and code-sharing marketing agreements.

Table 7.8 Passenger traffic and revenue of members of the Star global alliance, 2005. *Source: Airline Business*

Member	Date joined	Passenger traffic		Passenger revenue
		RPK (millions)	Passengers (millions)	(US $) (millions)
Adria Airways[a]	Dec 04	1019	1	167
Air Canada	May 97	75 290	30	8422
Air N.Zealand	Mar 99	25 568	12	2512
All Nippon	Oct 99	58 949	50	12 040
Asiana	Mar 03	19 225	12	3003
Austrian	Mar 00	22 894	10	3078
Blue1[a]	Nov 04	908	1	226
bmi	Jul 00	5558	6	1570
Croatia Airlines[a]	Dec 04	1200	2	226
Lot Polish	Oct 03	6284	4	853
Lufthansa	May 97	108 185	51	22 371
SAS	May 97	26 487	24	8225
Singapore Airlines	Apr 00	82 742	17	8030
South African	Apr 06	24 300	7	3034
Spanair	Apr 03	5974	7	1225
Swiss	Apr 06	20 469	10	2860
Tap Air Portugal	Mar 05	14 536	6	1683
Thai Int'l	May 97	49 930	18	4056
United	May 97	183 262	67	17 379
US Airways	May 04	62 582	40	10 610
Varig	Oct 97	28 506	13	2810
Alliance total		823 866	387	114 379
Share of world total		20.9%	18.7%	25.4%
Air China		52 453	28	4681
Shanghai Airlines		8780	7	976
Share if above carriers join		22.4%	20.4%	26.7%

[a] Associate/regional member.

Table 7.9 Comparison of global alliances' financial results, 2005. *Source: Airline Business*

Alliance	US $ millions		
	Revenue	Operating profit	Net profit
Oneworld	63 895	2969	1947
Skyteam	86 152	−1176	−5014
Star	114 379	2660	−20 151

Table 7.10 Comparison of global alliances' networks, 2006.[a] *Source: Airline Business*

	Destinations		Countries served	Frequencies (thousands)	ASK^b (billions)	Share of ASK^c
	Total	Duplicates				
Oneworld	591	163	128	57	15.9	14.5%
Skyteam	730	366	141	96	20.4	18.6%
Star	873	318	147	109	22.6	20.6%

[a] Analysis based on weekly global operations August 2006.
[b] ASK denotes available seat kilometres.
[c] Shares are of total (global) non-stop scheduled capacity offered.

If Emirates, and the two other carriers in the Middle East specializing in the carriage of sixth freedom traffic, have not joined one of the global groupings, nor have shown much intention in participating in a new regional alliance of Arab airlines known as Arabesk. This was formally inaugurated in January 2006, with the following six members Egyptair, Gulf Air, Middle East Airlines, Yemenia, Saudi Arabian Airlines, and Royal Jordanian Airlines. With the exception of the last named, which is due to become full member of oneworld in 2007, none of the Arabesk members has any connection with a global alliance. Arabesk is still in its infancy, but its main activities are likely to be focused on joint ventures to reduce costs, code-sharing marketing agreements, and special 'prorate' arrangements for dividing up revenues earned jointly.

The *Airline Business* surveys contain details of the diverse areas covered by alliances. They include: joint sales and marketing; joint purchasing and insurance; joint passenger and cargo flights; codesharing; block spacing; links between frequent flyer programmes; management contracts; and joint ventures in catering, ground handling and aircraft maintenance. To some extent the proliferation of bilateral deals within groups of airlines is a partial substitute for multilateral collaboration through the International Air Transport Association on interlining and revenue proration. Interlining and proration agreements continue but are becoming less significant for traffic transferring between alliance partners.

The interest in alliances shown by airlines mirrors the interest that firms in some other industries have been displaying. The growth in alliances between otherwise separate enterprises is a prominent feature of contemporary business across the world. One analysis of this development, in referring to the explosion of alliances worldwide, talks of the 'revolution amongst us' (Lynch, 1993, p. 1). It is difficult to be precise on the quantitative extent of alliances, for the relevant statistics are deficient in various ways. Nevertheless, the evidence overall certainly supports the contention that the last two decades have witnessed a mushrooming growth in alliances in a great many different industries, ranging from electronics to retailing. One estimate

(Krubasik and Lautenschlager, 1993) is that the annual growth rate in alliances in hi-tech industries, such as electronics, computers, aerospace, pharmaceuticals and telecommunications, has risen about four-fold.

Not only have alliances boomed in number over the past few years, they have also proliferated in type. Joint ventures and licensing arrangements have long been a feature of international business, and they are now a fairly common phenomenon in domestic commerce as well. Other alliances take on a wide variety of forms; such as co-operation in research and development, management servicing, training agreements, agreements on franchising, contact assembly, supply chains, etc. Sometimes these alliances are backed by minority equity holdings and sometimes they are not.

How does the pattern of alliances developing in the airline industry compare with those observed in other industries? To explore this question it is useful to categorize alliances accordingly to three main criteria:

- Whether they are horizontal, vertical or external alliances.
- Whether they are motivated more by technological factors than by market forces.
- Whether the mode of interfirm governance is of a relatively strong or relatively weak kind.

Horizontal, vertical, and external alliances

Horizontal alliances are those between firms selling in the same product or service market. Vertical alliances are those with suppliers, distributors, or buyers. External alliances are drawn up with potential entrants or with the producers of substitutes or complements in other industries.

Prize examples of horizontal alliances are to be found in the pharmaceutical and telecommunications industries. In July 1993 the giant triad in the pharmaceutical industry, Glaxo, Welcome, and Warner-Lambert, announced that they were forming an alliance to develop and market over-the-counter (non-prescription) drugs across the world. There has also been a considerable flurry of activity in the telecommunication industry, with a number of major transatlantic alliances being struck. Three large rival alliances emerged: Worldsource, Concert, and Atlas. Each of these groups sought to compete in the market for one-stop international telecommunications contracts. It seems likely that competition for the lucrative business of multinational companies will replace the traditional cartel-like arrangements that have governed international telecommunications for many years. Something similar may well be occurring in international air transport. In many ways the links in telecommunications resemble the European and transatlantic links formed in air transport.

In the airline industry there have been horizontal agreements of one kind or another for a great many years. Before liberalization, and before government authorities took steps to eliminate them, international airlines often had pooling agreements with each other. Under these arrangements the revenue earned by different carriers operating a particular route was shared between them in accordance with a specific formula. In some cases revenues were divided up in proportion to the capacity offered by each carrier. In others, airlines pooled revenues only up to a certain percentage of seats sold, or by some other more complex revenue allocation scheme. Pooling agreements also often provided for co-operative scheduling and joint marketing, two things that are important aspects of the alliances airlines are currently entering into. But there is an essential difference: the old pooling agreements were between carriers co-operating the *same* route, whereas the current alliances are mostly between airlines operating *different* routes. Two of the most important strategic objectives behind the current alliances are traffic feed and access to new markets. Airlines are now tending to ally themselves with partners that have complementary networks rather than services against which they are in head-to-head competition. Major airlines operating trunk routes seek alliances with small regional carriers flying short-haul routes; international airlines with no cabotage rights seek to be associated with airlines serving large domestic networks in foreign countries; and airlines with a large presence in one part of the world often wish to team up with others in areas where they are not all that well represented. Thus the alliances of today are not so horizontal in nature as inter-airline pooling agreements used to be in the past; and, to the extent that the partners supply each other with traffic and other kinds of business the alliances do have something of a vertical nature about them. This is also what appears to be happening in the telecommunications industry. And it is also, to a certain extent, a feature of alliances in the motor industry.

In the motor industry – and also in electronics – a major focus over the past decade has been to develop vertical alliances in order to match the perceived benefits of good relations with suppliers, such as those enjoyed by the Japanese Keiretsu. In the computer industry the development of vertical alliances has had the effect of intensifying competition in the product market, there being little in the way of horizontal collaboration between the main manufacturers of computers.

The clearest example of vertical alliances in the airline industry are the collaborative arrangements that exist between carriers and hotels, car hire firms, travel agents, and other companies involved in travel and tourism. For a while some airlines diversified into these travel-related businesses, in attempts to offer total travel products and thereby secure for themselves higher proportions of consumers' total expenditure on travel. But generally speaking these ventures were unsuccessful, because of the strain they put on airlines' capital and managerial resources; and in times of financial stringency these kinds of investment are often among the first to be curtailed. For example, in 1980, Pan American sold its chain of Intercontinental Hotels to Grand Metropolitan, in order to meet a high deficit on its airline operations. For similar reasons TWA transferred its interests in Hilton International to its holding company, Trans World Corporation (which subsequently sold it to Ladbroke). And more recently Air France sold its Meridien hotel chain to Forté, and Aer Lingus divested itself of its Copthorne Hotel group. Airlines now prefer alliances instead, leaving other travel and tourism business to specialist managements with long experience in these industries. BA, for instance, is in partnership with a number of hotel chains including Marriot, Hilton Mandarin Oriental, the Ritz-Carlton Group, the Savoy Group, Radisson Edwardian, the Taj Group in India, and the Southern Sun Group in South Africa. Apart from hotels, BA is also in partnership with Hertz for car hire and with Diners Club for charge cards.

Few airlines have been able to integrate vertically with airport authorities, usually because airports are almost always in public ownership and because governments usually prohibit airlines from taking equity stakes in them. One exception is Alitalia, one of whose subsidiaries is responsible for the management of Aeroporti di Roma, Italy's main airport. Another is Cathay Pacific with its investment in Xiamen airport in China, about 500 miles south west of Shanghai.

These few cases apart, the only instances in which there is a significant degree of vertical integration between airlines and airports is where airlines own their own airport terminals. This is not unusual in the US and also applies in the case of domestic terminals in Australia. Governments also intend to constrain airlines' equity holdings in undertakings running air traffic control facilities if and when these are transferred to the private sector. The UK government for example put limitations on the maximum number of shares that airlines could hold in the National Air Traffic Services (NATS) company.

External alliances – or, as they are sometimes known, 'diversification' alliances – are seen only relatively infrequently. Over the past decade the chemical industry has shown a lot of interest in developing external collaboration, especially with small biotechnology firms in search of new products. So far as airlines are concerned, external alliances have traditionally been limited largely to joint ventures in marketing promotions (e.g. special offers on fares, frequent flyer bonuses, package holidays, insurance, etc.). But there are now some indications of airlines hiving off other specialized activities to external alliances. The 50/50 joint venture between Delta Airlines and AT&T, under which AT&T handles much of Delta's internal computing requirements – although not its reservations system – is a good case in point.

In short, the main kind of alliance in the airline industry is that formed amongst carriers themselves, although this has perhaps become less horizontal and more vertical in nature as markets have become more and more liberalized. This reflects similar developments in other industries like telecommunications.

Technological and market motives

What fundamentally accounts for the proliferation of alliances, both generally in business and in airlines in particular? This is an interesting question in its own right. It is also central to the formulation of business strategy. This is so because the potential for sustainable advantage to be achieved via interfirm collaboration will depend on the nature and strength of the underlying forces motivating alliances, and these may vary from industry to industry and from case to case.

Some accounts of the growth in strategic alliances visualize it as the result of a large number of different forces at work (Lynch, 1993). It is helpful, however, to refer to a prominent analysis that sees the main explanation in terms of a small set of forces of a pervasive nature. This is the globalization thesis of the Japanese business guru, Kenichi Ohmae.

According to Ohmae it is the sheer scale of contemporary global industries and global markets that requires interfirm collaboration, as opposed to the establishment of large global enterprises. In Ohmae's words:

> globalization mandates alliances, makes them absolutely essential to strategy. Uncomfortable perhaps – but that's the way it is. Like it or not, the simultaneous developments that go under the name of globalization make alliances – [business] entente – necessary
>
> (Ohmae, 1993)

The simultaneous developments Ohmae identifies are:

- The convergence of consumer preferences across the world.
- The fact that modern products require access to, and control of, so many critical-edge technologies that many companies (however large) cannot maintain a leading competence in all of them at the same time.
- The need with global products to incur immense fixed costs, for example in research and development, in information technology, in building transnational brand loyalty, and in setting up worldwide sales and distribution networks.

Ohmae emphasizes the last factor so far as alliances are concerned:

> the need to bolster contribution points in a single, clear direction: towards the forging of alliances to share fixed costs. This is a fundamental change from the competitive world of 15, or even 10, years ago. . . This new logic forces managers to amortize their fixed costs over a much larger market base . . . this logic mandates alliances that both enable and facilitate global, contribution-based, strategies
>
> (Ohmae, 1993)

The fundamental question here concerns the significance of fixed costs. Most of the costs incurred in airline operation are escapable and therefore variable; and it is generally accepted that the airline industry is one in which the ratio of fixed to variable costs is relatively low. As argued in Chapter 3 it is not fixed costs in general but more specifically sunk costs that represent the critical dimension to be considered in this regard. The relevant point is that, if sunk costs are zero, what would be the underlying motive for alliances? Where sunk costs are zero – as the model of 'perfect' contestability has it – firms could make go-it-alone hit-and-run entries to, and exits from, given industries to earn a stream of net returns, without needing to go through all the costs and difficulties of forming complex alliances with other firms. In other words, Ohmae's point may be more appropriate, especially in the airline context, if it is recast in terms of sunk costs.

In a major empirical study of some 10 000 co-operation agreements between firms in various industries (but not including airlines) over the period 1980–89, Hagedoorn (1993) identified the existence of two broad sets of reasons why firms join alliances: motives associated with technology, such as that required for basic or applied research; and motives concerned with market access and/or with influencing the structure of the market. Hagedoorn's study concentrated specifically on alliances in which there were at least some technology motives, but even within this constrained data set, it was found upon detailed examination that market motives often predominated over technology ones. This was particularly the case in mature industries such as automobiles, food and drink, chemicals and consumer electronics; and, more surprisingly, it was also the case in hi-tech growth industries like telecommunications, computers, and microelectronics. But it would not ordinarily be expected that essentially service-based industries – even some of those that make extensive use of hi-tech equipment – would find much reason to form alliances based on the technology motive. Almost by definition the scope for technological collaboration is smaller in a service industry than it is in manufacturing.

There are however some instances in the airline industry in which technological factors are strong motives for alliances. Back in the 1960s two groups of European airlines formed international consortia with the objective of economizing on aircraft maintenance. With the introduction of large aircraft like B747 and DC-10, airlines realized that a fleet size of at least 20 would be needed by each carrier to justify the necessary investments in hangars, equipment, and simulators. So, KLM, SAS, Swissair, and the former UTA got together to form KSSU in 1968, this organization becoming known as KSS following the merger of UTA with Air France. Air France itself, together with Alitalia, LH, and Sabena, set up Atlas, Iberia joining in 1972.

The purpose of these alliances was to permit airlines to specialize in certain aspects of maintenance, whether airframes, engines, avionics or landing gear, or to concentrate on particular aircraft types, so that for example, Air France specialized on 747 airframes and landing gear plus GE CF6 engines; LH on A300 airframes and landing gear plus JT9D engines; Sabena on A310 engines; and Alitalia on DC-10 airframes. In this way savings in aircraft maintenance of the order of some 10 to 20 per cent were achieved. The KSSU and Atlas consortia evolved to encompass other aspects of technical co-operation and co-ordination. In 1989 three of the Atlas members – LH, Air France, and Iberia – signed a more comprehensive agreement covering, among other things, harmonization of aircraft purchasing policies, establishment of a joint catering company, joint training of pilots, and increased collaboration in the development of computer reservations systems (CRSs). The Atlas consortium is now formally disbanded, but some co-operation continues on a bilateral subcontracting basis. The KSS consortium remains more or less in being, with KLM maintaining 747 airframes and CF6 engines; SAS maintaining JT9D engines; and Air France maintaining landing gear (a task originally assigned to the former airline UTA). But a number of developments are limiting the usefulness of these two European consortia. The fleet sizes of the airline partners have now reached levels sufficient to justify each carrier investing in its own maintenance facilities. At the same time membership of the maintenance consortia does not correspond to membership of the global alliances, the three members of Atlas ending up in three separate global alliances (LH in Star, Air France in SkyTeam, and Iberia in oneworld). Indeed there is now often closer co-operation across the Atlas/KSS divide than there is within Atlas or KSS. LH and SAS, for example, both members of the Star global alliance but one originally in Atlas and the other in KSS, have entered a maintenance joint venture with each other. And it seems likely that future co-operation on maintenance is going to be more with partners in the global alliances than in the traditional maintenance consortia. One disadvantage with maintenance consortia is the time taken up transporting parts and spares from one centre to another; and a further development is the growing trend for some major airlines to set up and run specialist maintenance subsidiaries (e.g. LH Technik) which undertake third-party maintenance for other carriers, including some against which they are in competition for passengers.

Besides Atlas and KSS there have been other technical consortia with similar objectives. The decision of Cathay Pacific, SIA, Garuda, and Thai Airways International to establish SEAMA (the South East Asian Maintenance Alliance) formed the first multi-airline collaborative venture of its kind in Asia. This was intended to reduce costs by eliminating duplication of equipment, training, and spares inventories. There are now many examples of technical collaboration between established airlines in Western countries and carriers in developing countries. Western airlines often have comparative advantages in technological expertise while developing countries' airlines have much lower labour costs. The recent opening up of the aviation sector in the People's Republic of China seems likely to presage a lot of joint ventures between international airlines and Chinese regional carriers. Among international airlines seeking to collaborate in China are LH,

Qantas, SIA, Cathay Pacific, and Japan Airlines. The last three, along with Air China and the Boeing aircraft company, have all invested in a joint maintenance facility in Xiamen, to service the fleets operated by Xiamen Airlines. LH Technik also has a joint venture with Air China, Aircraft Maintenance and Engineering (AMECO) based in Beijing, to carry out D checks on Boeing aircraft. And Qantas has been in discussions about setting up something similar with airlines in Shenzhen, Shanghai, and Yunan. The indications are that these initiatives are merely the start of more extensive links between Chinese and foreign airlines, especially given the explosive growth of air travel in China.

Alliances to achieve savings in cost are important but so far they have been far less common than market-motivated alliances. In a survey of some 200 alliances the Boston Consulting Group found the most common objectives to be traffic feed, access to new markets, defence of current markets and economies in marketing generally (Flanagan and Marcus, 1993). The emphasis in many marketing alliances on code-sharing, block space agreements, franchising, links between frequent flyer programmes, etc. comes from airlines seeking to reap economies of scope by extending route networks, as discussed in Chapter 4. The motive behind many marketing agreements stems from the belief that the airlines that will be in the best position to compete in the future will be those that can offer the most extensive global networks. Co-operating with other airlines is a means of tapping into worldwide traffic flows and enhancing the 'global reach' of a carrier's network, which might otherwise be limited by the traffic rights which its national government had been able to negotiate.

One of the most important marketing objectives of alliances is to encourage interline hubbing by facilitating co-operation between domestic and international services where restrictions on cabotage prevent the international carrier from serving domestic routes and where, under existing bilateral air service agreements, the domestic carrier had no traffic rights on the relevant international routes. They also encourage closer links between the services of two international carriers. It is possible through forming alliances to make good fits between the networks of the partners and to provide swift connections at the hub airports each partner serves.

Interfirm governance

Modes of governance in alliances vary greatly from case to case. There are some 'strong' forms of governance, where the directors of one company sit on the board of the other. But some alliances merely involve informal understandings with no exchange of managerial control. Hagedoorn (1993) suggests that strong modes of interfirm governance tend to be associated with a more long-term strategic dimension to the collaborative relationship; and that 'weaker' forms of interfirm governance reflect more limited objectives.

Strong modes of governance are often backed up by the partners taking stakes in each other's equity capital.

7.4 Experience of alliances

A number of studies have investigated the effects of alliances, with a view to estimating their impacts on both airlines and passengers. Gellman Research Associates (1994) conducted a counterfactual scenario analysis – comparing outcomes with what might have been expected to have happened had the alliances not been struck – and drew the conclusions summarized in Table 7.11 in relation to the BA/USAir and KLM/Northwest alliances. The findings on the BA/USAir case indicated that both partners gained in terms of net profit, although BA gained much more (almost five times more) than USAir; and that most of the extra profits came at the expense of other carriers, especially other US carriers. In total US airlines lost as a result of the alliance while non-US airlines (mainly BA) gained. Passenger benefits were estimated in terms of reduced fares and improved services

Table 7.11 Estimated effects of the BA/USAir and KLM/Northwest alliances (first quarter, 1994). *Source*: Gellman Research Associates (1994)

Airline	Change in net profit ($ million)	Change in passenger benefits ($ million)	Change in social benefits ($ million)
BA/USAir alliance	27.2		
USAir	5.6		
Other US carriers	−26.7		
Other non-US carriers	−0.8		
US total	−21.1	4.9	−16.2
Non-US total	26.4	5.4	31.8
Grand total	5.3	10.3	15.0
KLM/Northwest alliance			
KLM	10.6		
Northwest	16.1		
Other US carriers	−15.7		
Other non-US carriers	−8.6		
US total	0.4	13.0	13.4
Non-US total	2.0	14.1	16.1
Grand total	2.4	27.1	29.5

and both US and non-US passengers gained, so that in overall terms the change in social benefits (change in airlines' net profits plus change in passenger benefits) was positive. Similar findings were made in respect of the KLM/Northwest alliance, except that the gain to Northwest more or less cancelled out the loss to other US carriers, so that US airlines as a whole broke even on the alliance, unlike in the BA/ USAir case where they lost heavily.

A later study by the US General Accounting Office (1995) was not an econometric analysis, being based mainly on interviews with airline representatives and government officials. In addition to the BA/USAir and KLM/Northwest alliances, the General Accounting Office also looked at three alliances involving United, those with LH, Ansett, and British Midland. Its conclusions were similar: all airlines in these alliances benefited in terms of net profits, albeit to varying degrees; and a lot of the gains came from carriers outside the alliances. For example, some representatives of Continental told the GAO that their airlines had lost an estimated $1 million in 1994 because of some traffic it would normally have carried between the US and Europe had transferred to the KLM/Northwest alliance. Some estimates were produced of increased passenger numbers travelling on alliance partners, for example United gaining 600 passengers a day from its alliance with LH, 120 passengers a day from its alliance with Ansett and 30 000 passengers a year from its alliance with British Midland.

There is little doubt that some airlines have experienced some significant revenue enhancement from alliances. And some more recent estimates are given in Table 7.12. What is more open to doubt is the effect of alliances on airline fares. An extensive investigation aimed at casting some light on this was conducted by Park (1997) who estimated a number of econometric models on annual panel data for North Atlantic routes for the 1990–94

Table 7.12 Estimated revenue enhancements from alliances, 1997.[a] *Source: Aviation Strategy*

Airline	Route group	Revenue (millions)	Enhancement (millions)	Enhancement as percentage of revenue
Delta	Atlantic	US $2223	US $138	6.2
KLM	Atlantic	DFL 2011	DFL 400	19.9
LH	Atlantic	DM 3000	DM 300	10.0
Northwest	Atlantic	US $644	US $65	10.1
Qantas	Kangaroo[b]	A$ 723	A$ 35	4.8
United	Atlantic	US $1745	US $120	6.9

[a] The estimates refer to claims made by the airlines.

[b] Australia/Europe routes.

period. In this study a distinction was drawn between 'complementary' and 'parallel' alliances, the former being one where the main purpose is to link up two partners' complementary, or non-overlapping, networks and the latter one where the networks do overlap. Most alliances involve a mix of overlapping markets (e.g. the inter-continental routes) and non-overlapping markets (e.g. routes in two different continents). There was some evidence in the Park study that complementary alliances (e.g. KLM/Northwest) led to lower fares while predominantly parallel alliances (e.g. Delta/Swissair/Sabena) had something of an opposite effect in increasing them; but, overall, Park's findings suggest that passengers in North Atlantic markets are generally better off as a result of alliances and that most alliance partners experience greater traffic increases on their alliance routes than they do on their non-alliance routes.

Airline alliances have attracted a lot of interest from transport economists undertaking econometric research using empirical data – rather in the same way that airline deregulation once did! Econometric studies investigating the effects of airline alliances include those by Youssef and Hansen (1994), Dresner, Flipcop, and Windle (1995), Oum, Park, and Zhang (2000), Bruckner and Whalen (2000), and Bruckner and Pels (2005). Broadly speaking, the results of these studies suggest that passengers have gained from lower interline fares, but that the net benefits to the airlines involved were not especially large. Reviewing a number of these studies, Morrish and Hamilton (2002) could find no conclusive evidence that alliance membership put airlines into a position from which they could make much in the way of monopoly profits.

7.5 Pro- and anti-competitive effects

It is widely expected that the growing number of alliances, possibly followed by some outright mergers, will result in the airline industry continuing to become more and more highly concentrated. Forecasts may vary on exactly how many airlines will survive or on how far the industry will be dominated by just a few large carriers, or consortia of carriers bound together in some form of global alliance. But what is generally agreed is that the number of major airlines operating as entirely separate entities may fall quite sharply. This once again raises the question of what will happen to inter-airline competition.

Increased concentration is often associated with a higher risk of collusion or with firms being able to set wider price–cost margins, whether because of enhanced market power exerted by individual firms or because of the umbrella effect under which market power carries over to other firms in the industry as well. Where airlines are lining up in alliance groupings there is also the possibility of certain groupings dominating certain market areas. Much may depend on how far the alliances are complementary, linking airline networks in different areas, and how far they are parallel, with airlines operating head-to-head on the same routes. Emphasizing that his airline needs partners with complementary rather than overlapping networks, the Vice President of International Relations at LH claimed that, of 3000 services covered by the alliance with United, only two had been operated by both airlines before the alliance (Schulte-Strathaus, 1994). In cases like this alliances are likely to increase market power only on routes between the market areas. But here they could increase it quite a lot, creating virtual monopolies on routes between the hubs of alliance partners, permitting the exercise of considerable market power in hub-to-hub markets. In the international context entry to such routes is inhibited not just by airport capacity constraints but often by government regulation as well; and, in addition to the monopolization effect, alliances may inhibit competition in hub-to-hub markets that might otherwise have come from airlines seeking to expand their networks through internal expansion.

In a study of the market power effect of alliances, Youssef and Hansen (1994) examined the former alliance between Swissair and SAS (1994) and examined the former alliance between Swissair and SAS, an alliance which, on account of the specially close relationship between the airlines, had been dubbed an 'alliance within an alliance', both airlines being members of what was then the broader European Quality Alliance. What Youssef and Hansen found was that in hub-to-hub markets (between Copenhagen, Stockholm and Oslo in Scandinavia and Geneva and Zurich in Switzerland) competition was virtually eliminated; and that on non-stop hub-to-hub routes fares increased much more than fares on other non-alliance non-stop routes in the same region over the same period. The conclusion drawn was that the airlines had taken advantage of the increased concentration in hub-to-hub markets to earn higher profits on these routes. The alliance between Swissair and SAS now no longer exists. As a member of Star, SAS now has a close relationship with LH, which is possibly reflected in some relatively high fares on hub-to-hub routes between Germany and Scandinavia.

A statistical analysis undertaken by the author sought to identify routes on which fares charged are unusually high. The samples were limited to routes within the European Union and the focus of attention was on the levels of fully flexible fares charged by major EU airlines (in July 1997). Fare levels taper with route distance in a manner indicated in a study by the Civil Aviation Authority (see Figure 6.1 in Chapter 6). An appropriate way of representing this is to regress fare level upon route distance by estimating the equation:

$$\hat{Y}_i = \hat{a} = \hat{b}X_i$$

where Y denotes fare level (expressed here in ECUs), X denotes route distance (in kilometres), a is an intercept term, b the slope of the relationship, $i = 1, 2, \ldots, n$ are sample observations across routes, and where the hat ($\wedge$) indicates estimates. The coefficients were derived by first estimating the slope as:

$$\hat{b} = \frac{n\sum X_i Y_i - \sum X_i \sum Y_i}{n\sum X_i^2 - (\sum X_i)^2}$$

which was then substituted into the following equation to find the intercept:

$$\hat{a} = \frac{\sum Y_i - \hat{b}\sum X_i}{n} = \bar{Y} - \hat{b}\bar{X}$$

The degree of statistical explanation was assessed by the coefficient of determination r^2, calculated as:

$$r^2 = \frac{\sum(\hat{Y}_i - \bar{Y})^2}{\sum(Y_i - \bar{Y})^2}$$

where $\bar{Y}$ is the sample mean. The level of statistical explanation was considered satisfactory if $r^2 > 0.7$, implying that over 70 per cent of the variation in the dependent fare variable is explained statistically by variation in the independent distance variable. In testing for observed fares that are unusually high or unusually low, the standard error of estimate, S, was used, where:

$$S = \sqrt{\frac{\sum Y_i^2 - \hat{a}\sum Y - \hat{b}\sum X_i Y_i}{n}}$$

On the assumption that the errors, the differences between the observed fare levels and the levels predicted by the equation $(Y_i - \hat{Y}_i)$ are normally distributed, 68 per cent of the sample of observed levels should lie between plus and minus S either side of the estimated regression line. Hence any observed level outside this range can be considered either unusually high or unusually low. An unusually high fare level would be where $(Y_i - \hat{Y}_i) > S$.

Separate regressions were run for each airline studied; and the results for LH and SAS (SK) were as follows:

LH: $\hat{Y}_i = 125.42 + 0.32824X_i$ $r^2 = 0.856$
$S = 56.90$
$n = 204$

SK: $\hat{Y}_i = 113.60 + 0.24690X_i$ $r^2 = 0.724$
$S = 86.90$
$n = 137$

These equations imply that fares on the following hub-to-hub routes were unusually high:

	X_i	Y_i	$\hat{Y}_i$	$(Y_i - \hat{Y}_i)$ as % of $\hat{Y}_i$
LH: Frankfurt–Copenhagen	678	404	348	16
LH: Frankfurt–Stockholm	1221	601	526	14
LH: Munich–Stockholm	1316	680	557	22
SK: Copenhagen–Frankfurt	678	329	281	17
SK: Copenhagen–Munich	809	401	313	28
SK: Stockholm–Frankfurt	1221	502	415	21

The comparisons here are affected by fluctuations in currency conversion factors, but nonetheless it is clear that fares between the two largest hubs in Germany and the two largest hubs in Scandinavia are well above the estimated regression lines. Apart from a very few flights by other operators, all six routes were effective LH/SK duopolies and so the hub airlines were in a position to exert some market power.

When two airlines serving the same route enter into an alliance it is only to be expected that they will take steps to co-ordinate their marketing of that route. The alliance usually includes reciprocal arrangements for the carriers to act as sales agents for one another at each end of the route. In these circumstances there is a natural suspicion that the airlines will not compete against each other head-to-head and will prefer to fix mutually acceptable fares, to schedule services at mutually convenient times and, where code-sharing agreements apply, to arrange joint listings in CRSs. There is then some fear that competition will be curtailed in some important travel markets. There are for instance some hub-to-hub markets in which the majority of passengers flying the route have both origins and destinations in the hub cities concerned. Where entry is restricted, by the terms of the relevant bilateral air service agreement for example, and where alternative routeings are of much greater circuitry and consequently involve much longer journey times, the alliance partners could indeed be left with considerable market power on the route in question.

Market power is often a major concern for government competition authorities; and concerns of this nature have caused governments to intervene in two of the alliances struck by BA. The Australian Trade Practices Commission blocked a proposal by the BA/Qantas alliance for the joint fixing of passenger fares and freight rates on Europe–Australia services. And the original BA/USAir deal was only approved by the US government after USAir was divested of its UK–US route authorities, these being passed to other US carriers. The policy of the UK government has for many years been to foster and promote the entry of third-carriers on routes that would otherwise remain as duopolies (Civil Aviation Authority, 1993b).

This may be an eminently suitable policy for some heavily trafficked hub-to-hub routes, but the question is whether it should be applied generally. Where partner airlines seek to fix fares and co-ordinate capacity in a hub-to-hub market, this threatens a return to the old horizontal pooling agreements of the past. Competition authorities are always likely to oppose moves in this direction, but then it is hard to see any (eventual) outcome other than the withdrawal of one or other of the partners from the route in question. The maintenance of competition on the route will then depend heavily on the entry of airlines outside the alliance. But this may be seriously inhibited by capacity constraints at either or both the hubs involved.

Alliances, in effect, enable each airline to extend its marketable network to cities served by its partner. If this results in each member of the alliance being able to attract more traffic without increasing the number of routes operated, then each member's marginal cost may fall through economies of density. And this cost reduction may be achieved very soon after the forming of the alliance, thus reducing the significance of the timing qualification to Williamson's trade-off analysis in this instance. For there is no reason to expect the density economies to take all that long to come through. However, if competition authorities foster new entry on some of the routes within an alliance's hub and spokes system, this may benefit passengers flying the routes in question, but at the same time it may cause some loss of density economies for the alliance partners, resulting in an increase in marginal cost. Competitive pressure may counteract the higher marginal cost on routes on which new entry has occurred, but not of course on those on which there has been no increase in competition. In this sense the entry of new competition on an individual spoke may generate negative externalities across the network as a whole.

Across the network as a whole competition may be increasing anyway. As argued above (in Chapters 3 and 5) any reductions in competition in hub-to-hub markets may be offset, or more than offset, by increased competition in through markets via hubs. Alliances are clearly stimulating competition in through markets by, among other things, encouraging 'double hubbing'. An illustrative example of this is given in Figure 7.1. Around the world there are a great many city pairs not served by direct flights. One such city pair in the North Atlantic market is Kansas City– Gothenburg, but passengers wishing to travel between these two cities have a fairly wide choice of indirect services: all four transatlantic alliances provide multiple connection options, making up a grand total of 89 services a week (albeit services that entail two connections to be made, one at a hub in the US and one at a European hub). And this is not an isolated example of where all four alliances compete. In Autumn 1997 Stuttgart in Germany had no less than 22 transatlantic city pairs in which all four alliances competed (ter Kuile, 1997).

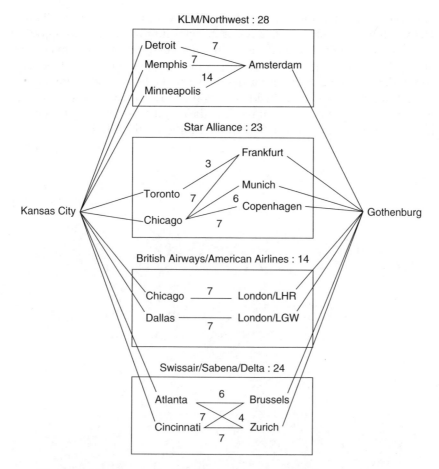

KLM/Northwest : 28

Detroit ╲ 7

Memphis ⁷ ⟶ Amsterdam

14

Minneapolis

Star Alliance : 23

Frankfurt

3

Munich

Toronto 7 6 Copenhagen

Kansas City

Chicago 7

Gothenburg

British Airways/American Airlines : 14

Chicago — 7 — London/LHR

Dallas ⟶ London/LGW

7

Swissair/Sabena/Delta : 24

Atlanta 6 Brussels

7 4

Cincinnati ⟶ Zurich

7

This chart shows the number of weekly frequencies which offer connecting times of 2 hours or less through the hubs

Figure 7.1 Competition between hubs: an example of double hubbing on routes between Gothenburg and Kansas City, Autumn 1997 (*Source: Airline Business*)

Where mergers and alliances increase market power on routes to and from hubs, but at the same time induce greater competition in through markets via hubs, there is a further trade-off to consider. Passengers in hub-to-hub markets may lose while passengers in through markets gain. As argued in Chapter 5 (Section 5.6) the balance between these two effects will depend on: the relative widths of price–cost margins on short- and long-haul routes; own- and cross-price elasticities of demand in through markets as compared with those in hub-to-hub markets; and the distribution of passenger gains and losses by income or journey purpose. Ideally all these factors should be taken into account in determining the balance between pro- and anti-competitive effects. While mergers and alliances may often appear anti-competitive, in practice some of their effects will be pro-competitive. Competition authorities then face the following dilemma: how to curb the market power wielded on routes to and from congested hubs without at the same time impairing the ability of merged airlines or alliances partners to compete for through traffic via these hubs.

8

Transnational airlines

8.1 Are airlines losing their nationalities?

The so-called 'flag carrier' concept is now out-dated, mainly because it is incompatible with the need to make the European airline industry competitive on a global scale

(Comité des Sages, 1994)

It is possible that alliances are, in certain cases, simply precursors to outright mergers. The signs are there. With the same logo, joint advertising and close co-ordination of service schedules, KLM and Northwest have already gone quite some way in the direction of merger (and might still sometime in the future find themselves in a merger situation, despite the fact that KLM has already merged with Air France). In other cases the fact that alliances have adopted common air-craft liveries, or common uniforms for cabin staff, is possibly a portent of some more fully con-summated relationships to come. Also there are some instances in which equity purchases have earned investing airlines options to acquire further shares in the future. The scope for cross-border shareholders seems certain to increase as state ownership declines and as privatized airlines seek greater access to foreign capital in a deregulated or liberalized environment. But there are still some formidable impediments to cross-border mergers.

It is true that some national governments are beginning to relax restrictions on foreign ownership, but if foreign ownership goes beyond a certain point, this raises serious questions regarding traffic rights on international routes. Ownership clauses in bilateral air service treaties restrict the grant of the relevant freedoms of the air to airlines owned and controlled by nationals of the state concerned. As things stand, if an airline of one state takes over the airline of another state, then this could invalidate the third, fourth, and fifth freedoms held by the airline being taken over, on the ground that it no longer qualifies as a national airline of the state concerned. In terms of Figure 4.6, if the airline of State B took over the airline of State A, this could mean the loss of third and fourth freedoms between State A, and States X and Y.

It is possible for one airline to buy up another. A US airline could in principle buy shares in any publicly quoted European airline and might, for a time, acquire a controlling interest. But would such control be worth anything? The ownership and control provisions in air service agreements mean that the acquired company would cease to be a 'national' airline. It would then risk losing international rights negotiated under air service agreements with states outside the European Union; and, incidentally, it would also lose its right to an operating licence for routes within the EU (since the EU's definition of a 'community carrier' excludes majority ownership by non-EU citizens). Thus the new owner of the airline 'would have acquired an impressive but costly static aircraft display' (Staniland, 1998).

A consideration of this kind became a central issue in the bid SAS made for British Caledonian in 1987. If the SAS bid had succeeded, and SAS had acquired a majority stake and effective control of BCAL, other countries might not have accepted the merged airline as a UK designated airline on international routes. Other countries have separate agreements on traffic rights with Scandinavia and they might not have been prepared to grant SAS rights on former BCAL routes out of London, which in this context they might have interpreted as seventh freedoms. Similar concerns were felt by the Dutch and German governments when KLM and Lufthansa were being privatized. Both adopted procedures designed to protect the airlines' status as national carriers. The Dutch government insisted on having the option to buy back KLM shares if there was any danger of non-nationals acquiring a controlling position. And in Germany the shares of all publicly listed German airlines (not just Lufthansa) must be registered shares whose transfer is subject to the consent of the company, which enables the company to force the sale of foreign owned stock if in aggregate it approached 50 per cent of the total. Doubts about what might happen to traffic rights could be a serious deterrent to full cross-border mergers. For often the main objective of such mergers is to achieve economies of scope by extending marketable networks, enhancing access to through markets by combining rights held separately by the airlines involved. If there is some risk of either or both parties to the merger losing some of these rights, then the perceived advantages in merging are going to be that much less. This partly explains the current preference for alliances over mergers. There is much less risk of losing traffic rights as a result of an alliance.

However, one aspect of alliances that can have important implications for traffic rights is code-sharing. There has been some debate over whether or not code-sharing should require specific authorization, in the same way that third, fourth, and fifth freedom traffic rights do. The vast majority of inter-governmental bilateral agreements were drawn up and signed long before code-sharing became commonplace on international routes; and in many of these agreements, like for example the Bermuda II agreement between the UK and the US, there is no reference at all to code-sharing. Some countries have argued that code-sharing should be regulated, on the ground that airlines are in fact holding out services to the public as if they had the traffic rights concerned. This has been the view of the US, which has been worrying that code-sharing might give the appearance of foreign airlines possessing cabotage rights on internal US domestic routes. US policy on code-sharing has been evolving through several stages (de Groot, 1994). When code-sharing first became a matter of international aeropolitical concern, the US sought to restrict it to routes on which the foreign carrier held the appropriate rights, effectively limiting its use to routes to/from gateway airports specified in the applicable bilateral agreement. In 1988, the US adopted the position that code-sharing has to be covered by an express statement of authorization; the next step was to introduce traffic rights for the sole purpose of code-sharing. Code-sharing with carriers operating US domestic routes then became part of the 'Open Skies' concept: the US was prepared to be fairly liberal in granting permission for code-sharing in exchange for foreign countries agreeing to liberal bilaterals on traffic rights and the associated issues of market access, frequencies, and pricing freedom. For example, the US–The Netherlands Open Skies bilateral led to extensive code-sharing possibilities for the Northwest/KLM alliance. But bringing code-sharing into bilateral negotiations has turned it into another bargaining chip which some countries have used to demand reciprocity. Some countries whose airlines see relatively few opportunities for code-sharing have tended to argue that code-sharing infringes traffic rights, especially restrictions on fifth freedom. Germany, Greece, Israel, and Saudi Arabia, for example, have all complained of the disadvantage at which they perceive their airlines to be in competition with code-shared services of the Northwest/KLM alliance via Amsterdam. The governments of these countries have argued that through traffic carried on routes east of Amsterdam should be regarded as beyond-point fifth freedom traffic and therefore should not exceed a certain proportion (e.g. 15 or 20 per cent) of third and fourth freedom traffic on the route concerned. At one time Germany considered applying frequency limitations on such connecting services. But the main response has been to demand aeropolitical concessions in exchange for permitting code-sharing. For example, Finland granted Northwest code-sharing authority only after it obtained traffic rights to San Francisco.

Complex negotiations over code-sharing hark back to the old disputes over sixth freedom traffic and point up once more the tensions between airlines pursuing commercial interests and governments pursuing national interests. If the trends towards liberalization, privatization, foreign ownership and ultimately cross-border mergers continue, the long-term future of present bilateral system must be in some doubt.

Nationalism in civil aviation may die hard, but die it probably will – eventually. This is certainly the view (or hope?) of a number of airline executives. A former Chairman of British Airways (BA) expressed it as follows:

> National interest is no longer the same as producer interest. The producer is less an arm of state and more of a normal international business that happens to be based in the country. If the choice boils down to what is good for the consumer against what is good for the indigenous airlines, how is a nation to decide? And if a country wishes to maintain a multi-airline policy, but its market is too small to support more than one airline efficiently, should airline competitiveness or national policy be sacrificed? . . . the nationality principle is weaker today than it has ever been.
>
> (Ayling, 1993)

On one view, if any industry should be leading the drive towards globalization, it should be civil aviation (Skapinker, 1999). After all, airlines are in the business every day of transporting millions of people across international boundaries, dealing with dozens of different currencies and languages. Airlines are under some considerable pressure to become global firms, given that their most important customers, international business travellers, want to be able to fly anywhere in the world without having to check in their luggage at every stopover or to switch terminals at every airport where they change flights. On any given flight there could be a broad cosmopolitan mix of passengers by nationality, as illustrated in Figure 5.5. It was largely in recognition of this that BA decided to remove the Union Jack flag design from its tailfins in favour of ethnic designs from around the world. As the Chairman of BA's alliance partner American Airlines has put it, there are no flag companies in the oil, pharmaceutical, chemical, motor, tobacco, or hotel industries, nor even in telecommunications. So why should there be flag carriers in air transport?

It may be some time yet before governments retreat from pursuing mercantilist policies 'in the national interest'. Although the role of airlines as a form of military reserve is not so important these days, many countries still see their flag carriers as part of their national identity, as a means of promoting trade and developing tourism, and as an earner of foreign currency. For benefits of this kind many countries are prepared to protect their airlines from the full force of international competition, supporting them with state aids and adopting restrictive stances over traffic rights. But the costs of this are rising, both in terms of the magnitude of subsidies required and in terms of lost opportunities, as more and more airlines elsewhere are privatized and follow purely commercial objectives. Public opinion is increasingly against the idea of airlines being subsidized and there is mounting pressure for the bilateral system of traffic rights to be reformed so as to remove many of the restrictions on where airlines may fly.

The latter is the key to whether – or when – transnational airlines will emerge in any true sense. One might foresee the bilateral system gradually falling away for the very reason that it may soon become rather difficult to say exactly which nationality an airline actually has, that of the country in which it is (or was originally) based or that of the country of the carrier owning a controlling share of its equity. For we are now beginning to see foreign airlines taking majority control of carriers based in other countries. One suggestion is that the present system under which bilateral negotiations are conducted between individual countries will be replaced, at least in part, by one in which negotiations take place between groups of countries or regional blocs. It is possible to envisage bilaterals being negotiated between the European Economic Area (which includes EFTA countries) and the North American Free Trade Area (US, Canada, and Mexico). And other possible blocs for this purpose might include the ASEAN countries in South East Asia, the Andean Pact countries in Latin America, the Australian and New Zealand Single Market and, conceivably, various associations of African, Middle East countries, etc. There are bound to be some fundamental problems with regional negotiations. For instance, how would any traffic rights successfully negotiated by the bloc be allocated among carriers from different countries within the region? In the absence of political union, the regional bloc may have no sovereignty over this and therefore no mandate to trade off the interests of airlines in one member state against those of airlines in others.

More importantly, the cross-border alliances and investments airlines are now making or not limited geographically to the particular region in which they are based. Indeed, in their search for partners with complementary networks, airlines are more interested in alliances and investments *outside* their region rather than within it. It is true that many of the alliances and cross-border investments airlines have made so far have in fact been with airlines of the same region: the Air France/KLM merger, the Lufthansa/Swiss merger, the stakes SAS and Lufthansa have taken in bmi British Midland, the merger of JAL and JAS, and so on. Increasingly however, there are close relationships between airlines in *different* regions: the transatlantic pairings of Northwest/KLM, United/Lufthansa, American/BA, for example.

Airlines' global ambitions will make any attempt to substitute regional aviation agreements for bilaterals signed by individual countries a rather difficult matter. More and more airlines will want to be released from the constraints that their nationalities impose on what they want to do. Nothing is likely to happen suddenly in the near future. But in the longer term it would not be altogether surprising to find that firm's nationality is of no more importance in the airline industry than it is in many other transnational industries.

8.2 Bilateral, multilateral, and plurilateral approaches to route access

Predicting the future is always a hazardous business, especially so in respect of an industry in the process of some profound change. It is always difficult to forecast exactly which airlines will fail, which airlines will survive and which will merge. One in three marriages end in divorce and a similar fate might well befall a large number of the inter-airline links that are being forged in the current wave of alliance formation. The alliance groupings may undergo a lot of changes in the months and years to come. But what is more certain is that the building of alliances will fairly swiftly result in the emergence of some truly global airlines. What is much harder to see is how the current system of traffic rights, presently negotiated under the Chicago Convention in terms of freedoms of the air, will change, or at least evolve, to accommodate transnational airlines operating under the flags of several different nations at one and the same time.

To mark the Silver Jubilee of the Chicago Convention the International Civil Aviation Organization (ICAO) convened a special world conference in Montreal from 23 November to 6 December 1994, almost exactly 50 years to the day from the signing of the original agreement. This, the most important meeting on international aviation for half a century, was attended by over 800 delegates from 137 ICAO contracting states. The object of the conference was to consider whether, in the light of changing attitudes towards various forms of regulation, some new internationally established regulatory arrangements are necessary, or whether indeed they are even possible. No radical decisions were reached. There was, for instance, no consensus on the question of whether the rule that a country's airlines must be owned and effectively controlled by interests based in that country should be changed to allow increased foreign investment. But on one matter there was a consensus, the meeting agreeing that global 'open skies' is not at the present time a feasible option. The most controversial issue discussed concerned the possibilities of some kind of multilateral system replacing, at least in part, the present bilateral regime.

Under a bilateral regime one individual country negotiates with another; under a multilateral system the negotiations would take place between groups of countries (Kasper, 1988). The ICAO conference, while recognizing that there is for the foreseeable future no prospect of a global multilateral agreement in the exchange of traffic rights, accepted that the two kinds of system could co-exist. The US, which because of the vast size of its air travel market could constitute a 'group' on its own in this context, clearly wants to see multilateral open skies agreements being developed, believing that its airlines would fare better under such a regime. Some countries in Europe also want a multilateral system, as does the Transport Directorate of the European Commission (EC). But other European countries do not. Nor is the concept of multilateralism especially appealing to countries in Africa, the Middle East or the Asia–Pacific region. Many of these countries still prefer to retain sovereignty in their negotiations of air transport agreements, and it seems likely that the concept of multilateralism will take longer to develop than the US and some other countries might wish. Given that many countries still jealously guard their own national interests in international air transport, it is difficult to see how a body representing a group of separate countries could be given a mandate to trade the interests of one against the other. For example, if the EC is to negotiate traffic rights on intercontinental routes to and from the European union, it could frequently find itself in the position of having to trade concessions for one country in order to get traffic rights for another. That could become very difficult. Would, for instance, the Italians be willing to sacrifice some market opportunities for Alitalia so that the Greeks could gain some additional rights for Olympic? Or would the Spanish government accept certain limitations on Iberia in order that the EC could secure more openings for TAP Air Portugal? Negotiations of such a kind would clearly involve a lot of hard bargaining, not just between the different groups of countries but among individual countries within the groups as well. EU countries might well find themselves in a stronger bargaining position vis-à-vis the US and other groups of countries if they negotiated as a bloc. But even if bloc negotiations could be conducted successfully at government level, there is still the problem that they could conflict with strategies being pursued at airline level.

As explained earlier, airlines are seeking to reap economies of scope by extending their marketable networks. This they seek to achieve through franchising, block spacing and code-sharing, and by taking equity stakes in, and forming alliances with, airlines operating complementary networks in other parts of the world. As most people envisage them, multilateral negotiations are most likely to take place on an inter-regional basis, where the countries represented in each group are either contiguous or at least

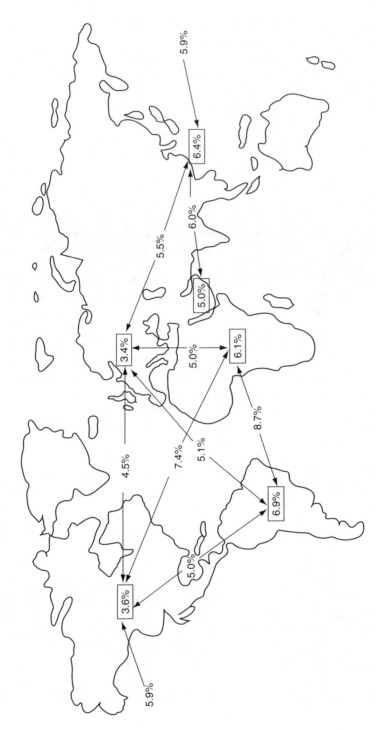

Figure 8.1   Forecast growth in passenger traffic by region, 2005–2025 (*Source:* Derived from data published by Airbus)

neighbouring states in close proximity. But inter-airline marketing agreements and alliances are now less likely to be drawn up between airlines within a particular regional bloc. For airlines are seeking to maximize their 'global reach', in the belief that those that will be in the best position to compete in the future will be those that can offer the most global service.

The most important air travel markets, and their forecast rates of growth, are shown in Figure 8.1. To be a truly global airline a carrier needs to have a substantial presence in as many of these markets as possible. This is clearly the central objective of the global alliance groupings now forming. Airlines' ambitions to become global firms may well in the end lead to the complete removal of controls over international route entry, if not across the entire world, then at least among groups of like-minded states (with group membership not limited to states within particular regional blocs). This concept has been termed 'pluralateralism' and it seems to have more potential as a step in the direction of open skies than either bilateralism or multilateralism (when that is seen as negotiations between regional blocs).

A more freely competitive regime in international air transport is likely to lead to increased market concentration, but that in itself will not necessarily reduce the intensity of competition. There will be places where competition intensity might be expected to increase, despite greater concentration. Where it is likely to increase the most is on those long haul through routes on which airlines' price–cost margins have been at their widest. As such this would be a most beneficial effect, but it may often come only at the expense of increases in monopoly power on shorter routes to and from hubs. Hence there may often be trade-offs to consider.

8.3 A global competition authority?

Who should assess these trade-offs? When controls over entry and pricing are relaxed, it would seem very important that greater attention should be paid to competition policy issues of this kind, especially when the scope for predatory behaviour is as great as it appears to be in air transport. The extra-territorial application of national competition laws is not always appropriate when dealing with international competition taking place at the level of the network. The problems were highlighted when BA and American announced their intention to form an alliance in June 1996.

As originally announced the BA/American alliance would involve:

1   The co-ordination of passenger and cargo services between the US and Europe, with revenue pooled according to the profitability of individual routes.

2   Code-sharing across both airlines' global network of about 36 000 city pairs.
3   The establishment of a fully reciprocal, worldwide frequent flyer programme.

There was to be no exchange of equity or any other form of cross-shareholding; and the arrangement was to last for at least 6 years in the first instance. With such an alliance there would be a particularly complementary fit of the two airlines' networks. One is strong where the other is weak, BA being strong in Europe and the East, American being strong in the US and in Latin/South America. But in order to implement the alliance fully, BA and American needed regulatory approval from three separate competition authorities, the UK Office of Fair Trading in London, the EC in Brussels, and the US Department of Transportation in Washington, DC. The UK Office of Fair Trading would grant its approval if the alliance were to surrender 168 weekly slots in London, but the EC's requirement was for the surrender of 267 weekly slots (a reduction of 86 from its original recommendation of 353). The surrender of 267 slots would permit other airlines (Delta, TWA, British Midland, Virgin Atlantic, Continental, or US Airways) to operate an additional 19 flights a day. BA and American considered this too great a sacrifice and offered to release 196 slots a week (sufficient for 14 new daily flights). But a further bone of contention arose over the disposal of the slots: should BA (or American) be able to sell them? The Office of Fair Trading recommended that selling them should be permitted, but this was opposed by the EC. The US Department of Transportation also required greater access to slots at Heathrow as a condition for approving the alliance but in addition it wanted the UK government to agree an 'open skies' air service agreement with the US as a kind of quid pro quo for granting antitrust immunity. Under this condition the US had already granted antitrust immunity to the other (at that time) three transatlantic alliances, Lufthansa/United, Northwest/KLM, and Delta/Sabena/Swissair/Austrian. The EC, which wanted to negotiate an EU–US open skies agreement, started taking to the European Court those member states which had negotiated their own bilateral agreements with the US, on the basis that, by unilaterally granting US carriers traffic rights within the EU, they were distorting competition. Nonetheless the other three alliances were already operating and offering network benefits that the BA/American alliance was still prevented from offering. Naturally enough, BA and American questioned this, BA pointing out that, increasingly, competition is between airline networks rather than individual airlines, and claiming that the delay in gaining regulatory approval for the alliance was causing it to lose corporate business travel contracts to airlines whose alliances were already fully operational (House of Commons Environment, Transport and Regional Affairs Committee, 1999). It is, however, understandable why the BA/American alliance has worried competition authorities more. The UK–US market with more than 12.5 million passengers a year is more than twice as big as the next largest North Atlantic market, that between Germany and the US. It is thus a very important market per se. Also, the combination of BA and American would give the alliance a high market share, 60 per cent of UK–US sched-uled passenger traffic, and this, together with the importance of Heathrow as a hub airport, may be sufficient for the authorities to regard the BA/American alliance as especially challenging to competition.

However, it is, at the time of writing, a full 10 years since the airlines announced their alliance and the matter is still not resolved, one way or the other. So far as the industry is concerned, the regulatory regime, or regimes, might be seen as something of a mess in this context. A dog's breakfast! There must be a case for some institutional change in the interests of speedier deci-sion-making and in order to prevent airlines having to make multiple appli-cations for regulatory approval from several different competition authorities. If airlines are going to become global entities, then (ideally) the competition authority should be global too. This might suggest an additional role for ICAO or perhaps for the World Trade Organization, if that body is to assume responsibility for competition issues in international trade generally.

Whichever body ultimately becomes responsible for administering them, competition laws are likely to be applied more rigorously. In many inter-national markets airlines still co-ordinate tariffs through the machinery of the International Air Transport Association (IATA). The IATA system still survives in a few parts of the world, because governments, especially those that still own airlines, find it a convenience and because it facilitates the set-ting of joint fares for interline passengers. Fares agreements at IATA Traffic conferences are subject to government approval and are presently granted block exemption from the competition rules of the Treaty of Rome and also immunity from US antitrust legislation. But in an increasingly deregulated and liberalized environment there is pressure to remove these concessions. Antitrust authorities in the US are becoming increasingly reluctant to grant immunity to IATA airlines and would like to see the laws governing inter-national air transport to be much like those they apply domestically. In Europe, the Comité des Sages considered the borderline between consult-ations on tariffs and a price cartel to be a sensitive issue requiring careful handling by competition authorities. During difficult times of weak demand consultations on fares can do much to prevent revenue yields falling to such low levels as to prejudice the financial stability of the whole industry. But at the same time colluding on price offers airlines opportunities to limit the spread of competition. This has been a particular concern of the UK Civil Aviation Authority (CAA) (1994) especially in relation to routes on which there is intrinsically less scope for competition from smaller airlines that do not participate in IATA Traffic Conferences. The CAA feels that 'a watchful eye' needs to be kept on airlines' use of loyalty marketing schemes especially when the rebates and discounts incorporated in them are structured in such a way as to disadvantage smaller airlines. There is clearly much to concern competition authorities here, but in general terms the danger of widespread price collusion is much less than it was in the past. The justification for IATA fares co-ordination in terms of interlining benefits is clearly going to decline further. Experience on international routes is going to mirror that on US domestic routes, with more and more interline connections being substituted for by online ones, or at least by intra-alliance ones, through the increasing use of code-sharing, franchising and block spacing. And governmental interests in tariffs co-ordination is also going to decline as the number of airlines being transferred from state to private ownership increases.

8.4 Towards global airlines

The subject of an address made to the Atlantic Bridge Conference on 30 September 2003 by another former BA Chairman, Rod Eddington, was:

ARE GLOBAL AIRLINES INEVITABLE?

He began answering this question by saying:

> *If it were left to the market, there can be little doubt that international airlines would follow in the footsteps of other industries, and would seek the benefits of scale and scope that are currently denied to them.*
>
> *Banking, telecoms, car manufacturing and I.T. all suffered at one stage from the excessive fragmentation that we find today in the airline business, particularly in Europe*
>
> *Global businesses emerged in these industries to extend their market reach, access fresh sources of capital, and spread their investments over larger revenue bases*

So why does it appear so difficult to achieve global businesses in air transport? On this Eddington referred to what he described as the 'complex spider's web' of bilateral agreements which have the effect of trapping airlines in their home markets, unable to break out and compete in any markets other than those negotiated by their respective governments. But, as Eddington put it:

> A truly global airline. . .would be free to operate on a global basis on any route where its customers demanded

That's very far from the reality of the current regulatory environment based as it is on the freedoms of the air discussed in Chapter 4.

It is something inherent in the very nature of the bilateral system that tends to make it restrictive. When two countries sign an air service agreement, the opportunities opened up tend to be 'those considered acceptable by the less liberal of the two countries' (Doganis, 2006). This has for a long time been recognized by the US which has since 1992 has been vigorously pursuing its own brand of bilateralism known as 'open skies'. The main feature of an open skies agreement is the unlimited exchange between the two countries of third, fourth, and fifth freedom traffic rights. This is certainly more liberal than the traditional type of bilateral which only agrees the exchange of traffic rights between specified points. The US has been very successful in persuading countries to sign open skies agreements (see Table 8.1). Noticeably the list does not include the UK, with whom the US still has a relatively more restrictive bilateral (known as a 'Bermuda II' agreement). Nevertheless some significant liberalization of route access between the UK and the US has taken place over the past decade or so, as the comparisons presented in Figure 8.2 amply demonstrate.

Table 8.1 Open skies agreements, 1992–2005. *Sources*: World Trade Organization and various reports

1992 The Netherlands–USA	1997 Malaysia–USA
1995 Austria–USA	1997 The Netherlands Antilles–USA
1995 Belgium–USA	1997 New Zealand–Singapore
1995 Czech Republic–USA	1997 New Zealand–USA
1995 Denmark–USA	1997 Nicaragua–USA
1995 Finland–USA	1997 Panama–USA
1995 Iceland–USA	1997 Romania–USA
1995 Luxembourg–USA	1997 Singapore–USA
1995 Norway–USA	1997 Chinese Taipei–USA
1995 Sweden–USA	1998 Brunei–New Zealand[a]
1995 Switzerland–USA	1998 Chile–New Zealand
1996 Germany–USA	1998 Chile–Panama
1996 Jordan–USA	1998 Denmark–New Zealand
1997 Aruba–USA	1998 Ethiopia–UAE
1997 Brunei–Singapore	1998 Italy–USA
1997 Brunei–USA	1998 New Zealand–Norway
1997 Chile–USA	1998 New Zealand–Sweden
1997 Costa Rica–USA	1998 Peru–USA
1997 El Salvador–USA	1998 S. Korea–USA
1997 Guatemala–Panama	1998 Turkmenistan–USA
1997 Guatemala–USA	1998 UAE–Uganda
1997 Honduras–USA	1998 Uzbekistan–USA
1997 Kenya–USA	1999 Argentina–USA
1997 Malaysia–New Zealand	1999 Bahrain–USA

Table 8.1 *Continued*

1999 Chile–Costa Rica	2001 Cook Islands–Samoa
1999 Dominican Republic–USA	2001 France–USA
1999 Ireland–New Zealand[a]	2001 Oman–USA
1999 New Zealand–Peru	2001 Poland–USA
1999 New Zealand–Switzerland	2001 Samoa–Tonga
1999 Pakistan–USA	2001 Sri Lanka–USA
1999 Portugal–USA	2002 Cape Verde–USA
1999 Qatar–USA	2002 Chile–Peru
1999 Tanzania–USA	2002 Jamaica–USA
1999 UAE–USA	2002 New Zealand–Tonga[b]
2000 Australia–New Zealand	2002 Singapore–UAE[b]
2000 Benin–USA	2002 Uganda–USA
2000 Burkina Faso–USA	2003 Albania–USA
2000 Cook Islands–New Zealand	2003 Tonga–USA
2000 Gambia–USA	2004 Gabon–USA
2000 Ghana–USA	2004 Indonesia–USA
2000 Malta–USA	2004 Madagascar–USA
2000 Morocco–USA	2004 USA–Uruguay
2000 Namibia–USA	2005 Bosnia & Herzegovina–USA
2000 New Zealand–Samoa	2005 Cameroun–USA
2000 Nigeria–USA	2005 Canada–USA
2000 Rwanda–USA	2005 Ethiopia–USA
2000 Senegal–USA	2005 India–USA
2000 Slovakia–USA	2005 Maldives–USA
2000 South Africa–Zimbabwe	2005 Mali–USA
2000 Turkey–USA	2005 Paraguay–USA

[a] Includes the exchange of the seventh and eighth freedoms.
[b] Includes the exchange of the seventh freedom.

Despite its name, open skies does not mean completely free access to routes. Some important restrictions remain. To begin with, the US has resolutely refused to trade domestic cabotage rights, knowing full well that it has far more to give away than it could possibly hope to receive in return. Nor, as a bilateral, can an open skies agreement secure seventh freedom rights, because these necessarily require the approval of third countries.

Another restriction, common to a great many bilaterals, whether open skies or not, is the requirement that airlines designated by a country to exercise the traded traffic should be 'substantially owned and effectively controlled' by nationals of the designating country. What this means in practice can vary quite a bit from country to country. Many countries specify maximum limits on foreign ownership of share capital, like those

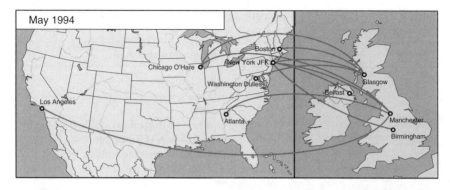

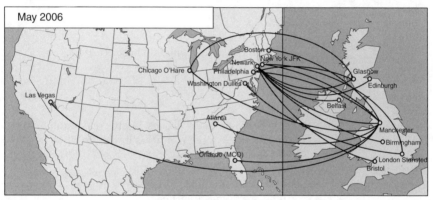

Figure 8.2 Increases in non-stop routes between the UK and the US (excluding routes to/from Heathrow and Gatwick) 1994–2006 (*Source*: Inter-Vistas)

represented in Table 8.2. This restriction denies foreign airlines the ability to control an existing airline or to establish a new one. The latter has proved to be a major impediment to Virgin Atlantic's plans to extend its overseas operations into the US by establishing a subsidiary there (in the same way it established Virgin Express in Europe and Virgin Blue in Australia).

In a report prepared for the EC the Brattle Group (2002) considered the effects of these restrictions on North Atlantic routes. It found that some enormous benefits – broadly of the order of some US $5 billion per annum – would flow from creating an 'Open Aviation Area' between the EU and the US, which would in effect mean a free trade area in air transport.

Given this, transatlantic mergers might become possible. Might we perhaps envisage BA merging with American, Lufthansa with United, the Air

Table 8.2 Limits on foreign ownership of airlines in selected countries. *Source*: Chang and Williams (2001)

Country	Maximum limits on foreign ownership
Australia[a]	49% for international airlines 100% for domestic airlines
Brazil	20% of voting equity
Canada	25% of voting equity. The maximum single holding in Air Canada by any investor is limited to 15%
Chile	Designation as a Chilean carrier (domestic or international) has 'principal place of business' as the sole requirement
China	35%
Colombia	40%
India	26% for Air-India 40% for privately owned domestic carriers
Israel	34%
Japan	One-third
Kenya	49%
Korea[b]	50%
Malaysia[c]	45% for Malaysian Airlines, but the maximum holding by any single foreign entity is limited to 20% 30% for other airlines
Mauritius	40%
New Zealand[d]	49% for international airlines 100% for domestic airlines
Peru	49%
Philippines	40%
Singapore	None
Taiwan	One-third
Thailand	30%
US	25% of the voting equity

[a] Australia's limit was revised in 1999.

[b] Korea's limit was revised from 20 per cent to 50 per cent in1998.

[c] Malaysia's limit was revised from 30 per cent to 45 per cent in 2000.

[d] New Zealand's limit for domestic carriers was revised in 1998 and the international limit was revised in 1996.

France-KLM Group with Northwest, etc.? Such mergers would represent major steps towards globalization. They may at this stage seem quite a long way off; but a survey of airline executives reported on in the August 2006 issue of *Airline Business* found that two-thirds of them expect that, if the industry moves towards mergers, these mergers will most likely be between airlines which are members of the same global alliance.

Recommendations for further reading

The airline industry

There are a number of very good books amplifying many of the points in Chapter 2. The second edition of *The Airline Business* by Doganis (2006) provides a very recent commentary on the industry covering the central issues in some depth. Another text in its second edition, Holloway's *Straight and level: Practical Airline Economics* (2003) is most useful on the basic economics of airline operation. Then there is a trilogy of books from the pen of Taneja: *Driving Airline Business Strategies through Emerging Technology* (2002), *Simpli-Flying: Optimizing the Airline Business Model* (2004) and *Fasten Your Seatbelt: the Passenger is Flying the Plane* (2005). All of these make interesting reading, especially the volume concerned with airline business models. On that subject there has been a whole host of thought provoking articles, a particular example being that by Tretheway in the *Journal of Air Transport Management* (2004). For some light but at the same time instructive reading on low-cost airlines, see Cassani (2003) Calder (2002) Creaton (2004) and Jones (2005). And for a case study of how a full-service airline might re-invent itself as a low-cost carrier, see Barrett (2006).

Competition issues

Airline deregulation spawned a vast literature on the arguments for and against regulation/competition, and on the effects of liberalizing the industry from controls over route entry, capacity, and fare levels. Much of this is summarized concisely in Williams (2002). Accounts of experience with deregulation in the United States, Canada and Australia and some discussion of prospects for liberalization in Europe are given in a book edited by Button (1991). For a critique of deregulation, see Dempsey and Goetz (1992) who challenge the view that US deregulation has been a success, in a book that contains much interesting material on the fortunes of particular airlines.

For some more in-depth analysis, there are two books with very similar titles, Morrison and Winston's volume on *The Evolution of the Airline Industry* (1995) being the result of some careful econometric work, and the volume by Ben Yosef (2005) being a by-product of the author's long experience of working in the airline industry. Two journal articles by Morrison and Winston (1987; 1990) are further references worth pursuing for those interested in econometric analyses.

Networks/hubbing

Some clear explanations of freedoms of the air and how they are traded in bilateral air service agreements are given in the books by Graham (1995) and Dobson (1995). The paper by Sealy (1992) contains interesting material on the development of international routes. The contributions of Doganis and Dennis (1989) and Dennis (1994) provide good treatments of the principles involved in scheduling through hubs. And the volume edited by Boyfield (2003) on *A Market in Airport Slots* contains a set of interesting papers, two of which – that by Starkie and that by Humphreys – are of particular relevance to the issues raised in this book.

Pricing power

A good explanation of the concepts and techniques airlines use in yield management is given in a short volume produced by the Institut du Transport Aerien (Daudel and Vialle, 1994). The Organisation for Economic Co-operation and Development (1998) has produced an excellent discussion of the economics of predatory pricing; and another very good discussion of predatory behaviour, this time specifically related to civil aviation, is presented in a report prepared for the European Commission by Dodgson, Katsoulacos and Pryke (1990). A book of readings edited by Forsyth, Gillen, Mayer and Niemeier (2005) is a valuable compendium of rich material on the subject of predation.

Mergers and alliances

Quite a number of papers in academic journals investigate the consequences of mergers for market concentration, competition intensity, fare levels, and so on, including those by Shepherd (1988), Hurdle et al. (1989), Borenstein (1991), and Morrison and Winston (1990). In addition there are important reports from two departments of the US Government, the Government Accountability Office and the Department of Transportation. On alliances, a book entitled *Globalisation and Strategic Alliances: the case of the Airline Industry* by Oum, Park and Zhang (2000) is a good place to find results of empirical investigations.

General

There are a few books on specialist aspects of air transport which contain much useful material. Two of them are on air law, one by Balfour (1995) and one by Goh (1997). Also on the subject of air law, there is a short volume by Lelieur on the *Law and Policy of Substantial Ownership and Effective Control of Airlines* (2003). This is very germane to some of the issues discussed here in Chapter 8. A book by Morrell (1997) on *Airline Finance* and one by Frechtling (1996) on *Tourism Forecasting* are also very worth reading. And a volume by Abeyratne contains much interesting and relevant material on the commercial, security and environmental crises facing the airline industry. There is also some interesting material in a book by Vogel (2001).

Finally, there are two periodicals to which many references have been made in the preparation of this book. First, the *Journal of Air Transport Management*, on whose Editorial Board the author is privileged to serve, contains some interesting, fully refereed academic papers, all related to air transport. Second, the magazine *Airline Business* is a veritable treasure trove of facts, data and statistics as well as a source of much well-informed and shrewd comment.

References

Abbott, K. and Thompson, D.J. (1989) 'Deregulating European aviation: impact of bilateral liberalisation', Centre for Business Strategy Working Paper, London Business School.

Abeyratne, R.I.R. (2004) *Aviation in Crisis*, Aldershot: Ashgate.

Airline Business (2006) 'Taking the sixth' editorial, March, **9**.

Airline Users Committee (1976) *European Air Fares*, London: Civil Aviation Authority.

Air Transport Action Group (2005) *The Economic and Social Benefits of Air Transport*, International Air Transport Association, Geneva.

Air Transport Users' Council (2004) *Booking a Flight: the AUC guide to cutting through the jungle of European Air Fares*, London.

Alamdari, F. (2004) 'Changes in the demand for air travel', *Airport International*, 3–8.

Alperovich, G. and Machnes, Y. (1994) 'The role of wealth in the demand for international air travel', *Journal of Transport Economics and Policy*, **28**(2), 163–73.

Areeda, P. and Turner, D. (1975) 'Predatory prices and related practices under Section 2 of the Sherman Act', *Harvard Law Review*, **88**(4), 697–783.

Ayling, R. (1993) 'National protectionism and world-wide competition', paper delivered to a conference on the Future Regulation of Air Transport, London: 5–6 October.

Bailey, E.E., Graham, D.R. and Baumol, W.T. (1984) 'Deregulation and the theory of contestable markets', *Yale Journal on Regulation*, **1**, 111–28.

Bailey, E.E., Graham, D.R. and Kaplan, D.P. (1985) *Deregulating the Airlines*, Cambridge, MA.: MIT Press.

Bailey, E.E. and Williams, J.R. (1988) 'Sources of economic rent in the deregulated airline industry', *Journal of Law and Economics*, **31**(April), 173–202.

Balfour, J. (1995) *European Community Air Law*, London: Butterworths.

Barnett, A., Curtis, T., Goranson, J. and Patrick, A. (1992) 'Better than ever: nonstop jet service in an era of hubs and spokes', *Sloan Management Review*, **33**(2), 49–54.

Barrett, S. D. (2006) 'Commercialising a national airline – the Aer Lingus case study', *Journal of Air Transport Management* **12**, 159–167.

Baumol, W.J. (1982) 'Contestable markets: an uprising in the theory of industry structure', *American Economic Review*, **72**(1), 1–15.

Baumol, W.J. (2005) *Regulation Misled by Misread Theory: Perfect Competition and Competition-imposed price Discrimination*, AEI-Bookings Joint Centre, Distinguished Lecture presented at the American Enterprise Institute, 22 September.

Baumol, W.J., Panzar, J.C. and Willig, R.D. (1982) *Contestable Markets and the Theory of Industry Structure*, New York: Harcourt Brace Jovanovich.

Beesley, M.E. (1986) 'Commitment, sunk costs and entry to the airline industry', *Journal of Transport Economics and Policy*, **20**, 173–90.

Belobaba, P.P. and Van Acker, J. (1994) 'Airline market concentration: an analysis of US origin–destination markets', *Journal of Air Transport Management*, **1**(1), 5–14.

Ben-Yosef, E. (2005) *The Evolution of the US Airline Industry: Theory, Strategy and Policy*, Dordrecht: Springer.

Berry, S.T. (1990) 'Airport presence as product differentiation', *American Economic Review*, **80**(2), 394–9.

Bisignani, G. (2005) 'State of the air transport industry', paper to 61st IATA AGM, Tokyo, May.

Bisignani, G. (2006) 'State of the air transport industry', paper to 62nd IATA AGM, Paris, June.

Boeing Commercial Airplane Company (1986) 'Overview of US Passengers' Connect Patterns under Deregulation', unpublished, Seattle.

Borenstein, S. (1989) 'Hubs and high fares: airport dominance and market power in the U.S. airline industry', *RAND Journal of Economics*, **20**(3), 344–65.

Borenstein, S. (1992) 'The evolution of U.S. airline competition', *Journal of Economic Perspectives*, **6**(2), 45–73.

Boston Consulting Group (2006) 'Understanding the demand for air travel: how to compete more effectively', *BGC Focus*, June.

Boyfield, K. (ed.) (2003) *A Market in Slots*, London: Institute of Economic Affairs.

Braden, K.A. (1990) 'Frequent flyer coupon brokering: a valid trade?' *Journal of Air Law and Commerce*, **55**, 727–62.

Brattle Group, The (2002) *The Economic Impact of an EU–US Open Aviation Area*, report prepared for the European Commission, London/Washington, DC.

Brenner, M.A., Leet, J.O. and Scholt, E. (1985) *Airline Deregulation*, Westport, CT: Eno Foundation for Transportation.

British Airways (1977) 'A Reply to the Airline Users Committee on European Air Fares', unpublished, London.

Brueckner, J.K., Dyer, N.J. and Spiller, P.T. (1992) 'Fare determination in airline hub-and-spokes networks', *RAND Journal of Economics*, **23**(3), 309–33.

Bruckner, J.K. and Whalen, T. (2000) 'The price effects of international airline alliances', *Journal of Law and Economics*, **43**(2), 503–45.

Bruckner, J.K. and Pels, E. (2005) 'European airline mergers, alliance consolidation and consumer welfare, *Journal of Air Transport Management*, **11**, 27–41.

Bundeskartellamt (2002) Decision in the Administrative Proceedings against Deutsch Lufthansa AG, 9th Decision Division, B9-144/01, 18 February.

Butler, R.V. and Huston, J.H. (1990) 'Airline services to non-hub communities ten years after deregulation', *Logistics and Transportation Review*, **26**(1), 3–15.

Button, K.J. (ed.) (1991) *Airline Deregulation: International Experiences*, London: David Fulton.

Button, K.J. (1996) 'Liberalising European Aviation: is there an empty core problem?', *Journal of Transport Economics and Policy*, **30**(3), 275–91.

Button, K.J. (2002) 'Debunking some common myths about airport hubs', *Journal of Air Transport Management*, **8**, 177–88.

Button, K.J., Haynes, K. and Stough, R. (1998) *Flying into the Future: Air Transport Policy in the European Union*, Cheltenham: Edward Elgar.

Button, K.J., (2004) *Wings across Europe: Towards an Efficient European Air Transport System*, Aldershot: Ashgate.

Cairns, R.D. and Galbraith, J.W. (1990) 'Artificial compatibility, barriers to entry and frequent flyer programs', *Canadian Journal of Economics*, **23**(4), 807–16.

Calder, S. (2003) *No Frills: the Truth behind the Low-cost Revolution in the Skies*, London: Virgin Books.

Cassani, B. (2003) *Go: an Airline Adventure*, London: Time Warner Books.

Caves, D.W., Christensen, L.R. and Tretheway, M.W. (1984) 'Economies of density versus economies of scale: why trunk and local service airline costs differ', *RAND Journal of Economics*, **15**(4), 471–89.

Caves, R.E. (1962) *Air Transport and its Regulators: an Industry Study*, Cambridge, MA: Harvard University Press.

CE Delft (2003) *Meeting External Costs in the Aviation Industry*, Report to the Commission for Integrated Transport, August.

Chambers, A. (1993) 'European regional airlines: cross-border alliances and feed consolidation', *Avmark Aviation Economist*, **10**(8), 12–17.

Chang, Y.C. and Williams, G. (2001) 'Changing the rules – amending the nationality clauses in air service agreements' *Journal of Air Transport Management*, **7**, 207–16.

Cherington, P.W. (1958) *Airline Price Policy: a Study of Domestic Airline Fares*, Cambridge, MA: Harvard University Press.

Civil Aeronautics Board (1973) *Domestic Passenger Fare Investigation Phase 5: Discount Fares*, Docket 21866-5, Washington, DC.

Civil Aeronautics Board (1982) *Competition and the Airlines: an Evaluation of Deregulation*, Washington, DC: Office of Economic Analysis, CAB.

Civil Aviation Authority (1977) *European Air Fares – a Discussion Document*, London.

Civil Aviation Authority (1988) *Business Air Fares: a UK Survey*, CAA Paper 88015, London, July.

Civil Aviation Authority (1992) 'Decision on Application 1A/10/34 by Loganair', unpublished report PH 1/92, April.

Civil Aviation Authority (1993a) *Passengers at London Airports in 1991*, CAP 610, London, January.

Civil Aviation Authority (1993b) *Airline Competition in the Single European Market*, CAP 623, London, November.

Civil Aviation Authority (1994) *Airline Competition on European Long Haul Routes*, CAP 639, London, November.

Civil Aviation Authority (1995) *Slot Allocation: a Proposal for Europe's Airports*, CAP 644, London, February.

Civil Aviation Authority (1997) *Passengers at Birmingham, Gatwick, Heathrow, London City, Luton, Manchester and Stansted Airports in 1996*, CAP 677, London.

Civil Aviation Authority (1998) *The Single European Aviation Market: The First Five Years*, CAP 685, London, June.

Civil Aviation Authority (2004) *The Effect of Liberalisation on Aviation Employment*, CAP 749, London, March.

Civil Aviation Authority (2005a) *An Economic Assessment of Granting Fifth-freedom Rights to Passenger Services from UK Regional Airports*, Report for the Department of Transport, London.

Civil Aviation Authority (2005b) *Demand for Outbound Leisure Air Transport*, Economic Regulation Group, London, December.

Civil Aviation Authority/Office of Fair Trading (2005) *Competition Issues associated with the Trading of Airport Slots*, a paper prepared for DG TREN, OFT 832, London, June.

Clinton Commission (1993) *Change, Challenge and Competition; a Report to the President and Congress*, The National Commission to Ensure a Strong Competitive Airline Industry, Washington, DC: Government Printing Office, August.

Clouatre, M.T. (1995) 'The legacy of Continental Airlines v. American Airlines: a re-evaluation of predatory pricing theory in the airline industry', *Journal of Air Law and Commerce*, **60**, 869–915.

Comité des Sages (1994) *Expanding Horizons, Civil Aviation in Europe: an Action Programme for the Future*, Brussels: European Commission, January.

Commission of the European Communities (1992a) 'Merger Procedure Article 6(1) Decision: Affaire No. IV/M. 157 – Air France/Sabena', Brussels, 5 October.

Commission of the European Communities (1992b) 'Merger Procedure Article 6(1) B Decision: Case No. IV/M.259 – British Airways/TAT', Brussels, 27 November.

Commission of the European Communities (1992c) 'Predatory pricing in air transport', draft discussion paper, unpublished, Brussels.

Commission of the European Communities (1993a) 'Council regulation on slot allocation at community airports', *Official Journal of the European Communities*, Regulation 95/93, Brussels, 22 January.

Commission of the European Communities (1993b) 'Frequent flyer programmes in the internal aviation market', consultation document, Brussels, March.

Committee of Inquiry into Civil Air Transport (1969) *British Air Transport in the Seventies* (the 'Edwards' report) Board of Trade, London.

Crane, J.B. (1954) 'The economics of air transportation', *Harvard Business Review*, **22**(Summer), 495–509.

Creaton, S. (2004) *How a Small Irish Airline Conquered Europe*, London: Aurum Press.

Crossair (1991) *Annual Report 1990*, Basel, Switzerland.

Daudel, S. and Vialle, G. (1994) *Yield Management: Applications to Air Transport and Other Service Industries*, Paris: Institut du Transport Aerien.

Davies, S., Coles, H., Olczak, M., Pike, C. and Wilson, G. (2004) *The Benefits from Competition, some illustrative UK cases*, DTI Economics Paper No. 9, Department of Trade and Industry, London.

de Groot, J.E.C. (1994) 'Code-sharing; United States' policies and the lessons for Europe', *Air and Space Law*, **19**(2), 62–75.

Dempsey, P.S. (1990) 'Airline deregulation and laissez-faire mythology', *Journal of Air Law and Commerce*, **56**(4), 305–412.

Dempsey, P.S. (2002) 'Predatory practices and monopolization in the airline industry: a case study of Minneapolis/St. Paul', *Transportation Law Journal*, **29**(2), 129–87.

Dempsey, P.S. and Goetz, A.R. (1992) *Airline Deregulation and Laissez-faire Mythology*, Westport, CT: Quorum Books.

Dennis, N.P.S. (1993) 'Introduction to hubbing', University of Westminster Conference on Hubbing, London: 10–12 June.

Dennis, N.P.S. (1994) 'Scheduling strategies for airline operation', *Journal of Air Transport Management*, **1**(3), 131–44.

Denton, N. and Dennis, N.P.S. (2000) 'Airline Franchising in Europe: benefits and disbenefits to airlines and consumers' *Journal of Air Transport Management*, **6**(4), 179–90.

Department for Transport (2003) *The Future of Air Transport*, White Paper, London, December.

Dobson, A.P. (1995) *Flying in the Face of Competition*, Aldershot: Ashgate.

Doganis, R.S. (1994) 'Impact of liberalisation on European airlines', *Journal of Air Transport Management*, **1**(1), 15–25.

Doganis, R.S. (2002) *Flying off Course: The Economics of International Airlines*, 3rd edn, London: Routledge.

Doganis, R.S. (2006) *The Airline Business*, 2nd edn, Abingdon: Routledge.

Doganis, R.S. and Dennis, N.P.S (1989) 'Lessons in hubbing', *Airline Business*, March, 42–5.

Dodgson, J.S. (1994) 'Competition policy and the liberalisation of European aviation', *Transportation*, **21**, 355–70.

Dodgson, J.S., Katsoulacos, Y. and Pryke, R.W.S. (1990) *Predatory Behaviour in Aviation*, Brussels: Commission of the European Communities.

Douglas, G.W. and Miller, J.C. (1974) *Economic Regulation of Domestic Air Transport*, Washington, DC: The Brookings Institution.

Dresner, M., Flipcop, S. and Windle, R. (1995) 'Trans-Atlantic airline alliances: a preliminary evaluation', *Journal of the Transportation Research Forum*, **35**, 13–25.

Economist, The (1992) 'A survey of the airline industry', 12 June.

Economist The (2006) 'Funny money: who will cheer loudest when frequent flyer miles celebrate their 25th birthday?' 24 December, 108–9.

Edlin, P.S. and Farrell, J. (2002) *The American Airlines Case: a chance to clarify predation policy*, Paper CPC 02033, Competition Policy Centre, Institute of Business and Economic Research, University of California, Berkeley.

European Regional Airlines Association (1991) *Yearbook 1991/92*, Burnham: The Shephard Press.

Federal Aviation Administration (1992) *FAA Aviation Forecasts 1992–2003*, Washington, DC: US Government Printing Office, February.

Flanagan, A. and Marcus, M. (1993) 'Airline alliances: secrets of a successful liaison', *Avmark Aviation Economist*, **10**(1), 20–23.

Forsyth, P., Gillen, D.W., Mayer, O.G. and Niemeier, H-M. (eds) (2005) *Competition versus Predation in Aviation Markets: a Survey of Experience in North America, Europe and Australia*, Aldershot: Ashgate.

Frechtling, D.C. (1996) *Practical Tourism Forecasting*, Oxford: Butterworth-Heinemann.

Frontier Economics (2006) *Economic Consideration of Extending EU Emissions Trading System to include Aviation*, report prepared for the European Low Fares Association, London.

Gellman Research Associates (1994) *A Study of International Airline Code Sharing*, Office of Aviation and International Economics, US Department of Transportation, Washington, DC.

Gidwitz, B. (1980) *The Politics of International Air Transport*, Lexington, MA: DC Heath.

Gillen, D.W. and Lall, A. (2005) 'Predation in Aviation: the North-American Divide' in Fosyth, P., Gellen, D.W., Mayer, O.G and Neimeier. H-M (eds) (2005) *Completion versus Predation in Aviation Markets: a Survey of Experience in North America, Europe and Australia*, Aldershot: Ashgate, 105-27.

Gillen, D.W., Morrison, W.G. and Stewart, C. (2004) *Air Travel Demand Elasticities: Concepts, Issues and Measurement*, report prepared for Department of Finance, Canada.

Goh, J. (1997) *European Air Transport Law and Competition*, Chichester: Wiley.

Gordon, R.J. (1965) 'Airline costs and managerial efficiency' in National Bureau of Economic Research, *Transportation Economics*, New York: Columbia University Press.

Gourgeon, P-H. (2005) 'Does the hub model have a future', mimeo, Air France-KLM, Paris.

Graham, A. (2000) 'Demand for leisure air travel and limits to growth', *Journal of Air Transport Management*, **6**(2), 109–18.

Graham, A. (2006) 'Have the major forces driving leisure airline traffic changed?' *Journal of Air Transport Management*, **12**(1), 14–20.

Graham, B. (1995) *Geography and Air Transport*, Chichester: Wiley.

Gregory, M. (1994) *Dirty Tricks: British Airways' Secret War against Virgin Atlantic*, London: Little, Brown and Company.

Hagedoorn, J. (1993) 'Understanding the rationale of strategic technology partnering: interorganizational modes of co-operation and sectoral differences', *Strategic Management Journal*, **14**, 371–85.

Hamilton, M.M. (1988) 'Airline pricing: highly complex, hotly competitive', *Washington Post*, 20 November, H1 and H16.

Hanlon, J.P. (1973) 'The demand for air travel: an econometric study of business travel over international routes', PhD Thesis. University of Birmingham.

Hanlon, J.P. (1981) 'Air fares and exchange rates', *International Journal of Tourism Management*, **2**(1), 4–17.

Hanlon, J.P. (1984) 'Sixth freedom operations in international air transport', *Tourism Management*, **5**(3), 177–91.

Hanlon, J.P. (1986) 'Indian air transport: factors affecting airline costs and revenues', *Tourism Management*, **7**(40), 259–78.

Hannegan, T.F. and Mulvey, F.P. (1995) 'An analysis of codesharing's impact on airlines and consumers', *Journal of Air Transport Management*, **2**(2), 131–37.

Hansen, M. and Kanafani, A. (1989) 'Hubbing and airline costs', *Journal of Transportation Engineering*, **115**(6), 581–96.

Holloway, S. (2003) *Straight and Level: Practical Airline Economics*, 2nd edn, Aldershot: Ashgate.

House of Commons Environment, Transport and Regional Affairs Committee (1998) *Regional Air Services*, Eighth Report Session 1997–98, HC Paper 589–1, London: HMSO.

House of Commons Environment, Transport and Regional Affairs Committee (1999) *Meeting with European Commission Officials to Discuss Air Transport*, Seventh Report 1998–99 Session, HC Paper 272, London: HMSO.

House of Commons Transport Committee (1988) *Airline Competition: Computer Reservations Systems*, Third Report Session 1987–88, London: HMSO.

Humphreys, B.K. (1991) 'Are FFPs anticompetitive?' *Avmark Aviation Economist*, July/August, 12–15.

Humphreys, B.K. (1994) *New Developments in CRSs*, Paris: Institut du Transport Aerien.

Humphreys, B.K. (2003) 'Slot allocation: a radical solution' in Boyfield, K. (ed.) *A Market in Airport Slots*, London: Institute of Economic Affairs.

Hurdle, G.J., Johnson, R.L., Joskow, A.S., Werden, G.J. and Williams, M.A. (1989) 'Concentration, potential entry, and performance in the airline industry', *Journal of Industrial Economics*, **38**(2), 119–39.

International Air Transport Association (2006) *Value Chain Profitability*, IATA Economics Briefing No. 4, Geneva, June.

International Civil Aviation Organization (1997) *Implications of Airline Codesharing*, Circular 269-AT/110, Montreal.

International Civil Aviation Organization (2003) *Regional Differences in International Airline Operating Economics: 1998 and 1999*, Circular 293-AT/125, Montreal, January.

James, G. (1993) 'US commercial aviation: a growth or mature industry?' *18th FAA Aviation Conference Proceedings*, FAA-APO 93–2, 182–203.

Jensen, R.B. (1990) 'US hubbing: the myth of the fortress-hub', *Avmark Aviation Economist*, October, 6–9.

Joskow, P.L. and Klevorick, A.K. (1979) 'A framework for analyzing predatory pricing policy', *Yale Law Journal*, **89**(2), 213–270.

Jones, I., Viehoff, I. and Marks, P. (1993) 'The economics of airport slots', *Fiscal Studies*, **14**(4), 37–57.

Jones, L. (2005) *easyjet: the Story of Britain's Biggest Low-cost Airline*, London: Aurum Press.

Kahn, A.E. (1970) *The Economics of Regulation: Principles and Institutions* (2 Vols), New York: Wiley.

Kahn, A.E. (1988) 'Surprises of airline deregulation', *American Economic Review*, **78**(2), 316–22.

Kahn, A.E. (1999) 'Comments on exclusionary airline pricing', *Journal of Air Transport Management*, **5**(21), 1–12.

Kasper, D.M. (1988) *Globalisation and Deregulation: Liberalising Trade in Air Services*, Cambridge, Mass.: Ballinger.

Keeler, T.E. (1972) 'Airline regulation and market performance', *Bell Journal of Economics*, **3**(Autumn), 399–424.

Keeler, T.E. (1991) 'Airline deregulation and market performance: the economic basis for regulatory reform and lessons from the US experience' in *Transport in a Free Market Economy*, (D. Banister and K.J. Button (eds)), London: Macmillan, pages 121–70.

Kleit, A. and Kobayashi (1996) 'Market failure or market efficiency? Evidence on airport slot usage', in *Research in Transportation Economics* (B. McMullen (ed.)), Connecticut: JAI Press.

Koontz, H.D. (1951) 'Economic and managerial factors underlying subsidy needs of domestic trunk line air carriers', *Journal of Air Law and Commerce*, **18**(1), 127–5.

Koontz, H.D. (1952) 'Domestic airline self-sufficiency: a problem of route structure', *American Economic Review*, **42**(1), 103–25.

Kotaite, A. (2006) Opening remarks, Aviation and Environment Summit, Geneva, April.

Krubasik, E. and Lautenschlager, H. (1993) 'Forming successful strategic alliances in high-tech businesses' in *Collaborating to Compete*, (J. Bleeke and D. Ernst (eds)), New York: The Free Press, pp. 55–65.

Lawton, T.C. (2002) *Cleared for take-off: Structure and Strategy in the Low Fare Airline Business*, Aldershot: Ashgate.

Lelieur, I. (2003) *Law and policy of substantial ownership and effective control of airlines: Prospects for Change*, Aldershot: Ashgate.

Levine, M.E. (1965) 'Is regulation necessary? California Air Transportation and National Regulatory Policy', *Yale Law Journal*, **74**(8), 1416–47.

Levine, M.E. (1987) 'Airline competition in deregulated markets; theory, firm strategy and public policy', *Yale Journal on Regulation*, **4**(Spring), 393–494.

Levine, M.E. (2006) 'Why weren't the airlines re-regulated?' *New York University Law and Economics Working Paper*, No. 54.

Lodge, D. (1984) *Small World. An Academic Romance*, Harmondsworth: Penguin Books.

Loy, F.E. (1968) 'Bilateral air transport agreements: some problems of finding a fair route exchange' in *The Freedom of the Air*, (E. McWhinney and M.A. Bradley (eds)), Doble Ferry, New York: Ocean Publications, pages 174–89.

Lyle, C. (1988) 'Computer-age vulnerability in the international airline industry', *Journal of Air Law and Commerce*, **54**(1), 161–78.

Lynch, R.P. (1993) *Business Alliances Guide: the Hidden Competitive Weapon*, New York: Wiley.

Mason, K.J. (2001) 'Marketing low cost airlines to business travellers', *Journal of Air Transport Management*, **7**(3), 107–19.

Mason, K.J. (2006) 'The value and usage of ticket flexibility for short-haul business travellers', *Journal of Air Transport Management*, **12**(2), 92–7.

McGowan, F. and Seabright, P. (1989) 'Deregulating European Airlines', *Economic Policy*, October, 283–344.

McKenna, J.T. (1993) 'American cleared of unfair pricing', *Aviation Week and Space Technology*, 16 August, 34.

McShane, S. and Windle, R.J. (1989) 'The implications of hub-and-spoke routeing for airline costs and competitiveness', *Logistics and Transportation Review*, **25**(3), 209–30.

Milgrom, P. and Roberts, J. (1982) 'Predation, reputation and entry deterrence', *Journal of Economic Theory*, **27**(August), 280–312.

Monopolies and Mergers Commission (1987) *British Airways Plc and British Caledonian Group Plc: a Report on the Proposed Merger*, Cm 247, London: HMSO.

Monopolies and Mergers Commission (1990) *British Airways Plc and Sabena S.A.*, Cm 1155, London: HMSO.

Morrell, P.S. (1997) *Airline Finance*, Aldershot: Ashgate.

Morrish, S.C. and Hamilton, R.T. (2002) 'Airline Alliances–who Benefits?' *Journal of Air Transport Management*, **8**, 401–07.

Morrison, S.A. and Winston, C. (1986) *The Economic Effects of Airline Deregulation*, Washington, DC: Brookings Institution.

Morrison, S.A. and Winston, C. (1987) 'Empirical implications and tests of the contestability hypothesis', *Journal of Law and Economics*, **30**(April), 53–66.

Morrison, S.A. and Winston, C. (1990) 'The dynamics of airline pricing and competition', *American Economic Review*, **80**(2), 389–93.

Morrison, S.A. and Winston, C. (1995) *The Evolution of the Airline Industry*, Washington, DC: The Brookings Institution.

Morrison, W.G. (2004) 'Dimensions of predatory pricing in air travel markets', *Journal of Air Transport Management*, **10**(1), 87–95.

Muirhead, G. (1993) 'Airport initiatives: the interline hub' unpublished, Manchester Airport.

Nuutinen, H. (1994) 'ValueJet: no tickets but amazing profits', *Avmark Aviation Economist*, November, 16–21.

Ohmae, K. (1993) 'The global logic of strategic alliances' in *Collaborating to Compete*, (J. Bleeke and D. Ernst (eds)), New York: The Free Press, 35–54.

O'Leary, M. (1994) 'The challenge of replicating Southwest Airlines in Europe', *Institute of Economic Affairs Second International Aviation Conference*, London: 14–15 November.

Organisation for Economic Co-operation and Development (1988) *Deregulation and Airline Competition*, Paris: OECD.

Organisation for Economic Co-operation and Development (1989) *Predatory Pricing*, Paris: OECD.

Organisation for Economic Co-operation and Development (1993) *International Air Transport: the Challenges Ahead*, Paris: OECD.

Oum, T.H., Park, J.-H. and Zhang, A. (1996) 'The effects of airline code-sharing agreements on firm conduct and international air fares', *Journal of Transport Economics and Policy*, **30**(2), 187–202.

Oum, T.H., Park, J.-H. and Zhang, A. (2000) *Globalisation and Strategic Alliances: the Case of the Airline Industry*, Oxford: Pergamon.

Oxford Economic Forecasts (2005) *Measuring Airline Network Benefits*, report prepared for the International Air Transport Association, Oxford.

Pagliari, R. (2003) 'The impact of airline franchising on air service provision in the Highlands and Islands of Scotland', *Journal of Air Transport Management*, **11**(2), 117–29.

Park, J.H. (1997) 'Strategic airline alliance: modelling and empirical analysis', PhD Dissertation, University of British Columbia.

Pickrell, D. (1991) 'The regulation and deregulation of US airlines' in *Airline Deregulation: International Experiences*, (K.J. Button, ed.), London: David Fulton, 5–47.

Plender, L. (1999) 'European Aviation: the emergence of franchised airline operations', *Journal of Air Transport Management*, **20**, 565–74.

Proctor, J.W. and Duncan, J.S. (1954) 'A regression analysis of airline costs', *Journal of Air Law and Commerce*, **21**(2), 282–92.

Regional Airline Association (1993) *Annual Report 1993*, Washington, DC: RAA.

Reichheld, F.F. (1996) *The Loyalty Effect: the Hidden Force behind Growth, Profits and Lasting Value*, Boston, MA: Harvard University Press.

Richmond, S.B. (1962) *Regulation and Competition in Air Transportation*, New York: Columbia University Press.

Rhoades, D.L. and Tiernan, S.D. (2005) 'The viscous cycle of growth and declining quality in the US airline industry: some lessons for new start-ups' *World Review of Entrepreneurship, Management and Sustainable Development*, **1**(1), 31–44.

Schulte-Strathaus, U. (1994) 'Strategies for success and survival of airlines in the European market', paper presented to the Institute of Economic Affairs Second International Aviation Conference, London, 14–15 November.

Sealy, K. (1992) 'International air transport' in *Modern Transport Geography*, (B.S. Hoyle and R.D. Knowles (eds)), London: Belhaven, 233–56.

Shenton, H. (1993) 'Frequent flyer programmes: what next in Europe?' *Avmark Aviation Economist*, November, 20–22.

Shepherd, W.G. (1988). 'Competition, contestability, and transport mergers', *International Journal of Transport Economics*, **15**(2), 113–28.

Simons, P. (1994) 'From hard values to outside-in marketing', *Avmark Aviation Economist*, **11**(2), 8–9.

Skapinker, M. (1997) 'easyJet withdraws KLM complaint', *The Financial Times*, 22/23 November, 2.

Skapinker, M. (1999) 'National flags keep flying', *The Financial Times*, Special Survey on Global Business Outlook, 29 January, III.

Small, N.O. (1993) 'Hub airports: the regional economic implications', *University of Westminster Conference on Hubbing*, London: June 10–12.

Snow, J. (1990) 'The future for regional airlines in a liberalised environment' unpublished paper presented to the 'Montreaux Event' a conference on Regional, Commuter and Business Aviation, Montreaux, Switzerland, 21 June.

Staniland, M. (1998) 'The vanishing national airline?' *European Business*, **10**(2), 72–77.

Starkie, D. (1994) 'The US market in airport slots', *Journal of Transport Economics and Policy*, **28**(3), 325–29.

Starkie, D. (1998) 'Allocating airport slots: a role for the market?' *Journal of Air Transport Management*, **4**(2), 111–16.

Starkie, D. (2005) 'A capacity lock-in rule', in Forsyth, P. et al. (eds) *Competition versus Predation in Aviation Markets: a Survey of Experience in North America, Europe and Australia*, Aldershot: Ashgate.

Straszheim, M.R. (1969) *The International Airline Industry*, Washington, DC: The Brookings Institute.

Taneja, N.K. (2002) *Driving Airline Business Strategies through Emerging technology*, Aldershot: Ashgate.

Taneja, N.K. (2004) *Simple-Flying: Optimizing the Airline Business Model*, Aldershot: Ashgate.

Taneja, N.K. (2005) *Fasten your Seatbelt: the passenger is Flying the Plane*, Aldershot: Ashgate.

Taylor, L. (1988) *Air Travel: How Safe is it?* Oxford: BSP Professional Books.

Telser, L.G. (1978) *Economic Theory and the Core*, Chicago: University of Chicago Press.

ter Kuile, A. (1997) 'Hub fever', *Airline Business*, (December), 66–71.

Thomson, A. (1990) *High Risk: the Politics of the Air*, London: Sidgwick and Jackson.

Times, The (1989) 'The eagle and the ugly duckling', 1 December.

Tirole, J. (1988) *The Theory of Industrial Organisation*, Cambridge, MA: MIT Press.

Tretheway, M.W. (2004) 'Distortions of airline revenues: why the network airline business model is broken', *Journal of Air Transport Management*, **10**(1), 3–14.

US General Accounting Office (1990) 'Airline competition: higher fares and reduced competition at concentrated airports', Washington, DC.

US General Accounting Office (1995) *International Aviation: Airline Alliances Produce Benefits but Effect on Competition is Uncertain*, GAO/RCED-95–99, Washington, DC.

US General Accounting Office (1996) *Airline Deregulation: Barriers to Entry Continue to Limit Competition in Several Key Domestic Markets*, Report to US Senate, Washington, DC.

US General Accounting Office (2002) *Airline Service Trends at Small Communities since October 2000*, GAO-02-432, Washington, DC, March.

US Government Accountability Office (2005) *Bankruptcy and Pension Problems are Symptoms of Underlying Structural Issues*, GAO-05-945, Washington, DC, September.

US Government Accountability Office (2006) *Airline Deregulation: Reregulating the Airline Industry would likely Reverse Consumer benefits and not save Airline Pensions*, GAO-06-630, Washington, DC.

US Department of Transportation (1988) *A Study of Airline Computer Reservations Systems*, Washington, DC: Government Printing Office.

US Department of Transportation (1990) *Secretary's Task Force on Competition in the U.S. Domestic Airline Industry*, Washington, DC.: Government Printing Office.

US Department of Transportation (1998) *Statement of Enforcement Policy Regarding Unfair Exclusionary Conduct*, Office of the Secretary, Docket No. OST-98-3713, 6 April.

US Department of Transportation (1999) *Competition in the US Domestic Airline Industry: the need for a policy to prevent unfair practices*, Washington, DC, May.

Vickers, J. (1985) 'The economics of predatory practices', *Fiscal Studies*, **6**(3), 24–36.

Vickers, J. (2005) 'Abuse of market power', *Economic Journal*, **115**(June), F244–F261.

Vogel, H.L. (2001) *Travel Industry Economics: a Guide for Financial Analysis*, Cambridge University Press.

Walker, K. (1997) 'When the wolf's at your door', *Airline Business*, May, 62–67.

Wassengbergh, H. (1993) *Principles and Practice in Air Transport Regulation*, Paris: Institut du Transport Aerien.

Wheatcroft, S.F. (1964) *Air Transport Policy*, London: Michael Joseph.

Wheatcroft, S.F. and Lipman, G. (1986) *Air Transport in a Competitive European Market*, London: Economist Intelligence Unit.

Wheatcroft, S.F. and Lipman, G. (1990) *European Liberalisation and World Air Transport*, London: Economist Intelligence Unit.

White, L.J. (1979) 'Economies of scale and the question of natural monopoly in the airline industry', *Journal of Air Law and Commerce*, **44**(3), 545–73.

Windle, R.J. (1991) 'The world's airlines: a cost and productivity comparison', *Journal of Transport Economics and Policy*, **25**(1), 31–49.

Williams, G. (2002) *Airline Competition: Deregulation's Mixed Legacy*, Aldershot: Ashgate.

Williamson, O.E. (1968) 'Economies as an antitrust defense', *American Economic Review*, **58**(1), 18–36.

World Tourism Organization (1994) *Aviation and Tourism Policies: Balancing the Benefits*, London: Routledge.

Youssef, W. and Hansen, M. (1994) 'Consequences of strategic alliances between international airlines: the case of Swissair and SAS', *Transportation Research*, **28A**(5), 415–31.

Index